THE EMERGENCE OF OLIGOPOLY

Alfred S. Eichner, a specialist in economic history, teaches at Columbia University, from which he holds the Ph.D. He turned to the study of economics after a brief career in journalism which brought him, while still an undergraduate, a Pulitzer Prize nomination. He is the co-author, with Eli Ginzberg, of *The Troublesome Presence*, and has published a number of articles. He is presently at work on a book studying the theory of oligopoly.

The Emergence of Oligopoly

Sugar Refining as a Case Study

::

ALFRED S. EICHNER

THE JOHNS HOPKINS PRESS
Baltimore and London

Manufactured in the United States of America

The Johns Hopkins Press, Baltimore, Maryland 21218
The Johns Hopkins Press Ltd., London

Library of Congress Catalog Card Number 74-79300

Standard Book Number 8018-1068-X

In memory of my mother . . .

whose sustenance and encouragement
mark the beginning

PREFACE

THE stimulus for this monographic study was a remark by Professor Donald Dewey in his industrial organization course that no satisfactory history of the 1895–1907 merger movement had as yet been written. What follows can hardly be said to fill this gap; but perhaps it can be said to mark the first step in a necessary second look at and reinterpretation of that crucial decade in American history, a decade which witnessed a sudden and dramatic change in the structure of this country's manufacturing sector. While this monograph covers only a single industry, it would seem to be a reasonable working hypothesis—at least until complementary studies in other industries show otherwise—that what occurred in sugar refining provides an instructive guide to what happened contemporaneously in other industries.

It is currently fashionable in some quarters to talk about the "new economic history."[1] Whether this monograph falls under that rubric is for others to judge. Certainly it does not make use of the econometric techniques which have come to be associated with that phrase. On the other hand, it does attempt to apply—for the first time, really—current industrial organization theory to the substantial body of information which exists on the 1895–1907 merger movement. Previous studies of this period, numerous as they have been, have generally suffered from the lack of such a theoretical structure for organizing and evaluating the available materials. In terms of technique, the use of industrial organization theory to help interpret a historical epoch may be the most important contribution which this monograph has to make.

The application of economic theory to history, however, has its dangers as well as its advantages. For while the theory can provide

[1] See the discussion "Economic History: Its Contribution to Economic Education, Research and Policy," 77th Annual Meeting of the American Economic Association, reprinted in *American Economic Review*, 55 (May, 1965), especially the contributions of Douglass C. North and Robert W. Fogel, pp. 86–98.

many important insights, it can also blind one to the process of cumulative change, an awareness of which is the *sine qua non* of a "historical" sense. It is the lack of such a historical sense which vitiates some of the most noted examples of the "new economic history." This monograph, it is hoped, has exploited the possibility without falling victim to the trap.

To Donald Dewey I owe much more than just the subject of this monograph, originally a dissertation written under his supervision and completed in the spring of 1966. He has influenced my approach to this and other economic questions in ways that I am only dimly aware of but for which I am deeply grateful. The relationship between a graduate student and his faculty sponsor is a unique one, and, like all meaningful human relationships, is best appreciated only as it comes to an end.

In revising the original manuscript for publication I have been most fortunate to have the benefit of criticisms and comments by Professors Alfred D. Chandler, Jr., of The Johns Hopkins University, and Louis D. Galambos, of Rice University. As a result of their helpful suggestions, the manuscript has been improved considerably, as any reader of the original version will be able to testify. Among other things, they are responsible for the monograph's being more sharply focused on its main themes.

Professor Louis Hacker served as the second reader of the original dissertation and, it would appear to me, carried out that office with a devotion far beyond the normal call of duty, reading through the entire manuscript with careful attention to every detail. To him I am truly indebted for a historian's keenly critical review, as well as for many helpful suggestions. However, as in the cases of Professors Dewey, Chandler, and Galambos, he should not be held responsible for the errors, omissions, and faulty judgments that still remain in the manuscript. Professor Julius Rubin, now of the University of Pittsburgh, performed a similar service when the original dissertation was in its early stages of development, and I wish to acknowledge that substantial debt. I also want to thank Professors Carter C. Goodrich, also now of the University of Pittsburgh, and Joseph Dorfman for their help and encouragement. This list of intellectual obligations would not be complete without mention of Professors Aaron W. Warner and Eli Ginzberg. Their contribution to this monograph has been indirect rather than direct: the opportunity I have had to work closely with them both over the last eight years has comprised the equivalent of several graduate and post graduate educations.

This monograph would have been far more difficult to write had it not been for the co-operation I received from the American Sugar Company, its president, William F. Oliver, and, most important, Robert T. Quittmeyer and Ernest P. Lorfanfant of the company's legal department. I wish to express my gratitude to them, and to Courtney C. Brown, former dean of the Columbia Graduate School of Business, for his interest and assistance. In addition to the materials received from the American Sugar Company, Henry L. Huelin, of Willett & Gray, Inc., publisher of the *Weekly Statistical Sugar Trade Journal,* was kind enough to put at my disposal his firm's copies of its early issues. Since these early volumes are not to be found at any library—though they are an important source on the early history of the sugar refining industry—I am very grateful to him. Lastly, I would like to thank the librarians at the many collections I visited during the course of my research for their help and advice, particularly the librarians at Columbia University, the New York Historical Society, the National Archives, and the Stimson Collection at Yale University.

The final, and perhaps most important, acknowledgment must be to my wife, Barbara, who not only had to suffer through the agony of the dissertation process but also, to compound matters, typed the entire final copy. I would also like to thank Miss Jane Stein, Mrs. Robert Stein, Mrs. Belle Joyce Kass, and Mrs. Eva Gilleran for typing earlier drafts of various chapters.

Alfred S. Eichner
Columbia University

CONTENTS

Preface · *vii*

CHAPTERS

1 · The Larger Framework · *1*

2 · The Emergence of a Competitive Industry · *26*

3 · Competition and Instability · *50*

4 · The Trust is Born · *70*

5 · Why Consolidation · *93*

6 · A Change in Legal Form · *120*

7 · Culmination and Condonation · *152*

8 · The Problem of Entry · *188*

9 · The Exercise of Control · *229*

10 · The Old Order Passeth · *264*

11 · The Acceptance of Oligopoly · *291*

12 · Historical Perspectives · *332*

APPENDIXES

A · Sugar Refineries Located in New York City, 1868–87 · *339*

B · Sugar Refineries Located in Philadelphia, 1869–87 · *341*

C · Sugar Refineries Located in Boston, 1868–87 · *342*

D · Average Prices of Raw and Refined Sugar for Selected Years, and the Margin between Them · *343*

E · Domestic Sugar-Market Shares · *344*

F · Havemeyer and American Sugar Refining Company Holdings in Sugar Beet Companies, 1907 · *345*

Bibliography · *351*

Index · *365*

MAPS

1 · The American Sugar Refining Company and the Railroads, 1906 · *198*

2 · Beet Factory Sites in California, 1907 · *231*

3 · Beet Factory Sites in the Utah-Idaho Area (Intermountain Region), 1907 · *236*

4 · Principal Cane-Refining Centers and "Natural" Market Territories, 1907 · *252*

5 · Beet Factory Sites in the United States, 1907 · *346*

1 :: THE LARGER FRAMEWORK

BETWEEN 1895 and 1907 the American economy experienced a momentous organizational convulsion. It was not only that the pace of merger activity increased, that over this thirteen-year period an average of 266 firms a year were absorbed by competitors.[1] Much more important was the fact that the surviving enterprises were of a radically different nature. Whereas, before, scores of firms had competed somewhat independently in these various industries, now in many cases a single firm controlled a major share of the market. In 60 per cent of the consolidations that took place between 1895 and 1904, a single large corporation gained control of at least 62.5 per cent of its industry's market as measured by capitalization. And in another 10 per cent of the consolidations it gained control of 42.5–62.5 per cent.[2] By 1904, it was estimated, 318 corporations owned 40 per cent of all manufacturing assets.[3]

This Corporate Revolution, as it has been termed, marked the birth of what Adolph A. Berle and Gardiner C. Means later described as "the modern corporation."[4] From this period of consolidation came many of the large corporations that today play such an important role in the American economy. Of the 100 largest corporations in 1955, 20 were born in consolidation during this period; another 8 were the court-ordered offspring of the pre-1895 Standard Oil trust which had provided the model for the Corporate Revolution.[5]

From this Corporate Revolution have flowed many important political and social consequences, from the "trust busting" of the Progressive era to today's organization man. The economic consequences, though not always so clearly recognized, have been at least equally

[1] Ralph Nelson, *Merger Movements in American Industry, 1895–1956*, p. 37.
[2] *Ibid.*, p. 102.
[3] Henry R. Seager and Charles A. Gulick, Jr., *Trust and Corporation Problems*, pp. 60–61.
[4] Adolph A. Berle and Gardiner C. Means, *The Modern Corporation and Private Property*.
[5] Nelson, *Merger Movements*, p. 4.

important. In many an industry, including the most important ones, the Corporate Revolution spelled an end to competition, at least as economists have defined the term.[6] Instead were created first monopoly, and then, later and more enduringly, oligopoly. It is important to understand this history because it reveals how the industrial structure of the American economy has evolved in the past, posing a challenge to both the economic theorist and the national policy-maker. The large bureaucratic corporation, or "megacorp,"[7] that emerged from the Corporate Revolution to dominate nearly every oligopolistic industry was a quite different social institution from its predecessor, Alfred Marshall's representative firm.[8] It was no longer subject to the same life-and-death cycle which had previously applied to business firms. A professional, self-perpetuating management and an almost impregnable market position assured the megacorp of virtually continual existence, and this in turn forced the megacorp's executive group to base its decisions increasingly on longer-run considerations. But it was not only along the time axis that the previous human limitations on a firm's growth were transcended. The reorganization of production and new management techniques made it possible for the megacorp to expand to any size it might wish without suffering diseconomies of scale, and this in turn reinforced the megacorp's already considerable market power. For the economic theorist the challenge posed was to adapt the traditional models of market behavior to the new institutional form; to the national policy-maker it was to see that a satisfactory degree of social control was maintained. That neither has met the challenge with complete success may well reflect a failure to understand the process by which oligopoly emerged from the Corporate Revolution.

::

While students of the 1895–1907 period do not deny that something approximating a Corporate Revolution did, in fact, occur, they are quite divided over its causes. The simplest explanation comes from those who wistfully look back to the days when competition was the general rule, even in key industries. "Few of our gigantic corporations," Henry Simons wrote, "can be defended on the ground that their present size is necessary to reasonably full exploitation of pro-

[6] George J. Stigler, "Perfect Competition, Historically Contemplated."

[7] "Megacorp" is used by the author as a better term to indicate what has variously been called the "large" or "modern" corporation. See his "Business Concentration and Its Significance," esp., pp. 188–89.

[8] Alfred Marshall, *Principles of Economics*, bk. 5.

duction economies; their existence is to be explained in terms of opportunities for promoter profits, personal ambitions of industrial and financial 'Napoleons,' and the advantages of monopoly power."[9] This view had earlier found support from a one-time Princeton University professor, who gave this explanation for the Corporate Revolution: "It is not competition that has done that; it is illicit competition." Added Woodrow Wilson, "It is competition of the kind that the law ought to stop, and can stop—this crushing of the little man."[10]

The theory that the Corporate Revolution was caused by the machinations of evil, ambitious, and money-mad men suffers, however, from a major defect. Such men have never been in short supply throughout history. Why, in the years between 1895 and 1907, should they suddenly have been capable of transforming the structure of the American economy? The answer, in part, has been supplied by those who trace the Corporate Revolution to the growth and maturation of the American capital markets. "Our theory," George Stigler has written,

> . . . is that mergers for monopoly are profitable under easy assumptions that were surely fulfilled in many industries well before the mergers occurred. The only persuasive reason I have found for their late occurrence is the development of the modern corporation and the modern capital market. In a regime of individual proprietorships and partnerships, the capital requirements were a major obstacle to buying up the firms in an industry. . . .
>
> I am inclined to place considerable weight upon one . . . advantage of merger: it permitted a capitalization of prospective monopoly profits and a distribution of a portion of these capitalized profits to a professional promoter. The merger enabled a Morgan or Moore to enter a new and lucrative industry: the production of monopolies.[11]

At first glance, the empirical data seem to bear out this contention. By 1895, the New York Stock Exchange "had reached a sufficiently advanced stage of development to be capable of playing an important role in the [subsequent] merger movement. The quantitative and qualitative growth of the New York Stock Exchange from the early 1880's to the late 1890's was appreciable and was apparently based largely on factors other than the financing of mergers."[12] Moreover, a large proportion of the corporate consolidations later had stocks listed by an organized capital market. Of the various consolidations

[9] Henry Simons, *Economic Policy for a Free Society*, pp. 59–60.
[10] Edward C. Kirkland, *A History of American Life*, p. 424.
[11] George J. Stigler, "Monopoly and Oligopoly by Merger," pp. 28–30.
[12] Nelson, *Merger Movements*, p. 91.

which took place between 1897 and 1902, 68.4 per cent were listed on the New York, Boston, Philadelphia, or Baltimore exchanges.[13]

To connect the growth of the stock market with the Corporate Revolution, however, poses the nearly impossible task of separating cause and effect. One group of authors, for example, has attributed the growth of the stock market, or at least the market for industrial securities, to the consolidation movement.[14] Even if this view is not accepted, it may well be that the growth of the capital market was a necessary precondition for, but not necessarily the primary cause of, the Corporate Revolution. And since it is difficult to believe that the strong-willed, independent owners of the many businesses that were consolidated agreed to merge their firms simply to enable promoters to foist overvalued stock on the public, one is inclined to look for that primary cause elsewhere.

One possibility frequently suggested is that economies of scale were growing more rapidly at this time than was the market, making economically feasible larger firms relative to the market. Alfred D. Chandler, Jr., for example, has pointed out the advantages which new marketing arrangements and vertical integration, together with the possibility of large-scale production, offered certain firms. "These pioneers in high volume manufacturing and distribution of both perishable and relatively complex durable goods," he has written, "demonstrated the clear economies of scale. They provided obvious models for manufacturers who had until then found the existing wholesale network quite satisfactory."[15] While Chandler distinguishes the role played by economies of scale in the growth of large firms before 1895 from that which they played during the subsequent Great Merger Movement—economies of scale in his view being only a necessary precondition for, but not a sufficient cause of, the latter phenomenon—others, especially defenders of the giant enterprises thus created, have seen the need to exploit the advantages of greater size as creating the underlying pressure for consolidation throughout the entire period.

As Nelson has noted, however, the data are inadequate to determine the precise role played by economies of scale.[16] What little evidence there is disputes the view that economies of scale were the

[13] *Ibid.*, pp. 92–93.

[14] T. R. Navin and M. V. Sears, "The Rise of a Market for Industrial Securities, 1887–1902."

[15] Alfred D. Chandler, Jr., "The Large Industrial Corporation and the Making of the Modern American Economy."

[16] Nelson, *Merger Movements*, p. 103.

precipitating factor in the Corporate Revolution, though they may, as Chandler suggests, have been a necessary precondition. Nelson himself cites the great diversity of industries involved in the Corporate Revolution. "It is hard to believe," he concludes, "that such a variety of technological developments as would be needed to bring production economies of scale to these diverse industries could have converged in the same short period of time."[17] And although Donald Dewey, in analyzing the data on average plant size from 1869 to 1909, found a significant increase during this period, he could find no evidence of an acceleration in the trend after 1895 or shortly before. As for the specific role played by new marketing arrangements and the other means of achieving economies of vertical integration, it would appear that in many cases, as Chandler himself indicates,[18] they came into being only after an industry had already been consolidated. To the extent that this was the case, the creation of new distribution networks was a result rather than a cause of the Corporate Revolution.

Another version of the above argument cites the completion of the national railroad network at this time. This development, it is held by Jesse Markham, increased the market area of the typical firm and enabled it to take advantage of potential economies of scale previously unrealizable. ". . . It can be crudely estimated," he says, "that the area served by the average manufacturing establishment in 1900 was about 3.4 times as large as it was in 1882."[19] Joe S. Bain also links the Corporate Revolution to railroad development, but emphasizes a somewhat different effect. "Competition," he says,

> was intensified by the continuing growth of the railroad systems, which tended to bring all of the principal firms together in direct competition for a single national market. The economy was passing from a situation where a fairly large number of small manufacturers sold their products, each in a limited local market somewhat protected by high costs of transportation, to a situation where a few large firms vied among themselves for sales in a single market. In the new environment, price competition was potentially ruinous to all.[20]

---

[17] *Ibid.* Nelson also points to the fact that most of the mergers that took place were horizontal, between competing firms in the same stage of production. He then concludes that since most economies of scale result from vertical integration, the 1895–1907 consolidations were not designed to achieve economies of scale. I think Nelson errs in attributing most economies of scale to vertical integration.

[18] Chandler, "The Large Industrial Corporation," pp. 80–82.

[19] Jesse Markham, "Survey of the Evidence and Findings on Mergers," p. 156.

[20] Joe S. Bain, "Industrial Concentration and Government Anti-Trust Policy," p. 618.

According to Nelson,[21] industries with high transport costs were, in fact, the ones mainly involved in mergers and consolidations. Moreover, the number of miles of railroad track in America increased substantially from 1882 to 1916, while the cost of rail transportation declined steadily. However, as Nelson also points out,[22] at the time of the Corporate Revolution there was no sharp acceleration in the trend toward increased railroad trackage and falling freight rates. More important, much of the increased railroad mileage represented not an extension of the railroad network but an intensification of it—the double-tracking, for example, of an already existing line. Except in the non-industrial Southwest and Northwest, the era of railroad pioneering had come to an end at least a decade before the Corporate Revolution.

The Bain version of the railroad development hypothesis finds little support in the empirical data as well. For Nelson discovered that, in the case of many of the industries consolidated, plants were already concentrated within a narrow geographical area.[23] Therefore, the completion of the national railroad network could not have led to ruinous competition by bringing previously separated local markets together in one large national market, because the markets had not previously been separated by high transport costs.

The Bain hypothesis does touch on another explanation of the Corporate Revolution, however, one that is frequently advanced by businessmen or the defenders of consolidation. "In the United States as elsewhere," say Seager and Gulick,

> the combination movement has resulted from the efforts of businessmen to throw off the restraints and avoid the wastes of unregulated competition. It is one of our conclusions that even after all of the economies of large-scale production have been realized, there remain wastes and losses that can be avoided only through the exercise of sufficient control over output to secure the highest attainable regularity in the operation of plants. The combination movement is therefore a natural and indeed inevitable business development, which is not in and of itself opposed to the public business.[24]

This argument, that businessmen agreed to consolidation in order to avoid ruinous competition, keep production levels steady, and maintain reasonable profit margins, has much in common with the explana-

[21] Nelson, *Merger Movements*, pp. 82, 83.
[22] *Ibid.*, p. 82.
[23] *Ibid.*, pp. 85–87.
[24] Seager and Gulick, *Trust and Corporation Problems*, p. ix.

tion, rhetoric aside, that the consolidation movement was fostered by the desire for monopoly profits. Ignoring for the moment the question of whether or not monopoly results in certain economies, one should realize that the only difference between these two views is their difference of opinion as to what constitutes a "reasonable" profit. But whether the objective was, in fact, a "reasonable" or a "monopoly" profit, it was attained in much the same way—that is, by gaining control over an industry.

The evidence to support this thesis, that the Corporate Revolution was caused primarily by the desire to avoid "ruinous" competition, is quite substantial, if only on the basis of the actual results. As already noted,[25] a substantial percentage of the consolidations, if market control was actually the motive behind them, achieved their objective. But this still does not solve the problem of timing. Like the evil-men explanation, which it closely resembles, the market-control hypothesis does not explain why businessmen should have become more highly motivated by this desire in 1895 than in previous times, or even why they should have been more successful in satisfying it.

The ruinous-competition explanation for the Corporate Revolution has sometimes been linked to the decline-of-growth argument, namely, that the American economy at the end of the nineteenth century experienced a fall in its rate of growth and that the slackened demand led to ruinous competition among firms fighting for their former share in a reduced market. As Myron Watkins has explained:

> The opening of a new and wider market involves pioneering costs which call for the compact association of producers. But once a market has been opened by the joint action of the associated producers, its development attracts the ambition and varied talents of many producers, the prize for successful competition being high. The third and final phase is reached when the limit of the expansion of a given market has been touched, and the amount and character of its consumption have become settled and known. The gains from initiative and ingenuity are then no longer sufficient to hold producers upon an independent course, and they fall in together for their common enrichment at the expense of consumers.[26]

Nelson's empirical study, however, throws great doubt on this explanation. Analyzing the data on production trends, Nelson found that the Corporate Revolution took place at a time of increasing growth rather than of decline. In fact, he discovered a high correlation between growth and merger, not only for the turn-of-the-century period,

[25] See p. 1 above.

[26] Myron Watkins, *Industrial Combination and Public Policy*, pp. 12–13.

but also for subsequent periods of high merger activity. He also found that those industries which experienced consolidation or merger generally had higher growth rates than did the economy as a whole.[27]

A final economic explanation for the Corporate Revolution points to the high American tariffs in effect at this time. From 1883 to 1897, Republican-controlled Congresses steadily revised American tariffs upward, and they remained at a high plateau until the Underwood Tariff of 1913. For many years the belief was widely held that "the tariff is the mother of trusts."[28] Nelson attempts to dispose of this explanation by citing a similar British merger movement, also at the turn of the century, which, since Great Britain at this time was still deeply committed to a policy of free trade, occurred without the protection of tariffs.[29] Even disregarding Nelson's argument,[30] the question of timing still remains. Why would high tariffs not have induced a wave of industrial consolidations before 1895?

Two non-economic factors have also been cited as explanations for the Corporate Revolution. One of these was the change in corporate law which took place in the late 1880's. Before then, corporations were generally prohibited by common law from owning shares in other corporations, a prohibition which largely precluded the possibility of using the holding company as a means of effecting industrial consolidation. Then, in 1888, New Jersey enacted a new law permitting corporations chartered in that state to purchase stock in other corporations. Dewey, however, contends that this was no more than a contributing factor to the Corporate Revolution. Even before 1888, he says, other states conferred the same privilege on corporations or could do so by simple legislative enactment.[31]

The second non-economic explanation for the Corporate Revolution points to the changing legal attitude toward cartels and other forms of industry price control. The Corporate Revolution erupted, it is held, when the U.S. Circuit Court of Appeals in 1898 ruled in the *Addyston Pipe & Steel* case that cartel agreements were illegal under

[27] Nelson, *Merger Movements*, p. 78.

[28] Ironically, the author of this phrase was Henry O. Havemeyer, one of those responsible for consolidating the sugar refining industry, which was itself a major beneficiary of the tariff. See Havemeyer's testimony before the U.S. Industrial Commission, *Reports*, 1, pt. 2:101.

[29] Nelson, *Merger Movements*, pp. 132–33.

[30] Tariffs, while obviously not a factor in the British merger movement, still might have played an important role in the American Corporate Revolution. They may be part of the explanation why what was only a movement in Great Britain was a revolution in the United States.

[31] Donald Dewey, *Monopoly in Economics and Law*, pp. 53–54.

the Sherman Act. With this method of avoiding ruinous competition closed to them, businessmen were forced to turn to consolidation as the only alternative. "This contention has its grain of truth," notes Dewey. "The condemnation of a cartel in the *Addyston Pipe* case . . . coincided with the start of the eighteen-month period that saw merger activity reach its peak, and at least two major consolidations—the mergers creating the United States Pipe and Foundry Company and the United Shoe Machinery Company—were precipitated by this decision, the promoters having previously inclined to some less irrevocable arrangement."[32] But, as Nelson points out, the Corporate Revolution had already begun, even before the *Addyston Pipe* decision was announced. Moreover, in Great Britain, where a similar merger movement was occurring, British courts were simultaneously declaring that cartel agreements were not necessarily illegal, even if they were unenforceable in a court of law.[33]

Thus, of the numerous explanations that have been offered for the great merger movement in American industry at the turn of the century, none seems wholly adequate.[34] The evidence in support of any one of the explanations is, at best, inconclusive. Clearly, there is need for a better understanding of what actually happened during this critical phase of American economic development.

This monograph represents the beginning of an effort to provide that better understanding. It will attempt to place the events occurring between 1895 and 1907 in a larger historical context, that of the long-run evolution of the structure of American industry. It will do so by re-examining the historical evidence from the period as it pertains to a single industry, sugar refining, in light of present economic theory. Too often this evidence has been framed in moralistic terms, either decrying or defending the events reported. But the time has long since passed when such an approach serves any useful purpose. Like it or not, the Corporate Revolution is a fact of our historical experience, the precursor of today's economic world. The time has now come to try to understand that revolution with the aid of modern economic analysis.

Recent developments in economic theory, especially in the field of

[32] *Ibid.*, pp. 54–55.

[33] Nelson, *Merger Movements*, p. 136.

[34] It should be noted that the various explanations cited may not necessarily exhaust all the possibilities, but they do cover the explanations most frequently advanced by students of the Corporate Revolution and, more to the point, they cover the explanations that have been subjected to quantitative investigation by Nelson in *Merger Movements*.

industrial organization, provide the guide. The pre-conditions of competition, the behavior of cartels, the importance of barriers to entry, and other aspects of industrial organization are much better understood now than when the Corporate Revolution was actually taking place. The older historical evidence, meanwhile, stripped of its moralistic overtones, supplies the raw data. This evidence, much of which has been ignored previously, is to be found in business records, government documents, court papers, trade journals, newspaper accounts, and biographical materials. Together, these two elements—recent economic theory and the older historical evidence—make possible a comprehensive explanation of the Corporate Revolution, such as the one presented below.

::

The changes that have occurred in the structure of the American economy over time, the most dramatic of which was the Corporate Revolution itself, can best be understood in terms of a four-stage model. Each of the last three stages, while evolving directly out of the previous stage, has nonetheless, like the first stage, been characterized by a unique market structure. The number of competing firms, the importance of barriers to entry, and the extent of product differentiation are the factors that have determined the nature of each typical market structure, and since these are the factors that determine which theoretical model of pricing behavior is applicable in any given situation, they also indicate the nature of the competitive processes that have been at work during each successive stage.[35] The exogenous force—that is, the engine of change throughout—has been technological progress, each stage representing the adaptive response of market structure to the evolving technical basis of economic activity. But technological progress as the engine of change should not be thought of as simply the effect of new production methods on an industry's cost structure. It must be viewed in the larger sense of being the factor which historically has made possible entirely new industries, rising output per worker, reduced transportation and communications barriers, and more complex social organization—these developments both influencing and in turn influenced by the nature

[35] For a description and analysis of the various models of pricing behavior, see Donald Watson, *Price Theory and Its Uses*, pts. 4–6, and Leonard W. Weiss, *Case Studies in American Industry*.

of demand in a subtle interplay of forces.[36] It is only in this broader sense that technological progress may be said to be the independent variable in the four-stage process described below.[37]

The first of the four stages was the initial Period of Imperfect Competition. This was essentially a preindustrial stage during which handicraft techniques largely prevailed in the manufacturing sector—insofar as there was a manufacturing sector. The stage lasted from the time of the first colonial settlements in this country until the triumph of the factory system sometime during the two decades preceding the Civil War. While the precise timing varied in each industry, a useful bench mark was that parallel technological achievement, the transportation revolution, which by creating a vast domestic market both was stimulated by and in turn stimulated large-scale manufacturing. The typical market structure during this initial Period of Imperfect Competition reflected the conditions that underlie the theory of monopolistic competition today. Production was generally carried out by firms which, if not individually owned proprietorships, were at most only two- or three-man partnerships. Entry into any particular field, moreover, was moderately easy, being limited primarily by the skill required to perform the various handicraft operations and secondarily by the working capital needed to keep the business solvent. The distinguishing characteristic of the period, however, was the lack of uniformity among the goods produced. Because of the handicraft techniques employed, the quality of the product varied both among firms and even within the same firm over time. This gave rise to a product differentiation not unlike that achieved in more recent times by advertising and other forms of sales promotion. Each firm became known for the particular quality of its own product and the extent to which that quality varied. This product differentiation, together with the regional segmentation of markets, in turn provided

[36] Thus, while Douglass C. North is correct in stressing the importance of the nature of demand in the American growth process (*The Economic Growth of the United States, 1790–1860*), it is difficult to see how the nature of demand itself would have changed had it not been for prior changes in technology, in Europe if not in the United States. More generally, it may be suggested that consumer preferences are too stable a factor to produce by themselves any significant movement away from the static conditions of a long-run equilibrium.

[37] The four-stage model, it should be stressed, is taxonomic rather than analytic. Thus there is no intention of suggesting that the separate stages have a specified time dimension or even that each necessarily led to the subsequent stage. The model is merely descriptive of what happened in the American economy cover a certain period of time, and the separate stages indicate which theoretical model of market behavior most closely approximates the market behavior actually observed.

the firm with partial protection against the forces of competition, thereby assuring some degree of stability and security.

The second stage in the development of industrial organization was the Golden Age of Competition, so called because of the tendency of so many persons in later years to look back on it with nostalgia. The first phase of this stage represented the culmination of a series of striking technological innovations, the effect of which was to make possible large-scale, low-cost production of manufactured goods. In addition, the new mechanical techniques, together with improved measuring devices, made it possible for the first time to turn out articles of uniform quality. The interaction of these developments with the transportation revolution and the creation of a vast domestic market has already been touched on. Together they led to an unprecedented expansion of manufacturing activity, variously timed in individual industries but most generally occurring in the years immediately after the return of prosperity in 1843.[38]

Two groups of entrepreneurs rushed to take advantage of the resulting opportunities: those who among the older artisan group were able to adapt to the new mechanical techniques and those who among the commercial classes were willing to risk their capital in less liquid enterprises. The former brought with them a tradition of workmanship, the latter the habits of commodity dealing. The characteristic business spirit of the period derived from both sources, producing a condition similar to that underlying the model of perfect competition later developed by economists. The large number of separate enterprises created to take advantage of the rapidly expanding market meant that no one firm could hope to influence the market by its actions alone. Technological improvements meanwhile created a degree of product homogeneity dictating the same type of independent pricing which had long characterized commodity markets. Each firm was forced to take the industry price as given and to seek to maximize its net revenue by varying output—even if from time to time it might bring about a change in that very industry price through its testing of the market. The countervailing power exercised by brokers, commission merchants, and wholesale dealers served to keep

[38] North, *Economic Growth*, pp. 204–8. Economic historians are currently divided over the question of whether the decade beginning in 1840 marked a discontinuity in the growth rate of the American economy. Cf. George R. Taylor, "American Economic Growth Before 1840"; Paul A. David, "The Growth of Real Product in the United States Before 1840." What is being suggested here is not that the over-all growth rate necessarily accelerated at about that time but rather that the pace of manufacturing activity suddenly spurted.

the new manufacturing markets "honest," a true barometer of short-run supply-and-demand forces. In the long-run the still-relative freedom of entry—absolute capital requirements had increased but the wealth of the country had increased even more—performed the same function. Finally, the drive on the part of at least some individuals to continually improve both the product and the way in which it was manufactured meant that those who failed to adopt the new techniques found themselves at an increasing disadvantage—even if this disadvantage was not always immediately apparent.

The Golden Age of Competition, however, like many another heroic era, contained within it the elements of its own destruction. The same force of technology which so greatly reduced the costs of production and made it possible to turn out goods of uniform quality in large numbers also required a substantial investment in fixed assets, thereby making the capital-output ratio significantly high. This meant that whenever the demand for a firm's product fell, it was under considerable economic pressure to try to expand its sales by cutting its price and in this way spread its overhead costs over a larger volume. As long as the revenue received more than covered the variable or "out-of-pocket" costs, it was to the advantage of the individual firm to shade its price in this manner—even if, as a result, the industry price fell below long-run average total costs.

In the long period of prosperity that lasted through the Civil War and on into the second term of the Grant administration, this proclivity toward price cutting posed no serious problem. The times of falling or stagnant demand, when they occurred, were relatively brief and soon forgotten in the subsequent further expansion of the economy. But in the years after the Panic of 1873—though here again the precise date varied for each industry—secular conditions changed. The times of falling or stagnant demand were now much more frequent.[39] Equally important, the forces of supply—that is, the ability of new or existing firms to increase production—proved more vigorous than those of demand. Manufacturing firms no longer found it unusual to be forced for considerable periods of time to sell their output at prices below their long-run average total costs. This was particularly true of the marginal firms, those enterprises which had been less willing to modernize their plants during the earlier period of prosperity. For these firms there ensued a desperate struggle for survival, and in the process of that struggle they significantly influenced industry price levels. Somehow a few of them managed to hang on, shut-

[39] Rendig Fels, *American Business Cycles.*

ting down when the price fell below a certain point but starting up again whenever it rose sufficiently to cover their out-of-pocket expenses. The result was to keep the industry price from reaching much higher than the average variable costs of the marginal firms. While a few of the more efficient enterprises could nonetheless earn an adequate return, the majority of firms could not.[40]

For the owner-entrepreneurs associated with these enterprises it was an entirely unsatisfactory state of affairs. In the long run, unable to cover their total costs, they faced probable economic extinction. The loss of both their capital and the social position which that capital afforded them was too great a blow to accept, and so these businessmen resolved to do something about their plight. The years from 1873 to 1895, the second phase of the Golden Age of Competition, thus constituted a period of transition presaging the Corporate Revolution as those who had invested their capital in manufacturing assets sought in various ways to mitigate the expropriating effects of competition.

The period as a whole was one of instability, for the ad hoc solutions that businessmen devised to cope with the situation inevitably failed to solve the underlying problem of excess supply relative to the demand. In most cases the first response of the manufacturing firms was to agree among themselves not to sell below a certain price or produce in excess of a given quantity. But like all such agreements heretofore, they were soon violated, sometimes even before they could be put into effect.[41] The advantages of cutting the price were so great and the ability to police the agreements so limited that this result was all but inevitable—and the knowledge that the agreements would soon be violated was itself a factor contributing to their abrogation. While these cartel arrangements gradually grew more sophisticated with the creation of pools and common sales agencies, they nonetheless continued to suffer from a generally fatal defect: the agreements, obviously designed to suppress competition, were unenforceable in a court of law. Thwarted along these lines, businessmen turned to legal

[40] On the destructive effects of competition, see the testimony of various manufacturers before the U.S. Industrial Commission, *Reports*, 1, pt. 2.

[41] As a producer of wallpaper later testified before the Industrial Commission, after first describing how an agreement in his industry had succeeded in raising prices: "The greed of a number of manufacturers, however, did not allow this favorable condition of affairs to continue. They sold goods at less than scheduled prices and to cover up the transactions failed to report the sales to the [pool]. Fines were imposed for such violations when discovered, but they failed to check the evil, . . . and this dishonesty finally led to abandonment of the scheme" (*ibid.*, 13:283).

and extralegal alternatives. In some cases they simply sought additional tariff protection or even export subsidies. In others they tried to enlist the support of politicians and government officials for whatever scheme promised to bring relief from competition—and in the process helped set the tone for what has come to be known as the Gilded Age of Politics. Even so, in most cases the only real alternative was a more furious struggle for survival, the tactics employed becoming less restrained as the contest itself became more desperate.[42]

While instability was the general rule, the period was also one during which the solution to the problem of how to mitigate the effects of competition was gradually being worked out as a result of the cumulative experience in a few key industries. Even before 1873 the firms active in anthracite coal mining learned that control over transportation could be used to obtain control over the entry of new firms into the industry and thus to provide a check on competition from without.[43] Earlier, Cornelius Vanderbilt and the organizers of the Western Union Company had demonstrated that the exchange of stock was an effective means of gaining control over the firms already in the industry and thus of assuring a check on competition from within.[44] The Standard Oil Company, under the direction of John D. Rockefeller, then combined both these lessons to achieve an unprecedented degree of control over prices in the petroleum industry. With low-cost methods of production and railroad rebates providing the Standard Oil Company with an unmatchable advantage, rival refiners were left with the choice of either selling out to the Rockefeller group—generally for stock but, if they insisted, for cash—or facing competitive ruin.[45]

The importance of the Standard Oil example was not only the success it achieved on so large a scale but, even more important, the new legal device it created for controlling the various properties acquired. That new legal device was the trust form of business organization. It consisted of a group of trustees, the functional equivalent of a board of directors, in whom the stock of different corporations

[42] See the studies of particular industries to be found in William Z. Ripley, ed., *Trusts, Pools and Corporations*; Seager and Gulick, *Trust and Corporation Problems*.

[43] Eliot Jones, *The Anthracite Coal Combination in the United States*; Jules Bogen, *The Anthracite Railroads*; Pennsylvania, Legislature, Senate, Committee on the Judiciary, General, *Report in Relation to the Anthracite Coal Difficulties with the Accompanying Testimony*; Chester A. Jones, *The Economic History of the Anthracite-Tidewater Canals*; Marvin B. Schlegel, *Ruler of the Reading*.

[44] Allan Nevins, *Study in Power*, 1:364.

[45] *Ibid.*, chaps. 4–14.

could be vested, giving the trustees absolute control over the management of the properties. In return for handing over their stock to the trustees, the shareholders in the various companies received trust certificates, the functional equivalent of common shares. This arrangement, besides making it possible to get around the common law prohibition on holding companies, enabled the very existence of the trust to remain a secret, since, unlike a corporation, the trust did not have to obtain a state charter.[46] In the late 1880's, as knowledgeable businessmen gradually became aware of the Standard Oil trust's formation, a number of other industries were quick to follow petroleum's example. The certificates of these trusts, traded in the New York Stock Exchange's unlisted department, created the first significant market for industrial securities in this country.[47]

The trust form proper, however, was to have only a brief existence. Even as the Sherman antitrust law was being enacted into law in the summer of 1890, a New York court decision was rendering the trust form illegal.[48] It was a decision soon to be confirmed by judicial rulings in other states.[49] But the several combinations which had been organized as trusts were unwilling to return to the *status quo ante*. As was to be seen again many times in the years that followed, a competitively structured industry, once destroyed, was not easily resurrected. Instead, the several combinations took advantage of a change in New Jersey's corporation law which conveniently permitted one corporation to own stock in another and thus gave sanction to the holding company.[50] Still, before other industries were willing to follow the example of the trusts that were now transformed into New Jersey–chartered corporations, two questions had to be answered. The first was whether such corporations were legal under the Sherman Act. While the majority of distinguished corporate lawyers was convinced that they were consistent with the law, a definitive answer had to wait until the Supreme Court itself ruled on the issue. The second question was whether combinations of that type were sound from a business point of view. Doubts of this sort were greatly increased when the National Cordage Company, one of the trusts which had been reorganized as a New Jersey corporation, suffered a finan-

[46] *Ibid.*, chap. 21; John Dos Passos, *Commercial Trusts*, pp. 12–14.

[47] Navin and Sears, "Market for Industrial Securities," pp. 106–12.

[48] *People* v. *North River Sugar Refining Co.*

[49] *Railway & Corporate Law Journal*, 7 (January 18, 1890); *State* v. *Standard Oil Company*.

[50] New Jersey, *Statutes*, 1889, chaps. 265, 269; see also Edward Q. Keasbey, "New Jersey and the Great Corporations"; Russell C. Larcom, *The Delaware Corporation*, chap. 1.

cial collapse which marked the onset of the 1893 Depression. The cordage combination had been victimized by rivals who organized new enterprises almost as quickly as they were bought out.[51]

Somewhat ironically, it was the 1893 Depression which conclusively demonstrated the advantages of industrial consolidation to businessmen. They could not help but notice that prices fell less rapidly and that their fellow capitalists suffered less severely in those industries which had been successfully consolidated. By the time economic conditions began to improve in 1895 and the stock market had regained its buoyancy, many businessmen no longer doubted the practical soundness of combination. Meanwhile, in its decision in the *E. C. Knight* case, the Supreme Court had removed whatever legal uncertainty still remained.[52] Implicitly—or so it seemed at the time—the New Jersey holding company had passed the scrutiny of the law. If some businessmen still hesitated, preferring less formal and less permanent price-fixing arrangements even if they were unenforceable in the courts, they were less likely to hold back after the *Addyston Pipe* decision made such cartel practices a positive criminal offense.[53]

The first phase of the Corporate Revolution and the change it wrought in the structure of the American economy have already been mentioned. The long-frustrated desire of businessmen to avoid the expropriating effects of competition built up a pressure for consolidation which was suddenly released in 1895 by the coincident return of prosperity and the Supreme Court's implicit approval of the New Jersey holding company. The by-this-time well-developed market for industrial securities greatly facilitated the process of combination and merger as investment bankers such as J. P. Morgan used the stock exchange to float the issues of the many newly created corporations. In fact, Morgan and his associates, with the wealth and experience gained in consolidating the nation's railroads, and Rockefeller and his partners, with the even greater wealth and experience acquired in building up the Standard Oil empire, provided the impetus and leadership for a significant number of the consolidations. The culmination of this Great Merger movement, at least symbolically, came in 1901 when Rockefeller agreed to sell his Mesabi Range properties to Morgan, thus enabling the latter to go ahead with his plans to form the United States Steel Corporation, a combination of previous

[51] Arthur S. Dewing, *A History of the National Cordage Company*, pp. 4–32.
[52] *United States* v. *E. C. Knight et al.*, 156 U.S. 12 (1895).
[53] *United States* v. *Addyston Pipe & Steel Co.*, 175 U.S. 211 (1899).

consolidations in the steel industry and this country's first $1 billion company.[54]

The important point about this first phase of the Corporate Revolution is that its effect was to create in a large number of industries a single giant enterprise or, in other words, conditions closely approximating those underlying the economist's theoretical model of monopoly. The second phase of the Corporate Revolution witnessed the transformation of this market structure into oligopoly and the consequent emergence of the modern corporation—or megacorp—characterized by multiplant operation and the separation of management from ownership. This second phase lasted roughly from the Rich Man's Panic of 1907, following the federal government's prosecution of the Standard Oil and American Tobacco companies, through the 1920's—though once more it must be stressed that the dates varied for each individual industry, with the structure of some even relapsing into an earlier form rather than evolving into the next stage.

While the possibility of organizing as a holding company largely eliminated the problem of how to control competition from within an industry, the problem of how to control competition from without still remained. The groping for a solution to this problem was one of the distinguishing features of the second phase of the Corporate Revolution. The method adopted by the petroleum industry—forced rebates from the railroads—was not necessarily applicable to other industries. Moreover, as a result of the gradual strengthening of the Interstate Commerce Act and the new-found willingness of the executive branch under Theodore Roosevelt to enforce the law, the exaction of rebates involved an increasingly unacceptable degree of risk. The consolidation of an industry into a single enterprise, if it were to prove endurable, thus required that new ways of forestalling the entry of firms into the industry be devised. A few of the combinations ignored the problem entirely or else dealt with it inadequately. Bankruptcy and reorganization tended to be their fate.[55] Most of the consolidations, however, were able to protect their market positions by erecting substantial barriers to entry.

This came about in a variety of ways, depending on the circumstances prevailing in each industry. Some of the monopolistic firms created were able to establish exclusive distribution systems by either

[54] Frederick Lewis Allen, *The Great Pierpont Morgan*, chap. 9; Nevins, *Study in Power*, chap. 32; John Moody, *The Truth About the Trusts*, pp. 490–93.

[55] Arthur S. Dewing, *Corporate Promotion and Reorganizations*.

taking over an existing dealer network or creating their own.[56] Others managed to obtain sole control over strategic raw materials and thereby put themselves in a position to deny these materials to others.[57] Of course, the older techniques of patent control and selective price cutting continued to be employed.[58] To supplement and reinforce these methods of limiting entry, a new technique offering substantial economies of scale was developed and expanded. This new technique was national advertising.

These methods, however, could not suppress all outside competition. In some cases, firms had been allowed to remain outside the combination because their owners refused to join and, after they had given assurances that they would match the combination's prices, it had not seemed worthwhile to press them further. To their numbers were soon added other firms, some established to take advantage of a specialized or geographically separated segment of the market, others formed by persons who, after selling out to the combination, found the enforced retirement unbearable. It seemed as though the sight of a single large corporation dominating an industry and enjoying substantial profits presented too tempting a target for outside interests to ignore; and while most of the efforts to invade the industry might fail, still a few firms managed to gain a foothold and survive at the fringe. As a result it was not unusual for the single large corporation created during the first phase of the Corporate Revolution to find itself coexisting with numerous but relatively insignificant smaller rivals.

This competitive "tail" of the monopolistic industry generally had little or no effect on the ability of the consolidation to control prices. But it did provide the basis for the later growth of firms able to match the original combination in size and strength. The emergence of powerful rivals was then given a considerable boost by the political and legal reaction which the first phase of the Corporate Revolution produced in its wake, a reaction that was to impose an upper limit on the share of the market which any one firm could control. This political and legal reaction, identified with the Progressive movement, was a second distinguishing feature of the second phase of the Corporate Revolution.

[56] William S. Stevens, *Industrial Combinations and Trusts*, chap. 7; Ripley, *Trusts, Pools and Corporations*, p. 273; Watkins, *Industrial Combination and Public Policy*, pp. 73–76; Richard Tennant, *The American Cigarette Industry*, pp. 305–6.

[57] Watkins, *Industrial Combination and Public Policy*, pp. 184–90; Eliot Jones, *The Trust Problem in the United States*, pp. 222–24.

[58] Stevens, *Industrial Combinations and Trusts*, chap. 12; Ripley, *Trusts, Pools and Corporations*, pp. 280–303.

The fears and apprehensions to which the consolidation movement gave rise did not find a meaningful political expression until the presidency of Theodore Roosevelt. The concern, however, was not so much over the actual changes in economic structure as over the implied threat to the democratic order. The question, as many persons including the president saw it, was whether an economic power had been created which could and would dictate to the political institutions of the country.[59] It was for this reason that Roosevelt, at a very early point in his administration, moved pre-emptorily in the *Northern Securities* case to reassert the primacy of the government—and in the process succeeded in reviving the moribund Sherman Act.[60] Initially Roosevelt felt that eliminating railroad rebates was all that would be required. Denied any unfair advantage in transportation costs, only those consolidations which truly reflected economies of scale would be able to survive. But to his chagrin Roosevelt soon learned that simply eliminating railroad rebates was not enough. Other barriers to entry also existed, or were quickly devised to replace those found to be illegal. To attack what he viewed as "bad trusts," that is, combinations whose market power rested on some unfair advantage, Roosevelt found himself forced to fall back on the Sherman Act—despite fears that it might subsequently be used indiscriminately against all combinations, whatever their social value.[61] The dissolution and dismemberment of the Standard Oil, American Tobacco, and DuPont companies was the eventual result of this campaign.[62]

While Roosevelt sought to break up only the "bad" trusts, hoping in this way not to lose the benefits of large-scale production, his successor, the jurist and former law professor William Howard Taft, felt it was necessary to dissolve any consolidation formed primarily to achieve control over prices. Only those combinations whose market power was ancillary to some other purpose were, in his view, immune from prosecution under the Sherman Act. Taft's successor, Woodrow Wilson, went one step further. All consolidations representing monopoly power, whatever the reason they were organized, were

[59] Richard Hofstadter, *The Age of Reform*, pp. 227–38.

[60] *Northern Securities Co.* v. *United States*; see also William Letwin, *Law and Economic Policy in America*, chap. 6.

[61] John M. Blum, *The Republican Roosevelt*, pp. 107–21; George E. Mowry, *The Era of Theodore Roosevelt*, pp. x–xi, 112, 130–34.

[62] *United States* v. *Standard Oil Co. of New Jersey*, 221 U.S. 1 (1911); *United States* v. *American Tobacco Co.*, 221 U.S. 106 (1911); *United States* v. *E. I. DuPont de Nemours & Co.*

in his eyes illegal.[63] But while the presidential attitude toward industrial consolidation was growing increasingly hostile, the judicial response continued to be equivocal. More to the point, the process of building up a body of case law on the subject was extremely time-consuming. Years of investigation and pretrial testimony were required before a suit could even be filed, and this preliminary work had to be done by the already overworked U.S. attorneys in a few major cities. Then, many more years were to pass before the case reached the Supreme Court and a final decision was handed down.[64] Thus, when World War I broke out, the Wilson administration was still awaiting the results of an appeal to the Supreme Court brought by the International Harvester Company, defendant in a suit testing Taft's theory that all combinations formed to exercise control over prices are illegal.[65] The war was to change dramatically the larger social and political attitudes toward industrial consolidation.

The co-operation and material support in prosecuting the war which the Wilson administration received from many of the very same combinations that it had only a short time before planned to break up seemed to confirm the argument long advanced that the consolidations were necessary to achieve certain desirable social goals in general and the realization of operating economies in particular. Even the Wilsonian Democrats' ardor for trust-busting cooled noticeably. Moreover, the growing repute with which the large industrial combinations now came to be held gave added weight to a concern long felt by the judiciary in weighing the merits of dissolution. Was it fair, they were forced to ask themselves, to impair the equity of the many stockholders who had invested in the combinations long after they were formed when there was every reason to believe that they were not illegal? The answer clearly depended on how great a social evil the combinations were.

The changing attitude toward industrial consolidation became evident in the Supreme Court's decision in the *United States Steel* case, which was handed down in the spring of 1920.[66] While the steel combination had not been guilty of the "unfair" tactics attributed to

[63] Letwin, *Law and Economic Policy*, pp. 250–53; Henry F. Pringle, *The Life and Times of William Howard Taft*, 2:654–59.

[64] It took five years to prosecute successfully the Standard Oil Company and three years to do the same to the American Tobacco Company. Suits with lower priority in the eyes of the Government generally required even longer to complete; the case against the American Sugar Refining Company, for example, required four years before it was even ready to go to trial.

[65] *United States* v. *International Harvester Co.*, 274 U.S. 696 (1927).

[66] *United States* v. *United States Steel Corp.*, 251 U.S. 441 (1920).

the petroleum and tobacco companies, its head, Judge Elbert Gary, had just the same taken the precaution of allowing U.S. Steel's share of the market to fall from the more than 80 per cent it had controlled at the time of its formation to somewhat less than 50 per cent. The Supreme Court, in absolving the company of any violation of the Sherman Act under the "rule of reason," seemed to be taking into account these specific facts as well as the larger social and political trends. Whatever the court's specific motivation, however, the precedent was established that a corporation which accounted for less than half of an industry's market and which avoided aggressive tactics to discourage competition was relatively safe from dissolution under the antitrust laws. It was this ground rule, together with the tendency of the smaller firms that managed to survive in the various consolidated industries to merge during the 1910's and 1920's in order to provide stronger competition, which was to transform the monopoly originally created by the Corporate Revolution into oligopoly. Meanwhile, an organizational transformation was also occurring within the giant corporations that were emerging during this period. This organizational transformation was the third and final distinguishing feature of the Corporate Revolution.

When first created the consolidations were generally little more than strong cartel arrangements, with the previously independent owner-entrepreneurs continuing to direct the operations of their own plants free of all outside interference except with respect to prices or output. As time passed, however, the central board of directors gradually increased its authority. The least efficient plants were scrapped entirely, marginal plants were held in reserve for peak periods of demand, and production was concentrated in the remaining plants where costs could be held to a minimum. As a result the consolidations were able to expand or contract production—the way in which changes in industry demand were now adjusted to—largely by starting up and closing down entire plants or plant segments. In this way, with the judicious management of inventories, it was possible to operate with something approaching constant marginal costs.[67]

Paradoxically, in order to exercise increased authority, the central board of directors had to delegate responsibility. The details of managing so large an enterprise were simply too great to be handled by any one small group of men. Managers for the various plants had to be appointed, charged with seeing to it not only that the plant was

[67] See Watson, *Price Theory*, chap. 11.

operated efficiently but also that over-all company policy was carried out down the line. In time these new plant managers replaced the former owner-entrepreneurs who had initially brought the properties into the consolidation. In addition, men knowledgeable in the ways of corporate law, finance, sales, and other specialized areas had to be brought into the central office to oversee the various staff functions, with new techniques of business administration being developed to co-ordinate their as well as the line executives' actions.[68] The result was the emergence of a managerial group whose power, derived from specialized knowledge of how the company was run, grew as that of the stockholders waned. The former owner-entrepreneurs who had originally joined together to form the consolidation found that as time passed it was to their interest to sell off their holdings of stock. In some cases this was done to diversify an investment portfolio. In other cases it was done to take advantage of inside information. In still other cases it was done out of pique over the loss of influence within the company. Whatever the reason, the tendency over time was for the stockholders to become more numerous and scattered, with a consequent growth in the management group's power. This eventual separation of management from ownership, together with multiplant operations in an oligopolistically structured industry, was to produce the typical large corporation—or megacorp—of today.

The fourth stage in the development of industrial organization is the one in which we are presently participant-observers. This is the Era of the Conglomerate, in which the megacorps that have arisen in specific industries have branched out into various other industries through diversification. Since the phenomenon is still too recent for proper historical perspective, any analysis must be tentative. This is particularly true since theoretical models for understanding the behavior of oligopolistic industries are still lacking. Still, as a preliminary hypothesis, it may be suggested that the conglomerate form of industrial organization reflects the need of megacorps in maturing oligopolistic industries to find new outlets for the investment funds they are able to generate internally through their control over prices. On the one hand, the continued technological progress which has led to the expansion of certain markets and brought a decline in others has meant that a megacorp, no matter how formidable its position in any particular industry, could expect to maintain an adequate growth rate in the long run only by periodically shifting its resources and energies into an entirely new area of economic activity. Often,

[68] Alfred D. Chandler, Jr., *Strategy and Structure.*

the technological change has been given a prodding by the megacorp's own research and development efforts, which, if not actually responsible for creating the new products or new techniques, have at least enabled the megacorp to keep abreast of the evolving state of the industrial arts, thereby reducing the time lag between the discovery and the exploitation of new knowledge. On the other hand, the further advance of management techniques—a form of technological progress the importance of which has not always been sufficiently appreciated—has made it possible for multiproduct firms to avoid the predicted handicaps of bigness.[69] In this current stage of the evolution of industrial organization in the United States, the megacorp has finally transcended the limits of its own original industry; and the economic theory which perhaps may be most relevant to its situation is that dealing with investment planning by nation-states.

::

The chapters that follow attempt to describe this evolution of industrial organization as it occurred in a single industry, sugar refining. This industry is of special interest for several reasons. First, it was intimately involved in many of the critical events of both the transition phase of the Golden Age of Competition and the subsequent Corporate Revolution. One of the first major industries to be consolidated, sugar refining was the center of the legal battles over the trust and holding-company forms of organization. Its securities were among the first of any manufacturing firm to be traded on the New York stock exchanges. Most important, it experienced many of the same challenges and tribulations as the other consolidated industries, eventually falling victim to the antitrust sentiment that was to help transform monopoly throughout the American economy into oligopoly.

On the other hand, the sugar refining industry has been virtually ignored by economic historians, despite the wealth of information which exists. The one attempt to describe the industry's consolidation is a 121-page monograph written in 1907,[70] but it probes neither widely nor deeply. It is in part this gap which the present monograph will attempt to fill. What follows, then, is in one sense simply the history of a particular business enterprise, the American Sugar Refining Company. It contains an account of the entrepreneurial activ-

[69] *Ibid.*, chap. 1, n. 27; Louis D. Brandeis, "Trusts and Efficiency," pp. 223–24.
[70] Paul L. Vogt, *The Sugar Refining Industry in the United States.*

ities of Henry O. Havemeyer and his colleagues in the sugar refining industry, a description of parallel developments in other industries, and an overview of antitrust and related legal actions. These various elements, however, are presented as part of a single, complex, interrelated process in order to illuminate more clearly what is, after all, the central focus of this study, the emergence of oligopoly in one industry as a result of the Corporate Revolution.

It would, of course, be silly to suggest that the chapters which follow "substantiate" in any meaningful sense the general historical model of the evolution of industrial organization outlined above. First, that model has been formulated by taking into account all available empirical evidence, which in this particular case means the original source material uncovered pertaining to sugar refining, as well as the extant secondary literature.[71] It is thus fallacious to infer that any test of the model has been conducted. Second, a sample size of one industry, even if inflated to include the few other industries for which a comparable historical account already exists, is not very impressive. This is the basic weakness of all case studies. Still, it can—and will—be argued that the model presented above does provide a useful working hypothesis for the subsequent industry studies which it is hoped this monograph will stimulate. For on this question of what factors were responsible for the Great Merger movement at the turn of the century, the point has been reached where only in-depth investigations of individual industries over time are likely to shed further light. Surprisingly, only a few of the industries involved in the Corporate Revolution have been studied in this manner.[72] The one merit that will be claimed for this monograph is that it adds yet another industry to the list.

[71] See the Bibliography in this volume.

[72] These are the petroleum and tobacco industries. See Harold F. Williamson *et al.*, *The American Petroleum Industry*; Nevins, *Study in Power*; Tennant, *American Cigarette Industry*. Alfred Chandler and Stephen Salsbury are presently at work on a study of the DuPont Company and the gunpowder industry.

2 :: THE EMERGENCE OF A COMPETITIVE INDUSTRY

FOR the American sugar refining industry the Period of Imperfect Competition lasted from 1730 to the early 1850's, the Golden Age of Competition from the early 1850's until the late 1870's. What separated the two stages of industrial organization was a series of technological improvements—charcoal filters, the vacuum pan, steam power, and, finally and most important, the centrifugal machine—which made it possible to produce for the first time sugar of uniform quality on a mass scale. These cost-reducing innovations, together with the growth of population and income, as well as a transportation revolution which both created a vast new domestic market and shifted the flow of interregional trade, led to the sudden emergence of a competitive industry which displayed all the characteristics of the theoretical model: numerous firms pursuing independent pricing policies, relative ease of entry and exit, and product homogeneity.

::

On August 10, 1730, the *New York Gazette* carried an advertisement announcing the completion of the first sugar refinery on Manhattan Island:

> Public Notice is hereby given that Nicholas Bayard of the City of New York has erected a Refinery House for Refining all sorts of Sugar and Sugar-Candy, and has procured from Europe an experienced artist in that Mystery. At which Refining House all Persons in City and Country may be supplied by Whole-sale and Re-tale with both double and single Refined Loaf-Sugar, as also Powder and Shop-Sugars, and Sugar Candy, at Reasonable Rates.[1]

Two years later the London Board of Trade, investigating the extent to which colonial manufactures were competing against home prod-

[1] Rita S. Gottesman, *The Arts and Crafts in New York, 1726–1776*, p. 316.

ucts, reported that "several . . . sugar bakeries had been established in New England," most probably referring to Boston and Providence.[2] Soon thereafter refineries had also been erected at Philadelphia, the fourth of the four major cities which dominated the commerce and trade of colonial America.[3]

Although sugar had been refined in England as early as the sixteenth century,[4] the methods employed in America at this early date, and for nearly a century afterward, were extremely crude. The only major source of sugar, aside from the irregular and undependable flow of maple syrup, was sugar cane, grown throughout the tropical world but principally in the West Indies. In its natural state the sugar cane contained numerous undesirable elements, including dirt, living organisms, wood fibers and uncrystallizable glucose. The purpose of refining was to separate these various impurities from the sugar crystals.

This was accomplished in several stages. The first was to place the raw sugar that had been imported from the West Indies in large, open kettles, then melt it in a white lime solution to neutralize certain acids and prevent fermentation. Next came filtration, a process intended to remove as much of the foreign matter from the raw sugar as possible. In the primitive technology of the eighteenth century any floating particles which failed to settle to the bottom of the kettle were sifted out by pouring the liquid solution through blankets or linen bags. The sugar was then further clarified "by the use of bullock's blood, albumen and clay" as filtering agents.[5] As the final step in the refining process, the liquid solution was placed over an open fire and boiled until the sugar began to recrystallize. Then, at the proper moment, it was removed from the flame and allowed to cool. The result was what was known as loaf sugar, a large cylindrical roll from which lumps of various shapes could be cut to meet individual customers' orders.

[2] J. Leander Bishop, *A History of American Manufactures from 1608 to 1860*, 1:340; Moses Brown, Providence merchant, to John Dexter, Treasury Department official, July 22, 1791, in *Industrial and Commercial Correspondence of Alexander Hamilton*, ed. Arthur H. Cole, p. 72.

[3] ". . . By 1739, the sugar houses of Philadelphia were well enough established in the refining of loaf sugar to cause quotations for the local product to appear regularly in the list of commodities in newspapers." By 1762 the Philadelphia product had completely displaced the loaf sugar imported previously from London. See Anne Bezanson *et al., Prices in Colonial Pennsylvania*, pp. 181–82.

[4] John E. Searles, Jr., "American Sugar," p. 259.

[5] American Sugar Refining Company, *A Century of Sugar Refining in the United States, 1816–1916*, pp. 11–12.

This last stage of recrystallization was a crucial moment in the refining process, for if the sugar was allowed to boil too long, it came out very brown and the taste was unsatisfactory. On the other hand, if the liquid solution was not allowed to boil long enough, too few of the impurities were removed. It required great skill to strike the proper balance, knowing just when to remove the sugar from the fire.[6] For this reason, most of the early sugar refinery owners, following the example of Nicholas Bayard, brought "an experienced artist in that Mystery" over to this country from England, where the refining art was further advanced. Two of the skilled sugar men who came to America in this way were William and Frederick Havemeyer, progenitors of the family that was to play so important a role in the history of the American sugar refining industry.[7]

Yet, despite the skill of these European masters, sugar refining remained a most imperfect art. Before 1830, the owner of a refinery considered himself fortunate if from one hundred pounds of raw cane he produced fifty pounds of refined sugar; within half a century the loss of more than 7 per cent in the refining process would be considered intolerable.[8] As a result of these crude manufacturing methods, refined sugar was an expensive commodity. Its price during the later colonial period ranged from the equivalent of 7.1 cents a pound to the equivalent of 17.8 cents a pound.[9] At Philadelphia, for which the most comprehensive data are available, the average price of loaf sugar from 1762 to 1775 was just a little over one Pennsylvania shilling (or the equivalent of 13.5 cents) a pound.[10] Since, in Phil-

[6] J. Carlyle Sitterson, *Sugar County*, pp. 145–46. While this refers specifically to the manufacture of sugar on the plantations of Louisiana, the technological problems were the same as those which confronted the early refiners on the Atlantic coast. In many respects the Louisiana planters on the eve of the Civil War were in the same primitive stage of manufacture that the Atlantic coast refiners had faced in 1830.

[7] Henry O. Havemeyer, Jr., *Biographical Record of the Havemeyer Family, 1606–1943*, pp. 25–26.

[8] American Sugar Refining Company, *A Century of Sugar Refining*, p. 8.

[9] Unfortunately, comprehensive price quotations for refined sugar during the colonial period are available only for Philadelphia, occasional price quotations only for Boston. The highest price noted after 1761 at the former city was 1 shilling and 4 pence, the lowest price, 11 pence, while the highest price noted at Boston after 1752 was 6 shillings and 6.7 pence, the lowest price, 3 shillings and 2.6 pence. However, the Philadelphia and Boston shillings were not equal, the first being equivalent to six times the latter. In later U.S. monetary units the Philadelphia shilling was equal to 13.3 cents, the Boston shilling, 2.22 cents. See Bezanson, *Prices in Colonial Pennsylvania*, pp. 184–85, 423; Carroll D. Wright, *History of Wages and Prices in Massachusetts, 1752–1860*, pp. 45–49.

[10] Bezanson, *Prices in Colonial Pennsylvania*, p. 423.

adelphia, skilled laborers such as carpenters and bricklayers earned at most the equivalent of only 80.0 cents a day during this period, while unskilled laborers earned at most the equivalent of only half that amount,[11] refined sugar was beyond the means of all but the wealthier classes. This was true not only in Philadelphia but in other major cities as well, for instance, Boston, Providence, and New York.[12]

Although output was greatly limited by crude refining methods and attendant high prices, the sugar business could be highly remunerative. Cost figures have not survived the years,[13] but there is evidence of several sugar refiners who, after a relatively short time, were able to retire with what in those days was considered a substantial fortune and either spend the rest of their lives in rural retreat or go on to more venturesome economic and political pursuits.[14] This was especially true in New York, where many of the leading families —beginning with the Bayards and later including the Livingstons, the Cuylers, the Van Cortlands, and the Roosevelts—were at one time or another during the colonial period interested in refineries.[15] To erect a "sugar house" and bring a skilled master over from Europe required a considerable capital outlay, and this fact not only made these prominent merchant families the most likely ones to undertake such enterprises but also served to limit the potential competition. In sum, then, sugar refining on the eve of the American Revolution was a business in which a man residing near a major seaport with considerable financial resources could, in a small way, hope to earn a

[11] U.S., Department of Labor, Bureau of Labor Statistics, "History of Wages in the United States from Colonial Times to 1928," p. 53.

[12] While detailed price data, comparable to that available for Philadelphia, have not been gathered for any of these cities, what little data there is fails to reveal any basis for considering sugar to be any less of a luxury item in those localities.

[13] Based on the price data available in Bezanson, *Prices in Colonial Pennsylvania*, it is possible to estimate with some degree of reliability the margin between raw and refined sugar at Philadelphia for the years 1762–75. During this period the price of raw sugar was slightly less than half the wholesale price of refined, leaving a margin equivalent to approximately 6.9 cents a pound. Since each pound of raw sugar produced only half a pound of refined, it seems that the expense of refining, plus any profit that was to be made, had to come from the sale of the one-quarter pound of molasses which was a by-product of the refining process. From 1762 to 1775 the average price of molasses was 24.2 cents a gallon. However, without any knowledge of refining costs per pound, the analysis of profits cannot be carried any further, even for this one city.

[14] See *Pennsylvania Magazine of History and Biography*, 21 (1897): 505, and pp. 30–31 below.

[15] Gottesman, *Arts and Crafts in New York*, p. 186; I. N. Phelps Stokes, *The Iconography of Manhattan Island*, 4: 646, 662, 790; Karl Schriftgiesser, *The Amazing Roosevelt Family, 1612–1942*, p. 110.

substantial return on his capital. It was a well-established type of enterprise, though not one which bulked large in the trade and commerce of that day. Finally, while sugar refining was among the first of this country's manufacturing industries, it had not as yet advanced much beyond the handicraft stage. It was thus a manufacture in the original sense of that word.

::

Despite the disruptions of the Revolutionary and Napoleonic wars, the nature of the industry remained essentially the same. The census of 1810, unreliable as it was in regard to manufactures, provides the first evidence of the sugar industry's relative importance. It noted that of the $127.7 million in manufactured goods produced that year, refined sugar accounted for only $1.4 million, or just a little over 1 per cent.[16]

Meanwhile, sugar continued to be a luxury item, the price of refined sugar in the years just prior to 1820 being approximately twenty cents a pound, twice the price of raw.[17] This represented nearly 14 per cent of the daily wages a skilled laborer could expect to earn.[18] A three-cents-a-pound duty on raw sugar helped to keep the price of refined sugar high.[19]

The typical transaction in sugar was still small. Although a substantial wholesale trade had existed from the very beginning, many of the wealthier families in the large cities where refineries were located continued to send their servants to the sugar house in person to purchase the weekly supply.[20] The quality of the sugar varied greatly, depending on the skill of the refiner himself. But under the crude manufacturing methods of that day, sugar produced even by the same refiner varied considerably over time.

The one thing that changed significantly before 1820 was the type of person operating the refineries. In New York the old, prominent merchant families had all gone on to more prestigious pursuits. Isaac Roosevelt, for example, had become president of the Bank of New York, the city's first such financial institution.[21] The Livingstons, meanwhile, were preoccupied with their steamboat monopoly and

[16] Trench Coxe, *Arts and Manufactures of the United States of America for the Year 1810*, p. 37.

[17] H. Havemeyer, *The Havemeyer Family*, p. 98.

[18] U.S. Bureau of Labor Statistics, "History of Wages," p. 57.

[19] David A. Wells, *The Sugar Industry and the Tariff*, pp. 22–23.

[20] H. Havemeyer, *The Havemeyer Family*, p. 98.

[21] Schriftgiesser, *The Amazing Roosevelt Family*, pp. 118–19.

extensive land holdings.[22] They and the others were succeeded in the refining business by the Rhinelanders and the Seamens,[23] the latter being the ones responsible for bringing William C. Havemeyer over to this country from England in 1802 to take charge of their refinery. In 1807, when his contract expired, the thirty-seven-year-old Havemeyer went into business for himself, forming a partnership with his younger brother, Frederick C.[24] But though these newer and younger persons had come into the industry, the same crude refining methods continued to be employed.

Then, beginning about 1830, a series of important technological innovations, all of them originating in Europe, began to be introduced into this country. Perhaps the first of these was the use of "bone black," or animal charcoal, as a filtering agent instead of albumen, bullock's blood, or clay. Bone black is the product obtained by burning animal bone in an airtight oven in much the same way charcoal is produced. Its unique purificatory powers were first discovered in 1811 by a Frenchman[25] who found that while other materials were equally capable of destroying the organic coloring matter found in raw sugar, only animal charcoal was able to remove the brown stain caused by continued exposure to high temperature. The use of bone black made it possible not only to obtain a final product that was pure white and free of most impurities but also to derive a larger percentage of refined sugar from the same amount of raw cane. In 1832, animal charcoal was just beginning to be used in the United States.[26]

While French refiners were experimenting with the use of animal charcoal as a filter, an Englishman, Edward C. Howard, was developing a greatly improved device for boiling sugar. Known as the vacuum pan, it was based on the well-known principle that liquids will boil at a lower temperature if the atmospheric pressure is reduced. Howard's apparatus, which he patented in 1812, consisted "of a globular copper vessel, enclosed within an iron or copper jacket."[27] Hot steam was forced into the latter, while an air pump attached to

[22] Patricia J. Gordon, "The Livingstons of New York," *passim*.

[23] Stokes, *Iconography of Manhattan Island*, 4: 790, 5: 1454.

[24] H. Havemeyer, *The Havemeyer Family*, pp. 25–26.

[25] M. Figurer of Montpelier, according to *ibid*., pp. 96–97. According to a Dr. Evans, in an article in *DeBow's Review*, the use of bone black was first introduced by a M. Deroane and then perfected by a M. Dumont; see Evans, "Sugar Refining," p. 388.

[26] U.S., Treasury Department, *Documents Relative to the Manufactures in the United States*, 1: 468.

[27] Evans, "Sugar Refining," p. 397.

the inner vessel, or concentrator as it was called, created a partial vacuum. This enabled the syrup to boil at a much lower temperature than would otherwise have been possible. But more than that, as the water in the syrup turned to steam, the effect was to force air from the concentrator. Then, as the steam was drawn off through a pipe and condensed by a jet of cold water, an additional vacuum was created. Thus the boiling process, once initiated, tended to maintain its own vacuum.

A number of improvements were later made in Howard's apparatus, the most significant being the introduction of a long steam pipe into the heart of the concentrator, but the advantages of even the first model were clearly evident. For one thing, the use of steam meant that the temperature could be more closely controlled than it had been when the syrup was simply boiled over an open fire. It also meant a considerable saving on fuel. But even more important, a thermometer and pressure gauge within the concentrator enabled the refiner to know exactly when the liquid was about to boil. If, after comparing the temperature shown on the thermometer with the temperature at which sugar would boil under the pressure indicated by the barometer, the refiner was still uncertain, he could, through a special device, examine the syrup itself without destroying the vacuum. This, along with the fact that the syrup could be boiled at a much lower temperature, meant that the discoloration of the final product which had often occurred in the past could now largely be avoided. As one enthusiastic report later noted, "There is no mode of concentrating syrups at present known which offers advantages equal to those of the vacuum pan. . . ."[28] Nor were there to be any in the future. Although sugar refining now required even greater skill and knowledge than before, it had ceased to be a mystery dependent on the intuition and artistry of a single master.

Several attempts were made before 1832 to adapt steam to sugar refining in the United States, but none of these proved successful.[29] American mechanics seemed unable to learn how to control steam effectively. Then, in 1832, two brothers, Robert L. and Alexander Stuart, succeeded where others had failed. Their father, a small though moderately prosperous confectioner on New York's lower West Side, had died in 1826, leaving the business to his wife and two sons. When Robert, the older, turned twenty-one a year later, he took charge of the business and the following year invited his brother

[28] *Ibid.*, p. 398.
[29] *Biographical Sketch of Robert L. and Alexander Stuart*, p. 5.

Alexander to join him as a partner. No longer content to buy their sugar from others as their father had done, the two brothers decided to enter the refining end of the business for themselves. Instead of using the old methods, however, they began experimenting with the use of steam. (Their building on Greenwich Street was later the first in New York to be supplied with gas.) Practically everyone in the refining business, including William F. Havemeyer, son of the founder of the Havemeyer refinery, predicted failure. One day, when Havemeyer passed by, he saw a large steam boiler being carried into the Stuarts' refinery. Accosting Alexander, who was in charge of the manufacturing end of the business, he is supposed to have said, "Don't do it, it will ruin you!"[30]

Yet within a year the Stuart brothers had secured a patent for their system of steam refining.[31] In 1834 their sugar, exhibited at the American Institute Fair, became the envy of all the other refiners, and a year later the capacity of their refinery was increased fourfold, from three thousand pounds to twelve thousand pounds daily.[32] The Stuarts were able to apply the steam not only to the refining process itself but also to many of the ancillary operations, such as lifting the raw product to the top of their six-story building before it began its descent through the various refining stages. The Stuarts adopted several other recent technological advances, but their competitors found it difficult to follow their example. "It seems curious," one writer later observed, "that these new processes, which . . . completely revolutionized the business, should have been resisted, and adopted with great reluctance. Heating by steam met with very determined resistance on the part of many old refiners, and in some cases partnerships were dissolved because the members of firms could not agree respecting the practicality and advisability of its adoption."[33] Among the partnerships dissolved was that of William F. and Frederick C. Havemeyer in 1842, the former to go into politics and the latter to devote full time to other business affairs. The refinery built by their fathers, a plant which had never produced more than one million pounds in any one year, was sold to their respective brothers, Albert and Diedrich.[34]

Meanwhile, the firm of Robert L. and Alexander Stuart prospered. "The business increased so rapidly . . . that the two brothers were

[30] *Ibid.*, p. 5.
[31] J. L. Bishop, *History of American Manufactures*, 2: 380.
[32] *Ibid.*, 3: 150–51.
[33] H. Havemeyer, *The Havemeyer Family*, pp. 95–96.
[34] *Ibid.*, p. 46.

compelled to build extensive quarters, first at the corner of Greenwich and Chamber Streets, and then in 1849, at Greenwich and Reade Streets."[35] The latter building, a nine-story structure, contained eight large steam boilers, which together consumed eight thousand tons of anthracite coal a year. It was flanked by several other buildings used for storage. By 1853 the Stuart firm had become the predominant sugar refinery in America, producing about forty million pounds of sugar annually and employing a labor force of approximately three hundred men. That year, finding that the refinery required all their energies, the two brothers gave up their confectionery business.[36]

Only the East Boston sugar refinery in Massachusetts rivaled the Stuart works. Erected in 1834, it was the venture of John Brown, who had gone to England to learn the advanced techniques, including the use of steam, which the refinery employed. Though the firm was forced to suspend operations during the Panic of 1837, it subsequently reopened and thereafter waxed continually stronger. In 1852 the refinery was modernized, and its capacity increased to 25 million pounds annually.[37] Together with the Stuart works, it presaged the next stage in the sugar refining industry's evolution, the Golden Age of Competition.

::

For many years the Stuart and East Boston refineries were the only substantial sugar works in the United States. Then, beginning in the early 1850's, the number of refineries suddenly began to increase. "No longer ago than the year 1848," reported *Hunt's Merchant Magazine* in 1856, "there were but two refineries in New York city, . . . and now, notwithstanding the depression experienced last season, when two or three houses ceased operations, there are ten refineries, some of which cost from $500,000 to $800,00 or more, and two others will soon be added."[38] In Philadelphia, between 1853 and 1857, four new refineries were added to the one already in existence.[39] Various factors lay behind this rapid expansion of the sugar refining

[35] William M. MacBean, *Biographical Register of Saint Andrew's Society of New York*, p. 124.

[36] *Biographical Sketch of Robert L. and Alexander Stuart*, p. 6.

[37] Justin Winsor, ed., *The Memorial History of Boston*, p. 87.

[38] *Hunt's Merchant Magazine*, 35 (1856): 500. The article lists only the Stuart and Woolsey firms, failing to mention the old Havemeyer refinery, which was still in operation.

[39] Edwin Friedley, *Philadelphia and Its Manufactures*, p. 386.

industry, including, once again, several important technological and entrepreneurial innovations.

The final step in the refining process, once the syrup had boiled, was to separate the sugar crystals from the molasses, or that part of the syrup which would not crystallize. This process, known as "claying," consisted of "running the sugar into conical molds, and placing on top a layer of moist clay or earth. . . . The moisture from the clay percolating through the mass of sugar, would wash away the adhering molasses and leave the crystals comparatively free and clear."[40] It was a lengthy and expensive process, requiring large curing sheds, much labor, and at least three weeks to complete. After the adoption of steam, it became the principal factor limiting the amount of sugar which a refinery could produce.

Then, in 1851, a new machine was patented which could perform the same function in a fraction of the time the claying process required. Boiled syrup was "placed in a revolving sieve, the wires of which are so fine that nothing but the liquid part of the sugar is allowed to pass. This sieve . . . is made to revolve with the tremendous velocity of two thousand revolutions per minute. By this means a centrifugal force is attained, sufficient to cause the liquid and impure portions of the sugar instantly to fly off, leaving the sugar itself behind, entirely purified and white. . . ."[41] The invention of the centrifugal machine, no larger in size than an ordinary wash tub, helped to revolutionize the industry. It "opened the way for an almost unlimited amount of business in a given time, easily doing in a few hours work which before required many days."[42] By 1857 the centrifugal machine was reported to be in use by most refineries.[43]

Meanwhile, William Moller had developed a new type of cloth filter, as well as a way to restore used bone black.[44] The latter invention was extremely important, since the rapid growth of the industry was leading to such a large increase in the price of animal charcoal that it was becoming a major item of expense. Now that the same bone black, after being cleaned with certain chemicals, could be used over and over again, that expense greatly diminished. Moller had worked for refineries in Boston and New York before joining the old Havemeyer firm in 1849. The new firm, Havemeyer & Moller, soon became famous for its "Cut Loaf Sugar," produced by a machine

[40] *Encyclopedia Britannica*, 11th ed., s.v. "sugar."
[41] *Hunt's Merchant Magazine*, 24 (1851): 121.
[42] H. Havemeyer, *The Havemeyer Family*, p. 96.
[43] *Hunt's Merchant Magazine*, 37 (1857): 250.
[44] J. L. Bishop, *History of American Manufactures*, 3: 152.

which Moller had also invented. "This sugar," an early history of American manufacturing noted, "is well known throughout the continent, and is preferred by families because of its good quality, and the uniform size and shape of its lumps, at even a higher rate than the market price of 'broken' or 'crushed' sugar, or that cut into squares or cubes by hand labor."[45] Soon after the Civil War began, the firm became simply William Moller & Sons.

These new technological processes made possible a substantial reduction in the price of refined sugar. In the early 1830's, soon after the Stuarts had begun producing sugar with their new steam process, the wholesale price of refined sugar had ranged on the average between 15 and 17 cents a pound. By 1851 it had fallen to between 8½ and 9½ cents a pound,[46] which represented primarily a fall in the real price.[47] This sharp drop, coupled with a rise in personal incomes, was to lead to a significant increase in the demand for refined sugar. From a figure of 18 pounds per person in 1850, sugar consumption in the United States was to jump to 24 pounds in 1853 and 31½ pounds in 1858.[48] Meanwhile, fed by a steady stream of Irish and German immigrants, the population was rapidly expanding, especially in the northeastern states. Between 1840 and 1850 the population of the United States rose from 17.1 million to 23.2 million, an increase of 35.9 per cent. During the next decade it was to continue growing at about the same rate.[49]

Helping to broaden the market for sugar was the revolution in transportation which was taking place contemporaneously. By 1851

[45] *Ibid.*, p. 152.

[46] The average range of wholesale prices for refined sugar in New York City between 1831 and 1860 was as follows:

1831	15–16¾¢	1841	11–13¢	1851	8½–9½¢
1832	14–17	1842	10	1852	8
1833	14½–17¼	1843	10½–11	1853	8½
1834	15–16¾	1844	11	1854	9
1835	14–16	1845	11⅓–11½	1855	8⅔
1836	15½–17	1846	11	1856	10
1837	15–16	1847	10	1857	12⅔
1838	15–16	1848	8	1858	9½–10½
1839	15–16	1849	8½	1859	9–10
1840	11⅓–13⅔	1850	9½	1860	9¾–10

Source: U.S., Treasury Department, *Report of the Secretary*, 1863, pp. 368–96.

[47] The Pearson-Warren wholesale-price index fell from 94.3 in the years 1831–33 to 83.0 in 1851 (U.S., Department of Commerce, Bureau of the Census, *Historical Statistics of the United States, 1789–1945*, p. 115).

[48] *Hunt's Merchant Magazine*, 23 (1850): 216, and 31 (1854): 392.

[49] U.S., Department of Commerce, Bureau of the Census, *Fourteenth Census: Population, 1920.*

two separate rail lines, the Erie and what was later to become the New York Central, connected New York City with the Great Lakes. At the same time, the Pennsylvania Railroad gave the city of Philadelphia direct access to the Ohio River at Pittsburgh, while the Baltimore & Ohio Railroad did the same for Baltimore at Wheeling, West Virginia. Boston, though it lacked a major railroad to the West, nonetheless was the center of a rail network that tapped all of New England and joined the New York Central at Albany.[50] By these various routes the large eastern seaboard cities could for the first time reach the rapidly expanding Midwest markets cheaply and expeditiously. Meanwhile, the Midwest was experiencing a railroad boom of its own, one that would soon give it a rail system as extensive as that in the East. By 1860 Ohio, Illinois, and Indiana together would have 7,908 miles of railroad, an eightfold increase within a decade.[51] While it would take several decades more to integrate the eastern and midwestern systems completely,[52] the fact was that the railroad was significantly altering the flow of interregional trade.[53] This was especially true in the case of sugar.

Almost from the time the trans-Appalachian regions of the United States were first settled, they had been supplied with sugar from the plantations surrounding New Orleans. Inasmuch as a separate refining industry had failed to evolve,[54] the raw cane was processed on each plantation by means of the same crude methods that had been common in the East before the Stuarts built their steam-powered refinery. The Louisiana product, though far less satisfactory than the sugar refined in New York or Boston, had nonetheless pre-empted the Midwest markets, primarily because it was so much cheaper. Here transportation costs were a major factor. Bulk commodities, such as sugar, could be shipped up the Mississippi River at a fraction of what it cost to carry them overland from the eastern seaboard. Even after the Erie Canal was built, Louisiana sugar continued to enjoy a substantial freight advantage.[55]

[50] George R. Taylor, *The Transportation Revolution, 1815–1860*, p. 84.

[51] *Ibid.*, p. 79.

[52] George R. Taylor and Irene D. Neu, *The American Railroad Network, 1861–1890.*

[53] Albert Fishlow, "Antebellum Interregional Trade Reconsidered."
The Economic Growth of the United States, 1790–1860.

[54] For an interesting analysis of why this happened, see Douglass C. North,

[55] According to Taylor (*The Transportation Revolution*, pp. 136–37), as late as 1850 the freight rate from New Orleans to Cincinnati was twenty cents a hundredweight compared to eighty cents a hundredweight from New York City to Buffalo by way of the Erie Canal.

With the coming of the railroad this situation began to change. It was not just that the steam locomotive brought about a reduction in overland transportation rates, though certainly this was a significant factor. Whereas, before, it had cost between twelve and seventeen cents per ton-mile to transport goods by wagon, by 1851 it cost only four cents per ton-mile to haul them by rail.[56] Nor was it just that the railroad was a more expeditious form of transportation, that, whereas it required eighteen days for goods to reach Cincinnati from New York by canal, it required only six to eight days by rail.[57] Probably more important than either of these two advantages was the fact that the railroad was now able to reach many communities previously inaccessible by boat when river and canal waters were low or frozen, and thus assured steady and dependable delivery.

Gradually the surplus products of the Midwest—grain, meat, dairy items, wool, and lumber—were diverted from their natural course down the Mississippi River through the port of New Orleans and were sent instead across the Appalachians to the Atlantic seaboard cities.[58] Once established, the same channels of trade were then used for eastern manufactured goods, including refined sugar, on the return trip west. This change in the flow of internal commerce, first initiated by construction of the Erie Canal, was made permanent by the advent of the railroad.[59]

Still, eastern refined sugar probably would not have been able to gain a foothold in the Midwest had it not been for the fact that the Louisiana cane sugar industry had just about reached the limits of its expansion. This fact was not immediately obvious, for Louisiana cane production—protected by a substantial tariff[60]— had grown steadily through the years up to 1853. After that, however, climatic conditions and lack of transportation facilities limited the normal Louisiana crop to 250 million pounds a year.[61] This meant that whatever additional suger cane was needed to meet the growing demand

[56] *Ibid.*, pp. 134–35.

[57] *Ibid.*, p. 139.

[58] Economic historians are presently at odds over how great the diversion was. See Fishlow, "Antebellum Interregional Trade Reconsidered," as well as the "Comment" by Robert Fogel and the "Reply" by Fishlow in the same issue of the *American Economic Review.*

[59] Louis B. Schmidt, "Internal Commerce and the Development of the National Economy Before 1860," pp. 811–17.

[60] Wells, *The Sugar Industry and the Tariff*, p. 22. The tariff on imported raw sugar was 2½ cents a pound until 1846, when it was changed to 30 per cent ad valorem. In 1857 the tariff was further reduced to 24 per cent ad valorem.

[61] Henry A. Brown, *Statement Made Before the Committee of Ways and Means on the Sugar Question*, p. 7.

in this country had to be imported from Cuba. Because of the even higher tariff on refined products—six cents a pound until 1846 and 30 per cent ad valorem thereafter—this Cuban sugar was imported in a nearly raw state, then further processed at one of the Atlantic seaboard cities. The fact that the Louisiana cane industry had just about reached the limits of its expansion augured well for the East Coast refineries.

All these factors together, then—the demonstrated superiority of the steam refining process, the more recent technological improvements, the rising per capita consumption of sugar, the growth in the nation's population, the transportation revolution and the resulting shift in the flow of interregional trade, the opening of the Midwest markets, and the end of the Louisiana sugar industry's expansion—served to create a favorable climate for investment in sugar refining.

The early 1840's had been largely a period of depressed business activity following the Panic of 1837.[62] Prosperity returned in 1843, and the reviving economy received an added stimulus when, in 1849, gold was discovered in California, touching off one of the great expansionary decades in American economic history.[63] It was over these years that sugar refining first developed into one of this country's most important industries. According to an 1856 account, "the sugar refining interest of New York has increased, within a few years, to a business of great magnitude, till the city is nearly encircled by enormous refining establishments, easily recognized by their lofty walls and chimneys. . . ."[64] By that year there were twelve refineries in New York City and vicinity, five in Philadelphia, five in New England, two in Baltimore, and one each in St. Louis, Cincinnati, and New Orleans. Together they produced 385 million pounds of refined sugar annually,[65] a fourfold increase since 1850.[66]

::

In 1857 several additional refineries were completed, including one by Frederick C. Havemeyer. After selling out to his brother Diedrich in 1842, Frederick had devoted himself mainly to managing his

[62] Willard L. Thorp, *Business Annals*, pp. 123–25.

[63] North, *Economic Growth*, p. 205.

[64] *Hunt's Merchant Magazine*, 35 (1856): 500.

[65] *Ibid.*, p. 501.

[66] The 1850 census of manufacturing recorded the value of refined sugar produced in that year at $9.9 million. Estimating the average price to have been ten cents a pound, this would indicate an annual output equivalent to approximately 99 million pounds (U.S., Department of Interior, *Abstract of Statistics of Manufacturing According to the Returns of the Seventh Census*, p. 109).

father's estate. But he had also found time to make several trips to Europe, where he was able to inspect the latest improvements in sugar refining. In 1856 Frederick decided to re-enter the refining business, in part, no doubt, because of the attractive prospects which the industry at that time seemed to offer and in part because he wished to assure his four young sons a place in the mercantile world. The oldest, Frederick C. Havemeyer, Jr., proved unsuited for business and the next oldest, George W., was killed soon thereafter in an accident at the refinery, but the two youngest sons, Theodore A. and Henry O., were both to become active partners in the firm, along with their brother-in-law, James L. Elder, and their cousin, Charles H. Senff. This firm eventually came to be known as Havemeyer & Elder.[67]

Frederick C. Havemeyer, together with a series of partners (including for a brief period William Moller), began erecting a refinery across the East River in Brooklyn, the first such establishment in what was then a separate city. Soon after construction of the plant was begun, Frederick sent his son Theodore to Germany and England to see what further advances had been made in the refining process since his own last trip to Europe. On his return, Theodore assumed an active role in laying out and building the new plant. The seven-story structure, when finally completed in 1860, was among the most modern sugar refineries in the world, incorporating within its walls all the recent technological improvements which Theodore had encountered in Europe, as well as those which had previously been developed in this country.[68]

The new Havemeyer refinery differed from the plants of other firms in one important respect. It was located on the water's edge, which meant that the raw sugar could be unloaded from the boats directly into the refinery's warehouses. Other refineries had to incur the extra expense of carting the raw sugar from the customs house to their respective places of business. Thus the Havemeyers were able to take advantage of an 1854 law sanctioning a system of private bonded warehouses.[69] Under the new law it was possible to store imported goods not only in warehouses owned or leased by the federal government, as had previously been required, but in private warehouses as well, without paying duties on the goods until they were removed from the warehouses for domestic consumption.[70] By

[67] H. Havemeyer, *The Havemeyer Family*, pp. 46–49, 52.
[68] *Ibid.*, pp. 51–52.
[69] John D. Goss, *History of Tariff Administration in the United States*, p. 52.
[70] *Ibid.*, pp. 51–52.

having their own refinery sheds designated as acceptable private warehouses for strong dutiable sugar, the Havemeyers were able to avoid the expense of dealing through regular customs warehouses.

In Boston, Seth Adams was imitating the Havemeyers' example. Before 1849 he had owned a machine shop where he produced, among other things, the Adams printing press that his brother had invented. Then a refinery which owed him money for machinery became insolvent, and to recoup his loss he entered the sugar refining business. When, in 1858, the old refinery burned down, Adams decided to build a new one along the harbor's edge in South Boston. More than twelve thousand piles were driven into the soft, reclaimed land, and a nine-story refinery capable of turning out five hundred pounds of refined sugar daily was erected on the site.[71]

Small though this output was, the sugar could be produced at a very low cost because of the refinery's waterfront location. How significant this advantage was for both the Havemeyer and Adams refineries was not at first appreciated, however, for the coming of the Civil War made the sugar refining industry so profitable that cost considerations became relatively unimportant.

At first it appeared that the outbreak of hostilities would have the opposite effect. Access to the Louisiana crop was immediately cut off, and this had the effect of raising the price of raw sugar. Increased quantities of cane were imported from Cuba, but that island could not hope to make up so great a deficiency on such short notice. Nor were the other centers of world production equal to the task. East Coast refiners soon found that they could not obtain additional quantities of raw sugar at any price.[72] On top of that, in order to help finance the war, Congress began levying additional duties on imported sugar. By late 1862 the tariff on raw sugar was three cents a pound, more than double the immediate prewar rate.[73] Yet, despite these and other vicissitudes, the sugar refining industry managed to thrive. Although the Stuarts were able to operate their refinery at only half its normal capacity, the profits on even that reduced output were greater than those earned before the war, when they operated at full capacity.[74] The war-induced boom, reinforced by large govern-

[71] J. L. Bishop, *History of American Manufactures*, 3: 303; Winsor, *Memorial History of Boston*, p. 91.

[72] *Biographical Sketch of Robert L. and Alexander Stuart*, p. 6.

[73] Wells, *The Sugar Industry and the Tariff*, p. 24. The prewar tariff had been 24 per cent ad valorem, or approximately 1.44 cents of the average prewar price of 6.0 cents a pound for raw sugar.

[74] *Biographical Sketch of Robert L. and Alexander Stuart*, p. 6.

ment purchases, assured a strong demand for refined sugar even at the much higher prices.

Lee's surrender at Appomattox did not change this situation significantly. The demand for sugar, stimulated by the immediate postwar prosperity, continued strong. Meanwhile, the forces of supply had readjusted themselves. Sugar cane from Cuba and the other Caribbean islands more than made up for the raw sugar no longer received from Louisiana. For though the Civil War had ended, the Louisiana sugar industry was still in a state of disruption. For one thing, the labor supply was thoroughly disorganized. The planters, long accustomed to slave labor, were now faced with the necessity of dealing with free Negroes. It would take many years for both sides to adjust to the new relationship. In the meantime the productivity of labor, when labor could be obtained, fell sharply.[75] But perhaps equally important, the planters found themselves faced with a shortage of capital. Seed, sheds, and mills had all been destroyed in the war, and short-term funds were needed to replace them as well as to pay wages. Unable to secure credit except at exorbitant rates, the planters had no choice but to restrict the amount of acreage planted in cane.[76]

By 1872 the Louisiana sugar industry still had not fully recovered from the effects of the war, the statistics on imported raw sugar attesting to the diminished importance of Louisiana cane. Whereas, in the five years preceding the Civil War, foreign imports accounted for 63 per cent of the raw sugar consumed in the United States, by 1872 they accounted for over 90 per cent of domestic consumption.[77] Thus the Civil War reinforced a trend already apparent before 1861, the growing dominance of eastern refined sugar.

Among the various refining centers in the East, New York reigned supreme. In 1872 its sugar houses processed 59 per cent of the raw sugar imported from abroad; two years earlier they had processed only 55 per cent. Soon the percentage would rise even higher, reaching 68 per cent in 1887.[78] Many factors accounted for New York's

[75] Sitterson, *Sugar County*, pp. 213ff.; for a somewhat broader view of the problems posed by Reconstruction in the South, see Eli Ginzberg and Alfred S. Eichner, "The Reconstructed South," in their *The Troublesome Presence*, pp. 199ff.

[76] Sitterson, *Sugar County*, pp. 291–94.

[77] New York, N.Y., Chamber of Commerce, *Annual Report*, 1872–73, pt. 2, p. 11. Foreign imports account for over 90 per cent of domestic raw sugar consumption whether one surveys the five years preceding 1872, the two years preceding 1872, or 1871 alone.

[78] *Ibid.*; New York, N.Y., Chamber of Commerce, *Annual Report, 1887–88*, pt. 2, p. 10.

dominant role in sugar refining: its long pre-eminence as the nation's leading port, its numerous credit institutions for financing large importations of raw sugar,[79] the availability of inexpensive anthracite coal for powering its refineries, and the large pool of relatively cheap unskilled labor to man them. But perhaps the most important factor was the city's extensive transportation facilities. Not only did two independent railroads provide year-round service to Chicago and other midwestern points, but a canal offered even cheaper carriage during the summer months, helping to force down railroad rates. None of the other seaboard cities were so adequately supplied with transportation facilities for tapping the trans-Appalachian regions, the fastest-growing market area for refined sugar. In addition, other railroads reached out from New York to the south and southwest, providing inexpensive transportation to those areas as well. By 1870, sugar refining had become New York's most important manufacturing industry.[80]

::

It was during these immediate post–Civil War years that the sugar refining industry most closely approximated the conditions underlying what economists were later to define as the purely competitive model.[81] There was, first of all, the large number of refineries, not just in New York, but in Philadelphia and Boston as well. In 1869 there were forty-nine independent refining establishments in those three cities, including twenty-eight in New York and its vicinity.[82] There were, in addition, two refineries in Baltimore and one in St. Louis.[83] By 1878 there were still thirty-eight independent establishments in the three major refining centers, New York, Philadelphia, and Boston.[84]

[79] Although sugar refiners were heavily dependent on credit institutions to finance their large importations of raw sugar, investment bankers apparently played only a minor role in the growth of the industry. The capital to build the refineries seems to have come entirely from the refiners themselves.

[80] J. L. Bishop, *History of American Manufactures*, 3: 150.

[81] Frank H. Knight, *Risk, Uncertainty and Profit*, pp. 78ff. For a discussion of the historical elicitation of the assumptions underlying the competitive model, see George J. Stigler, "Perfect Competition, Historically Contemplated," pp. 1–17.

[82] See Appendixes A, B, and C of this volume.

[83] Their names were affixed to a petition addressed to Congress, a copy of which can be found in the New York Historical Society Library, New York, N.Y.

[84] See Appendixes A, B, and C of this volume.

No one of these refineries, moreover, controlled a disproportionately large share of its market. As Hugh N. Camp, one of the men active in the refining business during the period right after the Civil War, later testified before a congressional committee: "They were all pretty small then to what they are today. Some averaged only seven tons a day and some 400. My impression is that the average was about 200 tons a day."[85] The largest refinery at this time, Havemeyer & Elder, was capable of producing only five hundred tons of refined sugar daily.[86]

Entry into the industry was relatively easy, as evinced by its frequent occurrence. In New York, between 1869 and 1875, an average of from three to four new firms started business each year.[87] Of course, about an equal number of firms disappeared annually, but this, too, reflected the industry's fluid character.

Entry was easy because the barriers were few.[88] An up-to-date refinery, capable of producing sugar as efficiently as any competitor, required a capital investment of between $500,000 and $700,000, a sum not too great by itself to discourage entry.[89] Once a refinery had been built or purchased, the new entrant was on an equal footing with his competitors. Raw sugar could be bought in the open market from any one of the numerous importers or brokers that had emerged in the wake of the refining industry's growth. Depending, of course, on his bargaining skill, the new refiner could be certain that, as a result of the intense competition among these importers and brokers, he would have to pay no more than the going market price for raw

[85] U.S., Congress, House of Representatives, Committee on Manufactures, *Report on Trusts*, p. 73.

[86] H. Havemeyer, *The Havemeyer Family*, p. 101.

[87] See Appendix A of this volume.

[88] For a theoretical treatment of this concept, see Joe S. Bain, *Industrial Organization*, pp. 173–76.

[89] Havemeyer & Company, a refinery controlled by the same branch of the family that owned Havemeyer & Elder, represented a capital investment of $500,000 in 1872. Havemeyer Brothers & Company and Havemeyer, Eastwick & Company, two refineries controlled by the other branch of the family, the direct descendants of William F. Havemeyer, the former mayor of New York City, represented capital investments of $400,000 and $350,000 respectively in 1880 (H. Havemeyer, *The Havemeyer Family*, pp. 117–18, 123–24). Meanwhile, in 1877 Elisha Atkins of Boston was able to buy the old Waters refinery for $450,000, spending an additional $117,411 to recondition and modernize it. This renovated plant became the Bay State Sugar Refinery. See *United States* v. *American Sugar Refining Co. et al.: Testimony Before William B. Brice, Special Examiner*, pp. 4597–600; hereafter cited as *United States* v. *American Sugar Refining Co. et al.*, pretrial testimony, 1912.

sugar.[90] Similarly, the new entrant could dispose of his manufactured product through an extensive network of refined-sugar brokers and wholesale grocers without having to worry about setting up his own sales organization. In fact, the entire mercantile end of the business could be conducted within a few blocks' area of New York and the other major refining centers. Labor, coal, and bone black, the other inputs required, could also be obtained by new entrants on the same terms as any other refiner. While some technological processes were covered by patents, they were not important enough to put a refiner without access to them at a significant disadvantage. Actually, the most important technological processes not available to all comers were the trade secrets embodied in the skill of individual refining superintendents. The fact that men of such skill were limited in number was perhaps the most formidable barrier facing a new entrant. Still, it was often possible to hire the refining superintendent of a firm that had just gone out of business or to entice away the assistant from some active rival, frequently by making him a partner in the new venture.[91]

The fact that the various sugar refining companies were primarily partnerships was also important, for this implied a value orientation which was essential if the industry was to behave competitively.[92] As partnerships, the various sugar refining companies were interested primarily in maximizing their immediate profits.[93] It could hardly be otherwise, for the life of the typical firm was too brief to permit many long-term considerations. Not only death and retirement but even disagreement among the partners could, and sometimes did, bring a sudden end to a prominent refining firm.[94] While it survived, the firm was viewed by its members mainly as a vehicle for earning as large a

[90] As Willett & Gray's *Weekly Statistical Sugar Trade Journal* noted after the sugar trust was formed, ". . . the existence of a well-organized sugar business . . . heretofore included consignees, consignors, merchants, importers, bankers, brokers and agents who, in their combined capacities, helped the producer to carry his sugar and dispose of it, and naturally created a surplus of available stocks always existing in the consuming markets i.e., the refineries" (March 28, 1889). See also the later testimony of Wallace P. Willett, in *United States* v. *American Sugar Refining Co. et al.*, pretrial testimony, 1912, pp. 176ff.

[91] See the testimony of various former refining superintendents, such as Joseph Stillman, Julius A. Stursberg, and Max Wintjen, in *United States* v. *American Sugar Refining Co. et al.*, pretrial testimony, 1912, pp. 4561ff., 4711ff., and 7017ff. respectively.

[92] Economists have not sufficiently appreciated how closely associated the competitive model was with the non-corporate form of business organization.

[93] In Edith Penrose's terminology, their "expectational" horizon was quite limited; see her *The Theory of the Growth of the Firm*, pp. 41–42.

[94] See Appendix A of this volume.

return as possible on the capital which they had invested in it. As active members of the firm, they were at one and the same time both owners and managers. Some of the partners might have hoped that one day their sons would join them in the business, thus perhaps enabling the firm to survive beyond the life span of a single man, but this was a secondary consideration.

Of course, even by 1879, some sugar refineries had taken on the corporate form. The North River Sugar Refining Company, for example, had been organized under New York's general incorporation laws as early as 1857, DeCastro & Donner as early as 1871.[95] But although these firms assumed a corporate form, they remained essentially partnerships of a few active members. As an official of the sugar trust later testified: "Each one of these refineries was in the ownership of a limited number of persons. The Havemeyers, for instance, consisted of three partners, and others were in somewhat the same proportion."[96]

Competition during this period was fostered by the fact that refined sugar was essentially a homogeneous product. The new refining techniques had eliminated much of the variance in quality which had once been so characteristic of sugar. Centrifugal sugar was centrifugal sugar, and granulated was granulated. Each had its own easily recognizable characteristics. There were, of course, certain well-known brands, such as Havemeyer & Elder's or Matthiessen & Weicher's patent cut loaf sugar. These brands sold at a premium because of their reputation as consistently high-quality sugars.[97] But aside from this reputation they were the same as other granulated sugars, and the premium paid for them was not that high. Whatever confusion as to quality still remained after the new refining techniques were developed was eliminated by the growing use of the polariscope.[98] With this instrument it was possible to measure the exact saccharin content of sugar. While its greatest use was in the purchase and sale of the raw product, it also proved helpful in establishing a uniform quality for all lower grades of refined sugar.

It was not simply that the sugar refining industry was structured like a competitive industry. More importantly, it behaved like a competitive industry. There was, at any given moment in time, a

[95] *People* v. *North River Sugar Refining Co.: Record*, p. 54; see also H. Havemeyer, *The Havemeyer Family*, p. 119.

[96] New York, Legislature, Senate, Committee on General Laws, *Report on Investigation Relative to Trusts*, p. 8.

[97] J. O. Donner, letter to the *New York Evening Post*, March 13, 1880.

[98] The polariscope, although invented by the French optician M. Soleil as early as 1846, had only gradually been brought into commercial use; see *DeBow's Review*, 5 (1848) : 357.

single industry price determined by the interaction of impersonal supply and demand factors. This industry price was based on the latest quotation for standard "A" sugar, as reported by the brokers themselves. The prices of lower-grade sugars were obtained simply by subtracting the usual differentials.

This industry price then became the basis for each refiner's price and output decision. If he thought the market was growing stronger, he would try to obtain a better price for his sugar. Otherwise he would sell all he could at the current industry price. Sometimes, when the market weakened, he would have to accept a price below the last market quotation. In that case, his price soon became the new industry price.

If the price of refined sugar rose, the refiner would increase his meltings until the additional cost he incurred threatened to wipe out any additional revenue he might earn. If, on the other hand, the price of refined sugar fell, he would reduce his output. As long as the industry price was greater than the cost of raw sugar, labor, fuel, bone black, and other direct costs, the refiner would keep his plant going, even though he was not fully covering his overhead costs, including a return on the capital invested in the business. But if the industry price fell so low that he could not even cover his direct costs, he would then shut down the refinery until the price once more rose to profitable levels. During the winter months, when the Louisiana crop was being harvested, many of the less efficient, marginal refineries found themselves forced to suspend operations temporarily.[99]

What was most significant about the sugar refining industry's pricing behavior was the frequency with which the margin between raw and refined sugar changed.[100] Since the price of raw sugar itself

[99] See the early volumes of Willett & Gray's *Weekly Statistical Sugar Trade Journal*, available only at the New York offices of Willett & Gray, Inc. Although the earliest issues still extant date only as far back as 1883, they nonetheless are indicative of the industry's pricing situation several years previous to that. See also the testimony of Stursberg, Claus Doscher, William Havemeyer, and others, in *United States* v. *American Sugar Refining Co. et al.*, pretrial testimony, 1912, and the testimony of Henry O. Havemeyer, in U.S. House Committee on Manufactures, *Report on Trusts.*

[100] The importance of frequent price changes as an indication of competitive price behavior was first pointed out by Gardiner C. Means in a memorandum to the Secretary of Agriculture in 1934. The memorandum was subsequently published as Senate Document No. 13 under the title *Industrial Prices and Their Relative Inflexibility* (74th Cong., 1st sess., 1935), and has now been republished in a collection of Means's essays, *The Corporate Revolution in America.* Unfortunately, this point has been somewhat obscured by the attacks on Means for asserting in the same memorandum that not only the *frequency* of price changes, but also the *magnitude* of price changes, is indicative of competitive price behavior. The latter point has been effectively refuted, on both theoretical and empirical grounds.

fluctuated continually as a result of various competitive pressures in that market, the margin between raw and refined sugar was the true guide to the refineries' pricing practices. That margin changed almost daily as each refiner sought, independently, either to increase his own sales by undercutting the market price or to raise his total sales revenue by forcing up the industry price.[101] Any member of the industry might be the initiator of these price changes.

Finally, the performance of the sugar refining industry was what one would expect of a competitive industry. The high profits in the years immediately after the Civil War not only attracted new firms into the industry but also encouraged the existing refineries to expand their output.[102] As a result of the increased supply of sugar, as well as of continued improvements in technology, the margin between raw and refined sugar gradually narrowed. Before the Civil War it had been approximately 5 cents a pound;[103] by 1869 it had fallen, on the average, to 3.59 cents a pound. The decline then continued as follows:

AVERAGE MARGIN BETWEEN "MUSCOVADO" RAW SUGAR AND STANDARD "A" REFINED[104]

Year	Margin (per pound)
1870	3.47¢
1871	3.21
1872	2.88
1873	2.55
1874	2.28
1875	2.22
1876	2.07
1877	1.62

Moreover, the industry continued to adopt more improved methods of production, thereby penalizing those refineries which failed to keep

[101] See the early volumes of Willett & Gray's *Weekly Statistical Sugar Trade Journal.*

[102] *United States* v. *American Sugar Refining Co. et al.*, pretrial testimony, 1912, p. 5914.

[103] Donner, letter to the *New York Evening Post,* March 13, 1880.

[104] Wells, *The Sugar Industry and the Tariff*, p. 70. During the earlier period, from 1860 to 1869, when sugar margins were declining, wholesale prices in general, according to the Warren-Pearson index, rose from 93 to 151, using 1910–14 as the base period. During the latter period, from 1870 to 1877, when sugar margins continued to decline, wholesale prices fell from 135 to 106 on the Warren-Pearson scale. The secular decline in sugar margins would thus appear to have been independent of general wholesale price movements.

up with the evolving technology. Of the three or four firms that were forced to leave the industry each year, the majority were handicapped by out-of-date equipment.[105] No major technological breakthroughs occurred such as those which had, in effect, created an entirely new industry shortly before the Civil War, but the improvement in production techniques was nonetheless steady.[106] For example, the Havemeyer & Elder firm was able to increase its output substantially simply by curtailing the authority of its foremen and reducing the boiling time from 4 to 2½ hours.[107] As a result of this and other improved methods, such as double filtration, the direct cost of refining fell from approximately 3 cents a pound during the Civil War to 1½ cents a pound in the decade and a half immediately following, even for an average refinery.[108] Meanwhile, the most efficient firms were able to refine sugar for only ⅝–⅞ of a cent a pound.[109]

Thus the sugar refining industry seemed to be performing in the manner that economists have predicted a competitive industry would perform—it passed along to consumers the benefits of improved production techniques and thus assured, in the economic sphere, the greatest good for the largest number. But even as the sugar refining industry was most clearly manifesting its competitive character, it was going through a series of convulsions which seemed to suggest that a competitive industry was inherently unstable, for the convulsions were themselves the product of that same competitive character.

[105] Wells, *The Sugar Industry and the Tariff*, p. 70.

[106] U.S. House Committee on Manufactures, *Report on Trusts*, p. 145.

[107] *United States* v. *American Sugar Refining Co. et al.*, pretrial testimony, 1912, p. 302.

[108] Testimony of Lawson N. Fuller before the Lexow committee (New York, Legislature, Joint Committee to Investigate Trusts, *Report and Proceedings*, p. 449; hereafter cited as Lexow committee investigation, 1897).

[109] *Ibid.*; U.S. House Committee on Manufactures, *Report on Trusts*, p. 73; *United States* v. *American Sugar Refining Co. et al.*, pretrial testimony, 1912, p. 4559.

3 :: COMPETITION AND INSTABILITY

As in the case of other manufacturing industries, the years from the late 1870's until 1887 were a period of transition for sugar refining. Although the industry still retained its basically competitive structure—indeed, improvements in communications made it all the more competitive—it was now marked by increasing instability. This instability was manifested in various ways: in charges that extensive frauds were being perpetrated against the customs revenue of the United States, in efforts to change the tariff laws, in complaints that certain firms were adulterating their sugar, and in accusations that varying groups of refiners were conspiring to drive other groups out of business. The underlying cause of the instability, however, was the failure of the demand for refined sugar to expand as rapidly as the potential supply. Given the large fixed investment required in sugar refining, this meant that all but the one or two leading firms found themselves no longer able to cover their full costs, if an adequate return on invested capital is included as part of these costs. Agreements to limit output or fix margins brought, at most, only temporary relief. More drastic measures, it was finally realized, were required.

::

The first public manifestation of trouble in the sugar refining industry was a headline in the *New York Tribune* of September 6, 1878, hinting at extensive corruption in the collection of sugar duties. ". . . It is no longer a question of doubt," the accompanying article declared, "that for years there has been a systematic movement among certain importers and refiners of sugar to defraud the government. . . ." Estimating the losses in customs revenue at $5 million, the *Tribune* added, "Many refiners and importers, who refused to go into this combination, have been driven out of business and no honest man can successfully compete with the combination."[1] The charges had a familiar ring.

[1] *New York Tribune*, September 6, 1878.

Still fresh in everyone's mind were the recent revelations with regard to the so-called whiskey ring, which it was estimated had defrauded the government of approximately $3 million annually during the four years it had operated.[2] One of the scandals that were to give the Grant administration its reputation for corruption, the "ring" was actually a pool, similar in its purpose to the combinations that arose in other industries during the immediate post–Civil War period to cushion the effects of a growing disequilibrium between supply and demand.[3] The whiskey combination was, in fact, different from other pools only in its ability to enlist the co-operation of prominent government officials in its efforts to restrict output and prevent the entry of new distillers into the industry. With the connivance of Federal agents, certain favored distillers were able to avoid paying the seventy-cents-a-gallon excise tax on at least 50 per cent of the whiskey they produced, half the money saved going to the distillers themselves and half to the leading Republican politicians who had organized the scheme in each of the three major distilling centers, St. Louis, Chicago, and Milwaukee.[4] Not only did the thirty-five-cents-a-gallon cost disadvantage make it extremely difficult for any firm not a member of the ring to survive in business, but also the federal revenue agents, with access to the records of any distiller, were able to see to it that the production quotas set by the pool were scrupulously honored. Yet the scheme originally intended to fill party coffers gradually became more and more a scheme to line the pockets of the prominent politicians involved, and it was this fact, as well as the growing brazenness with which the ring's operations were conducted, that eventually led to its undoing.[5] The resulting disclosures were among the reasons that the Grant administration fell into such bad repute during its final years.

Grant's Republican successor, Rutherford B. Hayes, in an effort to improve his party's image following the disputed election victory of 1876, sought in various ways to meet the public demand for polit-

[2] H. V. Boynton, "Whiskey Ring," p. 300.

[3] See Arthur S. Dewing, *A History of the National Cordage Company*, pp. 5ff.; Allan Nevins, *John D. Rockefeller*, 1: 310; Jeremiah W. Jenks, "The Michigan Salt Association," pp. 3–10.

[4] Testimony of David P. Dyer, the U.S. attorney who helped prosecute the whiskey frauds (U.S. Congress, House of Representatives, Select Committee Concerning the Whiskey Frauds, *Whiskey Frauds*, p. 31). See also Jeremiah W. Jenks, "The Development of the Whiskey Trust"; Lucius E. Guese, "St. Louis and the Great Whiskey Ring."

[5] Boynton's "Whiskey Ring" is still the best account of how the ring was finally broken up. See also Guese, "The Great Whiskey Ring," pp. 168ff.; Matthew Josephson, *The Politicos*, pp. 198–202.

ical reform. One of his first moves upon taking the oath of office was to appoint a presidential commission, headed by John Jay, grandson of the illustrious Founding Father and a well-known civil service reformer, to investigate the New York customs house, long regarded as a hotbed of corruption. The Jay commission, while condemning certain patronage practices and calling for various reforms, noted in its report, delivered to the president late in 1877, that it had found evidence of dishonesty on the part of only a few minor customs-house officials. The Democrats, however, sensing that the extent of corruption was much greater than the Jay commission had indicated, launched their own investigation of the New York customs house through the House Ways and Means Committee, which they then controlled. In the back of their minds, undoubtedly, was the hope that they might uncover further scandals, rivaling those which had so shocked the nation in the case of the whiskey ring.

It was this new investigation, conducted by Representative Fernando Wood, the aged former mayor of New York City, which brought to the surface the charges of widespread fraud in the collection of sugar customs. The article in the *Tribune* first reporting these charges appeared only two weeks before Wood formally opened hearings in New York, and that first article was followed by others.

Once the committee actually began its hearings, on September 17, 1878, the charges of fraud were repeated by many of the smaller refiners, especially those who had already been forced out of business. "Fraud has run through the sugar business here for ten years," said William T. Booth, a partner in Booth & Edgar, a refinery which was on the verge of going out of business permanently. He then added, "I have been in and out among men and have preserved a good reputation; and when I say I know a thing to be so, no one will be found who will doubt my word. Now I say I know of frauds on the revenue in the importations of sugar which, when they are fully disclosed, will furnish reading that will astonish the people of this country."[6]

Employing a crude statistical analysis, witnesses before the committee were able to offer circumstantial evidence that the federal government was indeed being deprived of substantial sugar duties. The tariff on sugar was levied according to a color standard first developed by the Dutch. Until the invention of the polariscope, this so-called Dutch standard provided the only recognized means of determining the saccharin content of sugar. The lighter the shade of

[6] *New York Tribune*, September 19, 1878.

brown, the higher in saccharin content the sugar was supposed to be and the higher the absolute duty levied. Pure sugar was, of course, pure white and was taxed at the rate for refined sugar.[7] Applying the tariff rate for each of the different grades of sugar to the quantities of each grade thought to be imported into this country, witnesses estimated that the customs collections from sugar were falling short of what they should have been by approximately $4 million a year,[8] a rather significant sum. The question was whether the deficiency was due to systematic fraud or to the obsolete manner in which the government assessed the saccharin content of imported raw sugar.

As other witnesses before the committee testified, the invention of the centrifugal machine meant that growers in tropical areas were now able, with a modest capital investment, to produce sugar that was virtually free of all impurities. This sugar, sold in the United States on the basis of saccharin content as measured by the polariscope, commanded a top price. Yet because the duties on imported raw sugar were still levied according to hue, it was possible to pay the lowest duty simply by artificially coloring the sugar brown. A leading importer of sugar, after pointing out to the committee the resulting loss of revenue to the government, asked rhetorically, "Did the refiners get it? Certainly not, for the reason that the refiners buy all their sugars here upon their saccharin strength. . . . the planters—the manufacturers of centrifugal sugars—are the ones, of course, that got [the benefit]."[9] Undoubtedly, as everyone agreed, the law had to be changed, for the tariff on sugar accounted for nearly 30 per cent of all customs revenues, the major source of federal funds.[10] But as to what form the changes should take, the industry split into two opposing camps.

[7] The colors of the Dutch standard (D.S.) ranged in number from 1 to 25, the higher the number the lighter the shade of brown. Sugars classified D.S. No. 20 or higher were considered to be refined and were taxed at the full rate of five cents a pound. Those classified below D.S. No. 20 were taxed at a correspondingly lower rate as indicated below.

Classification	Rate
Raw sugars not above No. 7 D.S.	2.18¢
Raw sugars above No. 7 D.S. but not above No. 10	2.50
Raw sugars above No. 10 D.S. but not above No. 13	2.81
Raw sugars above No. 13 D.S. but not above No. 15	3.43
Raw sugars above No. 15 D.S. but not above No. 20	4.06

See David A. Wells, *The Sugar Industry and the Tariff*, pp. 22–29.

[8] Henry A. Brown, *Sugar Frauds*, pp. 3–9.

[9] Wells, *The Sugar Industry and the Tariff*, pp. 43–44.

[10] *Ibid.*, p. 9.

On one side were those who argued that the only change required was to substitute the polariscope test for the Dutch standard. If this were done, they said, the government would be assured of collecting whatever customs duties it was now losing.[11] On the other side were those who argued that the purported losses from artificially colored Demerara sugars were a "mere bagatelle,"[12] that adopting the polariscope test would not end the drain on government revenues. The Treasury Department was losing money, they charged, not because the wrong standard for determining the value of raw sugar was being applied, but rather because certain refiners, through deliberate underweighing and improper sampling, were systematically defrauding the government. If the drain on government revenues was to be halted, it was argued, far more fundamental reforms were required than the mere substitution of the polariscope test for the current color standards.[13]

The conflict, however, involved more than just the question of how the sugar duties could best be collected. Those making the charges of fraud were primarily the smaller refiners, those whose plants were located away from the water's edge. Allied with them were many of the raw-sugar importers, especially those representing Cuban and other Caribbean growers. What seemed to concern these two groups was not that the federal government was being defrauded, but that they, as a consequence, were being put at a certain disadvantage. As the *Commercial and Financial Chronicle*, which subsequently championed their cause, declared:

> . . . These methods which have hitherto proved so efficacious in depriving the Government of many millions of revenue, and in enriching the parties who have availed of them, are to a certain extent open to both importers and important refiners, but the latter have . . . the immense advantage of receiving their cargoes at their own refineries, where, within twenty-four hours from the arrival of the vessel, the sugars [can] be dumped into the boiling vats, thus rendering all identification impossible; whilst the merchant importer is obliged to land his cargoes at public bonded stores, where they remain for days subject to re-examination by the customs officers and to consequent exposure.[14]

It is interesting to note that, as an outgrowth of the various charges, the only person to be convicted of defrauding the government was an importer.[15]

[11] *Ibid.*, pp. 91–99.
[12] Brown, *Sugar Frauds*, p. 10.
[13] Wells, *The Sugar Industry and the Tariff*, pp. 99–100.
[14] *Commercial and Financial Chronicle,* November 16, 1878.
[15] *New York Tribune*, September 12, 1878.

The motivation of those making the charges of fraud was even more clearly indicated by the nature of the suggestions they offered for eliminating the supposed evils. These were that the government should permit no sugar to be landed at the refiners' private wharves and that a uniform rate of duty should be levied on all unrefined sugar.[16] These suggestions, if adopted, would have canceled out any cost advantage the major refiners might have had, and in some cases would even have placed them at somewhat of a handicap. Thus the battle over the tariff was actually a maneuvering for position within the industry. In fact, because of the industry's then current condition, it had become a bitter struggle for survival.

::

From the moment that the elder Havemeyer first built his new refinery on the East River in Williamsburg, it had been recognized that a waterfront site offered certain cost advantages over a location in the heart of Manhattan. As one refiner later remarked, "The difference in transportation, lighterage, warehousing, and harbor expenses alone is sufficient to pay a dividend."[17] Several of the refineries subsequently erected were also built on the water's edge, at various sites throughout the New York harbor, but many firms preferred to remain where they were. The expected savings did not seem to justify the additional capital expense that would have been necessary to relocate their plants. Besides, the margin between raw and refined sugar was more than sufficient to ensure a handsome profit even at the inland sites.

In 1870, refiners located on the water's edge had persuaded Congress to change the tariff on sugar so as to favor the importation of the lower grades. Previously, noted David A. Wells, one of the best-known publicists of his day, "owing to the policy of imposing but one . . . rate of duty on all sugars not above No. 12 [Dutch standard][18] the sugars of lower grades and prices were so discriminated against that none of them could be imported into the United States." This was because on the lower grades, such as No. 7 Dutch standard, importers were forced to pay, on an ad valorem basis, a much higher duty. As Wells added, "All such sugars, therefore, found their market almost exclusively in England, to the great benefit, in the absence of

[16] *Commercial and Financial Chronicle*, November 16, 1878; Brown, *Sugar Frauds*, p. 13.

[17] J. O. Donner, letter to the *New York Evening Post*, March 13, 1880.

[18] See note 7 above.

the world's competition, of British refiners and British commerce, and to the great detriment of the commerce and industry of the United States. . . .[19] To remedy this situation, Congress divided the old category, "not above No. 12 D.S.," into three separate categories, thus making the duty on the lower grades of sugar correspond more nearly to their value.

Several of the refiners promptly began installing the equipment necessary to process these lower grades. The savings on the raw material would, they hoped, more than justify the additional expense. "Previous to 1870," Theodore Havemeyer later pointed out, "the capital invested by these firms did not amount to $4,000,000; but since that date two very large new refineries have been built, and already existing ones have increased their works, to the amount of $9,000,000, . . . and this in order mainly to enable them to produce the cheaper grades of sugar which the public now so largely demands."[20] Again, many of the refiners refused to make the necessary capital investment. Profits, they felt, were sufficient without it.

But then the depression that followed on the heels of the Panic of 1873 accentuated a trend which had already been apparent for some time: the decline in the margin between raw and refined sugar. By 1874 this margin had fallen to 2.28 cents a pound, nearly a one-third decline in four years,[21] and many of the smaller, inland refiners began to feel the pinch. "Their refineries," said J. O. Donner, a close associate of the Havemeyers, "were old-fashioned, their former large profits were either squandered or tied up in outside speculations, leaving them no means to make the necessary radical changes." Some owner-entrepreneurs, like the Stuart brothers, prudently withdrew from the industry; but others, for a variety of reasons, tried to hang on.[22] Either they had sons who they hoped would one day succeed them in the business, or else they failed to perceive the changes that had taken place in sugar refining. In any case, they remained in the industry until it was too late to leave without taking a substantial loss. Their capital, they knew, could not be readily transferred to another industry, since the equipment in which it was tied up was of use only in sugar refining. Sold for scrap, that equipment would have brought only a fraction of its value as part of a going concern. More important, the skill and knowledge of these men also was limited to

[19] Wells, *The Sugar Industry and the Tariff*, p. 27.
[20] Theodore A. Havemeyer, *Letter to J. R. Tucker and Jas. G. Carlisle*, p. 4.
[21] Wells, *The Sugar Industry and the Tariff*, p. 70.
[22] Donner, letter to the *New York Evening Post*, p. 4.

sugar refining, and many of them were too old to learn a new business. Caught in a desperate situation, these refiners began looking around for any means which might enable them to survive.

One of the first areas to which they turned their attention was the drawback allowance on exported sugar. The government had always refunded the customs duties paid on imported goods that were subsequently exported. However, in the case of sugar, it was difficult to apply this rule, for in the refining process there was always a certain loss of raw material. It was up to the Treasury Department to take this factor into consideration when deciding what was a fair and reasonable drawback, but the difficulty in determining this had led to numerous disputes down through the years.

In 1875 the small, inland refiners, joined by their largest competitors, appealed to the secretary of the treasury to increase the drawback allowance. The current rate, they argued, was insufficient to reimburse them for the duties they were forced to pay on the raw sugar consumed in the refining process.[23] The secretary refused, but he did do something which had essentially the same effect. Previously, the government had retained 10 per cent of any drawback allowed, in order to cover the cost of collecting sugar duties. On March 3, 1875, Secretary of the Treasury B. H. Bristow, the man responsible for ferreting out and prosecuting the whiskey ring, reduced this fee to 1 per cent, the equivalent of raising the drawback allowance by thirty-four cents a hundred pounds.[24]

Whether the secretary's decision was reasonable or not was difficult to determine. Theodore Havemeyer later contended that the increased drawback allowance merely enabled the refiners to recover 99 per cent of the duties they were forced to pay on the sugar processed and shipped overseas,[25] but a statistical analysis by Treasury Department officials tended to show that the rate was excessive.[26] In any case, whatever its merits, the increased drawback allowance amounted, in effect, to an export subsidy, and it "at once placed refiners in a position for largely increasing their export business."[27] Whereas, before, American exports of refined sugar had been such an insignificant factor that no one had even bothered to keep a record of them, in the months following Bristow's decision they rose to a

[23] *Papers Relative to the Drawback Rates on Exported Sugar*, p. 1.
[24] *New York Times*, October 16, 1875.
[25] *Papers Relative to Drawback Rates*, p. 1.
[26] Henry A. Brown, *Revised Analysis of the Sugar Question*, pp. 17–18.
[27] *New York Times*, October 16, 1875.

rate of more than seventy-two million pounds annually (most of this going to Canada).[28]

This sudden blossoming of an export trade did bring the industry temporary relief from the downward pressure on margins. In its annual report for 1875–76, the New York City Chamber of Commerce reported that the increased drawback allowance was helping to take up some of the depression slack.[29] The increased allowance, however, proved too successful. British refiners soon complained that it was enabling Americans to undersell them by a third of a cent, and six months later, under pressure from the British foreign ministry, the secretary of the treasury reduced the drawback allowance from $3.75 to $3.21 per hundred pounds.[30] This drove American sugar from all but the Canadian markets, though in the latter the Americans' success was complete, forcing the refineries in that country to close down.[31] Even this limited success proved too great, however. Alarmed by the large amounts they were forced to pay out to refiners, Treasury officials became convinced that the drawback allowance was still too liberal, and late in 1877 reduced it to 3.14 cents a pound.[32] Exports of refined sugar soon fell to a trickle, aggravating the price squeeze on the industry.[33]

::

The hope of developing a large export market to augment the insufficient domestic demand having been disappointed, the small, inland refiners began turning to other tactics in their desperate struggle for survival. It was at this time that complaints of adulterated sugar first were heard.[34] Some of the refiners began mixing glucose made from corn syrup with their regular refinery products.[35] Since glucose was a much cheaper product than refined sugar, this amounted, in effect, to a disguised price increase. But such tactics

[28] Brown, *Revised Analysis of the Sugar Question*, p. 16. This, as well as all other figures on American exports during this period, must be viewed with a certain caution. Many of the figures not only contradict themselves but also fly in the face of other well-known facts.

[29] New York, N.Y., Chamber of Commerce, *Annual Report*, 1875–76, pt. 2, p. 9.

[30] *New York Times*, October 16, 1875.

[31] New York, N.Y., Chamber of Commerce, *Annual Report*, 1876–77, pt. 2, p. 12.

[32] Brown, *Revised Analysis of the Sugar Question*, p. 18.

[33] New York, N.Y., Chamber of Commerce, *Annual Report*, 1877–78, p. 2, p. 13.

[34] Brown, *Revised Analysis of the Sugar Question*, p. 16.

[35] Wells, *The Sugar Industry and the Tariff*, pp. 51–53.

offered no more than temporary relief to a few refiners. More drastic remedies were required.

The small, inland refiners soon began a determined effort to force all their rivals in New York to agree to a price-fixing scheme whereby the margin between raw and refined sugar would be maintained at 2¼ cents a pound,[36] for by 1877 the margin had fallen below 1¾ cents a pound.[37] However, the larger refiners, those whose plants were located on the water's edge, refused to go along with the scheme. Though there were no more than half a dozen of these refineries throughout the country, they produced 1.2 billion pounds of sugar annually, or three-fourths of the entire U.S. output.[38] Because of their locations and the more efficient refining methods they employed they were able to earn a return on their capital, even at the low margin then prevailing. On the other hand, any scheme to maintain prices would of necessity require a drastic curtailment of their output. And since these refineries embodied such a large capital investment, especially in comparison with the other plants, such a curtailment would lead to a disproportionate increase in their per unit overhead costs. It was for these reasons that the larger members of the industry resisted the price-fixing scheme.

More and more the struggle became one between these major firms and the small, inland refineries. When the former balked at the price-fixing scheme, the other members of the industry sought to bring pressure on them in other ways. "After the failure to establish a downright monopoly or combination as they proposed . . . ," said Donner, "an effort [was] made in the Board of Underwriters and the fire-insurance offices to enforce a cessation of all night-work at the refineries by the withdrawal of the insurances." Since the destruction of refineries by fire was a frequent occurrence, this seemed to be a justifiable action, even if it did lead to a reduction in output. But then it was shown "that no refinery had ever burned down *during*, but always *after* working hours,"[39] and the insurance companies reversed their stand.

When this gambit failed, the small, inland refiners tried another. "A little later," Donner explained, "a deliberate attempt was made by some members of the opposition, who held positions as bank presidents or directors, to enforce reduced work through the destruction of the credit of their opponents, thus preventing these firms from

[36] Donner, letter to the *New York Evening Post*, p. 4.
[37] Wells, *The Sugar Industry and the Tariff*, p. 70.
[38] T. Havemeyer, *Letters to Tucker and Carlisle*, p. 3.
[39] Donner, letter to the *New York Evening Post*, p. 4.

obtaining the required amount of raw material." In other words, the threat of being unable to finance the importation of cane from Cuba was used to try to force the larger refiners to agree to a price-fixing scheme.

This move, however, had an effect quite different from what had been intended. Denied access to local capital, the major refiners had no choice but to turn "to foreign credits, and as these could only be used in the form of drafts against shipments, it forced them into importations for their own account, and thus directly injured the importing merchants, who until then had this branch entirely in their own hands."[40] The possibility that the major refiners in deciding to do away with the services of importers were also motivated by other factors was later indicated by Theodore Havemeyer. "The refiners who commanded capital enough [to import] their own sugar wholly or in part," he said, ". . . not only saved the commission which would have been paid to the importer, but also sundries, such as dockage, storage, insurance, loss of interest on capital, etc." Havemeyer estimated these savings to be equal to approximately an eighth of a cent a pound.[41]

This bypassing of the importing merchants not only put the small, inland firms at a greater disadvantage but also made active opponents of many of the merchants. When, as a next step, the small, inland firms began charging fraud against the public revenues, these importing merchants quickly took up the cry. They also supported the demands that no more sugar be permitted entrance at refiners' private wharves and that a uniform tariff be levied on all unrefined sugars, for these demands, if adopted by the government, would have reestablished the business on its former basis. Only high-grade sugars, which all refiners were capable of processing equally well, would be imported, and these high-grade sugars would have to go through the regular customs house, thus returning control of the import trade to the same class of merchants which had held it previously, and eliminating whatever cost advantage the refineries located along the water's edge might have. This fight over the sugar tariff was to continue for many years, being waged before congressional committees, at public meetings, in the courts, and through the public prints.

The major refiners were led by Theodore Havemeyer, who, along with his brother Henry, held an interest in three of the nation's largest sugar houses. ". . . Firms like my own," he said, "which have been in

[40] *Ibid.*
[41] T. Havemeyer, *Letters to Tucker and Carlisle*, pp. 5–6.

existence for three-quarters of a century, and upon whose name the shadow of a stain has never rested, have been privately and publicly maligned, and for what reason?" Simply because, he told a congressional group considering changes in the sugar tariff in 1880, they had used the profits from their businesses to make their plants more efficient. "Many refiners," he said, "did not look at things in the same light. . . . [S]ome of them, situated in the heart of the city, were indisposed to seek other locations where savings in manufacture could be effected; others [were] unwilling to adopt the new methods of refining necessary for the large production of yellow [that is, the cheaper grade] sugars. . . . It is to these causes, and not to the frauds, . . . that the withdrawal of many refiners from business is really to be attributed."[42]

The other refiners also were led by members of the Havemeyer family—Hector and William, second cousins to Theodore and Henry. This branch of the family had re-entered the sugar business in 1870, purchasing a refinery located on a waterfront site, at Jersey City, New Jersey. Later, a second plant, located along the Brooklyn waterfront, was acquired.[43] Neither refinery, however, was equipped to process the lower-grade sugars, and it was this which led Hector and William to advocate a uniform duty on raw sugar. Yet seldom were their voices actually heard in support of such a measure. Preoccupied by their many investments in other fields, they left the lobbying for a change in the tariff laws to their associates in the sugar refining business, Edward P. Eastwick and John E. Searles, Jr.[44] The former was a veteran refiner, the latter, a young man of forty who was then in the process of reorganizing Hector's two previously independent refineries into the Havemeyer Sugar Refining Company.[45]

In testimony before the House Ways and Means Committee, Eastwick emphasized not his firm's inability to process the lower grades of sugar but rather the difficulty of preventing fraud under the existing system of levying tariffs. The various private wharves, he pointed out, had only a single customs inspector assigned to them, and all that was necessary to have incoming cargoes certified as being lower in grade than they actually were was to win that inspector's friendship. "The

[42] *Ibid.*, p. 7.

[43] Henry O. Havemeyer, Jr., *Biographical Record of the Havemeyer Family, 1606–1943*, p. 123; *United States* v. *American Sugar Refining Co. et al.*, pretrial testimony, 1912, p. 4504.

[44] See John E. Searles, Jr., *et al.*, *Memorial to the Committee on Ways and Means on the Sugar Tariff.*

[45] See the obituary for Searles in the *New York Times*, October 25, 1908.

business of sugar refining has been so far improved and the margin for profit so greatly reduced," said Eastwick, "that a very slight discrimination in favor of one importer at the expense of another must prove disastrous to the party discriminated against." To Eastwick this was such an important consideration that even though his own firm was located on the water's edge he preferred to see the system of private docks abolished rather than have the current method of collecting sugar duties retained. Far more preferable in his eyes, however, would be a single tariff rate on all grades of unrefined sugar.[46]

But a uniform tariff on sugar, Theodore Havemeyer pointed out with telling effect to the same committee,[47] would discriminate against the lower-grade sugars, once more driving them from the American market, since on an ad valorem basis they would be paying a higher duty. If, to prevent the loss of government revenues, it was necessary to change the tariff on sugar in any way, Havemeyer preferred to see the Dutch standard replaced by the polariscope test.[48] The latter remedy, however, was opposed by the smaller refiners, who continued to press Congress—to no avail, as it turned out—for a uniform sugar tariff. Bribery of congressmen was charged,[49] but the fact was that all tariff legislation, not just that relevant to sugar, was hopelessly stymied by the inability of the House and Senate to agree on any single measure.[50]

::

The fact that the tariff remained unchanged amounted, in effect, to a victory for the forces led by Theodore Havemeyer. This victory brought little rejoicing, however, for the underlying problem—the disequilibrium between supply and demand—had not been solved. As the New York City Chamber of Commerce noted in its 1879 report, "It would seem, judging from the mortality that continues to attend sugar refining establishments, several in this and other cities having closed last year, that the prosecution of this business is at-

[46] Searles *et al.*, *Memorial*, p. 35.

[47] Wells, for example, and many congressmen were greatly impressed by this argument; see Wells, *The Sugar Industry and the Tariff*.

[48] T. Havemeyer, *Letters to Tucker and Carlisle*, p. 15.

[49] *New York Times*, June 4, 1880.

[50] Meanwhile, Treasury officials, in an effort to close a proven loophole, began ordering the polariscope test in cases where discoloration of sugar was suspected. Although the Supreme Court was eventually to declare this action illegal (*Merritt* v. *Welch*), it did momentarily stem the losses in revenue, bringing protests from all refiners, large and small (*New York Times*, February 15, 1881).

tended with great hazard—and yet the quantity of sugar year by year steadily increases."[51] The better-situated, better-equipped refineries were still able to earn a respectable return on invested capital, but now they were beginning to find the severe competition increasingly unsuited to their own best interests. Most of the firms that were susceptible to competitive pressure had long since quit the industry; those marginal firms which still remained showed few signs of folding. The latter, whenever the margin between raw and refined sugar fell below their actual costs of production, simply shut down their refineries and waited until the margin rose again. As long as the plants themselves had no value except as scrap, and as long as no additional outlay was required to keep them running, they could continue in this fashion indefinitely.

Moreover, the price in a competitive industry such as sugar refining was at this time generally determined by whichever firm was willing to sell at the lowest price. In other words, the price was determined not infrequently by the marginal enterprises seeking to retain their foothold in the industry. As long as they were willing to supply the market at the quoted price, the price could rise no higher. Thus the tendency of these firms to resume production whenever the margin rose even slightly above a certain point served as a brake on the price level for the entire sugar refining industry. Production continued to expand, but the area of profitable operation narrowed. By 1880 the average margin between raw and refined sugar had fallen to 1.4 cents a pound.[52] It was for this reason that in the spring of 1880, when it became clear that Congress was not going to act on the tariff that year, the two opposing groups within the industry closed ranks in an effort to limit production by agreement.[53]

As pooling arrangements go, this was a fairly sophisticated one. At a meeting held on June 1 it was decided that each firm would pay into a common fund one cent for each pound of sugar it refined. The fund was to be divided at the end of each week among the various parties to the agreement according to the melting capacity of each, the latter figure being determined by taking the largest amount of raw sugar melted in any four consecutive weeks prior to the agreement. An executive committee, including Henry and William Havemeyer, was appointed to administer the pool, and refiners were to

[51] New York, N.Y., Chamber of Commerce, *Annual Report*, 1878–79, pt. 2, p. 14.

[52] See Appendix D of this volume.

[53] *New York Times*, June 13, 1880.

submit to it daily reports on their meltings. The committee also was given the power to close down certain selected refineries if the price of refined sugar fell below a certain figure. The agreement, signed by most of the refiners in New York, Boston, and Philadelphia, was to last for one year, beginning June 15.[54]

The fatal weakness of this and all similar pools was that the agreements which established them could not be enforced in any court of law. In New York the governing cases were quite explicit on this point. An 1839 decision had declared: "Contracts in restraint of trade are, for the most part, contrary to sound policy and are consequently held void. This is the general rule. There may be cases where the contract is neither injurious to the public nor the obliger, and then the law makes an exception. . . . [But] the general presumption is against all contracts in restraint of trade."[55] In subsequent decisions[56] the New York courts had specifically refused to uphold various pooling arrangements. Other courts in other states had done the same.[57] Although in periods of general economic depression the courts tended to take a more tolerant attitude toward such combinations,[58] the weight of judicial opinion throughout the country was clearly against compelling the parties to pooling agreements to abide by them.

Denied the protection of the law, these pooling agreements would inevitably break down. In order to force prices up to the desired level, production had to be curtailed; but this had the effect of increasing a firm's per unit costs. If a firm were to violate the pooling agreement, even just slightly, it would be able not only to take advantage of the resulting economies of scale but also to sell the extra output at the artificially higher price. The incentive to cheat was so great that eventually some firm would violate the agreement.

Although the exact details have been lost to history, this was essentially the fate that befell this first pool in the sugar refining industry. When, a little over a year later, another attempt was made to limit production artificially, the refiners did not even bother to put the agreement down in writing. Reporting an eighth-of-a-cent-a-pound increase in the price of refined sugar, *Bradstreet's Journal* attributed the rise to the action of three leading refining firms, including Havemeyer & Elder, "who induced the smaller refiners to join them in a

[54] *Ibid.*
[55] *Chappell* v. *Brockway.*
[56] *Hooker* v. *Vandewater*; *Stanton* v. *Allen.*
[57] See *India Bagging Association* v. *Kock.*
[58] Thomas S. Berry, "The Effect of Business Conditions on Early Judicial Decisions Concerning Restraint on Trade."

verbal agreement, no articles being signed, to curtail the production of their refineries one-third until there is an improvement in the demand. . . ." The lack of success which even this less intricate scheme was to enjoy was indicated by *Bradstreet's* added note that "the refiners of Boston and Philadelphia have refused to join these monopolists in their efforts to advance prices."[59]

Unexpectedly, however, fate intervened to reduce the supply of refined sugar far more effectively than any group of men could have done. On the night of January 9, 1882, the Havemeyer & Elder refinery, which produced nearly three-fourths of the nation's hard sugars, burned to the ground.[60] As a result, the downward pressure on prices eased somewhat. In fact, during the next twelve months the average margin between raw and refined sugar rose slightly, from 1.416 to 1.437 cents a pound.[61] In that year also, the Brooklyn Sugar Refining Company earned a $500,000 profit on its $1.2 million investment, its largest return in several years.[62]

But the relief from the severe price competition proved only temporary. The Havemeyers, Theodore and Henry, began immediately to rebuild their refinery, though not without travail. "The cost exceeded the early estimates," the family historian has noted, "and as a result the entire financial resources of the family were needed."[63]

When the new Havemeyer & Elder refinery was completed eighteen months later, Theodore and Henry owned the largest, most efficient sugar house in the world. It was capable of melting more than three million pounds of raw sugar daily,[64] twice as much as its next-largest competitor,[65] at an average cost (not counting capital) of 0.44 of a cent a pound.[66] When this added output began reaching the market, the margin between raw and refined sugar once more resumed its downward path. It fell to 1.032 cents a pound in 1883, then to 0.923 of a cent a pound the following year, and to 0.712 of a cent a pound the year after that.[67] Even at those low margins, because its costs were so low, the Havemeyer & Elder refinery was able to earn

[59] *Bradstreet's Journal,* 4 (July 16, 1881): 43.

[60] *New York Times,* January 11, 1882.

[61] See Appendix D of this volume.

[62] *United States* v. *American Sugar Refining Co. et al.,* pretrial testimony, 1912, pp. 471, 537.

[63] H. Havemeyer, *The Havemeyer Family,* pp. 67–68.

[64] *United States* v. *American Sugar Refining Co. et al.,* pretrial testimony, 1912, pp. 303–4.

[65] *Ibid.,* pp. 308–13.

[66] *Ibid.,* p. 320.

[67] See Appendix D of this volume.

a profit. But, as Henry Havemeyer later told a congressional committee, "I do not believe anyone else [could]."[68]

::

Winter had always been the slack season for the East Coast refineries. By that time of year sugar was no longer needed for preserving fruits, and the Louisiana crop was in the process of being marketed. Even the most efficient refineries hoped for nothing more than to break even during those months. But after the Havemeyer & Elder refinery was rebuilt, Julius A. Stursberg, who directed the manufacturing end of the business for the Brooklyn Sugar Refining Company, later testified, "the loss in the winter months became greater from year to year."[69] Whereas, before, the losses had usually lasted only until the first of March, they now began to extend into June. This was because, William Havemeyer said, "the refineries would all insist upon working full. No refinery wanted to [cut back], because the moment you reduce production you increase the cost."[70] And now that the much larger output of the new Havemeyer & Elder refinery was being added to that of the other refineries, it took longer for the heavy demand of the summer months to catch up with the excess supply of the winter.

A six-week strike by New York refinery employees in the winter of 1885–86 again brought temporary relief from the downward pressure on margins,[71] but by summer the various sugar houses found themselves as hard pressed as ever. To make matters worse, the secretary of the treasury in November reduced the drawback allowance by nearly 10 per cent, cutting off virtually all exports.[72] Although

[68] U.S. House Committee of Manufactures, *Report on Trusts*, pp. 107–10.

[69] *United States* v. *American Sugar Refining Co. et al.*, pretrial testimony, 1912, p. 552.

[70] *Ibid.*, p. 4543.

[71] *Ibid.*, pp. 4679–80.

[72] As the New York City Chamber of Commerce noted in reporting a decline in American exports of refined sugar in 1886:

> This falling off has been due entirely to the reduction in the drawback allowed by the Government, which took effect November 1st, and practically put a stop to this branch of the sugar trade. For several years the Government has been urged to make this reduction, it being claimed that the allowance of $2.82 per one hundred pounds was in reality equal to a bounty of about ¼ cent per pound, and hence the enormous increase that had been witnessed in such exports, which were principally absorbed by Great Britain. British refiners complained of the injustice, and were constant in their protests against the operation of this law, but it was not until October that the Treasury Department took any action, and then it was to reduce the drawback allowance to $2.60 per one hundred pounds, which was then announced as a provisional measure, as,

the amount of refined sugar sold overseas had not been substantial—and what was sold had to be sold at below cost—the secretary's order was a severe blow. As Henry Havemeyer later explained, these sales in foreign markets enabled the refiners to keep their plants operating at more efficient levels of output. ". . . The exportation diminished the cost of my work," he said, "and in that sense produced a profit."[73]

That year, 1886, the margin between raw and refined sugar was 0.781 of a cent a pound—higher than the previous year's margin but still not high enough to enable most of the refiners to earn what they considered a sufficient return on their investment. Joe Moller, the head of Moller & Sierck, complained to a colleague that "there was not much money in sugar refining" any more, that "business was bad." "Why don't you get out?" he was asked. "Well," Moller explained, "we are still making 5 or 6 per cent [return on our money], and if I go out I will only get 4."[74]

The refiners were thus faced, on the one hand, by unremunerative margins and, on the other, by the fact that they could transfer their capital to other branches of industry only at a considerable loss. Desperate to escape this predicament, they turned once again to the only other remedy they knew—an agreement to control prices and output. A meeting of all the leading refiners was called, and at that meeting a committee, consisting of Searles, William Havemeyer, and William Dick of Dick & Meyer, was appointed "to see what could be done."[75] The committee recommended closing down all the refineries for ten days—not just those in the New York area, but those in the

---

after investigation, it might be found necessary to make a still further reduction, in order to carry out fairly the spirit of the law. The drawback was never intended to be a source of direct profit to the shipper, but was for the purpose of reimbursing upon such sugar as was exported the duty which the Government had collected. Improved methods and greater economy in the process of refining had made it possible to obtain better results, so that the cheaper the cost of refining, the more profit was obtained from the drawback allowance. An adjustment that might have been fair and equitable fifteen or, even ten years ago, under new conditions became a source of profit, and hence the necessity for the reduction that has now taken place. The result has been a practical suspension of our export trade . . . [in refined sugar].

Annual Report, 1886–87, pt. 2, p. 13.

[73] U.S. House Committee on Manufactures, *Report on Trusts*, p. 142. Although most of the exported sugar was accounted for by Havemeyer & Elder, the impact of the secretary's order was nonetheless felt by the entire industry, since the sugar Havemeyer & Elder would otherwise have sold overseas was disposed of instead on the domestic market.

[74] *United States* v. *American Sugar Refining Co. et. al.*, pretrial testimony, 1912, p. 320.

[75] *Ibid.*, pp. 481–83.

other eastern seaboard cities as well.[76] The other refiners then agreed to this plan.[77]

But like all the previous agreements to limit production, this one was soon violated. Only a few of the refiners actually closed down their plants, William Havemeyer later testified, and "afterwards there was a red hot war."[78] The trouble, as everyone realized, was that there was no way of holding a man to his word. What was needed, from the refiners' point of view, was a better method of bringing the various members of the industry together, some mechanism by which they could be compelled to abide by whatever was the majority's will. As the winter of 1886–87 passed, this need became even greater. The Brooklyn Sugar Refining Company, one of the most modern refineries in the United States, found itself losing $200,000 during the first six months of the year.[79] Other firms found themselves in similar straits. From New Orleans and St. Louis came the plea that something be done about the narrowing margin between raw and refined sugar.[80] This margin, noted the New York City Chamber of Commerce, "has fallen to the lowest point in thirty years, and is in reality the lowest on record since the present methods of refining . . . [sugar came into] general use."[81]

[76] *Ibid.*, pp. 482, 4570–71.

[77] *Ibid.*, p. 317. While all those who later testified before various investigative bodies placed the dates of this attempt to limit production at one or two years before the actual formation of the trust, Willett & Gray's *Weekly Statistical Sugar Trade Journal*, which was usually well informed on such matters, made no mention of any such efforts during either 1885 or 1886. However, it did record various attempts to limit production in 1883 and 1884. ". . . The production [of refined sugar has been] regulated by a combination of refiners, to the demand" (February 8, 1883). "Arrangements have been made for curtailing the production of refined to some extent . . ." (March 6, 1884). Whether or not these were the same efforts to limit production cannot be ascertained.

[78] *United States* v. *American Sugar Refining Co. et al.*, pretrial testimony, 1912, p. 482.

[79] *Ibid.*, pp. 552–54.

[80] William Agar, in 1886 a director of the Planters Sugar Refining Company of New Orleans, later testified that on his way to New York in the winter of 1886–87 he had stopped off in St. Louis and seen R. J. Lockland, the president of a local bank and an influential director of the Belcher Sugar Refinery located in that city. Lockland, according to Agar, urged him to see Henry O. Havemeyer while he was in New York and suggest a consolidation of the sugar industry. Lockland told Agar to point out that a similar combination by the producers of steel rails had brought an end to the depressed prices in that industry. "We are losing money now in sugar," Lockland is reported to have said, "and I do not see why we do not come together. You suggest that from me and give [Havemeyer] my name" (*ibid.*, p. 7479).

[81] New York, N.Y., Chamber of Commerce, *Annual Report*, 1886–87, pt. 2, p. 9.

Sugar refining was still a competitive industry, behaving as one would expect a competitive industry to behave. In fact, it had become what some economists would call "perfectly" competitive[82]—that is, the various retail sugar brokers knew almost at once when a change took place in the price of refined sugar. This improved communication was due to the growth of the telegraph and cable, which created a single national market for refined sugar even though many of the buyers were located in distant cities.[83] To be sure of obtaining the latest quotations on both raw and refined sugar, a broker had simply to subscribe to Willett & Gray's statistical sugar-reporting service. This service, the offshoot of the two partners' own brokerage business, made it possible for a refiner to know instantly when a rival reduced his price,[84] and this knowledge helped to make the price competition during the winter of 1886–87 that much more severe.

Finally, alarmed by the continued decline in margins, William Havemeyer told Searles that he had better try to bring the various refiners together.[85] Searles, a banker with interests in many fields, had been one of the principal figures behind the earlier efforts to effect some sort of combination. This time, however, he went about his task with a different scheme in mind, one patterned after the new form of industrial organization which only recently had been applied by John D. Rockefeller to the petroleum industry.

[82] "Economists sometimes distinguish between 'pure' and 'perfect' competition. . . . [Besides the conditions] necessary for pure competition to exist [, p]erfect competition requires that one more condition be met. The additional condition is that all economic units possess complete knowledge of the economy. All discrepancies in prices quoted by sellers will be known immediately and buyers will buy at the lowest prices. This, of course, forces sellers charging higher prices to lower their prices immediately. . . . In the market for any particular product or resource, a single price will prevail" (Richard H. Leftwich, *The Price System and Resource Allocation,* p. 25). The distinction between pure and perfect competition can be traced back to Frank H. Knight, *Risk, Uncertainty and Profit.*

[83] New York, N.Y., Chamber of Commerce, *Annual Report,* 1885–86, pt. 2, p. 10.

[84] See the early issues of Willett & Gray's *Weekly Statistical Sugar Trade Journal;* see also *United States* v. *American Sugar Refining Co. et al.,* pretrial testimony, 1912, p. 4675.

[85] *United States* v. *American Sugar Refining Co. et al.,* pretrial testimony, 1912, p. 4513.

4 :: THE TRUST IS BORN

THE industry that provided a working model for consolidation of the various sugar refiners was petroleum. It too, had been plagued by the problem of excess supply relative to demand, but by 1882 John D. Rockefeller and his associates were able to bring the majority of oil refiners under unified control while simultaneously excluding new competitors.[1] To make this combination a legal entity, Rockefeller and his associates transformed the trust device from a means of simply holding property as fiduciary agent into an instrument of industrial consolidation.[2] But before this same solution to the problem of unregulated competition could be applied to sugar refining, a great many issues involving control of the trust had to be resolved. More than a year was to pass, with several setbacks along the way, before enough refiners could be persuaded to risk their status as independent businessmen to make the consolidation a success. Finally, however, eighteen of the twenty-three firms still left in the industry agreed to exchange stock in their own enterprises for the certificates of the newly formed sugar trust. With this act, the Golden Age of Competition in the sugar refining industry came to an end.

::

The spring of 1887 was a busy one for John Searles as he sought to duplicate in sugar refining what John D. Rockefeller had so recently accomplished in the petroleum industry. Searles' first task was to win over to such a scheme the other major refiners in the New York area. The smaller refiners did not require much persuasion. They could see at once the advantages that a combination of firms would offer. As George Moller, the manager of the North River Sugar Refining Com-

[1] Allan Nevins, *Study in Power,* vol. 1, chaps. 4–14; Harold F. Williamson *et al., The American Petroleum Industry,* chaps. 14–26.
[2] Nevins, *Study in Power,* vol. 1, chap. 21.

pany, later testified: "We were all practical men, all sugar refiners, . . . and as far as we were concerned, we did not consider any discussion necessary. We all knew that the only way to make sugar refining pay was to stop over-production."[3]

Even some of the larger refiners were easily persuaded to enter into the combination. As soon as Searles broached the idea to Julius Stursberg, one of the principal stockholders in the Brooklyn Sugar Refining Company, Stursberg offered to help convince some of the other refiners to go along with the scheme. He undoubtedly was influenced by the fact that the Brooklyn Sugar Refining Company was then losing several thousand dollars a month.[4] Claus Doscher, another major stockholder in the Brooklyn company, subsequently explained: "We might have gone on [indefinitely, trying to keep] that refinery working, but we were handling not only our own money but other people's money [as well. We felt] we could not go on losing other people's money."[5]

The difficulty was in winning over the largest refiners, the most important of which were the other Havemeyers, Theodore and Henry, and their cousin, Charles Senff, owners of both the Havemeyer & Elder and DeCastro & Donner refineries. The advantages of joining in such a combination were not as clear cut for them as they were for most of the other refiners. The Havemeyers' new, greatly enlarged plant enabled them to produce refined sugar for only 0.44 of a cent a pound in direct costs,[6] and thus, even with the average margin at 0.768 of a cent a pound, they were still in a position to earn a satisfactory return on their investment. Moreover, they were confident that no rival could produce sugar that cheaply; in any fight to the finish, they felt certain they would survive. In fact, as more and more firms were forced by competitive pressures to leave the industry, the two Havemeyer refineries could expect to reap the benefits of the reduced competition.

The proposed scheme of consolidation had many worrisome aspects as well. For one thing, it undoubtedly would require that the Havemeyers and Senff surrender some degree of control over their own enterprises. Although the three partners would have a large voice in the affairs of the new organization as a result of the large capacity they controlled, they still would represent only a minority interest, even among the New York refiners alone. There was, moreover, the

[3] U.S. House Committee on Manufactures, *Report on Trusts*, pp. 144–49.

[4] *United States* v. *American Sugar Refining Co. et al.*, pretrial testimony, 1912, p. 471.

[5] *Ibid.*, p. 587. [6] *Ibid.*, p. 320.

doubtful legality of the trust form itself. If later it were to be declared unlawful, control of the valuable Havemeyer properties might be jeopardized.

It was a difficult choice, whether or not to join the combination, and the partners in Havemeyer & Elder were at first divided on the issue. Theodore Havemeyer was anxious to join; Charles Senff advised against it. The deciding vote belonged to Henry Havemeyer, but he had not yet made up his mind. While his initial inclination was to oppose the combination, he felt that he, his brother, and his brother-in-law should discuss the scheme with some of their close associates in the sugar industry before making a final decision.[7]

Meanwhile, Searles continued to press the Havemeyers to join the combination. Later, recalling Searles' strenuous efforts during those many months, his associate William Havemeyer said, ". . . He went out among the different refiners, back and forth, in and out, and would come back and say so and so would not come in, and then we would get him started back again and . . . he would make a little further progress."[8] Although initially Searles concentrated his attention on gaining the support of the Havemeyer family, he was also anxious to win over the other major refiners. As William Havemeyer pointed out: "There is no use making a combination if you leave half [the firms] out. It is not a combination."[9] Havemeyer was aware of the distinction between consolidating an industry to form a single major firm and consolidating an industry to form several independent entities. The latter plan, he realized, might also be successful, but he felt it would "not make quite so much money." In periods of dullness, he said, one of the independent entities might be tempted to "refine too much sugar and sell pretty low." But he hastened to add that he did not think this would continue "for very long."[10] In the idiom of today's economist, William Havemeyer was comparing the advantages of monopoly with those of oligopoly, and he found the former much more attractive.

As a result of his further discussions with close associates in the sugar industry, as well as of Searles' continued visits, Henry Havemeyer, too, finally came to believe that the best interests of the family firm lay in joining the combination. (Andrew Carnegie, faced with a similar choice in the steel industry, was later to opt for a quite different solution, pursuing a policy of continuing competition until finally J. P. Morgan succeeded in buying him out.) Of the partners

[7] *Ibid.*, p. 7114. [8] *Ibid.*, pp. 4513–14. [9] *Ibid.*, pp. 4525–26. [10] *Ibid.*

in Havemeyer & Elder, however, Charles Senff continued to oppose amalgamation; and the two Havemeyer brothers, before finally committing themselves to the scheme, insisted that one condition be met. The success of the venture, they thought, depended on enlisting the support of all the leading refiners in all the major cities. Until this support was obtained, they told Searles, they would remain outside the combination.[11]

New York's only East Coast rivals as refining centers were Boston and Philadelphia. In the latter city there were only three sugar refineries of any consequence still in operation.[12] Of these three the largest and most important was the firm of Harrison, Frazier & Company. At one time Theodore Havemeyer had been among its partners, helping to build its new refinery in 1866. By 1879, however, Havemeyer had withdrawn from the firm, leaving Charles Harrison, his brothers, and his brother-in-law in control.[13] Meanwhile, the capacity of the refinery had increased to 4,000 barrels a day,[14] an output exceeded only by Havemeyer & Elder and by Matthiessen & Wiechers of New York. Harrison, Frazier & Company far overshadowed its two rivals in Philadelphia, and Searles knew that if it could be persuaded to join the combination the other two refineries would surely follow suit.

Just as the Harrison refinery was the key to the Philadelphia situation, so the Standard Sugar Refining Company was the key in the Boston area. There were six refineries still in operation in Boston in the late 1870's, but the Standard firm was by far the largest and most important. This was the same refinery that Seth Adams had erected in 1859, but now, greatly enlarged and modernized, it was owned and operated by Joseph B. Thomas.[15] With a water frontage of 620 feet, it was excellently located to transport its product either by rail or by sea. Its wharf facilities for handling both anthracite coal and raw sugar were said to be the best of any refinery in the country, while the plant itself was capable of melting 2,700,000 pounds of cane daily,

[11] *Ibid.*, pp. 7114–15.

[12] U.S. House Committee on Manufactures, *Report on Trusts*, p. 36.

[13] *United States* v. *American Sugar Refining Co. et al.*, pretrial testimony, 1912, p. 5912.

[14] *Ibid.*, p. 5914.

[15] See Chapter 2, p. 41; see also Albert P. Langtry, ed., *Metropolitan Boston*, p. 662. Very little biographical information on Thomas has survived. Practically all that has been discovered, aside from his ownership of the Standard refinery, is that he was apparently a retired army captain.

more than half again as much as its next largest competitor in Boston.[16]

Searles' initial efforts to win over Harrison and Thomas met with failure. Both men indicated that they were not interested in a combination such as the one Searles proposed.[17] Then Theodore and Henry Havemeyer agreed to see what they could do to get the two refiners to change their minds. Theodore was certain that if Thomas could be persuaded to enter into the combination Harrison would then fall into line.[18]

The Havemeyers called in Lowell M. Palmer, whose Brooklyn Cooperage Company supplied barrels to both their own refinery and the Standard, and asked him to approach Thomas about joining the combination. On receiving assurances that his company would continue to receive all of the Havemeyers' cooperage business, Palmer agreed to undertake the mission. "I found when I got to Boston," Palmer later recalled, "that the feeling on Captain Thomas' part was principally against H. O. Havemeyer. . . ." After first persuading Thomas that Havemeyer was not to be blamed for Thomas' brother being forced out of the old Harrison and Havemeyer firm in Philadelphia, and then carefully explaining to him the details of the consolidation plan, Palmer returned to New York with the news that Searles could go to Boston and complete the arrangements.[19] As expected, once the Standard agreed to join the combination, the other Boston refineries—the Bay State, Boston, Revere, and Continental—were easily persuaded to do the same.

With the Boston situation in hand, Searles was able to turn his attention to Philadelphia. He soon found that Theodore Havemeyer had been wrong when he predicted that Harrison would follow Thomas into the scheme. Having only recently bought out the Havemeyers in order to end their influence in his firm, Harrison had no intention of allowing himself to fall under their sway again, as would almost certainly happen if he were to enter into a combination which they, by virtue of their large refining capacity, would surely dominate. Though Searles made several trips to Philadelphia to try to persuade Harrison to change his mind, he returned each time with little to

[16] See note 55 below; see also U.S., Congress, House of Representatives, Special Committee on the Investigation of the American Sugar Refining Company and Others, *Hearings*, p. 2537 (hereafter cited as Hardwick committee investigation, 1911).

[17] *United States* v. *American Sugar Refining Co. et al.*, pretrial testimony, 1912, p. 4528.

[18] *Ibid.*, p. 7114. [19] *Ibid.*, pp. 7114–15.

show for his efforts. The most he was able to obtain was the promise from one of the smaller Philadelphia refineries, E. C. Knight & Company, that it would enter into the combination.[20]

Despite this setback, Theodore and Henry Havemeyer were now prepared to support the scheme of consolidation. They realized that the Harrisons—"with their means and knowledge in Philadelphia"[21]—might prove troublesome, but they were convinced that the combination would nonetheless succeed.

With the firm of Havemeyer & Elder fully committed to Searles' plan, those New York refineries which had not yet agreed to join the combination were quickly brought around. These included not only the larger firms, such as Matthiessen & Wiechers and Dick & Meyer, but also the more marginal enterprises, such as the North River Sugar Refining Company and Oxnard Brothers. The latter two refineries had already been forced by the falling margin on refined sugar to suspend production. Moreover, the North River refinery was on the verge of being condemned by the city of New York so that a public park could be built on its site, while the Oxnard plant was generally conceded by most persons in the industry to be hopelessly out of date. William Havemeyer later expained why, despite these obvious shortcomings, both firms were brought into the consolidation. The condemnation of the North River property, he said, was by no means certain; and the Oxnard refinery, though "very old fashioned," had proved its ability to survive on a very low margin, even if it could not make much money. Although it was true that both firms had been forced to suspend production, they would have no difficulty in starting up again, Havemeyer indicated, if the combination of refiners succeeded in raising prices. For this reason, the organizers of the consolidation scheme were determined to include every firm, no matter how small or inefficient. Havemeyer then added, "Sometimes we [took in refineries] to get the brains that were in the concern, to get the people themselves."[22]

By the first week in April, 1887, the task of winning over the various refiners in the three major refining centers had for the most part been completed. Though the Harrisons remained adamant in their refusal to join, most of the other surviving firms had agreed to the amalgamation. On April 7 Henry Havemeyer reported that eight refineries in New York and five in Boston—all that remained of the approximately

[20] H. O. Havemeyer to John Dos Passos, April 4, 1887, reprinted in *ibid.*, p. 4737.

[21] *Ibid.*, p. 7116. [22] *Ibid.*, pp. 4522–23.

twenty-five firms that had flourished as recently as 1878 in those two cities—as well as E. C. Knight & Company of Philadelphia, had agreed, in principle, to the proposed scheme of consolidation.[23]

::

What the organizers of the scheme had in mind, Havemeyer wrote to John R. Dos Passos, the lawyer retained by Searles to work out the details of the consolidation, was to form a corporation that would take title to all the refining properties involved. This corporation was to be capitalized at $19.5 million—$3.5 million in 10 per cent preferred stock and $16 million in common shares. Since it was the business rule-of-thumb at that time to issue preferred shares (considered the equivalent of first mortgages) equal to the assessed value of all the individual properties being brought into a combination of this type, the $3.5 million figure probably represented what the various refineries were thought to be worth as independent concerns. Thus the $19.5 million figure probably represented what those same refineries were thought to be worth when consolidated into a single entity. In his letter to Dos Passos, Havemeyer hinted that the total capitalization might later be increased to $50 million, depending on how many of the remaining sugar refiners throughout the country could be persuaded to join the combination. Fifty million dollars, then, was considered to be the capitalized value of a monopoly in sugar refining. Havemeyer told Dos Passos that he hoped the details could be worked out quickly enough for the scheme to be put into effect within ten days.[24]

Dos Passos was one of the nation's leading corporate lawyers and the father of the future novelist. A native Philadelphian who moved to New York soon after the Civil War, he had established himself as one of that city's outstanding criminal attorneys while still a young man. Gradually, however, his practice came more and more to involve matters of corporate and financial law, and he eventually became known as an authority on the laws governing securities trading.[25]

Undoubtedly it was because of his special background and knowledge that Dos Passos was retained by Searles to handle the legal aspects of the consolidation scheme. In fact, it was probably Dos Passos who first suggested the trust form of organization. As he later explained to the U.S. Industrial Commission: "A trust was not a novel

[23] *Ibid.*, p. 4737. [24] *Ibid.*

[25] This sketch of Dos Passos is drawn from the article in the *Dictionary of American Biography* and from Henry Woolman, "John R. Dos Passos," pp. 163–65.

proposition when it was recently introduced into dealings for the control of certain businesses. It was the application of an old principle of law to new conditions. The object of it was this: to keep people, who had no business to know, from discovering the secrets of that trust, and of the business which it controlled." He pointed out that, if a corporation had been formed for the same purpose—that is, to acquire control over several previously independent firms—its affairs would, as a matter of law, have been open to public scrutiny. The reason for forming a trust, he said, "was to avoid that publicity."[26]

Apparently this argument was sufficient to convince Henry Havemeyer, Searles, and the other principals that a trust was preferable to a holding corporation as a means of uniting their properties. The plans for consolidation were revised accordingly.

Dos Passos also explained the mechanics of forming a trust.

> Assume that certain persons . . . desire to become the owners of some manufacturing business or commercial enterprise which is owned by, say, six corporations; having bought the shares of these companies, they get together and they make what is called a trust deed, or a trust agreement. That trust agreement recites the terms under which the securities are held; that is, the stock, the shares of these six constituent companies, are taken and placed in the hands of a trustee, who has no actual or real ownership, except that he is the custodian—the shares belong, accordingly, to the trustee, to administer the trust.

The trustee, in turn, issues to the former holders of the stock a receipt called a trust certificate.[27]

Since, unlike the petroleum industry, no single individual or group of individuals owned all the sugar refining properties that were to be consolidated,[28] the terms of the trust agreement were extremely important, for they defined the respective shares and rights of those entering into the combination. Helping Dos Passos to draft this trust agreement was a second lawyer, John E. Parsons.[29]

Dos Passos' senior by fifteen years, Parsons had also begun his legal career as a criminal lawyer, serving for a time just prior to the Civil

[26] John R. Dos Passos, *Commercial Trusts*, pp. 13–14.

[27] *Ibid.*, pp. 12–13.

[28] In the petroleum industry Rockefeller and his associates in the Standard Oil Company had already acquired about 90 per cent of all rival refineries even before the trust was organized, and thus the trust arrangement represented a *fait accompli* as far as consolidation was concerned; see Nevins, *Study in Power*, 1: 617.

[29] Henry O. Havemeyer, Jr., *Biographical Record of the Havemeyer Family, 1606–1943*, p. 42.

War as an assistant district attorney for New York. Later he, along with the Havemeyer family, took an active part in ousting from their positions of power the various members of the notorious Tweed Ring. But for the most part, Parsons' was a general practice, and by 1887 the Havemeyer family had come to rely entirely on his counsel in all matters of law.[30]

The proposed trust deed, as worked out by Dos Passos and Parsons, included the following provisions.[31]

Each of the firms entering into the combination was to turn its capital stock over to a board, which "shall be designated by the name of The Sugar Refineries' Company." Since four of the parties to the agreement (including Havemeyer & Elder) were still partnerships, they were to take the additional step of first reorganizing themselves as corporations.

Each firm was to continue to "carry on and conduct its own business" as before. But thenceforth it was to be subject to the overriding authority of the trustee's board. This board was to consist of eleven members chosen for seven-year terms. However, to provide continuity, their terms were to be staggered: Henry O. Havemeyer, F. O. Matthiessen, John E. Searles, and Julius Stursberg were to serve initially for seven years; Theodore A. Havemeyer, Joseph B. Thomas, John Jurgensen, and Hector C. Havemeyer, for five years; and Charles Senff, Charles O. Foster, and William Dick, for three years. Thus the Havemeyer & Elder interests were to have three representatives on the board (Henry and Theodore Havemeyer and Charles Senff), the other branch of the Havemeyer family was to have two representatives (John E. Searles and Hector C. Havemeyer), and the Matthiessen & Wiechers interests were to have two representatives (F. O. Matthiessen and John Jurgensen). This left four representatives to be divided among the larger New York and Boston refineries (Julius Stursberg of the Brooklyn Sugar Refining Company, William Dick of Dick & Meyer, Charles O. Foster of the Boston Sugar Refining Company, and Captain Thomas of the Standard refinery). Finally, in case the Harrisons or some of the other refiners not yet included in the scheme later decided to join, provision was made for adding two members to the board.

This board was to exercise full control over the various refining

[30] See the sketch of Parsons in the *National Cyclopedia of American Biography;* see also Hardwick committee investigation, 1911, pp. 2065–66.

[31] The trust deed, except for the amount of trust certificates received by the respective parties, is reprinted in U.S. House Committee on Manufactures, *Report on Trusts*, pp. 3–7.

properties being brought into the combination, a simple majority of its members sufficing to carry any decision except the removal of one of the trustees during his term of office. The latter type of action required a two-thirds vote. A simple majority of the trustees could also fill a vacancy on the board, provided that the vacancy had occurred as a result of some member's resigning or dying before the expiration of his term. Aside from receiving their share of the pooled profits, the only right reserved for the actual owners of the properties, now designated as trust certificate holders, was the right to vote during the annual meeting each June to replace or continue in office those trustees whose terms had regularly expired.

The effect of these provisions was to forge an instrument for the highly centralized management of the various refining properties being brought into the combination. Yet, crucial as these provisions were, they were not the major source of contention. Most of the ensuing disagreements, which served to delay the establishment of the trust for nearly six months, arose as to what share each of the various parties to the agreement would receive in the new organization.

The plan had been to appoint a committee to appraise the value of the various properties being consolidated and then to distribute to the stockholders of each company trust certificates in the same ratio as that of the value of their refinery to the value of the whole.[32] The first part of this plan was actually carried out, with Hector Havemeyer, Henry Havemeyer, and J. O. Donner being chosen to serve on the committee.[33] In going about its task, the committee considered as the most important factor the relative capacity of the various refineries. But this was only one factor which the committee took into account. "Some plants were bought probably more on account of the real estate value," Henry Havemeyer later told the U.S. Industrial Commission; "others we took because they were going concerns; others we took for their standing; others have very valuable trade marks. All of these things were figured in. . . ."[34]

But the value that the appraisal committee placed on a refinery was not necessarily the amount that its owners were willing to accept. In an attempt to prevent invidious comparisons, negotiations were

[32] Testimony of H. O. Havemeyer before the U.S. Industrial Commission, *Reports*, 1, pt. 2: 124; U.S. House Committee on Manufactures, *Report on Trusts*, pp. 32–33.

[33] *United States* v. *American Sugar Refining Co. et al.*, pretrial testimony, 1912, p. 4518.

[34] U.S. Industrial Commission, *Reports*, 1, pt. 2: 110–11.

carried out with each refinery's owners separately, and the amounts offered to others were kept secret.[35] Still, in an industry as small and intimate as sugar refining, it was impossible to keep such matters secret for long. Invidious comparisons were made, and when certain refiners discovered how much in trust certificates other refiners had been offered, they began demanding additional amounts for themselves. Ultimately, then, the number of trust certificates which the owners of the various refineries received was determined by the give and take of bargaining between the parties. As William Havemeyer replied, when asked how these amounts were decided upon: "Not scientifically at all. A man simply said, 'I will not come in unless I get so much.' "[36]

::

By mid-June, 1887, it appeared that the trust agreement would soon be put into effect. Two of the firms that had originally agreed to join the consolidation had by now changed their minds. One was E. C. Knight & Company of Philadelphia; the other was the Revere Sugar Refining Company of Boston. "They said they were a small refinery," William Havemeyer later explained in connection with the latter, "[that] they had never increased their capacity, never intended to increase their capacity, and . . . only made one class of sugar, which was granulated . . . that they had a special trade in New England, . . . never sold out of New England, . . . had a certain pride in keeping their entity, and that they would not care to come in."[37] As for E. C. Knight & Company, its principal owner, the man whose name the firm bore, was unwilling to accept payment in trust certificates for his property, and the organizers of the trust were unwilling to give him cash as long as the more important Philadelphia refinery of Harrison, Frazier & Company remained outside the combination.

However, despite these defections, the consolidation did not appear

[35] So determined were the organizers of the trust to keep the actual shares in the organization received by the various parties secret that they later risked contempt proceedings by refusing to make these figures available to the several legislative investigating bodies appointed to look into the affairs of the trust. Although copies of the trust agreement itself were surrendered, the amount of trust certificates received by the various parties to the agreement was deliberately blocked out. See U.S. House Committee on Manufactures, *Report on Trusts,* pp. 3–7; Lexow committee investigation, 1897, pp. 384–90.

[36] *United States* v. *American Sugar Refining Co. et al.,* pretrial testimony, 1912, pp. 3514–15.

[37] *Ibid.,* p. 4529.

to be significantly weakened. It still had the support of all the refineries in New York and all the refineries, except one, in Boston. Moreover, it had by now succeeded in extending its influence westward, receiving promises from the two sugar refineries in New Orleans and the one in St. Louis that they, too, would join the trust.

Located as they were, close to the Louisiana cane fields, these three firms were capable of providing the eastern seaboard refineries with vigorous competition, especially in the surrounding areas where they enjoyed a slight advantage in transportation costs. Also, during the summer months, when the Louisiana crop was exhausted, they could import raw sugar from the Caribbean.[38] While their plants were as yet still relatively small,[39] their potential as rivals for the southern and western markets was clearly recognized by the organizers of the trust. It was for this reason that the latter were eager to have them become members of the amalgamation.

For their part, the New Orleans and St. Louis firms were just as eager to join. The Planters Sugar Refining Company had been organized in 1881, and for a time had been the only sugar refinery in New Orleans.[40] In 1884, however, the Louisiana Sugar Refining Company completed construction of that city's second refinery,[41] thereby touching off a bitter struggle between the two companies, not only over the sale of the final product, but also over the purchase of the raw material. The Planters refinery, as the older, better established firm, seemed to enjoy a slight advantage in obtaining its raw cane. But the Louisiana company, with its newer, more efficient plant, was able to process the cane at lower cost. Thus the two refiners were evenly matched, and for the next two years they continued to compete vigorously against each other, with neither earning the profits it had originally anticipated. Finally, late in 1886, they decided to call an end to the rivalry.

"Recognizing the depression which has continued for several years in the refining and manufacture of sugar in the United States, and particularly in the City of New Orleans, . . . and that a spirit of harmony will promote the mutual interest of the respective parties," representatives of the two companies met on November 18, 1886, and agreed to form a pool.[42] Each company was to continue to refine and sell sugar separately. However, "to secure similar prices for similar qualities, the Sales Book, as well as outgoing and incoming telegrams

[38] *Ibid.*, p. 7485. [39] *Ibid.*, p. 7467. [40] *Ibid.*, p. 7466.
[41] *Ibid.*, p. 7507; Henry Rightor, ed., *Standard History of New Orleans*, p. 528.
[42] *United States* v. *American Sugar Refining Co. et al.*, pretrial testimony, 1912, pp. 7471–72.

and letters of both companies, shall be open at all times to the inspection of the President of both companies." To further ensure co-ordination of prices, the two companies were to report their sales to each other twice daily. Meanwhile, all profits were to be pooled and divided equally between the stockholders in the two companies, even if, as was soon to be the case, production was concentrated in one refinery and the other refinery was shut down. This pooling agreement, subject to cancelation by either party on fifteen days' notice, was intended to run for at least a year.[43]

Thus, when Searles arrived in New Orleans late in the spring of 1887 to discuss his consolidation scheme, he found that city's two refineries already working closely together. By co-ordinating their prices and pooling their profits, they had finally been able to earn the return on their investment originally anticipated.[44] Having observed first hand the benefits of combination, they were easily persuaded to join the trust. The only dispute that arose was over how much in trust certificates they would receive in return for their properties. At first the Planters people agreed to accept $700,000, but when they learned that the Louisiana Sugar Refining Company's stockholders had been offered $837,000, they successfully demanded the same.[45]

The Belcher Sugar Refinery of St. Louis was just as easily persuaded to join the trust. Its plant had been completely rebuilt only two years earlier, but for some unexplained reason it continued to experience mechanical difficulties which made profitable operations almost impossible.[46] For more than a year its owners had been trying to unload the property, and when Searles promised them $500,000 in trust certificates, they readily accepted his offer.[47]

The owners of the Forest City Sugar Refining Company of Portland, Maine, for somewhat similar reasons were just as eager to sell out. The plant had originally been built in the hope that sorghum sugar could be grown successfully in that area. When this proved unfeasible, the owners had tried to operate their refinery by importing sugar cane from abroad. Since Portland lacked the commercial facilities and proximity to population that rival refining centers enjoyed, this had soon become a losing venture. The owners of the Forest City refinery were only too glad to receive what little in the way of trust certificates Searles was willing to offer them for their almost worthless property.

::

[43] *Ibid.*, pp. 7472–76. [44] *Ibid.*, p. 7481. [45] *Ibid.* [46] *Ibid.*, pp. 4549–50.
[47] *Ibid.*, p. 4517.

Thus the combination grew until it encompassed seventeen of the twenty-one sugar refineries still in business east of the Rocky Mountains. After considerable haggling, those seventeen finally agreed to the relative values placed on their properties, and the actual signing of the trust agreement was about to proceed when an unexpected complication arose. In the early morning hours of June 11, 1887, the Havemeyer Sugar Refining Company's plant at Greenpoint, which had a daily melting capacity of one million pounds, was destroyed by fire.[48] Searles was in Boston at the time to obtain the signatures of that city's refiners on the trust agreement, but when they heard what had happened they refused to sign.[49] Why, they argued, should they accept trust certificates for plants that were fully operable when the owners of the Havemeyer Sugar Refining Company were to receive trust certificates for a plant that was totally useless. Besides, they probably reasoned, now that the Greenpoint refinery had been eliminated as a factor in the market, the downward pressure on sugar margins would ease. As a result of this unforeseen circumstance, not only the refiners from Boston, but also some of those from New York, were reluctant to go through with the consolidation scheme.

It was to take another five months to bring the recalcitrants back into line. Searles and Havemeyer tried to point out that while the destruction of the Greenpoint refinery might bring temporary relief from narrow margins, it offered no long-run solution to the industry's problems. Just as the rebuilding of the Havemeyer & Elder refinery after it burned in 1882 led to even greater excess capacity, so the rebuilding of the Greenpoint refinery would eventually lead to more intensive price competition. But more than any argument, what probably convinced the other refiners was the fact that the Greenpoint refinery's lost output was easily made up for by other members of the industry without significant improvement in margins. Nevertheless, before the other firms would agree to go ahead with the consolidation scheme, Hector and William Havemeyer had to agree to take the insurance money they received and use it to erect a new refinery, even though the current level of demand was easily supplied without it.[50]

[48] *New York Times,* June 12, 1887. The fire was believed to have been set by workmen still disgruntled by the way in which the sugar refiners, and particularly the Havemeyers, had crushed a strike eight months earlier. Suspicion was heightened by the fact that a cooperage factory, also owned by the Havemeyers, had been set on fire several weeks earlier, though in that instance the arsonists had been apprehended. See *New York Times,* June 15, 1887.

[49] *United States* v. *American Sugar Refining Co. et al.,* pretrial testimony, 1912, p. 4547.

[50] *Ibid.,* p. 4548.

By August 16, 1887, this matter had finally been resolved, and all seventeen refiners had again expressed their willingness to enter into the combination. On that day, Henry O. Havemeyer, in behalf of Havemeyer & Elder and the DeCastro & Donner Sugar Refining Company, became the first company head to sign the trust agreement.[51] The tedious process of obtaining the necessary signatures, a process that was to take nearly two months, had begun.

::

Meanwhile, rumors of the consolidation appeared for the first time in the public prints. The story that the nation's sugar refiners were considering a plan to "curtail production," the *New York Times* reported on September 23, "is once more going the rounds." It added, "The talk now is that the principal refiners of the country are contemplating the formation of a sugar trust, as that sort of business combination seems to be in fashion just now." However, the same article noted, the refiners themselves deny the story. "The general opinion among New York sugar refiners seems to be that the formation of a trust would benefit the trade, but that the consummation of the scheme is hardly possible."[52] The refiners continued to deny the rumors of a consolidation until finally, on October 13, Willett & Gray's authoritative *Weekly Statistical Sugar Trade Journal* reported, "It may be considered a settled fact that a combination has been completed, . . . thus bringing under the management and control of a Committee of Eleven Refiners almost the entire consumption of raw sugar and production of refined sugar in the United States."[53]

The purpose of the combination, at least to the *Sugar Trade Journal*, was quite clear. "The committee," it pointed out, "have full control of the production of refined, so that it can always be regulated by the demand. . . ."[54] This control derived from the fact that the members of the trust supplied approximately 84 per cent of the refined-sugar market east of the Rocky Mountains.[55] "The new Sugar Trust is prospering," the *New York Times* reported on October 19, "and every day sees it nearer formal completion." Then, suddenly, the organizers of the trust found themselves faced with a new complication. The North River Sugar Refining Company's owners refused to approve the exchange of their refinery for $700,000 in trust certificates.

The North River stockholders originally had been led to believe

[51] U.S. House Committee on Manufacturers, *Report on Trusts*, p. 7.
[52] *New York Times*, September 23, 1887.
[53] Willett & Gray's *Weekly Statistical Sugar Trade Journal*, October 13, 1887.

that they would receive the same amount for their refinery as did Hector and William Havemeyer for their plant in Jersey City. But then they discovered that the Havemeyers actually were to receive substantially more.[56] "Our stockholders," explained George Moller, the active head of the North River firm, "were not happy with this arrangement. They thought our property was not valued as highly in

[54] *Ibid.* Although these details were not made public at the time, the companies signing the trust agreement, along with the capacity of their refineries and the approximate amount of trust certificates they received in exchange, were as follows:

Firm	Amount of Trust Certificates Received	Plant Melting Capacity (pound)
Havemeyer & Elder	$12,000,000[a, b]	3,500,000[c]
DeCastro & Donner	3,000,000[a, d]	800,000[c]
F. O. Matthiessen & Wiechers	6,500,000[b, d]	1,600,000[c]
Havemeyer S. R. Co.	5,500,000[i]	1,000,000[e]
Brooklyn S. R. Co.	3,500,000[a]	750,000[c]
Dick & Meyer	3,000,000[d]	650,000[c]
Moller & Sierck	900,000[f]	200,000[c]
Oxnard Brothers	700,000[b]	200,000[c]
North River S. R. Co.	700,000[b]	200,000[d]
Standard S. R. Co.	2,700,000[g]	600,000[g]
Boston S. R. Co.	1,800,000[g]	450,000[g]
Continental S. R. Co.	1,200,000[g]	400,000[g]
Bay State S. R. Co.	900,000[g]	350,000[g]
Planters S. R. Co.	837,000[h]	200,000[h]
Louisiana S. R. Co.	837,000[h]	250,000[h]
St. Louis S. R. Co. (Belcher)	500,000[b]	500,000[h]
Forest City S. R. Co.	unknown	unknown
Total	$44,074,000	11,300,000

Sources: (a) Julius Stursberg, *United States* v. *American Sugar Refining Co. et al.*, pretrial testimony, 1912, p. 497; (b) William Havemeyer, *ibid.*, p. 4517; (c) Ernest W. Gerbracht, superintendent of Havemeyer & Elder, *ibid.*, pp. 304–13; (d) John Moller of the North River Sugar Refining Company, U.S. House Committee on Manufactures, *Report on Trusts*, pp. 143–44; (e) Willett & Gray's *Weekly Statistical Sugar Trade Journal*, June 16, 1887; (f) John Moller of Moller & Sierck, *United States* v. *American Sugar Refining Co. et al.*, pretrial testimony, 1912, pp. 7092–99; (g) Joseph Stillman of Bay State Sugar Refining Company, *ibid.*, pp. 4556–76; (h) William Agar, *ibid.*, pp. 7460–81; (i) H. Havemeyer, *The Havemeyer Family*, p. 125.

[55] U.S. House Committee on Manufactures, *Report on Trusts*, p. 36.

[56] *United States* v. *American Sugar Refining Co. et al.*, pretrial testimony, 1912, p. 7021.

proportion as other properties which were taken in. They felt aggrieved about it, but under the circumstances they considered our chances as a corporation, if we wished to continue in the sugar business . . . would be better in going in even at that valuation than to stay out alone. . . ."[57] Convinced that the North River stockholders had no alternative, Moller prepared to sign the trust agreement.

At that point the company's principal owner returned from Europe firmly opposed to joining the trust. Rather than accept the $700,000 in certificates, he told his fellow stockholders, they might just as well wait and see what the city of New York would pay for the condemned North River properties. His fellow stockholders agreed, and on November 4 they voted to rescind the authority given Moller to negotiate the transfer of the North River refinery to the trust.[58]

The next day, however, Moller signed the trust agreement anyway.[59] Whether he was unaware of the stockholders' action, as he later claimed, or whether he was motivated by some other consideration, the evidence is not conclusive. In any case, Searles insisted that Moller's signature was binding on the North River company; if its owners refused to honor the agreement, they would be taken to court. The latter consulted a lawyer and learned that they could in fact be compelled to transfer their refinery to the trust.[60]

Still, some of the North River stockholders were reluctant to accept trust certificates for their property. The certificates were of uncertain value, they argued, and the trust itself might later be declared illegal. Other stockholders replied that "the sugar trust would likely have just as smart lawyers as the State," but they were in the minority.[61] The majority remained adamant in their refusal to accept the trust certificates, and not even Searles could persuade them to change their minds.

At the same time, the organizers of the trust were unwilling to allow the North River company to remain outside the combination, even though they knew the city might eventually take over the property. The condemnation proceedings, if they did occur, might take several years; in the meantime the North River company would benefit from the higher prices brought about by the formation of the trust without itself having to make any sacrifice.

[57] U.S. House Committee on Manufactures, *Report on Trusts,* p. 141.

[58] *People* v. *North River Sugar Refining Company: Record,* pp. 27–30; Lexow committee investigation, 1897, p. 214.

[59] *People* v. *North River Sugar Refining Company: Record,* p. 30.

[60] U.S. House Committee on Manufactures, *Report on Trusts,* pp. 142–43.

[61] *United States* v. *American Sugar Refining Co. et al.,* pretrial testimony, 1912, p. 7024.

Finally, to resolve the impasse, Searles offered to pay the North River stockholders $325,000 in cash, the value placed on their property by the appraisal committee, less $25,000 for six small lots which were part of the North River parcel but which the company had failed to purchase.[62] Searles himself would then transfer the property to the trust, receiving in return $700,000 in trust certificates. This arrangement was readily agreed to, and within three weeks the transaction was completed, thus removing the last obstacles to the trust's formation.[63] With this matter in hand, Searles and the Havemeyers turned their attention to the sugar refining industry west of the Rockies.

::

The dominant firm on the West Coast was the California Sugar Refining Company, owned by the colorful and energetic Claus Spreckels. Having immigrated to this country in 1846 from his native Germany, Spreckels operated grocery stores in Charleston, South Carolina, and New York City before deciding that his prospects would be much brighter in the gold-rush atmosphere of California. Upon reaching San Francisco in 1856, he first opened a grocery store, then a brewery, before finally entering the sugar refining business in 1863. Even at this early date Spreckels was unwilling to brook opposition, and when his fellow directors of the Bay Sugar Refinery refused to go along with his plans for expansion, he sold his interest in the company.

He was, however, anything but through with sugar refining. After spending two years in Germany learning the latest refining methods, he returned to San Francisco in 1867 and with the help of his family organized the California Sugar Refining Company. Beginning with a plant capable of refining only 25,000 pounds of raw cane a day, Spreckels gradually expanded the scale of his operations until in 1876 he was processing up to 250,000 pounds of raw sugar daily, a figure that was not large by East Coast standards but that nonetheless made him the largest sugar refiner west of the Rocky Mountains.

[62] U.S. House Committee on Manufactures, *Report on Trusts,* p. 143.

[63] *Ibid.;* Lexow committee investigation, 1897, pp. 200–14. To the last, Searles tried to persuade the North River stockholders to accept trust certificates for their property. "All I remember," Max Wintjen, superintendent of the North River refinery and a stockholder in the company, later testified, "is what John Searles said . . . that it was the greatest mistake in our lives that we didn't go in with them" (*United States* v. *American Sugar Refining Co. et al.*, pretrial testimony, 1912, p. 7023). Wintjen and the other North River stockholders were later prepared to admit that Searles had been right.

During this time he maintained a technological superiority over his rivals, inventing several new processes himself to reduce the cost of refining.[64]

In 1876 an event occurred that was to radically transform the West Coast sugar refining industry. Previously, sugars imported from the Hawaiian Islands had been taxed at the same rate as sugars from all other foreign countries. Consequently, they had enjoyed no particular advantage on the American market, despite the fact that most of the Hawaiian sugar growers were citizens of this country. In fact, since they were generally of high saccharin content, the Hawaiian sugars were placed at a disadvantage by the nearly prohibitive duties on higher-grade sugars. In 1876, however, as a result of pressure from American sugar growers in Hawaii and American expansionists on the mainland, the Senate ratified a reciprocity treaty which made it possible for Hawaiian sugar cane to be brought into the United States duty free.

Spreckels, as the West Coast's leading refiner, had vigorously opposed the reciprocity treaty. If Hawaiian sugar could be imported duty free, he pointed out, the manufacturing end of the business would inevitably move to the Islands.[65] Before the reciprocity treaty was signed, however, he and the other California refiners succeeded in having it amended so that only the lower-grade sugars were exempted from the tariff. With the future of the West Coast industry thus assured, Spreckels hurried off to Hawaii to take advantage of the reciprocity treaty himself. In fact, he was on the ship that brought the news of the treaty's ratification to the Islands.[66]

Spreckels' first coup was to buy up most of that year's sugar crop before the news of the treaty's ratification forced a price increase.[67] But this was only a taste of what he had in mind. Purchasing a large tract of arid land, he turned it into a prosperous sugar plantation by building a thirty-mile irrigation ditch. Then, according to one set of biographers, he took over a dubious land claim and, using his political influence to have it upheld, added it to his original tract so that it encompassed 40,000 acres, by far the largest plantation on the Islands. Meanwhile, he had formed a partnership with William G. Irwin, one of that small but important group of commercial factors who handled practically all the business affairs of the Hawaiian planters. Together, Spreckels and Irwin were able to direct the sale of more than a third

[64] This sketch is taken from Jacob Adler, "Claus Spreckels, Sugar King of Hawaii," pp. 29–34.

[65] *Ibid.*, pp. 20–22.

[66] *Ibid.*, pp. 1–2.

[67] *Ibid.*, p. 2.

of the sugar cane produced in the Islands. Still not satisfied, Spreckels acquired a fleet of vessels from a Philadelphia shipyard and soon was providing the only regular monthly service between Honolulu and San Francisco. But the key to control of the Hawaiian sugar-cane industry, Spreckels realized, was control of the West Coast refining industry.[68]

The size of the West Coast market was such that, as time went by and the melting capacity of refineries increased, it became increasingly difficult for more than one company to survive. Spreckels, with his greater command over the technical details of the business, together with his shrewd competitive sense, was more than able to hold his own against all rivals, and one by one they found themselves forced to quit the industry. By 1884 the only remaining competitor of Spreckels' Cailfornia refinery on the West Coast was the American Sugar Refinery.[69]

This was a relatively new firm, having been organized only four years before. Its plant, however, was an old one. It was, in fact, the same Bay refinery in which Spreckels had been interested when he first started out in the sugar refining business. For a year or so, the American Sugar Refinery had tried to compete independently, but finding this impossible it then reached a working agreement with the California Sugar Refining Company. Spreckels, meanwhile, had acquired a one-third interest in the company.[70] Faced with this united front, the Hawaiian planters had little choice but to accept the price that Spreckels was willing to pay for their sugar cane.

While the planters were, quite naturally, unhappy with the grip Spreckels had on their industry, they were not the only ones who felt unduly constrained. The majority stockholders in the American Sugar Refinery knew that the only way to reduce the expense of refining to less than the 1.63 cents a pound it was then costing them was to expand the scale of their operations.[71] But as the precondition for his co-operation, Spreckels had insisted that the American limit its output to 10,000 tons a year, or one-fifth of what the West Coast market could absorb at the then current level of prices. These prices were based on those prevailing in New York, plus the 2.0 cents a pound it cost to ship refined sugar from New York to the West Coast.[72]

[68] Shelley M. Mark and Jacob Adler, "Claus Spreckels in Hawaii," pp. 25–27.

[69] William W. Cordray, "Claus Spreckels of California," pp. 16–25. Meanwhile, Spreckels had built a new refinery, one capable of melting 750,000 pounds of sugar daily.

[70] Mark and Adler, "Claus Spreckels in Hawaii," p. 27; *United States* v. *American Sugar Refining Co. et al.*, pretrial testimony, 1912, pp. 3124–28.

[71] *Ibid.*, p. 3173. [72] *Ibid.*, pp. 3128, 5966–68.

In January, 1885, this market-sharing arrangement broke down. Spreckels' son Claus, Jr., later said that the falling out was caused by the American's insistence on having a larger share of the market.[73] But those associated with the American had a different explanation. Spreckels, they said, demanded that they reduce their meltings so that his own California refinery could expand its output. This they refused to do. "There was a great deal of discord in the company," Edmund C. Burr, the superintendent of manufacturing, later recalled, and finally Spreckels asked that he either be bought out himself or be allowed to buy out the others. The majority of the American's stockholders chose to buy him out. "Immediately after that, within a week," Burr testified, ". . . Mr. Spreckels dropped the price of sugar and the fight between the two refineries commenced. . . ."[74]

In this struggle the American Sugar Refinery soon found ready allies. Having long chafed under what they regarded as a monopoly in refining, the Hawaiian planters were only too willing to lend the American their support. The company was reorganized, its capital more than tripled to $1 million (with the Hawaiian planters supplying most of the additional funds), and the melting capacity of the refinery increased from 125,000 to 500,000 pounds a day.[75] The improvements enabled it to reduce the cost of refining to 0.9 of a cent a pound,[76] but the greatly increased output also caused prices to fall. Even the more efficient California refinery found itself losing money.[77] But with the Hawaiian planters backing the American, the fight continued.

It was at this point, in December of 1887, that Searles traveled west to see if the two San Francisco refineries could not be persuaded to join the sugar trust.[78] In line with the technique first developed by John D. Rockefeller in the petroleum industry, Searles approached the larger of the two firms first. If Spreckels' California Sugar Refining Company could be persuaded to join the trust, Searles believed that the American would eventually follow suit.

Meeting with the older and younger Spreckels together, Searles tried to explain the advantages of joining the trust. "He stated that the competition was very fierce in the Eastern states at that time," Claus Spreckels, Jr., later recalled, "that they could probably get better prices if there was not as fierce competition." The same, Searles said, was true in the West. Moreover, because the two San Francisco refineries were producing more sugar than they could profitably

[73] *Ibid.* [74] *Ibid.*, p. 3129. [75] *Ibid.*, pp. 3131–32.
[76] *Ibid.*, pp. 7173–74. [77] *Ibid.*, p. 5968. [78] *Ibid.*, p. 5970.

market on the Pacific coast, they were forced to sell in markets farther east, along the Missouri River, in competition with the New York, Boston, and Philadelphia refineries. With the formation of a trust, this competition would be better regulated. All the refineries "would make more money," the younger Spreckels remembered Searles saying, and "that was the object of the formation of the [trust]."[79]

Searles gave other reasons as well. He pointed out that, if the two Spreckelses entered into the trust, they would get a good price for their property. Also, their holdings in the industry would become more liquid. "We could get out of the business," Claus, Jr., recalled being told, "whenever we wanted to, as a market [would soon be] created for the stock." Finally, Searles told the Spreckelses that by joining the trust they would be better protected against fire. "He suggested . . . that in the event of one concern being put out of operation by . . . a fire, [its owners] would still have an interest in the other refineries and would not, therefore, be deprived of any revenue."[80]

These arguments, however, failed to sway the Spreckelses. As Claus, Sr., subsequently told a congressional investigating committee, if a trust is formed, "only one or two men will rule it. How about all that stock in there? They virtually hold that stock, and they will not acknowledge that Spreckels or anybody else has anything to say." Then, on a final note which drew applause from the spectators, Spreckels added, "I came to this country from Germany for liberty and liberty I shall maintain!"[81] To Searles, when he was in California the Spreckelses simply said that theirs was a family concern, that they "had no desire to go into the Sugar Refineries Company, and that perhaps the best arrangement would be if [they] would confine [them]selves to west of the Missouri River." When Searles threatened that he and his colleagues in the trust might decide to give the California "fierce competition by buying the American," the younger Spreckels warned that "they better let that alone."[82]

Thus rebuffed, Searles returned east, leaving Spreckels and his son with the impression that respective spheres of influence had been carved out, that the California Sugar Refining Company and the sugar trust would be able to coexist in peace. Not long after that, however, the two men were surprised to learn that the trust had, in fact,

[79] *Ibid.*, p. 5973. [80] *Ibid.*, pp. 5970–73.
[81] U.S. House Committee on Manufactures, *Report on Trusts*, p. 184.
[82] *United States* v. *American Sugar Refining Co. et al.*, pretrial testimony, 1912, pp. 5970–73.

carried through with its threat to buy the American Sugar Refinery.[83] Searles and his colleagues knew that this would probably precipitate a bitter fight between themselves and the Spreckelses,[84] but they reasoned that the great Hawaiian sugar magnate and his son eventually would be forced to sue for peace, for while the California refinery continued to suffer losses from its war against the American, the trust would be reaping the benefits of its monopoly position on the East Coast.

For their part, the owners of the American were only too willing to enlist additional allies in their struggle against Spreckels. Besides, they were afraid that Spreckels might sell out first, thus depriving them of a considerable part of the advantage they had in bargaining with the trust.[85] With these considerations in mind, they readily agreed to transfer their refining properties to the Sugar Refineries Company for $1.5 million in certificates.[86]

It was a move that the members of the trust were to regret many times over in the next several years, for Spreckels proved a more determined opponent than they had expected. Still, the American Sugar Refinery provided them with the eighteenth and final firm to join in the combination.

[83] *Ibid.; New York Times,* February 21, 1888.

[84] Ernest W. Gerbracht, the superintendent of the Havemeyer & Elder refinery, later reported the following conversation between himself and J. O. Donner.

GERBRACHT: I see they have acquired that company, the American. . . .
DONNER: Yes, they have to do that in order to go to work and compete with Spreckels.
GERBRACHT: Well, what does that mean?
DONNER: . . . they are going to pound Spreckels.

See *United States* v. *American Sugar Refining Co. et al.*, pretrial testimony, 1912, p. 330.

[85] *Ibid.*, p. 3133. [86] *Ibid.*, p. 4798.

5 :: WHY CONSOLIDATION

CHAPTER 1 of this volume listed the various explanations that have been offered for the Corporate Revolution. The following chapter will examine how well those explanations fit the case of sugar refining.

::

One of the explanations for the Corporate Revolution given in Chapter 1 cited the completion of the national railroad network in the period just prior to the Great Merger movement. According to one version of the argument, the railroads increased the market area of the typical firm, enabling it to take advantage of potential economies of scale. This meant that fewer firms were required to supply any given market, and thus that fewer firms could in the long run survive. According to the alternative version, the completion of the national railroad network led to increased competition by drawing various local markets, previously separated by high transport costs, together into one large market. The Great Merger movement followed as an attempt to mitigate this increased competition. These variations on the same theme, while pointing to quite different effects, are not necessarily incompatible.

As has already been pointed out,[1] the coming of the railroads did, indeed, increase the typical sugar refinery's market area. But the result was to strengthen, not destroy, the competitive nature of the industry. Because of lower transportation costs new markets opened up, and thus the railroads made it possible for many more refineries, given the then efficient scale of operations,[2] to survive than had previously been the case. It was, in fact, the decade immediately following the railroad boom of the late 1840's that saw the number of sugar refineries throughout the country increase from less than half a

[1] See pp. 36–38 above.

[2] The more specific role played by economies of scale will be discussed below.

dozen to more than thirty. For the first time in the industry's history there was effective price competition. Quality was standardized, and a whole new class of retail brokers arose to keep a close watch over the market. Even as late as the Depression of 1873, when the main outlines of the rail network east of the Missouri River had been completed, sugar refining still displayed all the characteristics of a competitive industry.

The second version of the argument—that the railroads obliterated previous market boundaries, thus creating intensified competition on a national scale—does not seem to fit the case of sugar refining any better. For this explanation implies that the coming of the railroads transformed a previously fragmented market, each fragment being supplied by a separate group of firms, into a single national market supplied by all firms together. Such a fragmentation of the market in sugar refining simply was not the case. It is true that before the coming of the railroads there were separate and distinct markets for refined sugar—the East Coast market, the Louisiana market, and, somewhat later, the West Coast market. But these remained separate and distinct, even after the completion of the national railroad network.

By its very nature, the business of refining sugar was necessarily confined to a few major seaports. Only such cities as New York, Boston, Philadelphia, New Orleans, and San Francisco had the necessary combination of direct ocean access to raw materials, ample credit facilities, and sufficient skilled labor; as a result, these cities controlled the sugar trade in their respective market areas. Thus, even before the coming of the railroads, sugar refining was geographically concentrated. The principal effect the new form of transportation had was to extend the market areas of these major refining centers. (In this respect, New York, Boston, and Philadelphia should be considered a single refining center, since transportation costs to the hinterlands were substantially the same for all three cities.) While the expansion of market areas did lead to some increased competition between the major refining centers, particularly in those regions where their market areas bordered (as in the southeastern states and the upper Mississippi valley), the increase was of only minor significance. It was the competition within these market areas—not between them—that inspired the efforts, even before the trust was formed, to bring about some sort of combination.

::

Another explanation that has been offered for the Great Merger movement cites the high American tariffs in effect at that time. It has been argued that without the protection which these import duties provided, the consolidation of American industry would not have been possible. Ironically, Henry Havemeyer himself offered this explanation. The tariff, he told the U.S. Industrial Commission in 1899, was the mother of trusts, though not, he hastened to add, the sugar trust specifically. "Economic advantages incident to the consolidation of large interests in the same line of business are a great incentive to their formation," Havemeyer testified, "but these bear a very insignificant proportion to the advantages granted in the way of protection under the customs tariff."[3]

At first glance this explanation seems to have relevance—despite Havemeyer's protestations—even to the sugar refining industry. The tariff on refined sugar was considerable, amounting to 89 per cent ad valorem in 1887.[4] Even when allowance was made for the fact that American refiners had to pay substantial duties on the raw sugar they imported, it nonetheless remained true that they were well insulated against foreign competition. This protection was equal to approximately 1.25 cents a pound, or 0.5 of a cent a pound more than the average direct cost of refining sugar in the United States.[5] And at least some of those familiar with the American industry were convinced that sugar could be refined as cheaply in this country as anywhere in the world.[6]

Yet, while it is possible to show that American refiners had the benefit of considerable tariff protection, it is difficult to link this protection to the formation of the sugar trust. After all, the American sugar refining industry had been protected against foreign competition long before 1887. The nation's first tariff, enacted almost a hundred years earlier, had levied a duty on refined sugar that was two cents a pound greater than the duty on raw sugar, and the differential, as a result of later tariff legislation, had grown even larger. By 1816 it amounted to thirteen cents a pound. While the degree of protection given American refiners was never again quite so large,

[3] U.S. Industrial Commission, *Reports*, 1, pt. 2: 101.

[4] U.S. House Committee on Manufactures, *Report on Trusts*, p. 84.

[5] *United States* v. *American Sugar Refining Co. et al.*, pretrial testimony, 1912, p. 195.

[6] As Hugh N. Camp, a former refiner, told a congressional committee in 1888: "I am satisfied that the sugar refineries of the United States can make sugar as cheap[ly] as any sugar refineries in the world. I do not suppose any house in the world can make sugar cheaper than the Havemeyers" (U.S. House Committee on Manufactures, *Report on Trusts*, p. 77).

and in fact declined steadily over the years, it nonetheless remained substantial.[7]

The tariff on refined sugar, like that on many other manufactured items, had been justified by the infant industry argument, though not always in exactly those words. And to the extent that the sugar refining industry did establish a foothold in this country, gradually growing stronger and more efficient until it was capable of holding its own against all foreign competition, this argument was eventually borne out. But it must be said that the tariff led to the formation of the sugar trust only in the sense that it enabled the sugar refining industry to survive. The fact that the industry was eventually consolidated was incidental.

This is not to say that the tariff was unimportant once the sugar trust was formed. Previously, when the industry was highly competitive, Congress did not have to worry about how high the duties on refined sugar were—except to allay political opposition to tariffs in general—as long as American firms were effectively protected against foreign competition. The impersonal workings of the domestic market set an upper limit on the price of refined sugar. After the trust was formed, however, this situation changed dramatically. Since the impersonal workings of the market could no longer be relied upon, Congress, in drawing up the schedule of sugar tariffs, had to recognize that it was also setting the upward limit on sugar prices.

Henry O. Havemeyer, in his subsequent testimony before various congressional committees, was quite candid on this point. To the House Committee on Manufactures in 1888 he conceded that the trust set its price by taking the London price of refined sugar and adding to it the amount of tariff protection.[8] Six years later, appearing before a special Senate committee investigating charges of bribery in connection with the tariff bill enacted that year, Havemeyer was asked, "Is not this . . . a fact, that the trust, being able to fix the price in America, [sets] it just low enough to keep out refined sugar made in other countries?" "That is the business, practically [speaking] . . . ," he replied. "And you have so fixed it as to practically exclude all foreign competition?" he was then asked. "Yes, sir; as protection to our own business."[9]

[7] Wells, *The Sugar Industry and the Trust*, pp. 22–23; 1 U.S. Stat. 24 (1789); 2 U.S. Stat. 768 (1812); 5 U.S. Stat. 558 (1842); 9 U.S. Stat. 46 (1846); 11 U.S. Stat. 192 (1857).

[8] U.S. House Committee on Manufactures, *Report on Trusts*, p. 108.

[9] U.S., Congress, Senate, Special Committee to Investigate Attempts at Bribery, *Report*, p. 360.

Of course, foreign competition was not the only consideration in setting the price of refined sugar. When asked what guarantee the consumer had that the price of refined sugar would not continue to be the London price plus import duties, Havemeyer replied, "There are a number of guarantees. . . . First, as I said before, the cheaper we can furnish sugar to the consumer the more he will eat and the more we will refine. [Second,] if we attempted to advance the rate of sugar [too much], we would increase the competition, by encouraging new firms to enter the sugar refining business."[10] But while these other considerations were important, it was still the amount of tariff protection which set the upward limit on sugar prices, especially in the short run. The key members of the congressional tax-writing committee were well aware of this fact, and they responded by seeing to it that the degree of protection embodied in the tariff bills of 1890 and 1894 was gradually reduced until it amounted to no more than 0.125 cents a pound.[11]

One could argue that the degree of tariff protection should have been lower, perhaps even eliminated altogether, but this would not have destroyed the trust; it would merely have made it less profitable. This conclusion, in fact, points to the true significance of the tariff. It had very little to do with the actual formation of the trust. But once the trust was established it was one of the major factors in determining how secure the market position of the consolidated industry would be.

::

Still another explanation for the Great Merger movement cites the growth of U.S. capital markets at that time. This development, it has been argued, made it possible not only for previously fixed assets to be converted into liquid capital but also for promoters such as J. P. Morgan to float industrial combinations on the basis of expected monopoly earnings. Some have even suggested that the merger movement was part of a gigantic stockjobbing scheme designed to enrich these same promoters.

In the case of the sugar refining industry, this explanation has several weaknesses. For one thing, the impetus for combination came, not from outside promoters, but from persons long and intimately associated with the industry. John Searles and the branch of the

[10] U.S. House Committee on Manufactures, *Report on Trusts*, p. 109.

[11] 26 U.S. Stat. 567 (1890); 28 U.S. Stat. 509 (1894); *United States v. American Sugar Refining Co. et al.*, pretrial testimony, 1912, p. 195.

Havemeyer family with which he was closely associated, although heavily involved in many outside interests, nonetheless were substantially involved in sugar refining. Their Havemeyer Sugar Refining Company could trace its origins back as far as 1870, and Searles himself had taken an active part in the tariff controversies of the late 1870's. Of the men actually responsible for organizing the trust, only John R. Dos Passos could be classified as an outsider. But his role was a relatively minor one, it being limited to advising what form the combination should take.[12]

For another thing, the organizers of the sugar trust—they and the others who had formerly comprised the industry—did not become rich from the sale of trust certificates. They became rich because the value of the certificates they received for their properties and then held on to gradually appreciated. The amount of these certificates was determined, not by any calculation as to how many the public would buy, but by an estimate of what the refining properties were worth as individual enterprises plus what they were worth when merged together into a single business entity. It was to take several years for these capitalized expectations to be realized. In the meantime, the value of the trust certificates fluctuated greatly, depending in part upon the economic fortunes of the sugar trust, but even more directly upon its current legal status.[13]

In other words, if the trust's organizers were to realize what they considered the certificates to be worth intrinsically, they would have to wait until the market confirmed their judgment. Of course, this still left considerable leeway for speculating on the rise and fall in the value of the certificates, an activity in which the trust's organizers undoubtedly engaged, although to what extent it is impossible to tell. Still, this speculation was incidental to the organizer's main task,

[12] Navin and Sears, pointing to the role Dos Passos later played in the formation of the American Thread Company, have described him as one of the major promoters responsible for the Great Merger movement. Insofar as the sugar trust was concerned, this is misleading. He was a technical adviser rather than an active promoter of that combination. See T. R. Navin and M. V. Sears, "The Rise of a Market for Industrial Securities, 1887–1902," pp. 129–30.

[13] Sales of sugar-trust certificates were, at first, infrequent. One of the first transactions noted was for 100 shares @80, and was reported by the *New York Times* on January 26, 1888. It was not until six months later that the *Commercial and Financial Chronicle* began reporting the trading in sugar-trust certificates on a regular basis. The initial listing showed 77 asked, 73 bid. In June, 1889, the certificates rose above par for the first time, but they began to decline soon thereafter, reaching 59 ¼ asked, 59 bid, in December when the news broke that the New York Court of Appeals had upheld the voiding of the North River Sugar Refining Company's charter.

that of making the trust a going concern. For it was on this last consideration that the profits from consolidating the sugar refining industry ultimately depended.

Perhaps the most serious weakness of the stockjobbing explanation is the fact that before 1885 not much of a market for industrial securities existed. Although there were well-organized exchanges already in existence both in New York and Boston, these dealt almost exclusively in railroad, banking, public utility, and government securities. Except for a few mining shares and the stocks of companies closely connected with the railroads, such as the Pullman Company, the only industrial securities traded were those of the large New England textile firms, and they were traded for the most part on the Boston exchange. There was not an extensive market for industrial securities, because many companies at that time, especially those outside of New England, were unable to meet the requirements for listing on one of the regular exchanges: large capitalization, widespread ownership, and a willingness to disclose pertinent information.[14]

In fact, it was the growing flood of trust certificates which led to the development of an industrial securities market of significant proportions. The Standard Oil trust, even though its certificate-holders tended at first to sell their shares only among themselves, had already prepared the way for public acceptance of this new type of security. Then came the formation of the cottonseed oil, lead-smelting, whiskey, and other trusts, not to mention the Sugar Refineries Company. All issued their own certificates.

At first the regular exchanges refused to have anything to do with this new type of security, largely because the trusts refused to provide information on their structures or operations. But the certificates were popular with the investing public, and in 1885 when the bottom dropped out of the market for most other types of securities, the New York Stock Exchange agreed to establish an unlisted department where the various trust certificates could be traded. This department functioned in much the same manner as the present over-the-counter market.[15] Despite the lack of protection which this unofficial arrangement afforded investors, the trading in trust certificates was brisk and soon exceeded the sales of the more conventional, regularly listed industrial securities. "The trade in sugar refining certificates alone by

[14] Navin and Sears, "Market for Industrial Securities," pp. 106–12.

[15] Francis A. Eames, *The New York Stock Exchange*, p. 65; see also the *Commercial and Financial Chronicle*, July 13, 1889, p. 52.

the last half of 1889," Navin and Sears have noted, "averaged 150,000 shares a week—in contrast to a volume of 2,000 in Pullman shares. . . ."[16]

It seems clear, then, that the consolidation of the sugar refining industry—and this was true of other industries as well—was due to factors far more fundamental than the existence of an industrial-securities market. For this early phase of the consolidation effort, the trust movement, proceeded without a market of significant proportions. In fact, it was the trust movement that was largely responsible for the market's growth and development.

This is not to say that the nascent industrial-securities market did not greatly facilitate the consolidation of the American sugar refining industry. Searles, in trying to persuade Spreckels to join forces with the other refiners, already was able to point to the greater liquidity Spreckels would have if his properties were part of a trust whose certificates were widely traded on one of the exchanges. And later, when other industries were consolidated—industries that did not lend themselves to consolidation as readily as sugar refining—this factor grew in importance. Businessmen who might otherwise have been unwilling to surrender their independence were persuaded to exchange their properties for trust certificates, and later for corporate stock, because such a move not only enabled them to shift their capital in and out of the industry more easily but also increased the value of their holdings. As Navin and Sears have pointed out, securities widely traded on one of the exchanges experienced a more than threefold increase in market value simply as a result of being listed.[17] Even today this is a significant factor in persuading a small firm to merge with a larger corporation.[18]

::

But what were those more fundamental factors responsible for the consolidation of American industries? They were perhaps best described in an article published in the *Commercial and Financial Chronicle* at the height of the trust movement. "The effect of competition in regulating the prices of manufactured articles is not, at best,

[16] Navin and Sears, "Market for Industrial Securities," p. 115.

[17] *Ibid.*, p. 108. This is based on the finding that unlisted companies generally could be sold for three times current earnings, while listed securities generally could be sold for between seven and ten times current earnings.

[18] Jesse W. Markham, "Survey of the Evidence and Findings on Mergers," p. 181.

wholly satisfactory," explained the editors of the *Chronicle,* who largely mirrored the views of businessmen.

> . . . It may prevent them from being too high or too low, but it does not prevent wide fluctuations from year to year which involve loss to both the producers and to the public. In fact, in the present workings it makes them inevitable. A man will not go into business unless prices are so high as to give him what he thinks a good prospect of interest on his investment after paying all other charges. But when he has once invested his money, he will not be able to withdraw it without loss. This plant, once established, must be kept in operation, even though the returns do not pay interest or fully cover maintenance charges. It then becomes a life and death struggle with him to maintain his position in the trade. He will compete all the more actively while prices are below cost, as long as his financial resources will stand the strain.
>
> Instead of establishing one natural or normal standard of prices, competition then furnishes two distinct ones. One, which includes all elements of cost, determines when new capital will come in; another, which only includes operating expenses in the very narrowest sense, determines when old capital will be driven out. One of these points may be very much higher than the other. The standard of prices of pig iron in a time of inflation is two or three times as high as in the period of depression which follows. For the concerns which have lived through the depression have a temporary monopoly in the "boom" which enables them to command the highest returns, while those which have afterwards been tempted to come in by these specially high prices throw their stock on the market just when it is not needed, and intensify the downward reaction.
>
> Now it is obviously for the advantage of the public as well as the manufacturers that these extremes should be avoided if possible. It is not desirable that the low prices should last so long as to drive concerns out of business if their work is needed in the long run. The temporary cheapness is dearly paid for on such terms. To a certain extent, then, the efforts to prevent this result are justifiable in the interests of the public. . . .[19]

In other words, the coexistence of a large-scale enterprise requiring substantial fixed investment and a regime of perfect competition led to results that businessmen found intolerable. The ensuing instability, they argued, was even detrimental to the public interest. The formation of trusts, then, like the formation of price agreements and pools at an earlier stage, was an attempt by businessmen themselves to deal with this problem by establishing some degree of control over prices and output. Realizing that technologically advanced methods of production and perfect competition were incompatible, businessmen were quite willing to discard the latter. Although not revolutionaries by nature, they were—at least some of them—prepared to overthrow

[19] *Commercial and Financial Chronicle,* July 28, 1888, p. 94.

the existing structure of markets when they could see no other alternative to their own eventual extinction. They knew that the rule "survival of the fittest" implied that every firm, no matter how strong at present, might eventually be forced to give way to an even stronger one. In this sense they could see the truth of the Marxist prophecy, even though they were not prepared to accept Marx's ultimate conclusions. The subsequent testimony by members of the industry before various investigative bodies clearly reveals the force of this motivation in bringing about the consolidation of the various refineries.[20]

::

For some students of this period, the principal explanation for the Great Merger movement was the desire not so much to gain control of prices and output as to take advantage of certain economies of scale. The resulting savings justified these consolidations, at least from society's point of view, even if an attendant consequence was the elimination of competition. Searles, in his testimony before the Senate committee, tried as best he could to bring out this point. The sugar trust, he stressed, was established "in order to save the waste of independent administration. . . ."

Economies of scale are of several types.[21] Most basic, perhaps, are the direct or "technical" economies of scale. These occur only at the plant level, and they determine how large a plant must be in order to produce goods efficiently, that is, with the least possible input of labor, capital, and raw materials. This type of scale economy is closely related to the state of the industrial arts, although changes in the relative price of inputs will affect it. There are also what might be called overhead economies of scale. These occur only at the firm level, and they arise from the fact that by expanding the scale of its operations a firm can economize on certain of its overhead costs—most important, the cost of management and sales promotion. This type of scale economy often reflects the "lumpiness" or indivisibility of such overhead costs. Finally, there are the "pecuniary" economies of scale. Once a firm reaches a certain size, it is able, simply by the dominant role it plays in the market, to force down the price of the inputs it must buy. This type of scale economy is always associated with some

[20] U.S. Senate Committee to Investigate Attempts at Bribery, *Report*, pp. 337, 383, 387; U.S. House Committee on Manufactures, *Report on Trusts*, pp. 102, 126; U.S. Industrial Commission, *Reports*, 1, pt. 2: 97.

[21] See Joe S. Bain, *Barriers to New Competition.*

degree of monopsony power, and economists tend to dismiss it as a true social savings, since it can come about only at the expense of some other group in society.

Insofar as the consolidation of the sugar refining industry was concerned, there apparently were not any significant direct or technical economies of scale.[22] Since this form of savings is to closely related to the state of the industrial arts, one would not expect it to have been otherwise. Put another way, the mere existence of twenty-two independent refineries would not have prevented the realization of direct economies of scale, were such economies possible. While some of the existing refineries undoubtedly were too small to operate efficiently, this shortcoming could have been corrected, had this been the real objective, simply by merging one refinery with another. It certainly did not require the consolidation of virtually the entire industry.

More important, however, was the fact that, at the time the sugar trust was organized, nearly all the technical economies of scale could be realized at a point below the plant level. The principal source of indivisibility in a sugar refinery, at least insofar as the equipment was concerned, was the vacuum pan. It, together with two defecating tanks, six bone-black filter tanks, two sugar coolers, and two centrifugal machines, comprised a single refining unit, and this single refining unit embodied virtually all technical economies of scale.[23] Typically, a refinery consisted of several such refining units, but this was in order to save on certain overhead costs, principally the expense of maintenance and management, not to save on any direct costs of manufacture. Since most technical economies of scale could already be realized at a point below the level of the existing firms, there would appear to be no reason for consolidation on those grounds.

What about the prospect of achieving further economies in overhead costs? The fact that it was possible to realize certain savings in this category by combining several refining units in a single firm suggests that an increase in the size of the firm itself might have led to even greater savings.

The historical evidence seems to indicate that there were no significant overhead economies of scale, at least not as that term is understood. John Jurgensen later testified that the formation of the trust did result in some savings, for it placed in two or three hands

[22] See Henry O. Havemeyer's testimony before the U.S. Industrial Commission, *Reports*, 1, pt. 2: 109–11.

[23] R. R. Bowker, "A Lump of Sugar," p. 84.

the buying of all raw sugar and the selling of all refined products,[24] but Henry Havemeyer called these, as well as all savings in management costs, "inappreciable."[25] In other words, whatever savings were achieved, they did not amount to much when spread over the millions of pounds of refined sugar produced each day. Since there was no source of sales expense other than these management costs—not even advertising—it was impossible to achieve any economies in that area.

Searles, in his subsequent testimony, laid particular stress on one type of overhead economy. ". . . Perhaps the greatest of all benefits" from consolidating the sugar refining industry, he said, was "the concentration of technical knowledge and ability of the people connected with the business. At the time the original sugar trust was organized each one of the refineries had some method or plans which it kept secret, which were supposed to be of value and which had value. When the trust was organized, these gentlemen were brought together and this technical knowledge and skill was concentrated and utilized for the common good."[26] Henry Havemeyer, however, minimized the importance of this overhead economy. The prospect of being able to pool the technical knowledge of everyone in the industry, he told the U.S. Industrial Commission, was realized only "in a measure."[27]

There was an important reason why the benefit from forming the trust which Searles cited should have turned out in practice to be insignificant. It was not the larger refineries, such as Havemeyer & Elder and Matthiessen & Wiechers, that were most likely to benefit from the pool of technical knowledge; they were already at a high level of technical efficiency. Rather, it was the smaller refineries that stood to gain. In most cases, however, these smaller refineries were subsequently shut down so that whatever economies were achieved in this area were not of lasting significance. That is probably the reason why Henry Havemeyer later minimized their importance.

::

Actually, the sugar trust was little more than a paper organization. It had no office and kept no records—except a list of certificate-holders.[28] It was really only a board of trustees that met two or three

[24] *United States* v. *American Sugar Refining Co. et al.*, pretrial testimony, 1912, pp. 4457–58.

[25] U.S. Industrial Commission, *Reports*, 1, pt. 2: 110.

[26] Lexow committee investigation, 1897, p. 439.

[27] U.S. House Committee on Manufactures, *Report on Trusts*, pp. 101–2.

[28] *Ibid.*, p. 39.

times a week, usually in the Wall Street chambers of Havemeyer & Elder. Although the board retained ultimate authority, the actual work of the trust was carried out by two committees, a mercantile group that included Searles, Jurgensen, Julius Stursberg, William Dick, Henry O. Havemeyer, and Joseph B. Thomas, and a manufacturing panel that included Theodore A. Havemeyer, Charles Senff, F. O. Matthiessen, and Charles Foster.[29] The functions of the mercantile committee were divided, with Jurgensen and Stursberg handling the purchase of raw sugars; the others, the sale of refined products. The manufacturing committee, meanwhile, decided how much sugar each refinery should melt.[30]

No attempt was made to control prices directly—either the price of raw cane or the price of refined sugar. Henry Havemeyer and others connected with the trust made quite a point of this in their testimony before the House Committee on Manufactures in 1888.[31] But the board of trustees very definitely did attempt to control physical quantities—the amount of raw cane purchased, the amount of raw cane melted, and the amount of refined sugar sold. And that, of course, was the equivalent of controlling prices.[32]

Each refinery had to file a daily report showing its purchases of raw sugar, its meltings, its sales of refined products, and the prices paid or charged.[33] To assure that the reports were accurate, an auditor was sent around to the various refineries periodically to check their books.[34] On the basis of these reports, the trustees then set general policy. Havemeyer and his colleagues tried to give the impression that these decisions of the trustees were merely recommendations and that the companies themselves did not have to follow them.[35]

[29] *Ibid.*, pp. 97–98.

[30] *United States* v. *American Sugar Refining Co. et al.*, pretrial testimony, 1912, pp. 4446–48.

[31] See Henry Havemeyer's and John Parsons' testimony, U.S. House Committee on Manufactures, *Report on Trusts*, pp. 27–29, 54; see also Foster's testimony, *United States* v. *American Sugar Refining Co. et al.*, pretrial testimony, 1912, pp. 4769–70.

[32] While the market for raw sugar was essentially a world market, the Atlantic seaboard refining cities imported most of their cane from Cuba. The United States was Cuba's most important customer, and a consolidation of buyers in this country was certain to have an effect on raw-sugar prices in Cuba, at least until the patterns of trade could be altered. Given the close commercial ties between Cuban sugar growers and American importers, however, this last possibility was not easily realized.

[33] *United States* v. *American Sugar Refining Co. et al.*, pretrial testimony, 1912, pp. 4769–70.

[34] *Ibid.*, p. 523.

[35] U.S. House Committee on Manufactures, *Report on Trusts*, pp. 128–29.

But as Parsons pointed out, "The board possess[es] this control, that if at the end of the current year they are dissatisfied . . . they can remove the officers of the particular corporation and put in others."[36]

Subject only to this over-all direction, each company was left free—in fact was instructed[37]—to manage its own business. "As I remember," Stursberg later testified, "every company continued to control its own affairs under the guidance of its officers who reported . . . to the respective committees of the Sugar Refineries Company."[38] The trust, then, was little more than a pool, but a pool with greatly expanded powers and more certain authority over its constituent members.

Having competed vigorously against one another for so long, the various refineries at first found it difficult to adjust to the new regime, especially since it still left them with a large measure of freedom. It sometimes happened, for example, that a member of the trust paid more for raw sugar or charged less for refined sugar than the price set by the board of trustees. Havemeyer, in fact, cited several such incidents in his efforts to prove that the Sugar Refineries Company did not actually control prices.[39] Stursberg later made the same point. Upon being asked if it were not correct that the trust sought to regulate prices he replied, "More or less." "Well," he was then asked, "in what respect is it not correct?" "Some of the corporations, especially [those] out of town . . . , did not live up to these suggestions at all times. . . . I refer especially to the Boston Houses," Stursberg explained.[40]

In fact, one of the few pieces of correspondence to survive from the sugar-trust era is a letter from Henry Havemeyer to Joseph B. Thomas complaining that someone in Boston was purchasing raw sugar at 1/16 of a cent above the New York price. Havemeyer asked Thomas to get together with Charles Foster, the other member of the board of trustees from Boston, to prevent anything like that from happening again.[41]

Although as time went on, these independent acts became less and less frequent, they nonetheless illustrate the extent to which the various companies that comprised the sugar trust continued to oper-

[36] *Ibid.*, p. 34.

[37] Henry O. Havemeyer to William Agar, January 9, 1888, reprinted in *United States* v. *American Sugar Refining Co., et al.*, pretrial testimony, 1912, p. 4740.

[38] *Ibid.*, p. 519.

[39] U.S. House Committee on Manufactures, *Report on Trusts*, pp. 128–29.

[40] *United States v. American Sugar Refining Co. et al.*, pretrial testimony, 1912, p. 519.

[41] *Ibid.*, pp. 4744–45.

ate as separate entities even after the trust was established. In so doing they precluded the possibility of achieving any significant direct or overhead economies of scale. This is not to say that some of the refineries were not later shut down while others increased in size. This happened, as circumstances and the state of the industrial arts permitted, but, generally, economies of scale were a later development. At the time the trust was organized there was little expectation of achieving them.

Thus, when one looks at the savings that mere size gave the sugar trust, they do not appear to have been important—at least not important enough to have led to the consolidation of the sugar refining industry. However, when one looks at the savings which a size sufficient to control price and output gave the trust, the picture is quite different. First of all, as a result of its monopsonistic power, the trust achieved certain pecuniary economies of scale, the most significant of which was a lower price for raw sugar.

Before the trust was established the market for raw sugar had been highly competitive, with many buyers (the twenty-two independent refineries) and many sellers (the various raw-sugar brokers). Upon the formation of the trust the number of buyers was suddenly reduced to five, with one of those five accounting for more than three-quarters of all purchases. In New York, Boston, and New Orleans the one buyer, the sugar trust, represented virtually the only potential customer. Moreover, it could command far greater resources than all the sellers combined. For the raw-sugar brokers to perform their economic function of maintaining an orderly market, it was necessary that they be able to buy and store raw sugar in their warehouses when the price was below normal, waiting for a rise in the price to release the extra stocks on the market. Yet, taking all the brokers together, the most raw sugar they could store was 25,000 tons. By the same token, it was not uncommon in the years that followed for the sugar trust to carry an inventory of from 150,000 to 200,000 tons of raw sugar.[42]

Faced with this great inequality in bargaining strength, the raw-sugar brokers could not hope to survive. The *coup de grâce* came with a sudden fall in raw-sugar prices, the world market's reaction to the news of the trust's formation. This fall in prices led to a heavy loss in the inventories that the raw-sugar brokers held, a blow from which they never recovered. The trust soon began to buy its supplies directly from overseas agents, while the raw-sugar brokers drifted into other

[42] *Ibid.*, pp. 184–85.

fields, some of them, in fact, becoming dealers in sugar trust certificates.[43]

Once the competitive market in raw sugar had been destroyed, the trust was able to bring its monopsonistic power to bear in forcing down the price of its most important input. The representatives of Cuban sugar growers found that they either had to deal with the trust or forgo selling their product in America.[44] The few remaining independent refineries were not able to provide a sufficient market, even though they generally paid ⅛ of a cent more per pound for raw sugar than did the trust.[45] One ship's captain, rather than accept the trust's price, sailed to London,[46] but others had no choice; they sold on the trust's terms. A person close to the industry estimated that the consolidation succeeded in knocking ⅜ of a cent a pound off the price of raw sugar,[47] and Havemeyer and Searles, in their testimony before the various investigative bodies, openly boasted of this fact. Since it was mainly foreign growers who suffered, no one in Congress seemed to mind. In fact, the nation's representatives seemed to agree that the ⅜ of a cent represented a gain for the American people.

In the same manner, the trust was able to secure a reduction in the cost of its other inputs. These were primarily labor, bone black, anthracite coal, barrels, and rail transportation.

In large part, the power that the sugar trust was able to bring to bear in reducing the cost of these other inputs was merely a reflection of its ability, on the product side, to limit output. For example, as refineries were closed down, large numbers of workers were discharged. One witness later estimated that altogether 5,000–6,000 employees lost their jobs as a result of the sugar refining industry's consolidation.[48] When several of the Boston refineries were shut down in the fall of 1888, officials of the trust took advantage of the opportunity to enforce a 10 per cent cut in wages among those refinery workers still holding jobs. In reporting this event the *New York Times*

[43] *Ibid.*, p. 219; Willett & Gray's *Weekly Statistical Sugar Trade Journal*, June 13, 1889.

[44] John Dodsworth, a reporter for the *Commercial Bulletin*, told the House Committee on Manufactures in 1888, "The common understanding is that the trust is the only buyer of raw sugar, and importers frequently hold themselves more or less at the mercy of the trust buyers" (U. S. House Committee on Manufactures, *Report on Trusts*, pp. 57–60).

[45] *New York Times*, November 11, 1888.

[46] *Ibid.*, February 1, 1888.

[47] Hugh N. Camp, testimony before the U.S. House Committee on Manufactures, *Report on Trusts*, p. 76.

[48] John Bergin, Lexow committee investigation, 1897, pp. 189–91.

noted: ". . . the only reason that could be advanced for [the wage cut] was that the Bay State employees [those whose refinery had been closed down] would probably be willing to accept employment at lower wages at the Boston Refinery [one of the refineries that remained in operation]. At all events, it would prevent a strike at the latter place."[49]

For political reasons, the trust subsequently reversed this policy of enforcing wage cuts, for it vitiated the trust's argument that it needed tariff protection because labor costs were higher in the United States than in Europe. In fact, the trust and its successor company began pursuing a policy of paying their workers wages that were slightly higher than the prevailing rates for similarly skilled laborers.[50] It was this sharing with their workers of part of the monopoly returns from consolidation which probably accounts for the divided opinion among labor leaders with regard to these industrial combinations. While many trade-union officials complained that the combinations led to reduced employment opportunities and higher prices, thereby injuring the workingman, others pointed out that the combinations often paid higher wages and provided steadier work.[51] Havemeyer himself cited this last factor, the steadier work, when replying to charges that the consolidation of the sugar refining industry had resulted in considerable unemployment.[52]

As for the trust's other inputs—in particular, anthracite coal and rail transportation—they were all supplied either by fellow monopolists or by firms with some independent pricing power and/or large overhead costs. This led to a situation best described as bilateral monopoly whereby the actual price reflected the respective economic strength and bargaining skill of the two parties.[53] While the amount of savings to the trust cannot thus be known, the cost of these inputs was cer-

[49] *New York Times*, October 3, 1888. It is interesting to note that one of the purposes of the sugar refining industry's consolidation, as stated in the trust deed, was "To furnish protection against unlawful combinations of labor" (U.S. House Committee on Manufactures, *Report on Trusts*, p. 7). This was probably no more than a residue of the bad feelings from the strike of 1886; see Chapter 3, p. 66 above. Still, the fact remains that the trust, and even its successor, the American Sugar Refining Company, was untouched by strikes during the period covered by this study.

[50] U.S. Industrial Commission, *Reports*, 1, pt. 1: 69. The policy was subsequently found to assure the sugar trust and similar consolidations of a more reliable and closely attached labor force.

[51] See the summary of trade-union testimony with regard to industrial combinations in U.S. Industrial Commission, *Reports*, 14: viii.

[52] U.S. House Committee on Manufactures, *Report on Trusts*, p. 103.

[53] For more on this point, see pp. 196ff.

tainly less than it would have been had the consolidation been without countervailing market power.

::

Pecuniary economies of scale, important as they might have been, were nevertheless of secondary importance compared to another source of savings from consolidation—the control over price and output which the consolidation made possible. As Searles explained it:

> Under the old regime, when the consumption was decreased, every refiner, in trying to keep his refinery in operation rather than close it up, was obliged to cut down his production 25 per cent, 40 per cent, sometimes 50 per cent at an enhanced cost of frequently one-eighth of a cent a pound on the entire product. . . . Under the existing arrangement, when the market will not take, that is, when the people will not buy the sugar, we reduce the production of sugar to the actual consumption of the country, not by trying to run all the houses at the increased cost . . . of one-eighth of a cent a pound, which means millions of dollars, but we close up the factories which cost the most per pound to operate, and only run those which can be run with the greatest economy, and run those to their fullest capacity.[54]

In other words, before the trust was organized the typical sugar refinery had a cost curve similar to the one shown in Figure 1. Because of the industry's seasonal nature the firm found itself operating to the left of point *A* a good part of the year. "The sugar consumption of the country," Searles pointed out, "is, during . . . [the winter], only about 60 per cent of what it is in the summer time. The consequence is that we have a surplus refining capacity, or sufficient refining capacity, to supply the whole country during the months of August and September, and carry as idle plant 40 per cent of that capacity during these other months of the year."[55] Ordinarily, the profits during the summer would have been sufficient to compensate for the losses during the winter, but as the nation's refining capacity proceeded to grow more rapidly than the demand, this became less and less the case.

With the sugar trust's formation the cost situation changed radically. As a multiplant firm, the Sugar Refineries Company had a cost curve similar to the one shown in Figure 2. Each refinery was now able to operate at its point of maximum efficiency, which corresponds to point *A* in Figure 1. When necessary, production was curtailed by

[54] U.S. Senate Committee to Investigate Attempts at Bribery, *Report*, p. 383.
[55] *Ibid.*, p. 382.

FIGURE 1

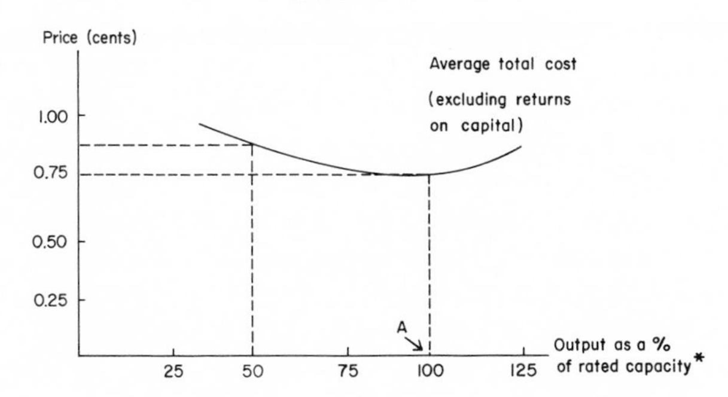

FIGURE 2

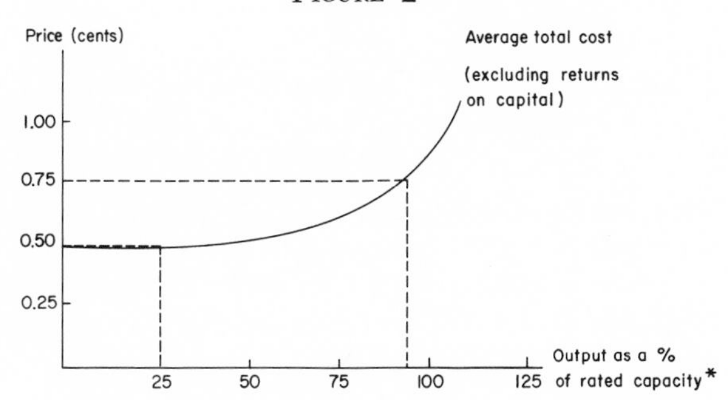

* *Rated capacity corresponds to the minimal point on the average total cost curve. It must be remembered that the horizontal scale in Figure 2 represents a much greater absolute quantity than does the horizontal scale in Figure 1. The trust was capable of producing more than 10,000,000 pounds of sugar daily, compared to the 500,000 pounds put out daily by the typical refinery before the trust's formation.*

closing down a refinery completely rather than by having it continue producing at less than full capacity. In this way no refinery was forced to operate to the left of point *A*, in the area of increasing cost. (Actually, the curve shown in Figure 2 represents the locus of these low-cost points.)

At first glance, since output could be altered only by somewhat large, discrete amounts, this would appear to be a somewhat clumsy way of regulating the supply. As a matter of fact, however, by judiciously juggling inventories, the process of adjusting supply to demand could be carried out quite smoothly. When production was greater than what the market could absorb at current prices, inventories of refined sugar were allowed to accumulate. On the other hand, when production was less than what the market could absorb at current prices, inventories were allowed to fall.

Searles later gave an illustration of how this regulating process worked, and of how, at the same time, it served to stabilize prices and output. Testifying before a Senate committee in the summer of 1894, he said:

> Now it happened last year in September . . . that there was in this country a sugar famine. The country had been afraid by reason of the panic (i.e., the panic of 1893) to buy anything; the grocers and all the wholesale dealers were unable to raise the money to carry the stocks of sugar they had been able to carry previous to the month of August. The question came with us whether we should stop our refineries, and some of our people felt as though we ought not to accumulate large quantities of sugar.
>
> But we did run our refineries until we had a stock of nearly 400,000 barrels of sugar, and in one week we had a call from the country for that entire 400,000 barrels. Under the old system of refineries, with sixteen [independent firms], the refiners could not have been found who would have dared to have accumulated any such stock of sugar with the possibility of a decline in raw sugars which we faced, and the result would have been that there would not have been in this country 100,000 barrels of sugar under any circumstances.
>
> Under this organization [i.e., the consolidated industry] we were able to accumulate and did have these 400,000 barrels of sugar, and when the demand came we had a call for 7,000,000 barrels of sugar in three weeks. We ran our refineries day and night in order to meet the demand of the people. We were bid from Chicago and all the larger cities of this country a premium of 1 cent a pound on our price if we would only send the sugar. The company turned out 1,000,000 barrels, and they sent every man 100 barrels where they could not otherwise have sent him 1 and kept the country going, and they did it without a farthing's increase in the cost to the consumer. That is a thing that would have been absolutely impossible under other conditions where there would have been active competition. It was only made possible by the fact that the American Sugar Refin-

ing Company [successor to the sugar trust], knowing it had the field, was able to accumulate this sugar with safety and carry it until the people wanted it.[56]

Searles contended that this was not an isolated incident. The trust and its successor, the American Sugar Refining Company, intend, he declared, "to provide all the sugar the consumers of this country will take. In order to economize [on] the cost of producing that sugar they [will] frequently . . . run their factories at a time when there is no sale of sugar, comparatively, for the sake of keeping their operatives employed and their refineries open. . . ."[57] In other words, the basis for regulating output was the expected long-run demand, not the short-run demand. This was also the basis for setting prices.

In sum, then, the consolidation of the sugar refining industry meant that fluctuations in demand, instead of being equilibrated primarily through changes in price as they had been before the trust was organized, were now equilibrated primarily through changes in output. But insofar as these changes in output were based on a longer time horizon, production and employment were greatly stabilized.

This new equilibrating mechanism was evident in the first winter after the trust's formation. Noting that the output of sugar was greatly below that of the previous year, Willett & Gray's *Weekly Statistical Sugar Trade Journal* reported on December 15, 1887, that "production [was] being kept down to consumption, by the closing of several refineries in New York and Boston. . . . Prices of refined are thereby kept steady. . . ." Three months later, when the full impact of the seasonal slump in demand would normally have been felt, that same journal recorded that the demand for "refined has remained firm at unchanged prices. All the elements which formerly caused frequent fluctuation are absent, and the whole sugar business has settled into a state of dullness and stupidity, which is a feature of the absence of all competition."[58]

As the cost curve in Figure 2 indicates, a reduction in output was apt to result in lower average total costs (excluding any return on capital), the opposite of what had been true before the trust was organized. This lowering of costs reflected the fact that as output was reduced, the least efficient plants were shut down first. However, as time went on, these least efficient plants were gradually replaced by improved facilities. As Searles explained, "Some of the plants, by

[56] *Ibid.*, p. 389.
[57] *Ibid.*
[58] Willett & Gray's *Weekly Statistical Sugar Trade Journal*, March 3, 1888.

reason of location and their character, [could] not be worked as economically as others, and the better refineries have been doubled in capacity and improved rather than . . . operate refineries which, through bad location or poor machinery, could not be operated as economically."[59]

In the New York area the Oxnard and North River refineries were shut down almost at once, just as soon as the stocks of raw sugar they had on hand could be worked off. The Moller & Sierck refinery met a similar fate soon thereafter. All three were subsequently dismantled, and their machinery was distributed to other members of the trust. The North River property, in fact, became a public park.[60]

The Havemeyer Sugar Refining Company's Greenpoint refinery was rebuilt as had been agreed, but following its completion in 1891 it was used only during peak periods of the year. The same was true of the DeCastro & Donner refinery. The Dick & Meyer plant burned down only a few months before the new Greenpoint refinery was finished, but in this case the board of trustees decided not to replace the destroyed facility.[61] Meanwhile, the Brooklyn Sugar Refining Company's plant had been connected by pipes to the adjoining Havemeyer & Elder refinery so that for all practical purposes they had become one and the same plant.[62] Similarly, the Havemeyer Sugar Refining Company's Jersey City refinery was connected to the adjoining Matthiessen & Wiechers refinery.

In Boston a similar winnowing-out process took place. The Bay State refinery was the first to close. Eight months after it joined the trust, its doors were shut permanently and its machinery was transferred to the Standard refinery. Not long after that the Continental refinery was connected by pipes to the Standard, which was located next door, and the operations of the two plants were completely integrated in much the same manner as those of the Havemeyer & Elder and Brooklyn refineries in New York and the Matthiessen & Wiechers and Havemeyer refineries in Jersey City. The Boston refinery, meanwhile, had been turned into a storage warehouse. Although its machinery was not dismantled, the plant itself was

[59] U.S. Senate Committee to Investigate Attempts at Bribery, *Report*, p. 382.

[60] *United States* v. *E. C. Knight et al.: Transcript of Record*, pp. 164–68; *New York Times*, January 1, 1888.

[61] *United States* v. *American Sugar Refining Co. et al.*, pretrial testimony, 1912, pp. 321–23.

[62] *Ibid.*, p. 515.

used thereafter only when the Standard-Continental was temporarily closed for repairs.[63]

In New Orleans the Planters refinery had closed down even before the trust was organized, and the entire output of the city had been concentrated in the Louisiana company's plant. Eventually, however, as the Planters' capacity was needed to meet the growing demand for refined sugar in the South, the two refineries were connected by pipes so that they, too, could be operated as a single plant. The *New Orleans Sugar Bowl,* in reporting this development in 1889, noted that "several of the 'Trust' refineries in New York and Boston have been similarly connected to work together, to the great advantage of the 'Trust' in the cost of manufacturing. . . ."[64] The savings, of course, were in overhead costs, since, as has already been pointed out, most technical economies of scale could be realized at a point below the plant level.

In St. Louis the trust made a sincere effort to keep the Belcher refinery in operation. William Havemeyer was even sent from New York to see if he could make it pay, but after eight months of steady losses the plant was finally shut down.[65] "In the first place, it was 1200 miles from a seaport town . . . ," Havemeyer later explained. "Every pound of sugar that I used had to come up from New Orleans. . . . Then, we had to compete with the eastern refineries on one side and the California refineries on the other side. We were between two firms all the time."[66] In the case of the Forest City refinery, in Portland, Maine, the trust did not even make an effort to keep it going. The competitive position was so hopeless that the refinery was shut down as soon as the trust took control.[67]

At the same time that these less efficient plants were being scrapped, the remaining refineries—Havemeyer & Elder in Brooklyn, Matthiessen & Wiechers in Jersey City, the Standard in Boston, and the Louisiana in New Orleans—were being expanded to meet the rising demand for refined-sugar products. This could be accomplished, without any increase in average variable costs, simply by

[63] *United States* v. *E. C. Knight et al.: Transcript of Record*, pp. 164–68; *United States* v. *American Sugar Refining Co. et al.*, pretrial testimony, 1912, pp. 4585–88, 4603–5; *New York Times*, October 2, 1888.

[64] The *New Orleans Sugar Bowl* article was reprinted in Willett & Gray's *Weekly Statistical Sugar Trade Journal*, August 8, 1889.

[65] *United States* v. *American Sugar Refining Co. et al.*, pretrial testimony, 1912, p. 4539.

[66] *Ibid.*, pp. 4549–50.

[67] *Ibid.*, p. 548.

adding entire refining units: vacuum pan and all. As this process continued, the tendency was for the cost curve shown in Figure 2 to level off until it was horizontal—or nearly so. Insofar as this process was typical of what happened in other industries that were later consolidated, it explains why the empirical study of cost curves has shown constant average variable costs and constant marginal costs over those ranges of output at which the modern corporation, or megacorp, customarily operates.[68]

::

This change in the shape of the sugar refining industry's cost curve represented a real saving—enough, argued Searles, "to pay a profit on the business."[69] More important was the fact that it represented a social as well as a private gain. Seager and Gulick made somewhat the same point in discussing the consolidation movement as a whole. "It is one of our conclusions," they wrote in their valuable study of the "trust" problem in 1929, "that after all of the economies of large-scale production have been realized, there remain wastes and losses that can be avoided only through the exercise of sufficient control over prices to maintain them at profitable levels and over outputs to secure the highest attainable regularity in the operation of plants. The combination movement is thus a natural and indeed inevitable business development, which is not in and of itself opposed to the public interest."[70] Even without following Seager and Gulick in all the conclusions they reach, one can still accept the basic point—that the consolidation of an industry may result in social savings other than the commonly recognized economies of scale, savings which reflect a more rational utilization of resources.

But these savings, it must be remembered, cannot be separated from the control over price and output which made them possible, because in order to achieve the former, it was first necessary to establish the latter. For that reason these savings should be regarded not as economies of scale but rather as economies of monopoly power. "Wasn't it a fact," Stursberg later was asked during the antitrust suit brought by the government against the American Sugar Refining Company, "that this consolidation was taking in a great number of refineries which you knew were not going to be operated, [and it was this] that put this doubt in your mind as to the earning of the trust

[68] J. Johnston, *Statistical Cost Analysis*, chaps. 4–5.

[69] U.S. Senate Committee to Investigate Attempts at Bribery, *Report*, p. 383.

[70] Henry R. Seager and Charles A. Gulick, Jr., *Trust and Corporation Problems*, p. ix.

certificates?" "Not in my mind," Stursberg answered, "because I felt that the advantages of working the modern and better refineries at their lowest cost and continuously instead of reducing with the variations of the market would more than make up what the cost would be for the amount spent on this property." "That is, you could afford to pay for the plants that were shut down in order to eliminate their competition?" the government's counsel continued.

"In a way," Stursberg replied.[71] In other words, it would have been impossible to keep some plants operating at full capacity and others idle without a considerable degree of monopoly power. Of course, the very act of becoming a multiplant firm in an industry the size of sugar refining resulted in a certain amount of control over price and output. But still, the organizers of the trust had to be sure there would not be so many other independent firms throwing refined sugar on the market that their efforts to manage supply would be disrupted.

The sugar refining industry's problem at the time of the trust's formation was excess capacity relative to demand. To solve this problem it was necessary, of course, to eliminate some of the excess capacity. It so happened that the best way to do this was to close down entire refineries, especially the older, more obsolescent ones. The advantage the trust form of organization had was that it provided a convenient way of compensating those whose refineries would have to be closed. They would simply be given their appropriate share of trust certificates. For this plan to be successful, however, those refineries which continued to operate had to earn sufficient profits to pay a dividend on the refineries that closed.

Henry Havemeyer and the others connected with the sugar trust later argued that the savings from stabilizing production were alone sufficient to justify the consolidation. "The output of the different refineries," Havemeyer told a congressional committee in 1888, "does not differ under the . . . [trust from what it was before]. It is [merely] concentrated in a few. By working these few to their fullest capacity, the economy is so great that it more than pays the expenses of the closed refineries. . . ."[72] Even if what Havemeyer said were true, the members of the trust would have had no way of knowing for certain before the trust was organized that such would be the case. They would have required some additional assurance, specifically the assurance of monopoly power, before agreeing to gamble their fortunes on the success of the consolidation. Looking at the record, it is clear

[71] *United States* v. *American Sugar Refining Co. et al.*, pretrial testimony 1912, pp. 550–51.

[72] U.S. House Committee on Manufactures, *Report on Trusts*, p. 60.

that the savings the trust realized from operating its plants at full capacity were not the only source of its profits.

There was, first of all, the trust's monopsony position, which enabled it to achieve certain pecuniary economies. Far more important, however, was its monopoly power. In the five years before the trust was formed, the average margin between raw and refined sugar had been 0.853 of a cent a pound. In the five years that followed the formation of the trust, the average margin was 1.01 cents a pound, an increase of 18 per cent.[73] This improved margin was the result almost entirely of the trust's ability to regulate price and output. But insofar as this ability led to certain economies, pecuniary or otherwise, the increase in profits was even greater than the increase in margin.

These profits were considerable. The trust declared its first dividend of 2.5 per cent in April, 1888,[74] and from that time on, until it was superseded by the American Sugar Refining Company in 1891, the trust continued to pay 2.5 per cent each quarter on the par value of its certificates. This constituted a return of 10 per cent per annum on the trust's capitalization—a capitalization which included not only the refineries that had been shut down but also the "water" in the trust certificates that represented expected monopoly earnings. Moreover, in 1889 the trust declared a special dividend of 8 per cent, payable in trust certificates.[75] But this still was not the whole profit picture. After paying out the above dividends, the trust had a surplus which in 1891 amounted to $7 million, or the equivalent of another 14 per cent dividend.[76]

It is difficult to say whether these were "monopoly" or "reasonable" profits. In testifying before various investigative bodies, Searles and Henry Havemeyer insisted that the profits were no greater than those earned by various independent firms before the trust was organized; they were simply more concentrated. In other words, they argued, the consolidation of the sugar refining industry had not led to any increase in the cost of refined sugar for the consumer. If the profits of sugar refining were greater, it was only because of the savings that the trust was able to realize. "We maintain," Havemeyer told the U.S. Industrial Commission, "that when we reduced the cost we were entitled to the profit, and that it was none of the public's business; we

[73] Lexow committee investigation, 1897, p. 274.

[74] *People* v. *North River Sugar Refining Co.: Record*, p. 51.

[75] U.S., Congress, Senate, Committee on Finance, *Replies to Tariff Inquiries on Schedule E, Sugar*, pp. 92–94.

[76] Paul L. Vogt, *The Sugar Refining Industry in the United States*, pp. 120–21; Willett & Gray's *Weekly Statistical Sugar Trade Journal*, January 18, 1891.

took it and paid it out to our stockholders; it may be business policy to share that with the public sometimes; we did not do that then; we have done it since."[77]

In making this claim, Searles and Havemeyer, aside from contradicting their own statements that the sugar refining industry had been forced to operate at a loss before the trust was organized, were not being completely honest. The price of refined sugar did fall after 1890, but only because the tariff on raw sugars was temporarily eliminated. Previously, in the period immediately after the trust was organized, not only the margin between raw and refined sugar, but also the price of refined sugar itself, had risen.[78] These facts had led many people to make their own judgments as to the causes of the sugar refining industry's increased profitability; and in some measure, that judgment accounted for the political and legal attack under which the sugar trust promptly found itself. Before turning to that reaction, however, it may be stated, briefly and in conclusion, that the sugar refining industry was consolidated for one reason alone: so that those who had survived the Golden Age of Competition would no longer be completely at the mercy of impersonal market forces. All other considerations, including possible economies of scale and windfall profits, were secondary.

[77] U.S. Industrial Commission, *Reports*, 1, pt. 2: 112.
[78] See Appendix D of this volume.

6 :: A CHANGE IN LEGAL FORM

WHILE the trust form of business organization offered a practical solution to the problem of how to unite diverse properties under a single management, it had yet to face the test of law and public opinion. When the test came, it failed—competition was still the unchallenged norm. A suit brought by the attorney general of New York to revoke the corporate charter of the North River Sugar Refining Company—on the grounds that its membership in the sugar trust was both a violation of the common-law prohibition against a partnership of corporations and contrary to the public interest in preserving competition—was successfully carried to the state's highest court, thereby destroying the legal basis of the trust device. This decision, which eliminated any need for federal action to fill the regulatory gap that was thought to exist in the case of trusts, was handed down just as Congress prepared to take final action on a revised antitrust law sponsored by Senator John Sherman. But though one legal basis for consolidation had been destroyed, another soon took its place. The Sugar Refineries Company, like many of the other trusts, subsequently reorganized itself as a holding company under the revised corporate statutes of New Jersey. This new legal entity, the American Sugar Refining Company, was in a position to exercise even stronger control over the various properties it commanded than had its predecessor.

::

The news of the sugar trust's formation in the summer of 1887 seemed to touch a raw public nerve, sending a shock through the body politic. That nerve had long been sensitive to the charge of monopoly. "As part of their Old World heritage," one historian has written,

> masses of Americans have been perenially obsessed with an ill-defined fear of monopolistic power. That fear was evident during colonial opposition to those exclusive privileges and royal patents which were granted in

accordance with the prevailing philosophy of mercantilism. It was expressed in continuing hostility to the banking, monetary, land and tariff policies of Alexander Hamilton which drove many citizens into the ranks of the Jeffersonian Republicans. In similar fashion a generation later, dissatisfaction with the privileges enjoyed by the Second Bank of the United States caused the Jacksonians to raise the magnetic shibboleths of antimonopolism once more. Likewise, amidst the growing pressures for homestead rights just before the Civil War, the cry against monopoly was echoed again and again, along with the audible reverberations of the natural rights of Man to a fair share in the bounties of his Creator.[1]

While those actively committed to these various crusades may have been no more than a small minority, they nevertheless represented a political force that candidates for elective office hesitated to offend. In expressing their opposition to special privilege in all its forms, the antimonopolists broadcast an appeal that met with a sympathetic response far beyond their own ranks, for the belief in equal opportunity for all lay at the heart of the American ethos.

In the years following the Depression of 1873, the special targets of those who rallied under the banner of antimonopolism were the railroads and their affiliates, the storage and terminal companies. To the farmer and his occasional urban allies, the common workingman and small-business proprietor, it seemed that these "behemoth" corporations were engaged in a "vast conspiracy" to take from them "the fruits of their labor."[2] The strategic position that many of these companies occupied, enabling them in certain cases to charge "what the traffic would bear," levy disproportionately higher rates for short hauls, and discriminate among individual shippers, seemed to threaten the economic freedom of those who found themselves dependent on rail transportation. Although the underlying cause of these alleged abuses—the large fixed investment that a railroad or terminal facility required—was the same as that which soon was to lead to industrial consolidation on a grand scale, the focus of protest was, for the moment, almost entirely on the railroads.

After 1882, this antimonopoly sentiment intensified—at least in the Great Plains and southern cotton states—because of depressed conditions in agriculture, the resulting discontent finding political expression in the Granger movement, and, to a lesser degree, in the Greenback-Labor party.[3] When efforts to regulate the railroads at the state level broke down, the antimonopolists turned to Congress for relief.

[1] Arthur P. Dudden, "Antimonopolism, 1865–1890," p. iii.

[2] G. Lee Benson, *Merchants, Railroads & Farmers.*

[3] John D. Hicks, *The Populist Revolt*, pp. 60–77; Chester M. Destler, *American Radicalism, 1865–1901*, pp. 17–19.

Although direct federal regulation of economic activity outside of banking was unprecedented, the railroads' opponents finally had their way. In 1887, after several years of studying and debating the matter, Congress passed the Interstate Commerce Act.[4]

Then came word of a new form of monopoly. In an article written for the March, 1881, issue of the *Atlantic Monthly,* Henry Demarest Lloyd told for the first time of how the Standard Oil Company of Ohio had succeeded in gaining control of an entire industry. The article, entitled "The Story of a Great Monopoly," was based for the most part on the testimony given two years earlier before the New York assembly's Hepburn committee. But, whereas that committee had concerned itself primarily with the reported abuses of railroads, probing into the affairs of the Standard Oil Company only insofar as they touched on that subject, Lloyd concentrated all his fire on what he termed the unprincipled drive of Rockefeller and his associates to destroy their competitors in the petroleum business. And while the Hepburn committee's five volumes of testimony had reached only a small, limited audience, Lloyd's article was read by thousands of influential persons across the nation. The issue in which it appeared ran through seven printings, with the *London Railway News* distributing reprints of the article throughout Europe. Many of the details were exaggerated, many of the accusations unwarranted, but the gist of the article—that the Standard Oil Company had succeeded in absorbing or otherwise eliminating all its rivals—could not be disputed. Perhaps almost as important, Lloyd had painted an indelible portrait of Rockefeller as a ruthless robber-baron.[5]

For the moment, however, the major thrust of political discontent was still directed at the railroads. Insofar as people were troubled by the reports of a monopoly in petroleum, they probably viewed the situation in that industry as merely one facet of the larger problem of

[4] John D. Clark, in *The Federal Anti-Trust Policy*, pp. 17–26, presents the interesting thesis that the Interstate Commerce Act was actually the first effort to deal with the problem of industrial combination on a national scale, its aim being to prevent the instances of rate discrimination which tended to favor one competitor over another. This interpretation, while true in a certain sense, in my opinion places too great an emphasis on what was, in fact, only one of many factors that led to passage of the Interstate Commerce Act. Gabriel Kolko, in *Railroads and Regulation, 1877–1916*, for example, has argued that the act was finally approved by Congress only because the railroads, recognizing that the regulatory machinery which it provided could be used to deal with their own problems of competition, supplied the necessary votes to assure passage. Discrimination in railroad freight rates was, of course, one manifestation of competition among railroads.

[5] Allan Nevins, *Study in Power*, 2: 140–41.

railroad regulation. Even after the *Atlantic Monthly* article appeared, not much was really known about the structure or organization of the Standard Oil empire—for example, that it was based on a new form of industrial organization, the trust device.

But then, just as Congress was preparing to enact the Interstate Commerce Act, the public began to hear of the formation of trusts in other industries. Late in 1886 it was revealed that seventeen cottonseed oil refiners, representing an alleged 88 per cent of the industry's capacity, had secretly organized a trust two years earlier.[6] In mid-summer of 1887, newspaper readers throughout the country learned that the nation's whiskey distillers, meeting in a Chicago hotel, had voted to establish a trust in that industry.[7] Soon the very word "trust" came to denote any combination of businessmen to control prices and output, whether it actually took the trust form or not. "These are the days of great combinations and monopolies," warned the *New York Times* editorially. "The baneful example set by the Standard Oil Trust has been followed in many fields of industry. Only a few weeks ago a Trust for controlling the rubber trade was organized. Now it is announced that firms representing 90 per cent of the productive capacity of the envelope business and controlling all of the potential machinery used in the manufacture of envelopes have united in a great corporation whose name—the Standard—is ominously suggestive of monopoly and of oppression and persecution for manufacturers who desire to maintain their independence."[8]

The *Times* was aware that the combination of envelope manufacturers was not actually a trust. "But the motives and intentions of its constituent firms are those of the Trust. Prices are to be raised, and if an independent manufacturer shall refuse to demand the raised prices for his goods he is to be crushed by destructive competition in his own market, just as the Standard Oil Trust has crushed independent refiners who dared to continue the sale of oil."[9]

In some cases there seemed to be a direct link between the members of the Standard Oil trust and combinations in other industries. The cottonseed oil trust, for example, was said to have been sug-

[6] The *Commercial and Financial Chronicle* had first reported the American Cotton Oil trust's formation in September; see *Commercial and Financial Chronicle*, 43 (September 11, 1886): 302. By early 1887 the attorney general of Louisiana was already taking steps to limit the trust's operations in that state; see *Railway & Corporate Law Journal*, 1 (April 23, 1887): 406–8.

[7] *Chicago Tribune*, July 20, 1887; *New York Times*, July 21, 1887.

[8] *New York Times*, July 16, 1887.

[9] *Ibid.*

gested by Henry M. Flagler, one of Rockefeller's oldest associates in the petroleum industry and a stockholder in one of the cottonseed oil companies that were combined. Colonel Oliver H. Payne, another Rockefeller partner, was reported to be involved in the whiskey business.[10] And when outside speculators began taking over control of Chicago gas and electric companies, it was rumored that Standard Oil money was behind the scheme. "The Oil Trust controls the supply of naphtha," the *New York Times* noted, "which is so largely used in modern processes of manufactured gas. By means of this product, it is said, the Oil Trust, or the millionaire holders of its certificates, propose to control the manufacture of gas through local Trusts, which seem to be independent but really are connected in some way with the present monopoly."[11] But even when it proved impossible to establish a link—direct or indirect—to the Standard Oil group, there was still a tendency to view each new instance of combination as yet another attempt to emulate Rockefeller.

Each month seemed to provide further grounds for the suspicion that all of American industry might soon go the way of the petroleum industry. There were reports of "trusts" being organized in lead, school slates, paper bags, linseed oil, paving pitch, salt, and cordage, among other industries. "It is the aim of those who make these combinations," an editorial in the *New York Times* declared, "to kill competition at home, and to exact from consumers a price high enough to invite competition from abroad—to make them pay to protected home manufacturers almost as great a tax as they must pay the Government when they buy the same kind of goods from foreign manufacturers."[12]

The very secrecy with which they conducted their affairs seemed to make the combinations all the more sinister. One advantage which the trust offered over the corporate form of organization was the fact that it required no charter or other form of approval by the state such as would have necessitated disclosure of its activities. As long as this secrecy could be maintained, it tended to avert public criticism, since what people do not know about they cannot fear. Once this secrecy was lost, however, the use of the trust form tended to have the opposite effect. What people know about only in part, they fear all the more.

[10] John T. Flynn, *God's Gold*, p. 278. Flagler did eventually become president of the cottonseed oil trust; see *New York Times*, November 1, 2, 4, 5, and 7, 1889.

[11] *New York Times*, July 8, 1887.

[12] *Ibid.*, December 26, 1887.

But beyond its secrecy, beyond its possible effect on prices, the trust aroused concern because it seemed to strike at the very heart of the prevailing business ethic. Competition, that ethic declared, was the order of life—the regulator of business activity as well as the arbiter of men's fates. That businessmen might from time to time violate this fundamental tenet did not negate its importance, any more than a man's having a mistress would necessarily belie his belief in the institution of marriage. Competition, like matrimony, was still the prevailing norm.[13] Of course, some businessmen—most notably Rockefeller and the Havemeyers—had already come to the conclusion that, from a social point of view, the disadvantages of competition far outweighed the benefits.[14] They were innovators, not only in the Schumpeterian sense, but in the Mertonian sense as well.[15] But those who held such a view were as yet numerically insignificant; and so pervasive was the majority sentiment, that they kept their thoughts on competition to themselves and their close business associates—at least for the time being.

The belief in the sanctity of competition was perhaps even more strongly held by that amorphous group in society, the molders of public opinion—especially those concerned with economic affairs. This small coterie of academicians and journalists was unwavering in its devotion to the general principle of laissez faire.[16] As Francis A. Walker later said, loyalty to that principle "was used to decide whether a man were an economist at all."[17] The state had no need to regulate economic activity, these laissez faireists would argue, because the market place would do the job better. Still, they recognized that such would be the case only if free competition were allowed to prevail. That is why they viewed the growth of "trusts" with such profound misgivings. If it were possible for a single firm to gain control of an entire industry, dictating the prices to be charged and the amounts to be produced, then competition could not be counted on

[13] Sidney Fine, *Laissez-Faire and the General-Welfare State*, pp. 109–11.

[14] Nevins, *Study in Power*, 2, chap. 24.

[15] Joseph A. Schumpeter, *The Theory of Economic Development*, pp. 57–94. Innovation in the Schumpeterian sense describes the act of developing and exploiting new technological processes and new methods of carrying on business. Innovation in the Mertonian sense describes the pursuit of socially approved goals through socially proscribed means; see Robert K. Merton, "Social Structure and Anomie," pp. 672–82.

[16] Support for tariff legislation marked the only heresy among the members of this group; however, the number of such heretics was small, especially among the academicians. See Fine, *Laissez-Faire*, pp. 47–73.

[17] Francis A. Walker, "Recent Progress in Political Economy in the United States," p. 254, quoted in Fine, *Laissez-Faire*, p. 48.

to regulate economic activity, and the intellectual foundations of laissez faire would collapse.

No event served to crystallize these fears so much as did the news of the sugar trust's formation. Perhaps it was the fact that seventeen previously independent firms had disappeared, firms which had been close to the large urban centers where these molders of public opinion were to be found. Perhaps it was the fact that prices had risen so quickly and sharply after the trust's formation. Perhaps it was the fact that sugar had become an important part of daily consumption. In any case, the news produced a sharp reaction. Previously, only the *New York Times* and *Chicago Tribune* had shown much interest in the "trust" problem. (Henry Lloyd was an editorial writer for the latter.) Now other newspapers began to express their concern. "Trusts ought to be investigated, thoroughly and unsparingly . . . ," the *New York Tribune* declared. "The public needs light about them all, their origin and methods, their influence upon production and prices, and their part in politics."[18]

In Congress a similar demand was heard for the first time. Noting that "some of the necessaries of life, particularly coal and sugar, are placed at an unreasonable price, by what are known as 'trusts,'" Congressman William E. Mason of Illinois, a Republican from Chicago, called for an investigation of "what effect said 'trusts' have upon the price of necessaries of life and whether the same are prejudicial to the interests of the people. . . ."[19] In supporting this request, his colleague Congressman Henry Bacon, a Democrat from New York, declared, "But here is a crying abuse, something that everybody understands, which the newspapers tell us daily is committing a serious injury to the [public]."[20]

As a result of this agitation, investigations were scheduled by both the Republican-controlled New York senate and the Democratic-controlled United States House of Representatives. The New York senate hearings, conducted by its Law Committee under the chairmanship of Frank S. Arnold, opened first. They began in New York City on February 20, 1888, and the leadoff witness was Henry O. Havemeyer.[21]

[18] *New York Tribune*, January 27, 1888.

[19] U.S., Congress, House of Representatives, *Congressional Record*, 50th Cong., 1st sess., 1888, 19, pt. 1: 210.

[20] *Ibid.*, p. 720.

[21] A resolution to investigate trusts was first introduced in the New York Assembly on January 31 (*New York Times*, February 1, 1888). Two weeks later, the *Times* charged that lobbyists for the Standard Oil Company and several of the other combinations involved (though not the sugar trust) were

The sugar trust's chief officer proved to be most unco-operative. After almost every question he would turn to his lawyer, John Parsons, for instructions; and the committee counsel, Colonel George Bliss, a leading Republican figure,[22] found it difficult to elicit information from him. The committee did learn that most, if not all, of the sugar refiners in New York State had signed an agreement whereby their stock was transferred to a board of trustees who exercised control over the properties in the name of all the stockholders. The committee even learned the names of the trustees. But when Colonel Bliss asked Havemeyer what companies outside of New York State were parties to the agreement, Havemeyer at first refused to answer, on the grounds that the committee had no jurisdiction to inquire into affairs beyond the state's borders.[23] Later, when pressed by the full committee to answer Colonel Bliss's questions on that subject, Havemeyer reluctantly did so. But he steadfastly refused to turn over to the committee a copy of the trust deed. It was in Parsons' possession, he said, and Parsons would not release the document.[24] Parsons was

---

working behind the scenes to block any investigation, especially one by a special committee of the New York legislature, and that the sponsor of the resolution, Assemblyman Austin A. Yates of Schenectady, after being subjected to the pressure of these lobbyists, had lost his ardor for any probe (*New York Times*, February 16, 1888). In light of the Standard Oil Company's history, these charges may well have been true (see Nevins, *Study in Power*, 2: 95ff.), although Yates vehemently denied them on the assembly floor. The next day, February 17, after the *New York World* had joined the *Times* in criticizing the legislature's failure to investigate the trusts, the senate instructed its Law Committee to conduct its own probe (New York, Legislature, *Legislative Journal*, 111th sess., 1888, pp. 82, 199–200). Members of the senate undoubtedly were uneasy because of the disposition the electorate had shown in the last several elections to vote out of office any politicians prominently identified with the "corporate" interests (see Benson, *Merchants, Railroads & Farmers*). Since the hearings began only three days later, the committee and its counsel could not possibly have had adequate time to prepare. The hurried preparation probably explains, in part, why the committee was relatively unsuccessful in eliciting information from the witnesses called to testify before it. The best account of these hearings, aside from the committee's report itself (New York, Legislature, Senate, Committee on General Laws, *Report on Investigation Relative to Trusts*), is to be found in the *New York Times*. The *New York Tribune* also covered the hearings extensively.

[22] Colonel Bliss had, incidentally, participated with the Havemeyers in the overthrow of the Tweed ring. The other counsel for the committee was Roger A. Pryor, but he did not play an important part in the sugar-trust portion of the hearings. He did, however, take a leading role in the later prosecution of the sugar trust. See pp. 132ff. below.

[23] New York Senate Committee on General Laws, *Investigation Relative to Trusts*, pp. 19–27; see also the *New York Times* and *New York Tribune*, February 21 and 22, 1888.

[24] New York Senate Committee on General Laws, *Investigation Relative to Trusts*, pp. 36, 64–69.

then called to the witness stand, and proved just as recalcitrant. The trust deed had been given to him in confidence as a lawyer, he said, and to surrender it to the committee would violate professional ethics.[25]

The only other member of the sugar trust called to testify was William Sierck. The others, including John E. Searles, had left town hurriedly in order to avoid the committee's subpoenas.[26] Sierck proved no more co-operative than Havemeyer, and even less informative. But what those two witnesses were reluctant to disclose, George Moller, the former head of the North River Sugar Refining Company, was more than ready to tell. He even revealed how much had been paid in certificates for some of the refineries.[27]

After the second day of hearings, the Arnold committee turned its attention to other industries. Brief as the spotlighting of sugar refining had been, it had nonetheless provided a glimpse of features likely to arouse public opposition to the trust's continued existence. Havemeyer had tried to make the point that the combination of sugar refineries was not intended to raise consumer prices, but the *New York Times* had only to call attention to the rise in sugar prices which had already taken place to cast doubt on that assurance.[28]

The sugar trust had probably followed the worst of possible courses. Although most of its salient features were brought out in the hearings, those members of the trust who testified gave the impression that there were still many more facts that had been concealed. The investigation seemed to show, the *Times* commented, "that if the sugar trust be the innocent organization that some of those

[25] *Ibid.*, pp. 70–74, 122–26. The trust deed was eventually surrendered to the Arnold committee, though not until the hearings had been completed and the amounts of certificates issued to the various refineries had been deleted (*ibid.*, p. 14). By then the issue had become somewhat academic, since the trust's officials had already decided to turn a copy of the trust deed over to the House Committee on Manufactures (see p. 130 below). In reflecting on this decision many years later, Henry O. Havemeyer said, "All this litigation and all this fuss about trusts was based upon that deed; if that deed had not been produced there would have been nothing to fight about or investigate." Havemeyer's view, of course, must not be taken too seriously, since the Standard Oil Company had turned a copy of its trust deed over to the Arnold committee even before the sugar-trust hearings, and in any case it is unlikely that a copy of the document could have been concealed from the public for long, once its existence was known.

[26] New York Senate Committee on General Laws, *Investigation Relative to Trusts*, pp. 48–49.

[27] *Ibid.*, pp. 102–15.

[28] *New York Times*, February 22, 1888.

who are interested in it claim it to be, it has features with which they do not propose the public shall become acquainted."[29] Rockefeller, in a later appearance before the same committee, was to create a much better impression, even if he could not dispel completely the feeling that trusts were synonymous with industrial monopoly.[30]

The Arnold committee was under instructions to report back to the senate no later than March 1, 1888. Six days after that deadline, the committee finally issued its report. Speaking of trusts in general, it declared that,

> however different the influences which gave rise to these combinations in each particular case may be, the main purpose, management and effect upon the public is the same, to wit: The aggregation of capital, the power of controlling the manufacture and output of various necessary commodities; the acquisition or destruction of competitive properties, all leading to the final and conclusive purposes of annihilating competition and enabling the industries represented in the combination to fix the price at which they would purchase the raw material from the producer, and at which they would sell the refined product to the consumer. In any event, the public at each end of the industry (the producer and consumer) is, and is intended to be, in a certain sense, at the mercy of the syndicate, combination or trust.[31]

The committee also noted that trusts were merely the latest in a long series of threats posed by aggregations of capital to the freedom of New York's citizens. "Colossal fortunes," it said,

> hastily accumulated, are always abhorrent and even in the hands of private individuals . . . are often considered a menace to good government. The people of this State have become alarmed at the constantly growing power of railroad, pipe-line, telegraph and other corporations; and the ease and boldness with which the great and powerful destroys or assimilates its weaker competitive neighbor, common carrier or manufacturer has become the scandal of the age. The end, if not the purpose of every combination, is to destroy competition and leave the people subject to the rule of monopoly.[32]

Despite these alarming conclusions, the committee's only recommendation was that it be given more time to pursue its investigation.

[29] *Ibid.*, February 21, 1888.

[30] New York Senate Committee on General Laws, *Investigation Relative to Trusts*, pp. 363–446; Nevins, *Study in Power*, 2: 221–23.

[31] New York Senate Committee on General Laws, *Investigation Relative to Trusts*, p. 5. The *New York Tribune* reprinted portions of the report.

[32] New York Senate Committee on General Laws, *Investigation Relative to Trusts*, p. 13.

Two days after this report was issued, the U.S. House Committee on Manufactures, under the chairmanship of Congressman Bacon, began its own inquiry into the formation of trusts. Once again, officials of the Sugar Refineries Company were the first to testify.[33] This time the hearings had been more adequately prepared. Also, the trust's organizers by now realized that they had made a mistake by refusing to co-operate with the New York senate investigation. They answered all the questions put to them and turned over to the Bacon committee whatever documents were requested—including a copy of the trust deed.[34] As a result of this closer co-operation and the greater length of time devoted to the sugar refining industry, the House investigators were able to bring out many more of the details surrounding the sugar trust's formation. The same was true of the other trusts and combinations the Bacon committee looked into. But the over-all picture that emerged was not very different from that already revealed by the Arnold committee. From both investigations it was clear that, in a number of industries, businessmen had joined together to stifle competition and control prices. It was not clear, however, what, if anything, could be done to halt or reverse the trend.

Many members of Congress were particularly concerned by the growth of trusts proper. It now appeared that passage of the Interstate Commerce Act the year before had not been enough, that despite the elimination of one gap in governmental powers, another still existed. For the trust, unlike the corporation, was responsible to no sovereign political body.

These fears were reflected in the congressional discussions of the trust problem. Congressman Bacon, when explaining to his House colleagues earlier in January why the Manufactures committee had amended the original resolution calling for an investigation of trusts, to broaden its scope, had said that the members of his committee wished to make sure that the investigation would "embrace every

[33] U.S. House Committee on Manufactures, *Report on Trusts; New York Times*, March 9, 1888. Counsel for the committee was Frank B. Gowan, the former president of the Philadelphia & Reading Railroad who had pioneered in the techniques of consolidating an industry when he helped to organize the anthracite-coal combination in the 1870's. The retention of Gowan as counsel foreshadowed the committee's eventual report, which, in the context of the day, was actually quite gentle toward the trusts. See, for example, the editorials in the *New York Times*, July 31 and August 1, 1888.

[34] Perhaps, too, they sensed that they were now in much friendlier hands (see note 33 above). Of course, the issue of limited jurisdiction could not arise in the same manner. Still, Searles had again prudently left town to avoid being served with a subpoena (U.S. House Committee on Manufactures, *Report on Trusts*, p. 48).

such trust or combination which, owing to the fact that it is not incorporated, is not within the reach, perhaps, of the laws of any State."[35] Certainly the objections that the members of the sugar trust raised to the authority of a state body to inquire into their affairs did not ease congressional fears on that score. Later, during the House hearings themselves, several members of the Manufactures committee pressed Parsons on just that point. Congressman Henry Smith, a member of the People's party from Wisconsin, noted that the sugar trust had not been incorporated by any state and declared, "It is outside the pale of the law, a thing without a name." To which Parsons replied, "It is a name without a thing—a mere convenient description." Congressman Smith nonetheless was inclined to compare the trust with wildcat banks in the West, while his Democratic colleague Congressman William D. Bynum of Indiana likened it to the proverbial flea. "When you want to put your finger on it," he said, "you can't find it."[36]

If it were true, as the evidence seemed to indicate, that the trust was beyond the jurisdiction of any state legislature, Congress might have no choice but to step in and fill the breach. This was not a cheering prospect, especially since so many members of Congress were reluctant to expand still further the powers of the federal government. Yet, as Congress debated the issue through the summer and on into the fall,[37] some members began to hope that federal legislation might not be necessary after all, that the states might already have sufficient powers to cope with the problem of trusts. The House Committee on Manufactures, in its report on July 30, 1888, had alluded to this possibility. Although it had made no recommendations itself for new legislation, it had pointed out that the attorney general of New York was then in the process of instituting a suit against the sugar trust. Apparently the members of the committee hoped that this would dispose of the matter.[38]

::

[35] House of Representatives, *Congressional Record*, 50th Cong., 1st sess., 1888, 19, pt. 1: 719.

[36] *New York Times*, March 9, 1888.

[37] Since Congress was then primarily occupied with the issue of the tariff, the time devoted to the trust problem was not very extensive. Yet, because of the inevitable tendency to link the two issues, the problem of trusts did crop up periodically. See House of Representatives, *Congressional Record*, 50th Cong., 1st sess., 1888, 19, pt. 4: 7261; pt. 8: 7512–13; pt. 9: 3483, 8559, 8645; and pt. 10: 9074.

[38] *New York Times*, July 31, 1888.

From the moment it had begun to deplore the growth of trusts, the *New York Times* had insisted that the various states had more than adequate remedies for dealing with this new form of industrial organization.[39] While the *Times* continued to argue in this vein during the many months of agitation over the trust question,[40] it began to receive support for its view only after the Arnold committee hearings. When that investigation was concluded, the executive committee of Tammany Hall, the governing body of the Democratic party in Manhattan, requested that the attorney general of New York proceed against the Sugar Refineries Company and its thirteen trustees.[41] A petition signed by Richard Croker and other Tammany chieftains charged "that these directors are exercising all the powers of a corporation without having been duly incorporated under the laws of this State." It further charged that "the Sugar Trust is injurious to trade and commerce."[42] Behind this petition lay the guiding hand of Roger A. Pryor, one of the leaders of Tammany Hall and Colonel Bliss's co-counsel on the Arnold committee.

The sixty-year-old Pryor had been born into a distinguished Virginia family that included among its forebears the names of Randolph and Bland. Moving to the North after serving as an officer in the Confederate army during the war, he had been admitted to the New York bar in 1866. The years that followed saw Pryor rise to a position of power within the Democratic party, his prewar contacts while a Virginia congressman serving him well. Although he held no elective office, he became one of the most influential members of Tammany Hall. Then, in 1888, his path crossed that of the sugar trust. Whether reflecting his Jeffersonian ancestry or indicating his political hopes, Pryor set his sights on destroying what had become in New York State the most notorious of consolidations.[43]

On instructions from Tammany Hall, Pryor prepared to travel to Albany to press Attorney General Charles F. Tabor to take action against the sugar trust.[44] That elected official, though a Democrat, was politically independent of the New York City machine and was

[39] *Ibid.*, July 8, 1887.

[40] See *ibid.*, November 28, 1887, and March 2 and 7, 1888.

[41] *Ibid.*, March 7, 1888.

[42] *Ibid.*, April 19, 1888.

[43] This sketch is drawn from the *Dictionary of American Biography*, the article which appeared in the *New York Times* on Pryor's eightieth birthday (July 19, 1908), and the obituary which ran in that same newspaper upon his death (March 15, 1919).

[44] *Ibid.*, April 19, 1888.

noticeably reluctant to bring suit against the Havemeyer interests.[45] In addition to putting pressure on the attorney general, Pryor's purpose in going to Albany was to line up support for a bill "to suppress trusts" which he himself had drafted and which the Tammany leaders were supporting.[46] Since the state legislature was then in the midst of a battle over antitrust legislation, the latter mission had first claim on his time.[47]

The Pryor, or Tammany, bill had been introduced in both houses of the state legislature even before the Arnold committee hearings opened. It prohibited all agreements—especially trusts—whose purpose was to control prices. Those who violated its provisions could be fined up to $5,000 or imprisoned for two years. However, except for these stiffer penalties and their specific application to the organizers of trusts, the Tammany bill did not differ significantly from the law already on the books. The latter made it a misdemeanor for "two or more persons [to] conspire to commit any act injurious to trade or commerce,"[48] and it was similar to the laws existing in a number of other states.[49] Like those laws, the New York statute, except for a few minor prosecutions, had never been invoked, for the reason that as a practical matter it was extremely difficult to obtain convictions under it. Since both houses of the legislature were firmly in the control of the Republicans, the Tammany bill, which might have made this statute more enforceable, stood little chance of passage.

Soon after his committee issued its report, Senator Arnold had introduced his own bill for dealing with the trust problem. It closely resembled the Tammany bill, except that the penalties provided were not so severe.[50] The only advantage it had over the Tammany measure was that it was sponsored by a Republican.

Still a third bill had been introduced by Senator Commodore P. Vedder, a Republican from Cattaraugus County. It took a different approach, proposing to tax all trusts and require them to file certain

[45] Tabor, a resident of Buffalo, was a close friend and political ally of President Grover Cleveland, whose support had been instrumental in securing Tabor's nomination as attorney general on the Democratic ticket (*New York Times*, September 29, 1887). As Democrats, the Havemeyers were also closely identified with the Cleveland wing of the party.

[46] *New York Times*, February 2, 1888, and July 3, 1888.

[47] At the last minute, Pryor became ill and another Tammany official, T. C. T. Crain, went in his place.

[48] *New York Penal Code*, 1888, sec. 168.

[49] Hans B. Thorelli, *The Federal Anti-Trust Policy*, p. 155.

[50] *New York Times*, March 15, 1888.

information with the state's attorney general. His measure, Senator Vedder argued, would at least enable the state to tax away the trusts' monopoly profits. It would also, its opponents were quick to point out, legalize trusts; and that was the last thing the majority of legislators wanted to see happen.[51] This bill's chances of passage appeared slimmest of the three.

It soon became apparent that both the Democrats and the Republicans were interested only in putting themselves in the best possible political light—without necessarily enacting any legislation.[52] Although it was questionable whether any new laws were needed, or even whether they would serve any useful purpose, the two parties were sensitive to the public clamor against trusts, and neither wanted to have it said that it had taken the trust's side against that of "the people." Antimonopoly sentiment was still a potent force in the state.[53]

The Democrats were perhaps somewhat more sincere in their efforts to obtain passage of an antitrust measure. Those from New York City, especially, were concerned by the inroads that various third-party candidates had been making in normally Democratic precincts, and they hoped that by sponsoring legislation to curb trusts they might prevent further defections from the party of Jefferson and Jackson. Even so, some of their fellow Democrats from upstate areas were to be found, on certain key votes, lined up with the opposition. In any case, since the Democrats were in the minority, they could not be held responsible for what the legislature did.

The Republicans, according to the usually accurate *New York Times* correspondent in Albany, had determined that no bill affecting the trusts would be enacted that session. Their problem, he pointed out, was how to kill the various measures that had been introduced without being tagged for doing so. In addition, Senator Arnold was honestly committed to the support of the bill that bore his name. The expedient the Republicans finally adopted was to permit the Arnold bill to reach the senate floor but to delay its passage until three days before the legislature adjourned so that the assembly would not have sufficient time to act on it. In that way, those senators who so wished could be recorded as voting against the trusts without any specific

[51] *Ibid.*, March 10 and 27, 1888.

[52] This legislative history is based on accounts which appeared in the *New York Times*, generally acknowledged by historians to be the most reliable source of information on the state legislature's activities during this period. See especially the May 3 and 9, 1888, issues.

[53] Benson, *Merchants, Railroads & Farmers*, pp. 174–203.

measure becoming law. However, even Pryor was not unhappy to see the Arnold bill defeated. As he confided to a *New York Times* reporter, he felt that Attorney General Tabor already had all the power he needed to proceed against the trusts, and that a suit against the Sugar Refineries Company specifically, for usurping and abusing corporate privileges, would turn out to be the most effective weapon against such combinations.[54]

Apparently the attorney general was now more sympathetic to this view. Within a week after the legislature adjourned, he scheduled a hearing on the Tammany charges against the sugar trust.[55] At that unusual session, both sides presented their arguments, with Pryor resting his case primarily on the evidence uncovered by the Arnold committee. When the hearing ended, Tabor said he would announce his decision after both sides had had a chance to submit additional briefs.[56]

Over a month passed without any word from the attorney general. The *Times* grew impatient, chiding Tabor for his lack of action.[57] But finally, on July 2, 1888, the attorney general announced that he had decided to heed the Tammany leaders' plea and would institute a suit against the sugar trust.[58] " . . . In view of the allegations contained in the petition before me," Tabor said, "and of the report of the Senate . . . it is important to ascertain by judicial investigation whether these things alleged . . . are true. If they are, a great public wrong has evidently been committed by them."[59]

The plan of legal attack ultimately decided upon was a suit by the attorney general to revoke the charter of the North River Sugar Refining Company on the grounds that, by becoming a member of the trust, it had usurped and abused its corporate franchise.[60] That the suit was to be limited to this one company seems to have been part of a deal worked out by the opposing counsel.[61] As their part of the bargain, lawyers for the trust appear to have agreed not to contest the attorney general's right to bring such a suit. In this way there

[54] *New York Times*, May 14, 1888.
[55] *Ibid.* [56] *Ibid.*, May 15, 1888. [57] *Ibid.*, June 26, 1888.
[58] *Ibid.*, July 3, 1888. [59] *Ibid.*, July 4, 1888.
[60] *Ibid.*, July 3, 1888. At first it was decided to bring a second action against the sugar trust, enjoining the members of the board from exercising the functions of a corporation. However, this second action, which rested on far less solid legal grounds, was later dropped (*ibid.*, November 13, 1888).
[61] John Parsons, in testifying before the Hardwick committee in 1911, said: "I will tell you what Tammany Hall did in respect to that litigation [i.e., the North River suit]. It arranged to test that question in a way that would do no harm to anybody . . ." (Hardwick committee investigation, 1911, p. 2073). The actual events strongly suggest such a deal.

could be a speedy court test of the main issue, that of the trust's legality, without directly jeopardizing the rights to the vast properties involved.

On the one hand, a suit against the North River Sugar Refining Company alone was sufficient to establish the legal precedent which the attorney general—or perhaps more accurately, Pryor—was seeking. For if that one company were dissolved, it would mean that the other members of the trust would be subject to similar proceedings, and thus the consolidation would not be able to continue under its current form of organization. On the other hand, it was to the trust's advantage to have the suit limited to the North River company. For if the suit were successful, dissolution of only that company, with its soon-to-be-dismantled refinery, would not have the same disruptive effect as simultaneous dissolution of all the trust's member corporations. Thus it was that the challenge to the trust's continued existence took the form of a suit to annul the charter of a single company which, for all practical purposes, had long since ceased to do business.

::

The ensuing legal battle, which opened in New York's Supreme Court on November 14, 1888, was fought on two levels.[62] One, very technical, involved the question of whether the North River Sugar Refining Company itself had become a member of the trust, or whether its stockholders (actually Searles alone) had merely transferred their shares in the company to a board of trustees. The question was important, for common law prohibited any form of partnership among corporations. Parsons, as was to be expected, argued that it was the stockholders, not the company, who had joined the trust. The North River company could not, therefore, be said to have entered into a partnership with other corporations. Pryor, of course, took the opposite view. Under the trust deed, he pointed out, a company first had to become a corporation before it could become a member of the trust, and it was the company, not its stockholders, that had to execute the trust deed. Technicalities aside, it was clear

[62] *People* v. *North River Sugar Refining Co.: Appellants' and Respondents' Briefs*, hereafter cited as *People* v. *North River Sugar Refining Co.*, briefs; see also the accounts of the oral arguments which appeared in the *New York Times* on November 15 and December 5 and 6, 1888. The papers in the *quo warrento* action were served on Searles August 8, and the trial was subsequently set for November 13, 1888. Under the New York State judicial system, the Supreme Court was an initial trial court, while the Court of Appeals was the highest appellate body.

that the North River Sugar Refining Company and its shareholders were one and the same.

On a more philosophical level, the question involved the social desirability of the trust. The issue, both sides agreed, was whether or not such an "agreement tends to stifle competition and enhance prices, and therefore to work an injury to trade and commerce."[63] For common law also provided that, if a corporation could be shown to have committed actions "prejudicial to the public interest," its charter could be revoked.

It was difficult for Parsons to argue that the formation of the sugar trust had not led to a decline in competition within the sugar refining industry. The evidence gathered by the two legislative investigations was overwhelming on this point. But he could, and did, argue that trade and commerce had not been injured thereby. The sugar trust, Parsons maintained, could not raise prices above their natural level without inviting new competition. Besides, competition already existed, for a number of refineries had remained outside the combination. The trust's control of the market was therefore partial, not complete, and it should not be considered a monopoly.

The trust, Parsons further maintained, was merely a new way of bringing together large aggregates of capital, and the attacks against it were attacks against such aggregates. Said Parsons in his brief, "Objections to combinations of capital upon the grounds that they are opposed to the public interest are at variance with the views entertained by leading political economists . . . ," and here he was able to cite the works of John Stuart Mill, Thorold Rogers, and Simon Newcomb. "Such combinations," Parsons' brief continued, "do not prevent competition. On the contrary, if they result advantageously, they stimulate, encourage and invite [competition]." They "enable producers to furnish a good article at a minimum of profit, and by reason of the scale upon which the business is done, at a remunerative return." But even if it could be shown that trusts prevented competition, this would not necessarily mean that they were against the public interest; for, as Parsons pointed out, "competition may be the death of trade." If such combinations of capital were to be declared illegal, he added, the same should be done to combinations of labor.[64]

For Pryor, there was no doubt but that the sugar trust constituted a monopoly. Its board of trustees, he pointed out, had sole control

[63] *People* v. *North River Sugar Refining Co.*, briefs, p. 36.
[64] *Ibid.*, pp. 5ff.

over all the sugar refineries in the state of New York. All competition between those refineries had been eliminated, and the profits and losses were to be shared equally among them. Moreover, the trust agreement provided for the purchase of any new refineries that might be built. Finally, high tariffs precluded the possibility of foreign competition. Citing the works of various economists to show what happened when a market was dominated by a single supplier, Pryor concluded, "Viewed in the light of these principles—axioms in the science of political economy—the agreement constitutes a strict and absolute monopoly."[65] Its effect, he said, was to raise prices at the consumers' expense. Even if the trust had not done so already, this would be its inevitable effect. The trust's undesirable character, he added, derived "from its organization, not necessarily from its operations."[66]

Pryor discounted the importance of potential competition. "Even after outside refineries shall be established, equipped and in operation," his brief said, "it by no means follows that they will compete with the combination in the reduction of prices . . . , and if they do, experience, notably of the Standard Oil Company, demonstrates that nascent rivals are invariably crushed by established and powerful combinations, which, for that purpose, reduce prices until their competitor is driven from the field, and then indemnify themselves by aggravated plunder of the public."[67] He also denied that economies of scale had resulted from the combination. "The combination does not bring a single additional dollar to the production of sugar. The principle of division of labor is not more available and operative than before. . . . The cost of running each company is precisely what it was before the combination, and the business of each is still under a separate and several management."[68]

The contention that the trust could have accomplished the same objectives just as well by forming a single corporation was not relevant, Pryor's brief went on to argue. For one thing, the legality of a single corporation did not make the trust itself legal. For another, a single large corporation controlling all the refineries in New York State would have been illegal for the same reason that the trust was—its effect would be to injure trade and commerce. Nor did labor's right to organize give owners of capital a corresponding right. "The mischief of oversupply and inadequate value in commodities," Pryor's brief declared, "the producer can and will correct by a reduced

[65] *Ibid.*, pp. 36–51. [66] *Ibid.*, pp. 32–34. [67] *Ibid.*, p. 51. [68] *Ibid.*

supply, thus restoring the equilibrium of prices. But sentient labor cannot withdraw from the market. It must eat or die. . . ."[69]

These various arguments were presented first before a single judge and jury, then before New York's various appellate courts. On January 9, 1889, Judge George C. Barrett of the New York Supreme Court, First District, directed the jury sitting with him to bring in a verdict for the plaintiff in the case of *People* v. *North River Sugar Refining Company.*[70] "It is the first time in the history of corporations," he declared in an accompanying opinion, "that we have heard of double trust in their management and control—one set of trustees elected formally to manage the corporate affairs, and a second set created to manage the first. . . ."[71]

On the narrow issue of whether the North River company or its stockholders had become members of the trust, Judge Barrett agreed with Pryor. "The accumulation of evidence," he said, "points irresistably to the complete identity of shareholders and corporations, and it is quite impossible to sever the acts of the persons solely interested in these corporations from that of the corporations themselves. . . . The form of the contract veil was thin enough, but the acts under it sweep away the gauze and leave the corporate body unclouded and in full view." Pointing out that common law prohibited any partnership between corporations, Judge Barrett declared: "It cannot be doubted that the arrangement in question amounted to a partnership between these corporations. . . . Such was the effect of the massing of all the profits of all the corporations. . . . Such, too, was the effect of uniting all the corporations under practically a single control."[72]

On the much broader issue of the trust's social desirability, Judge Barrett also agreed with Pryor. "It is not a case," he said, "where a few individuals in a limited locality have united for mutual protection against ruinous competition. It is the case of great capitalists uniting their enormous wealth in mighty corporations, and utilizing the franchises granted to them by the people to oppress the people." And he referred to the sugar trust as a "gigantic and irresponsible power, furnished with every delegated facility for regulating and controlling at will, not only in the state, but throughout the entire country, the production and price of a particular and necessary article of commerce." By "irresponsible," Judge Barrett hastened to add, he

[69] *Ibid.*, pp. 54–57.
[70] *People* v. *North River Sugar Refining Co.*, 3 N.Y. Sup. 401.
[71] *Ibid.*, p. 404. [72] *Ibid.*, p. 407.

did not mean the individuals who had organized the combination, but rather the combination itself, since it was subject to the regulation of no duly constituted authority.[73]

In his opinion Judge Barrett took note of the argument that to declare the trust illegal would be to interfere with the natural economic order. "Unfortunately for this argument," Judge Barrett declared, "it is the combination which has resorted to what it calls the unnatural thing. It was not content with natural partnerships or associations of individuals, but resorted to the device of corporate artificiality to effect its ends. Having asked and accepted the favor of the law, it cannot complain that it is taken to task for grossly offending its letter and spirit."[74]

Judge Barrett's decision was immediately appealed to the General Term of the New York Supreme Court, although it was to be another ten months before a three-member panel of that appellate body would hand down its decision. That ruling, delivered on November 7, 1889, upheld in full the lower court's decision revoking the North River company's charter, both on the narrow grounds that the trust was an illegal partnership of corporations and on the broader grounds that it represented an undesirable form of business organization.[75] This decision, too, was immediately appealed, this time to the Court of Appeals, the highest tribunal in New York; but the drift of judicial opinion was clear.

::

Even as the General Term of the Supreme Court was handing down its ruling, other states were following New York's lead in invoking common law to destroy the trust form of organization. California's attorney general, just as the case against the North River company was about to go to trial, had initiated a suit to annul the charter of the American Sugar Refinery, the one member of the sugar trust situated in his state.[76] The suit, a reflection of Claus Spreckels' political influence, was actually part of the struggle between him and the sugar trust for control of the West Coast industry,[77] but when Judge W. T. Wallace of California's Superior Court finally handed down his decision on January 6, 1890, the effect was to create another legal precedent for the suppression of trusts. Following the same line

[73] *Ibid.*, pp. 409–10.

[74] *Ibid.*, p. 413.

[75] *People* v. *North River Sugar Refining Co.*, 6 N.Y. Sup. 408.

[76] *New York Times*, November 6, 1888; *Railway & Corporate Law Journal*, 4 (December 15, 1888): 576.

[77] Hardwick committee investigation, 1911, p. 2097.

of reasoning as his lower-court colleague from New York, Judge Wallace vacated the American Sugar Refinery's charter.[78]

Meanwhile, the attorney general of Louisiana had begun action in the spring of 1887 to rescind the charters of those Louisiana companies which were members of the cottonseed oil trust.[79] When the companies involved proceeded to transfer all their property in Louisiana to a Rhode Island corporation, voluntarily surrendering their Louisiana charters, the attorney general sought and obtained an injunction barring the cottonseed oil trust from operating in his state.[80] Even the Chicago gas trust, which was not really a trust but rather a duly chartered corporation, found itself under legal attack. The Illinois Supreme Court on November 26, 1889, ordered its charter forfeited on the grounds that by acting as a holding company and acquiring a number of gas and electric companies in Chicago, it had abused its corporate privileges.[81]

By the spring of 1890 it was clear that the days of the trust as a legal means of consolidating an industry were numbered. Virtually all corporate lawyers recognized this fact. As Pryor commented when Judge Barrett handed down his decision in the *People* v. *North River* case, "The effect summarily is to break up this [and every other] trust, for upon the principles adjudicated . . . every corporation in the 'combine' had forfeited its charter. Of course, if you destroy the constituents, you destroy the combination."[82] It was in this climate of opinion that Congress met that spring to consider a bill (Senate 1) introduced by Senator Sherman at the beginning of the new session, which would "declare unlawful, trusts and combinations in restraint of trade."[83]

[78] *New York Times*, January 7 and 8, 1890; *Railway & Corporate Law Journal*, 7 (January 18, 1890): 41. Long before the decision was announced, and in anticipation of an unfavorable ruling, the American Sugar Refining Company's properties had been transferred to the firm of Havemeyer & Elder. In that way, control of the refinery itself was not endangered. The litigation continued for many months until finally Spreckels and the sugar trust reached a *modus vivendi* in their struggle for control of the industry (see below, pp. 165ff.).

[79] *New York Times*, June 21 and 22, 1888; *Railway & Corporate Law Journal*, 1 (May 21, 1887): 481, 509.

[80] *New York Times*, January 11 and February 9, 10, and 15, 1889; *Railway & Corporate Law Journal*, 6 (July 6, 1889): 1.

[81] *People* v. *Chicago Gas Trust Co.*

[82] *New York Times*, January 10, 1889.

[83] U.S., Congress, Senate, *Congressional Record*, 51st Cong., 1st sess., 1890, 21, pt. 1: 96. For the text of this and the various other bills offered in Congress during this period to deal with the problem of trusts, see U.S., Attorney General, *Bills and Debates in Congress Relative to Trusts*, pp. 69ff.; see also Thorelli, *Federal Anti-Trust Policy*, pp. 174–210.

Like the courts, Congress was under considerable pressure to do something about the trusts. The issue was not a partisan one, for both major political parties at their most recent conventions had denounced trusts and similar combinations.[84] Indeed, the trusts found few open advocates on the floor of Congress.[85] The problem was how to devise an effective remedy which would, at the same time, stand up as constitutional under the scrutiny of the U.S. Supreme Court.

One question was thus whether it would be best to base legislation on the power of Congress to levy taxes, regulate interstate commerce, or set rules governing the judiciary. Closely related to this first question was a second one: what remedies would be most effective, given the chosen constitutional basis for legislative action? Senator Sherman's bill, relying on the power of Congress to tax and applying only to industries producing those goods from which the federal government derived revenue, provided that those who organized trusts and similar combinations might be fined or imprisoned, while those who were thereby injured might sue in the federal courts to recover full damages. The measure also empowered U.S. attorneys to bring civil suits against the trusts, although the nature of the suits was not specified. In the subsequent debate, after being persuaded that his bill failed to cover some of the most notorious trusts, Sherman decided to let the bill rest instead on the federal government's judicial powers, the basis of action now being whether or not the combination affected the citizens of more than one state. Convinced that the bill's criminal penalties were useless, Sherman eliminated them altogether; at the same time, however, he changed the damages clause so that injured parties could sue for not just full, but double, compensation. He hoped that this latter provision, by the encouragement it gave to private suits, would make the law largely self-enforcing.[86]

But other senators, arguing that the amended bill lacked teeth, favored different remedies. The double-damages clause, they pointed out, was practically useless, since the group most directly injured by trusts, the consuming public, was in no position to undertake expensive litigation.[87] Some senators preferred to see the criminal penalties

[84] *Ibid.*, pp. 150–51.

[85] The only senators to defend trusts during the extended debate over the Sherman Act were Senators Orville H. Platt, Republican from Connecticut, and William W. Stewart, Republican from Nevada. "Combination, cooperation," the latter declared, "is the foundation of all civilized society." Senate, *Congressional Record*, 51st Cong., 1st sess., 1890, 21, pt. 3: 2564.

[86] See Sherman's defense of the revised measure, *ibid.*, pp. 2456–62, esp. pp. 2456–57.

[87] *Ibid.*, p. 2571.

reinstated;[88] others wished to give federal officers the right to confiscate any goods in interstate commerce which had been produced by trusts.[89] Still others proposed that the president be allowed to suspend the tariff on those articles which were manufactured by trusts,[90] that the courts be empowered to issue injunctions prohibiting trusts from carrying on business,[91] or that the trusts be barred from using the federal courts to collect their debts.[92]

During the week that the revised bill was debated, it became so loaded with amendments (many of them bordering on the frivolous) that the measure was referred to the Judiciary Committee for redrafting.[93] Reported six days later, the revised bill was barely recognizable as the measure Senator Sherman had originally introduced and then amended. Relying for its authority on the commerce clause of the Constitution, the committee draft declared illegal "every contract, combination in the form of trust or otherwise, or conspiracy, in restraint of trade or commerce among the several states, or with foreign nations." It retained both remedies Sherman had in the end advocated—the private suits for damages and the federal suits for equity relief—but it strengthened these provisions greatly. Injured parties were to be allowed to sue for triple rather than double damages, while U.S. attorneys were given the power to subpoena witnesses and obtain temporary restraining orders. Not satisfied that these remedies were sufficient, the Judiciary Committee added two others from the several that had been suggested. It wrote back into the bill the criminal penalties that Sherman had deleted, and it gave federal officials the right to confiscate any trust property that moved in interstate commerce.[94]

The committee's bill, the work of the Senate's leading constitutional

[88] *Ibid.*, p. 2601. [89] *Ibid.*, pp. 2613–14. [90] *Ibid.*, p. 2661.

[91] *Ibid.*, pp. 2640–41. [92] *Ibid.*, pp. 2657–58.

[93] Thorelli, *Federal Anti-Trust Policy*, p. 194; Senate, *Congressional Record*, 51st Cong., 1st sess., 1890, 21, pt. 3: 2731. Attempts had been made previously to refer the bill to the Judiciary Committee in order that it might be put in more satisfactory shape, but this had been opposed by the more vigorous supporters of antitrust legislation on the grounds that the measure would thus be buried. As Senator Pugh said: ". . . As a member of the Committee on the Judiciary I simply desire to say that in my opinion a reference of the bill to that committee will be the last of it for this session. I think I have knowledge enough to enable me to say that the enemies of the bill can not adopt more efficient action to destroy it than to send it to that committee" (*ibid.*, p. 2606). That is why when the Senate finally did send the bill to the Judiciary Committee it took the unusual step of requiring that the committee report back an amended version within twenty days (Thorelli, *Federal Anti-Trust Policy*, p. 199, n. 81).

[94] Senate, *Congressional Record*, 51st Cong., 1st sess., 1890, 21, pt. 3: 2901.

lawyers,[95] was intended to provide the most effective means possible for dealing with trusts and similar combinations within the limitations of what was then thought to be the extent of federal power.[96] With the support of both political parties, this revised measure then passed the Senate and House without a clause being changed and was subsequently signed into law by President Benjamin Harrison.[97] As Senator Sherman himself said in support of the committee's draft, while it was not "precisely what I want," it was "the best under all circumstances that the Senate was prepared to give."[98]

Although the bill finally enacted into law differed from the measure Sherman had originally proposed, it carried out his principal objective—to write into the federal statutes common-law prohibitions on monopoly and restraint of trade, to declare them "a rule of public policy."[99] For Sherman the trusts represented a threat to the existing economic system. Fearing that the individual states might lack the jurisdiction to cope with this new form of business organization, the Ohio senator proposed to give the federal government sufficient power to fill the gap. "The bill, as I would have it," he said in support of his own, earlier measure, "has for its single object to invoke the aid of the courts of the United States . . . to supplement the [efforts] of the several States. . . . It does not announce a new principle of law, but applies old and well-recognized principles of common law to the complicated jurisdiction of our State and Federal Government."[100] It was this purpose which marked the Sherman Act—named for the man who had pushed most vigorously for the passage of such a law—as essentially a conservative measure.[101]

What Sherman did not realize—or, if he did, he did not let on—was that federal legislation to curb the trusts qua trusts was no longer needed. The state courts had already done the job. (This is not to say that the state courts had come to grips with the problem of industrial consolidation, whatever form it might take. It is only to say

[95] Thorelli, *Federal Anti-Trust Policy*, pp. 210–14.

[96] This is the opinion of Thorelli, who has written the most thorough legislative history of the Sherman Act within recent years: see *ibid.*, pp. 220–21.

[97] *Ibid.*, pp. 199–210.

[98] Senate, *Congressional Record*, 51st Cong., 1st sess., 1890, 21, pt. 4: 3145.

[99] *Ibid.*, pt. 3: 2461. See the sketch of Sherman in the *Dictionary of American Biography.*

[100] For Sherman's major speech in support of antitrust legislation, see Senate, *Congressional Record*, 51st Cong., 1st sess., 1890, 21, pt. 3: 2456–62, esp. p. 2457. The first quotation has been changed slightly to put it in the plural rather than the singular.

[101] That is why efforts to demonstrate Sherman's insincerity with regard to antitrust legislation by pointing to his conservative voting record miss the mark.

that they had succeeded in dealing with a special type of legal arrangement which made consolidation possible. But then, it was this form of consolidation which the majority of those in Congress seemed to feel required federal legislation.) This fact may be one of the reasons why the Sherman Act met with so little legislative resistance. Those most likely to have opposed it—the Rockefellers, Havemeyers, and their congressional minions—recognized that the battle already had been lost. For on June 24, 1890, just as both houses of Congress were completing action on what came to be known as the Sherman Antitrust Act, the New York Court of Appeals handed down its decision in the matter of the *People* v. *North River Sugar Refining Company*.[102]

::

In its appeal to the higher courts, the sugar trust had decided to concentrate its defense on the broader issues involved. Recognizing the trust's vulnerability to the charge that it was an illegal partnership of corporations, Parsons, as lawyer for the appellant, laid particular stress on the trust's social desirability. To buttress his case, he quoted the works of various writers, including a speech by Gladstone which attributed England's agricultural depression to the lack of combination among farmers. Among the other works that Parsons quoted was an article in the *Political Science Quarterly* written by George Gunton, a well-known labor leader and economic writer.[103] Gunton had argued, in one of the first learned discussions of the problem, that trusts were essentially no different from other forms of industrial organization. "In what, for instance," he had asked, "do they differ, as industrial institutions, from corporations, individual capitalists, or even from hand workers? The more closely we examine the subject, the more clearly we shall see that they are fundamentally the same, that the difference is not one of principle, but solely of size and complexity of industrial organization."[104]

In its decision the New York Court of Appeals chose to ignore the broader questions entirely. Justice Francis M. Finch, speaking for a unanimous court, declared in upholding revocation of the North River Sugar Refining Company's charter, "that in this state there can be

[102] For another view of the Sherman Act's legislative origins—one which parallels the above account but ignores the *North River* case backdrop—see William Letwin, *Law and Economic Policy in America*, chap. 3. Letwin's volume appeared after the present chapter was first written.

[103] George Gunton, "The Economic and Social Aspects of Trusts," pp. 385–408.

[104] *Ibid.*, p. 386.

no partnership of separate and independent corporations, whether directly or indirectly, through the medium of a trust. . . ." Having reached this conclusion, he said, "it becomes needless to advance into the wider discussion over monopolies and competition and restraint of trade, and the problems of political economy."[105]

Pryor, who was soon to be appointed to the bench himself, had every reason to be proud of his brief. In reprinting that document many years later, he spoke of the case which it had helped to win as "the first effort in any court of the country, by judicial decision, to break up a trust-combination." It was especially important, he said, because "it established that the principles of the Common Law are adequate and effective to the destruction of such combinations."[106]

Although it meant the final death knell of the organization that for three years had enabled them to operate so successfully in concert, the members of the sugar trust were able to find some solace in the Court of Appeals' decision. That tribunal had not held the combination of refiners to be contrary to the public interest as the lower courts had done. As the trustees subsequently pointed out in a circular to certificate-holders: the Court of Appeals "bases its decision upon technical grounds. [It] nowhere condemns a union of interests of persons concerned in a number of manufacturing corporations carrying on the same business."[107] As for the next step, a new union of interests would have to be formed, this time under the cover of a single corporation duly chartered by one of the states. Both the various court decisions and the legislative debates had pointed to this procedure as the one most likely to afford a legal basis for continued consolidation. The only question was, in which state should the new corporation be set up?

As a precautionary measure, a few months after Judge Barrett's initial decision was announced, the leading figures in the sugar trust had secured a special charter from the Connecticut legislature.[108] This charter, incorporating the Commonwealth Refining Company of New Haven, gave to its holders the right to own stock in other corporations, a privilege denied to corporations formed under the general statutes not only of Connecticut but virtually of every other state in the

[105] *People* v. *North River Sugar Refining Co.*, 24 N.E. 891.

[106] Roger A. Pryor, *Essays and Addresses*, p. 151.

[107] *New York Times*, July 1, 1890.

[108] *Ibid.*, January 22, 1890; Connecticut, Legislature, General Assembly, *Special Acts and Resolutions of the General Assembly*, 1889, pp. 1095–97. The charter was reportedly obtained by including among the incorporators the relatives of certain prominent legislators.

Union.[109] Such a privilege was essential if the reconstituted sugar trust was ever to acquire any of the refineries in Philadelphia, for under Pennsylvania law no foreign corporation could hold real property in that state.[110] Thus, the only way that control over the Philadelphia refineries could be achieved (assuming that their owners were willing) was through the purchase of their stock, the corporations themselves being left intact.

The members of the sugar trust were prevented from taking advantage of this special Connecticut charter, however, by an injunction issued by Judge Barrett which prohibited them from transferring control of their refining properties.[111] This judicial order had created a legal impasse, for while the sugar trust was clearly unlawful as then constituted, it was at the same time barred from reconstituting itself in any other form.

In seeking the trust's dissolution, Pryor and those who had urged him on had probably hoped that the competitive situation previously existing in the sugar refining industry could be re-created. This, they now began to realize, was unlikely. Refineries had closed down, capitalist-entrepreneurs had left the industry, employees had found work elsewhere, and customers had developed other sources of supply. Once destroyed, competition was not easily revived.

About the closest that it was possible to come to resurrecting the old competitive order was to declare the charters of the New York refining companies forfeit, sell the physical properties for whatever they would bring on the open market, distribute the proceeds among the current certificate-holders, and hope that a new competitive sugar refining industry would emerge from the ruins.[112] The trouble with this approach, as Pryor pointed out, was that "such seizure and sale would not only involve a sacrifice of property but would be a serious

[109] For an analysis of where the law stood in this respect in 1890, see Russell C. Larcom, *The Delaware Corporation*, pp. 53–58. Fred Freedland has argued that New York State permitted intercorporate stockholding at this time; see his "History of Holding Company Legislation in New York State," pp. 369ff. But the provisions of the New York corporate statutes to which he refers were quite limited in scope and in general dealt with the types of investments that trust companies and similar financial institutions were permitted to make. Insofar as manufacturing companies were concerned, they were permitted only to hold stock in corporations "supplying or transporting materials required in the business of the holding company . . ." (*ibid.*, pp. 376–77). Needless to say, such a provision would not have given a reconstituted sugar trust the powers it would need to acquire stock in Philadelphia or other out-of-state corporations.

[110] Larcom, *The Delaware Corporation*, p. 12.

[111] *New York Times*, July 17, 1890.

[112] This was, in fact, the approach demanded by several of the minority certificate-holders; *see ibid.*, January 11, 1891.

detriment to the trade of New York. . . ."[113] For it was clear that as individual parcels the various sugar refining properties would bring only a fraction of their value as an integrated going concern. Thus, a forced sale might well lead to a large capital loss for the holders of sugar-trust certificates, many of whom had not taken part in the original consolidation but had merely purchased trust certificates during the intervening period. At the same time, it was by no means certain that it would be possible to find buyers for the properties who would be willing and able to operate them as separate and independent concerns. Many of the persons then employed by the refineries might therefore be thrown out of work, while the consuming public might ultimately find itself forced to pay higher prices for sugar. Neither Pryor, Tabor, nor any of the other public officials involved were willing to run those risks.

For this reason Attorney General Tabor began to think in terms of another approach. At a meeting with representatives of the sugar trust he let it be known that he would be willing to seek the removal of the injunction that was tying up the New York refining properties if the members of the trust in turn would agree to reorganize their companies under a single corporation chartered by the state. At least that way, if there was no alternative but to let the consolidation of the sugar refining industry continue, New York would be the tax beneficiary. When it was pointed out that under that state's laws one corporation was not permitted to own stock in another, Tabor promised to seek an end to that prohibition at the next session of the legislature.[114] The attorney general's proposal seemed to have met with a favorable response from the representatives of the sugar trust; Tabor even carried out his part of the bargain. But before the plan could be fully acted upon, the refining properties became tied up once more in litigation, this time as a result of lawsuits brought by minority certificate-holders.[115]

It was to take several more months for this latest legal snarl to be untangled. In the meantime, the members of the trust began seriously to consider a scheme for reorganizing their companies under the laws of another state.

::

New Jersey had by this time already acquired a reputation as a state friendly to corporate interests. As James Dill, the corporate

[113] *Ibid.*, July 18, 1890. [114] *Ibid.*, July 17, 1890. [115] See note 125 below.

lawyer who was to persuade so many corporations to relocate in that state, later commented, "Since 1875 it has been the announced and settled policy of the State of New Jersey to attract incorporated capital to the State, by the enactment of laws first wise and then liberal, and by like legislation to protect capital thus invested against attacks from within and from without." "The Legislature," Dill added, ". . . has never hesitated to pass promptly any law which tended to improve the general scheme of incorporation."[116]

In line with this policy, New Jersey's corporate statutes were revised in 1888 to permit a company chartered under the state's general laws to hold stock in another corporation.[117] The following year the statutes were further revised to permit a company chartered under the general laws of the state to purchase property outside the state with stock specially issued for that purpose.[118] These changes gave rise to what soon came to be known as the New Jersey holding company, a corporation that was able to gain control of other corporations located throughout the country, not only through the traditional method of purchasing their assets outright, but also now through the new method of acquiring either all or a majority of their outstanding stock. Such a holding device was essential for permitting various firms throughout the country to be consolidated within a single organization; and it came just as the trusts, finding themselves under increasing attack, were looking for some way to reconstitute themselves, a way that would stand up under the scrutiny of the law.[119]

The first trust to take advantage of this liberalization of the New

[116] James Dill, *Statutory and Case Law Applicable to Private Companies Under the General Incorporation Act of New Jersey*, p. v. As for Dill himself, see note 119 below.

[117] New Jersey, *Statutes*, 1889, chap. 269.

[118] *Ibid.*, chap. 265.

[119] Some historians have erroneously attributed this change in New Jersey's corporate laws to James Dill: William E. Sackett, *Modern Battles of Trenton*, 2: 121; H. W. Stoke, "Economic Influences Upon the Corporation Laws of New Jersey," pp. 510–11; *Dictionary of American Biography, s.v.* "Dill, James." According to these accounts Dill persuaded Governor Leon Abbett of New Jersey, who was seeking to raise additional state revenue without increasing taxes, to liberalize the corporate laws so as to encourage corporations to obtain charters in that state. Since Abbett was out of office when the laws were changed in 1888 and 1889, it is questionable whether Dill played the role attributed to him. Actually, Dill seems to have been responsible for certain of the later changes in the New Jersey corporate statutes, as well as for the consolidation of the statutes into a single code in 1893. He also seems to have played a leading role in persuading large corporations to locate in New Jersey, having organized a special trust company to assist in that purpose. However, this still leaves unanswered the question of who, if anyone, was responsible for the 1888 and 1889 changes in New Jersey's corporate statutes.

Jersey statutes was the cottonseed oil trust. In November, 1889, it was reorganized as a New Jersey corporation, the American Cotton Oil Company.[120] Five months later the lead trust reconstituted itself as the National Lead and Oil Company of New Jersey.[121]

As the leading figures in the sugar trust met throughout the summer of 1890 and on into the fall, pondering what course their own combination should take, a consensus began to emerge that it, too, should follow the example of the cottonseed oil trust by reorganizing as a New Jersey corporation. There were several advantages in doing so. Besides the ease with which a New Jersey charter could be obtained, there was no limit to the amount of stock which a New Jersey corporation could issue. The franchise fee was low, the directors could hold their meetings outside the state, and the company's property could not be taxed any more heavily than that of private individuals. Moreover, a New Jersey corporation was not required to divulge its financial condition either to the public or to its competitors—only to its own stockholders. Perhaps most important, as a contemporary noted authority on New Jersey law later pointed out, "Corporations were not considered as being hostile in any way to public interests."[122] While other states offered some of these same advantages, none except New Jersey offered them all.[123]

In the end, these considerations were overriding. As Henry Havemeyer later testified before a New York investigating committee: "there was less tax upon the franchise [in New Jersey]; and there was less scrutiny and investigating into corporate companies. There were many other advantages which the counsel [i.e., Parsons] stated."[124] By late October the decision to incorporate in New Jersey had already been made, but it was not until January 10, 1891, when the last of the private legal suits was finally settled, that members of the sugar trust were able to act. On that day the American Sugar Refining Company received a charter from the state of New Jersey, and control of the various refining properties was immediately transferred to the new corporation.[125]

[120] *Railway & Corporate Law Journal*, 6 (November 23, 1889): 420.

[121] *New York Times,* April 8 and 10, 1890.

[122] Edward Q. Keasbey, "New Jersey and the Great Corporations," p. 206.

[123] Larcom, *The Delaware Corporation*, p. 14.

[124] Lexow committee investigation, 1898, p. 126.

[125] *New York Times*, October 31, 1890, and January 11, 1891. The latter describes the complicated legal procedure by which the sugar trust was reorganized in the face of opposition by certain of the minority certificate-holders. In brief, the original trustees had petitioned the courts to be relieved of their fiduciary responsibilities preparatory to transferring control of the various re-

The financial arrangements had been worked out by the investment banking firm of Kidder, Peabody & Company, which was able to draw on its experience in handling railroad reorganizations.[126] Each holder of sugar-trust certificates was to receive in exchange an equal number of shares in the American Sugar Refining Company, half in the form of 7 per cent cumulative preferred shares and half in the form of common stock. The preferred shares were intended to represent the value of the new company's tangible assets; the common stock, the capitalized value of its expected profits. In addition, bonds worth $10 million were authorized to provide working capital, though they were never issued.[127]

Except for its new legal form, the combination of sugar refineries remained unchanged. Henry Havemeyer, the president of the trust, became president of the American Sugar Refining Company, while the former trustees became directors of the new company. If anything, the combination had been strengthened. Control over the various refining properties was now much more direct. All this had been accomplished while New York's officials—particularly Attorney General Tabor and his special assistant, Pryor—were forced to stand by helplessly. On the one hand, they could think of no way to bring about a return to the previous state of competition without destroying a considerable amount of private property and disrupting an important branch of trade. On the other hand, they were required by the principle of interstate comity to respect any company organized under the laws of another state. The consolidation of the sugar refining industry emerged from its first politico-legal crisis stronger than ever.

---

fining properties to a new corporation. The courts had granted this request, but then certain of the minority certificate-holders had intervened, obtaining an injunction to prevent the transfer of the properties. Eventually, these minority certificate-holders succeeded in having the courts appoint, in addition to Henry O. Havemeyer, two neutral receivers for the properties. Meanwhile, however, the original trustees had been soliciting proxies from the certificate-holders and when, in early January, it became apparent from the number of proxies obtained that the great majority of certificate-holders wished to see the trust reorganized as a New Jersey corporation, the minority certificate-holders withdrew their opposition, thereby permitting the reorganization to proceed.

[126] T. R. Navin and M. V. Sears, "The Rise of a Market for Industrial Securities, 1887–1902," p. 125.

[127] *New York Times*, October 31, 1890; *United States* v. *American Sugar Refining Co. et al.*, pretrial testimony, 1912, pp. 4540, 4799; Willett & Gray's *Weekly Statistical Sugar Trade Journal*, January 15, 1891.

7 :: CULMINATION AND CONDONATION

THE holding company—due to passage of the Sherman Act—was no less susceptible to legal attack than the trust form proper had been. As it happened, it was the culmination of the sugar refining industry's consolidation which set the stage for a test of the new law's applicability to a form of business organization other than that which the measure's sponsors had originally had in mind. The earlier attempt by the sugar trust to extend its influence to the West Coast had led to a protracted struggle with the Hawaiian sugar king, Claus Spreckels, the latter carrying the battle to the East by erecting a modern, highly efficient refinery in Philadelphia. The nearly two years of bitter price warfare that resulted were brought to an end only after the recently organized American Sugar Refining Company succeeded in absorbing all of its Philadelphia rivals, including those which had refused to join the original combination, while simultaneously recognizing Spreckels' suzerainty in the West. This latest merger, however, produced further public reaction, thereby forcing the federal government to bring suit against the American Sugar Refining Company for violation of the Sherman Act. The Supreme Court, when it handed down its decision in the *E. C. Knight* case in 1895, not only refused to annul the merger but, more important, seemed to strike down the antitrust law itself—at least insofar as it pertained to holding companies organized under the general statutes of New Jersey or of any other state to control manufacturing firms. This legal precedent, together with the subsequent court ruling in the *Addyston Pipe & Steel* case, was to give the judicial go-ahead to the ensuing Corporate Revolution.

::

As successful as consolidation of the sugar refining industry had been, unfinished business nonetheless remained. On the West Coast,

Claus Spreckels and his sons continued to provide vigorous competition, while on the East Coast the various Philadelphia refineries remained formidable rivals. As long as these firms retained their independence, Henry Havemeyer and his associates could not, with certainty, expect to control the price of refined sugar throughout the United States. It was for this reason that, once the trust had overcome its legal difficulties by reorganizing as a New Jersey corporation, Havemeyer and his fellow chief officers of the new company turned to the uncompleted task of consolidating the sugar refining industry.

The Havemeyer group, by its purchase of the American Sugar Refinery of California in the spring of 1888, had made clear its intention of driving Claus Spreckels out of business, and the challenge had been taken up immediately. As soon as he learned that his chief rival on the West Coast had been acquired by the trust, Spreckels began to wage an unrelenting campaign against what he termed "the Eastern combination." On the economic front, the price war with the American, which had been going on intermittently for nearly three years, was renewed with increasing ferocity.[1] Wholesale grocers were warned that if they bought from the American they would no longer be allowed to purchase sugar from the California refinery, and Spreckels even devised a special code for his barrels to make sure that no jobber who violated this edict would go unpunished.[2] On the political front, the attorney general of California was persuaded to bring suit to dissolve the American Sugar Refinery Company's charter on the grounds that by joining the trust it had entered into an illegal partnership.[3]

Fearing that Spreckels was more of an adversary than the current managers of the American Sugar Refinery on the West Coast were prepared to cope with, Havemeyer dispatched Robert Oxnard to San Francisco to take control of the company there. Acting on Havemeyer's instructions, Oxnard began immediately to make the refinery's operations more efficient by reorganizing them along eastern lines.[4] However, despite the several operating economies that he introduced, Oxnard found the competition rough going. In the person of the Hawaiian sugar king the trust had taken on a resourceful opponent, one who was not easily cowed.

[1] *New York Times*, February 7, 1888.

[2] William W. Cordray, "Claus Spreckels of California," p. 90.

[3] See pp. 140–41 above.

[4] *United States* v. *American Sugar Refining Co. et al.*, pretrial testimony, 1912, pp. 3134, 3546. Oxnard had been idle since the closing of his own refinery soon after the trust's formation.

For example, in line with the practice in the East, the American refinery began charging its customers the price that prevailed on the day an order for refined sugar was received—not, as had previously been the case on the West Coast, the price that prevailed on the day the refined sugar was actually delivered. Recognizing an opportunity to inflict a heavy financial blow on the trust's affiliate, Spreckels waited until the time of year when the West Coast refineries were almost wholly dependent on Hawaii for their raw-sugar supplies. Then he began cutting the price of refined sugar.

The American was forced to follow suit, and, as it did so, it became deluged with orders—in fact, with more orders than it could fill with the stocks of raw sugar it had on hand. To make up the deficit, it had no choice but to buy raw sugar on the open market. This was the moment Spreckels had been waiting for. Through his various Island connections he had already tied up the entire supply of Hawaiian sugar cane—all except the tonnage previously contracted for by the American. Since Spreckels was the only source of additional raw sugar, the American had to pay his price or do without—and, having orders to fill, it could not do without. Exploiting his advantage to the fullest, Spreckels began forcing up the price of raw sugar until it reached 6¼ cents a pound, the same price at which the American had taken orders to deliver refined sugar.

Not wishing to continue producing sugar at a loss, the American stopped taking orders. At that point, having the market to himself, Spreckels increased the price of refined sugar to its previous level. This encouraged the American to resume taking orders for refined sugar, but no sooner had it done so than Spreckels applied the same squeeze as before. The American found itself forced either to stay out of the market completely or to sell its product at a loss. This unhappy situation continued for several months until the trust was able to tap alternative sources of raw sugar.[5]

As sharp as the financial blow inflicted on the American was in this particular instance, it still was not sharp enough to persuade Havemeyer and the other top officials of the trust to give up their plan to control the West Coast sugar market. Nor were they any more persuaded when Spreckels, acting through the attorney general of California, succeeded in having the American's charter rescinded. As a precaution, the trustees had already taken the step of transferring ownership of the American refinery to the firm of Havemeyer &

[5] *New York Times*, August 9, 1888. It was usually possible to obtain raw sugar from the Dutch East Indies within six weeks.

Elder.[6] Although Spreckels, contending that this was a ruse, sought to have the plant shut down and a receiver appointed to dispose of the property, he was thwarted by the delaying legal tactics of the trust's lawyers. In the meantime, the former American refinery continued to turn out sugar in competition with Spreckels' California company.

Thus the struggle continued as before, with each side hoping to inflict whatever damage it could on the other. It was a battle of titans, the Hawaiian sugar king versus the Eastern Combination; and while each was able to strike a well-connected blow at the other from time to time over the next few months, neither could bring his opponent to his knees. If the trust found itself losing money as a result of the struggle, the same was true of Spreckels. The difference, however, was that while the trust could make up for the losses it suffered on the West Coast with the profits it earned in the East, Spreckels could not. This fact, as well as the greater financial resources which the trust commanded, put Spreckels at an increasing disadvantage. For example, when the three-year contract with the Hawaiian growers came up for renewal, the trust was able to outbid Spreckels, leaving him with only one-third of the Hawaiian sugar crop—that which he directly controlled.[7]

It was for this reason—the disadvantage of not being able to compete simultaneously on both coasts—that Spreckels had already begun to lay plans for building a refinery on the Atlantic coast, thus carrying the battle to the trust's home grounds. Rumors of this ploy had begun to circulate early in 1888. "Yes," said Spreckels on February 20, confirming the reports, "I shall leave next week for New York, and it is probable one or more refineries will be opened at Baltimore and at other Eastern points."[8] During the course of that trip east Spreckels testified before the House Committee on Manufactures, reaffirming his determination to build a refinery on the Atlantic coast in order to compete with the members of the trust. "I am going to start a refinery here," he said. "When they are fighting me there [in the West] they may say, 'We will undersell him and crush him out,' and they may hold the sugar at 5 cents a pound [an unprofitable level]. I will come here and start a factory, so that I will get my share [of

[6] Willett & Gray's *Weekly Statistical Sugar Trade Journal*, February 20, 1890.

[7] Cordray, "Claus Spreckels of California," p. 83. The custom was for the Hawaiian sugar growers to contract to sell their crop for three years at a time. Traditional hostility to Spreckels also explains why the trust was able to take over the major portion of the Hawaiian sugar crop. See pp. 90ff., 251–53, and 268–71.

[8] *New York Times*, February 21, 1888.

the profits] here."[9] Earlier, Spreckels had disclosed to reporters that he was prepared to spend up to $5 million to build his new refinery.[10]

Many persons began to see in the Hawaiian sugar king the instrument for curbing the power of the sugar trust. This attitude was especially marked among the congressmen who questioned Spreckels during his brief appearance before the House Committee on Manufactures.[11] Thus it was that the man who had monopolized the sugar refining industry on the West Coast for well over a decade came to be cast in the role of defender of the eastern consumer against the exactions of the sugar trust. Recognizing the irony in this situation, some persons contended that Spreckels' only purpose in building the refinery in the East was to force the trust to withdraw from the West, and that once this was accomplished he would abandon the project.[12] Spreckels himself, however, denied this accusation. "We mean business in this matter," he declared, "and will go right to work as soon as we have selected our site. Although it is our object to fight the sugar trust, we do not intend to expend $5 million merely for the luxury of a fight. The refinery will be a purely legitimate business venture, and will be run to make money."[13]

::

In his search for a suitable refinery location, Spreckels first visited New York, then Baltimore.[14] But it was in Philadelphia that he found a site which met all his requirements—a ten-acre parcel situated on the Delaware River, with excellent rail connections. The city of Philadelphia, anxious to attract a new enterprise that would add an estimated $40 million directly, and another $100 million indirectly, to its commerce, gladly agreed to grant Spreckels certain tax exemptions and a free water supply. On April 6, 1888, title to the property was transferred, and about a month later construction of the new refinery began.[15]

[9] U.S. House Committee on Manufactures, *Report on Trusts*, p. 181. Later, when the refinery was completed, Spreckels explained: "It was a move I had to make, and since I made it I am afraid of no man, company or association in the refining business. Before I had it, opposition was at work on me at both ends of the line, as it were, in the East and West, but as matters now are I am better prepared than ever to take care of myself" (*New York Times*, April 25, 1889).

[10] *New York Times*, March 5, 1888.

[11] U.S. House Committee on Manufactures, *Report on Trusts*, pp. 180ff.

[12] *New York Times*, March 24 and 27, 1888.

[13] *Ibid.*, March 5, 1888.

[14] *Ibid.*, March 31, 1888.

[15] *Ibid.*, March 5 and 7 and May 22, 1888; Lexow committee investigation, 1897, p. 403.

Although the work was pressed with great diligence, it was not until December, 1889, that the job was finally completed. In the meantime, of course, the price war on the West Coast had continued unabated. The new Philadelphia refinery, capable of melting two million pounds of raw sugar daily, was as modern and efficient as the science of sugar-making would permit. It consisted of eight separate buildings, the tallest of which was thirteen stories high. "Running on to the refining property," the *New York Times* reported,

> are three distinct lines of railroad, forming direct communications with every section of the country. On the river are three long wharves, each 80 feet wide and 600 feet long. Here a dozen of the largest-sized ships and steamers can load and discharge at the same time, there being ample depth of water at the lowest tide. The wharves are covered, forming immense warehouses where the raw sugar can be received and stored in bond . . . [and] a conveyor runs along the whole length of the dock, carrying sixty tons of sugar to the pans at a speed of eighteen feet per minute. The whole of the buildings are lighted by incandescent lights . . . supplied from a central station on the grounds. Automatic sprinklers for protection against fire are distributed throughout the buildings, and everything has been done to make the refinery the best equipped and most economically worked, as well as the largest in the world.

The entire plant was estimated to have cost $3 million.[16]

Rumors continued to persist that Spreckels intended to sell out to the trust, although the sugar king himself vigorously denied them. "No, Sir," he declared, "I have built that factory for my boys, and they, neither, will ever go into the trust. We will fight it for blood."[17] In fact, Spreckels announced plans to double the capacity of his Philadelphia refinery to four million pounds daily.[18] So far, however, the trust's only response to this challenge had been an attempt to put the same squeeze on Spreckels in the East that he had put on it in the West, by secretly buying up all the available supplies of raw sugar. But the wily Spreckels was not to be caught in such a trap. With typical prudence he had already arranged for the purchase of all the raw sugar he would need for his refinery. In fact, he was even able to sell part of his own stock to the trust, making a $20,000 profit on the transaction.[19] Unfortunately for Havemeyer and his associates, they did not have the same control over the sources of raw sugar on the East Coast that the Hawaiian sugar king had over those in the West.

[16] *New York Times*, May 22, 1888, and December 10, 1889.
[17] *Ibid.*, September 8, 1889.
[18] *Ibid.*, December 10, 1889.
[19] *Ibid.*, November 28, 1889.

Throughout that winter Spreckels worked to get his new refinery ready in time for the busy summer season. Although the first barrel of sugar was produced on December 9, 1889, it was to take several months more to test the equipment fully, making sure there were no mechanical defects. Spreckels—"stocky and strong, with a white beard and a healthy, rose-colored complexion"—personally supervised these preparations.[20] His son Claus, Jr., was to be in charge of the new plant once it actually got started, but the older Spreckels wanted to be on hand for the initial shakedown period.

For this reason he had set out from San Francisco late in October, accompanied by his wife, daughter, four servants, and several aides. Traveling by private railroad car, he had been greeted like visiting royalty at nearly every major stop by reporters requesting interviews. In answer to their questions, he had reiterated his determination to go on fighting the trust. He had even hinted that he was considering the construction of a second refinery in New Orleans to challenge the trust in that territory as well.[21]

Now that he was in Philadelphia, working to get his refinery ready for full operations, Spreckels found himself still pursued by reporters. The refinery, he said in reply to their queries, was in "splendid condition." He was particularly proud of the fact that the raw sugar could be unloaded from the ships and carried to the melting pans without being handled by any of the workmen. He confirmed reports that he had received several offers for the refinery, one for as much as $7 million, but he did not know whether they came from the trust. In any case, he said, he had no intention of quitting the struggle. When asked what tactics he would pursue, Spreckels said, "Why, when a man fights, he just fights, doesn't he?" "By cutting the price?" the reporters continued. "Certainly . . . ," he replied. "Can you stand cutting the price as well as the trust?" Spreckels was asked. "Oh, it may cost a million dollars or so, but I can stand it. I'm in business to stay."[22]

It was not surprising that reporters should have shown so much interest in Spreckels. Aside from the fact that their subject was such a colorful figure, they well understood that the opening of the refinery in Philadelphia signaled a new phase in the battle for control of the sugar refining industry.

Although the organizers of the trust had been disappointed when the two Philadelphia firms, Harrison, Frazier & Company and E. C.

[20] *Ibid.*, December 10, 1889, and February 12, 1890.
[21] *Ibid.*, October 20 and November 24, 1889.
[22] *Ibid.*, February 12, 1890.

Knight, refused to join in the consolidation, they had not considered the defections as fatal to their scheme. The capacity of the two Philadelphia refineries, even when added to that of the one small independent firm in Boston, amounted to only 2.2 million pounds daily, or 195,000 tons of refined sugar annually. This, the promoters of the consolidation had figured, would still leave nearly 1,000,000 tons of the total eastern market to be supplied by the various members of the trust. And if the average margin between raw and refined sugar could be increased to 1¼ cents a pound, thus affording a profit of ⅝ of a cent on every pound of sugar produced, the trust would stand to clear almost $13.5 million annually—enough to pay a 25 per cent dividend on the outstanding trust certificates.[23]

For the most part, these expectations had been realized. In 1888 the average margin between raw and refined sugar on the East Coast had been 1.258 cents a pound.[24] This high margin notwithstanding, the various members of the trust had been able to sell 987,570 tons of refined sugar.[25] The following year the returns had been a little less satisfactory. The average margin had slipped to 1.207 cents a pound, while sales had fallen to 863,305 tons.[26] Still, the results were not that far from the original calculations.

In setting its prices to achieve those margins, the trust had deliberately chosen to ignore its rivals in Philadelphia and Boston. During periods of peak demand, such as the summer, this created no difficulty. The market was able to absorb—at the prices set by the trust—all the sugar that both the trust and the independent refineries were capable of producing.[27] It was only at other times of the year, when the demand for sugar declined, that this policy had certain untoward consequences.

The independent refineries, by shading the trust's prices only slightly, could always be sure of selling whatever quantities of sugar they produced. Sugar being a homogeneous product traded by knowledgeable men, a difference of 1/16 of a cent in price was usually enough to give a firm all the business it desired. This meant that the

[23] Calculations similar to these were spelled out in the March 15, 1888, issue of Willett & Gray's *Weekly Statistical Sugar Trade Journal.* The only difference is that the Willett & Gray calculations were based on the national market instead of on the eastern market alone.

[24] See Appendix D of this volume.

[25] Willett & Gray's *Weekly Statistical Sugar Trade Journal* (Supplement), November 3, 1890.

[26] *Ibid.*

[27] To a certain extent, by closing down the marginal refineries and by taking into account the capacity of the independent firms, the trust had already adjusted its capacity to the expected market.

trust, unless it was prepared to engage in an open price war, had to be willing to accept what remained of the market after the independent refineries had filled all the orders they could handle.

An open price war, however, was not to the trust's liking. Its members had reached the conclusion that they stood to gain more by keeping margins high—even if this meant that the independent refineries were able to operate at full capacity while their own refineries were forced to curtail production and perhaps even shut down.[28] Thus, at certain times of the year, the members of the trust found themselves supplying little more than a third of the eastern market.[29] Willett & Gray's *Sugar Trade Journal,* in calling attention to this pricing strategy early in 1888, noted that in January the Sugar Refineries Company had held a price "umbrella" over the independent refineries.[30] "The 'Trust,'" reported the *Journal,* "maintained the prices of refined throughout the month, [while] the 'Non-Trust' companies undersold them to the extent of their capacity."[31] Although it fell somewhat short of being a monopolist, the Sugar Refineries Company was nonetheless disposed to act like one.

Both the firms which had entered the consolidation and those which

[28] This situation is depicted in the following diagram:

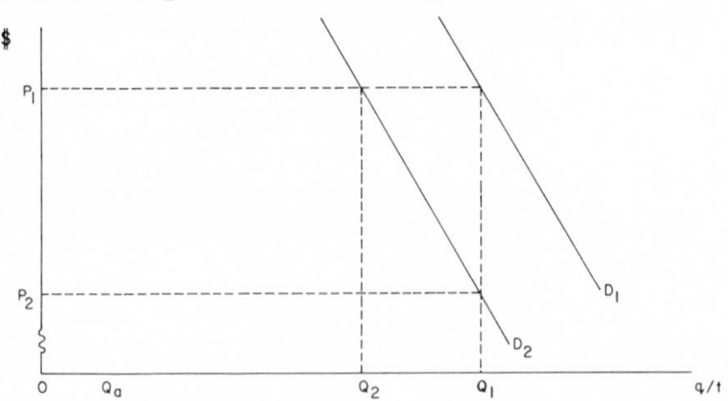

In periods of peak demand, as represented by curve D_1, quantity Q_1 was supplied to the market at price P_1. Of this quantity, Q_a represented the amount supplied by the independent refineries and Q_1-Q_a the amount supplied by the members of the trust. When, during a period of slackening sales the demand curve shifted to D_2, the price necessarily fell to P_2 if the trust was to continue producing at full capacity. Rather than have this happen, the trust preferred to reduce its output to Q_2-Q_a, thus enabling the price to remain at P_1. At the same time, the independent refineries continued to produce Q_a as before. Because of the change that had taken place in its cost curve (see pp. 110ff. above), the trust was able to produce Q_2-Q_a at the same, or perhaps even lower, average variable costs that were required for production of Q_1-Q_a.

[29] Willett & Gray's *Weekly Statistical Sugar Trade Journal,* August 15, 1889.

[30] *Ibid.,* February 9, 1888.

[31] *Ibid.,* February 2, 1888.

had stayed out benefited greatly from this state of affairs. The E. C. Knight company, for example, which had been on the verge of selling out to the trust in 1887 because the returns from sugar refining were so low, found itself earning a 50 per cent profit on its $1,000,000 investment,[32] and Harrison, Frazier & Company enjoyed a similar prosperity. However, with the opening of the new Spreckels refinery in the spring of 1890, this prosperous state of affairs promised to come to an end.

::

As Spreckels himself pointed out, the new Philadelphia plant would nearly double the capacity of the independent refineries in the East.[33] The trust, it seemed, had no choice but to abandon its previous pricing policy. For if it continued to set its prices without taking into consideration what its rivals in Philadelphia were doing, its share of the eastern market might well fall below 60 per cent. And if Spreckels carried out his announced intention of doubling the capacity of his new refinery, the trust's share of the market might fall even further. As Henry Havemeyer later told the U.S. Industrial Commission, in explaining why the trust reacted so vigorously to Spreckels' entry into the eastern market: "we did not fight [Harrison]; we could make our dividend without fighting him. But when Spreckels came in with his enormous capacity we either had to fight or make no dividend. We concluded to fight. . . ."[34]

By the end of January, 1890, the outlines of this new strategy were already beginning to emerge. Willett & Gray's *Sugar Trade Journal*, noting the unusually low prices for refined products, declared: "This is due to an apparent radical change in the policy of the Sugar Trust. Last year at this season, just the same as at other times, the prices obtained gave refiners ⅝¢ per lb. profit, but since the Spreckels refinery opened in December, the profit has been constantly lowered, and further reduction this week brings it down to within ⅛¢ per lb., which means that the country is now getting sugar at about the same relative prices to raw sugar that they paid before the Sugar Trust was formed." Estimating that the lower prices had resulted in consumer

[32] *United States* v. *American Sugar Refining Co. et al.*, pretrial testimony, 1912, pp. 6324–25; *United States* v. *E. C. Knight et al.: Brief for the United States*, pp. 20–21.

[33] *New York Times*, June 9, 1888.

[34] U.S. Industrial Commission, *Reports*, 1, pt. 2: 108.

savings of approximately $1 million a month, the *Journal* added, "Mr. Spreckels deserves the thanks of the country for his enterprise and patriotism."[35]

As much as the members of the consuming public might have welcomed this new element of competition in sugar refining, they were mistaken if they regarded it as signaling the re-emergence of a competitively structured industry. The competition being manifested in the early months of 1890 was oligopolistic price competition, which involved primarily two firms fully cognizant of the fact that their actions were necessarily interdependent. The competition deriving from a market structure of that type was apt to be little more than a momentary maneuvering for position, as subsequent events would demonstrate, rather than a permanent way of conducting business. Still, for the moment, the consuming public had no reason not to enjoy the unexpected windfall—so long as they did not deceive themselves as to its meaning.

As yet, Spreckels' influence on the industry's price level had barely begun to be felt, for his new refinery was turning out only 500–700 barrels of sugar daily. Two weeks later this figure had increased to 1,000 barrels a day, and Willett & Gray's *Sugar Trade Journal* reported: "The fight between the Trust, the non-Trust and the Spreckels refineries shows increasing animosity; the refiners' profits are now reduced to a minimum."[36] By the end of March, the new Spreckels plant was producing at full capacity, 3,000 barrels a day. The trust, matching Spreckels price, was succeeding in holding onto its former market share, but the profit from refining sugar had all but disappeared.[37] The same bitter price war that had prevailed on the West Coast for two years had finally come—as Spreckels had promised it would—to the Atlantic seaboard. As Willett & Gray's *Sugar Trade Journal* observed, "The power of monopoly may exist to the same extent as in 1888 and 1889, but it . . . has not been enforced thus far this year."[38]

That year, 1890, the average margin between raw and refined sugar fell by 40 per cent—to 0.72 of a cent a pound, the lowest it had ever

[35] Willett & Gray's *Weekly Statistical Sugar Trade Journal,* January 30, 1890.

[36] *Ibid.*, February 13, 1890.

[37] *Ibid.*, February 20, March 27, and July 31, 1890.

[38] *Ibid.*, April 3, 1890. Claus Spreckels, Jr., later complained of refinery machinery being sabotaged and of employees being bribed to disrupt operations (Hardwick committee investigation, 1911, pp. 2220–23, 2353–54). The charges, however, were never substantiated, and such actions would have been out of keeping with Havemeyer's character. But Spreckels' complaint illustrates the bitterness of the competition.

been except in the year 1885.[39] Claus Spreckels, Jr., in later recalling this period, said, "The competition, of course, was very keen, and whenever we had an accumulation of stock we cut the price."[40] The other independent refiners, who found themselves caught in the middle of this struggle, looked on the younger Spreckels, who by then was running the Philadelphia plant himself, as a "bull in the china shop" because of his vigorous price cutting.[41]

These independent refiners—especially the Harrisons and E. C. Knight—were badly pressed by the decline in sugar margins. The Spreckelses could recoup at least part of their losses on the western market (the former American refinery was temporarily shut down by court order, thus giving the Spreckelses a free rein in that territory for several months).[42] The trust could do the same on the Louisiana market, which it controlled almost exclusively. But the independents had to stand or fall on the business they were able to do in the one area in which they were active competitors. It was this total dependence on the eastern market which made their position so precarious.[43] Still, it was a member of the trust who first tried to bring the bitter price war to an end.

In the fall of 1890, Francis O. Matthiessen, the former head of F. O. Matthiessen & Wiechers, became concerned that the Sugar Refineries Company might not long survive if the price war with the Spreckelses continued. As a director he knew that the trust was not then earning its dividend,[44] and he therefore resolved to bring the price war to an end. Since he represented only a minority among the trustees, Matthiessen first took the precaution of buying up a majority of the trust certificates on the open market. This was easier than it might otherwise have been, because the legal cloud that then hung over the trust had depressed the price of certificates, and many of the original members of the trust—including the Havemeyers—had sold their holdings. Thus armed, Matthiessen went to see the younger Spreckels in Philadelphia.[45]

[39] See Appendix D of this volume.

[40] *United States* v. *American Sugar Refining Co. et al.*, pretrial testimony, 1912, p. 6086.

[41] *United States* v. *E. C. Knight et al.: Transcript of Record*, pp. 126–27.

[42] Willett & Gray's *Weekly Statistical Sugar Trade Journal*, February 20 and June 12, 1890.

[43] *United States* v. *American Sugar Refining Co. et al.*, pretrial testimony, 1912, pp. 6324–25.

[44] Willett & Gray's *Weekly Statistical Sugar Trade Journal* (Supplement), November 3, 1890.

[45] The incident was related by Claus Spreckels, Jr., in *United States* v. *American Sugar Refining Co. et al.*, pretrial testimony, 1912, pp. 5978–83.

"We might as well lay the cards on the table," Matthiessen said. Unless an agreement to raise prices could be reached, he told Claus, Jr., the Sugar Refineries Company would be ruined. Then he asked Spreckels what it was that he wanted. "I want to have peace in the sugar business," the latter replied. At that point Matthiessen informed his host that he had obtained absolute control of the trust, and that if he could make an arrangement to increase prices, he wanted to do so. Spreckels' answer to this was that he wasn't in business for his health, that he would like to make money also. "Now that I understand you," Matthiessen said, "if I go back and raise the price, will you advance yours?" "We certainly will," Spreckels replied. "We want to get all we can."

The next day, a Monday, prices were advanced as promised, and, as Spreckels later testified, "considerable money was made" for the next six weeks. "Then, suddenly," Spreckels continued, "without any warning whatsoever, the market broke, broke very severely, going back to the point where there was no profit."

It was not until several years later that Spreckels learned what had caused the price agreement to break down. Coming upon Matthiessen by chance one day, he questioned him about the incident and was told that when Matthiessen returned to New York and informed the Havemeyers (Henry and Theodore) that he had obtained absolute control of the trust, they threatened to resign and build competing refineries if the struggle with the Spreckelses were not continued. Matthiessen remarked that, "under the circumstances, if they were to build refineries in competition with the Sugar Refineries Company, [I] would be worse off than with the single competition of the Spreckels Company," and that for that reason he had finally given way.

A few months later, Spreckels heard the rest of the story. Mentioning the incident to the Havemeyers, he was told that they considered "it a huge joke on Mr. Matthiessen." "They told me," Spreckels said, "that if Mr. Matthiessen had only thought [about it he would have realized that] it would take them a couple of years to build a refinery, that they would not have built it because it would take too long. . . ." They had simply been bluffing, the Havemeyers admitted, hoping to force their colleague to "recede from his position." The only reason sugar prices had been advanced, even momentarily, was to enable Matthiessen to dispose of his trust certificates for more than he had paid for them.[46]

[46] *Ibid.*

The Havemeyers must have been greatly relieved by the success of their bluff, for of all the refiners who had joined in forming the trust, Matthiessen most probably was the one in the best position to challenge their hegemony. Next to the two Havemeyers themselves, he had received the greatest number of trust certificates,[47] and in addition possessed a substantial fortune on the side.[48] A Boston group, headed by Nash, Spalding & Company, the former sales agency for several of that city's refineries, had tried earlier that year to gain control of the trust, but when the crucial test came—on a vote to elect an independent slate of trustees—it could muster only 60,000 of the 380,000 trust certificates voted.[49] Matthiessen, however, had actually been able to acquire majority control, and only the Havemeyers' greater nerve had enabled them to remain on top. In a test of will the Havemeyers had triumphed, and while Matthiessen faded once more into the background, they were able to continue with their plans for reorganizing the sugar trust into a New Jersey corporation. Only when this first order of business was finally accomplished in January, 1891, were they able to turn their full attention to the problem posed by competition with the Spreckelses. By that time they were prepared to try a different tack.

::

One day, not long after the American Sugar Refining Company was organized, Claus Spreckels, Jr., was approached by John E. Searles. The newly named secretary of the American told Spreckels he would like to see him that night, if possible, in Philadelphia. Spreckels replied that he had made plans for dinner and the theater, but finally agreed to see Searles afterward. Recalling that midnight rendezvous many years later, Spreckels said: "He [Searles] stated that they were anxious to patch up a truce, and they were willing to recede from their position on the West coast and give us that if we would sell to Mssrs. Havemeyer and himself a half interest in the Philadelphia concern. I told him I would take the thing up by telegraph with my father, which I did. . . ."[50]

On receiving his son's wire, the elder Spreckels asked that Searles travel to the West Coast to discuss the matter with him personally.

[47] See Chapter 4, note 53.

[48] *New York Times*, March 10, 1901.

[49] *Railway & Corporate Law Journal*, 8 (July 12, 1890): 39; *New York Times*, October 31, 1890.

[50] *United States* v. *American Sugar Refining Co. et al.*, pretrial testimony, 1912, pp. 5985–86.

Searles suggested that they meet halfway—in New Orleans—instead, but Spreckels refused to leave San Francisco. Searles then confessed that he was under sentence for contempt of court in that city as a result of the litigation over the old American company, and so Spreckels agreed to meet him in San Diego.[51]

Out of that conference came an arrangement for ending the bitter price war between the two parties, an arrangement which differed somewhat from the one that Searles had proposed originally. On the West Coast a new company, Western Sugar Refining, was to be formed, with Spreckels and the American Sugar Refining Company each taking 50 per cent of its $1 million in common stock. In turn, this new company was to lease both the California (Spreckels) and the old American refineries, thus assuring a harmony of interests between the former competitors. Spreckels and the Havemeyers were each to choose two of the Western's directors, and, to resolve any deadlock which might occur, the cashier of the Bank of California was named as the fifth member of the board. On the East Coast the Havemeyers were to be given a 45 per cent interest in the Spreckels Sugar Refining Company of Philadelphia, enough to give them a voice in the company's affairs, but not enough to give them control.[52] For this minority interest the Havemeyers paid $2.25 million (par value based on the $5 million at which the company was capitalized).[53] Apparently this was as far as Spreckels was prepared to go at that time toward relinquishing ownership of the Philadelphia refinery.

Although certain of the details eventually leaked out to the public—it proved impossible, for example, to conceal the organization of the Western Sugar Refining Company[54]—this new working arrangement remained for the most part a secret.[55] To guard against disclosure, the

[51] *Ibid.*

[52] See the testimony of Oxnard, *ibid.*, pp. 3567ff., and the testimony of Spreckles, Jr., *ibid.*, pp. 5986ff.; see also Willett & Gray's *Weekly Statistical Sugar Trade Journal*, July 16, 1891.

[53] *United States* v. *American Sugar Refining Co. et al.*, pretrial testimony, 1912, pp. 6083–84.

[54] See, for example, Willett & Gray's *Weekly Statistical Sugar Trade Journal*, July 16, 1891. Rumors of the arrangement were published in the *New York Times* on March 31 and April 1 and 4, 1891, but that newspaper lacked the authoritativeness of Willett & Gray's *Journal*, and its rumors had often proved wrong on other occasions.

[55] Willett & Gray's *Sugar Trade Journal* strongly suspected a working agreement between Spreckels and the American in the East, although it could not be sure. On August 27, 1891, it noted, "Rumors persistently repeated of the sale of the Spreckels, or of its absorption into the American Sugar Refining Company, are beyond the facts, but a working arrangement exists between the two corporations which is satisfactory to each and more advantageous to the

Havemeyers insisted that the stock in the Spreckels Philadelphia refinery be endorsed over to them personally rather than simply transferred to the American.[56] By now the Havemeyers and Searles were aware of how damaging unfavorable publicity could be.

The bitter price war was thus brought to an end, but both sides found the new working arrangement a continual source of irritation. On the West Coast the strong-willed Spreckels proved a difficult man to work with. Oxnard, who had been named as one of the Western's directors, was instructed to avoid conflict with the irascible sugar king if at all possible. As Oxnard himself later testified, ". . . I endeavored to impress Mr. Havemeyer's views when I thought them correct on the Board of Directors, but in the last analysis I would defer to Mr. Spreckels."[57] Still, serious conflicts did arise. At one point, for example, Henry Havemeyer wrote to Oxnard complaining that it was folly to accumulate inventories of refined sugar as Spreckels was then doing, when the price was sure to fall in the next several months. But Spreckels apparently could not be made to accept this judgment.[58]

On the East Coast the friction was even greater. Joseph A. Ball, Henry Havemeyer's special assistant, was put on the board of directors of the Spreckels company to represent the American's interests.[59] In addition, Searles himself communicated regularly with the younger Spreckels. But the latter still did pretty much as he pleased.[60] As had been his custom, whenever the Philadelphia refinery began to accumulate a surplus of refined sugar, he would throw it on the market for whatever it would bring—despite the objections of Ball and Searles that this "spoiled" the market.[61] In October, for instance, after

---

American Sugar Refining Company than its ownership might prove to be at the present time." A week later it cited as proof of the "harmony among refiners" a 1/16-of-a-cent rise in the price of refined sugar despite an anticipated fall in demand. Aside from Willett & Gray's comments, however, no other journal showed signs of suspecting a working agreement between Spreckels and the American.

[56] *United States* v. *American Sugar Refining Co. et al.*, pretrial testimony, 1912, p. 5986.

[57] *Ibid.*, pp. 3721–22.

[58] Henry Havemeyer to Oxnard, July 13, 1891, reprinted in *ibid.*, pp. 3570–71.

[59] *Ibid.*, p. 6004.

[60] *Ibid.*, pp. 5992–96.

[61] *Ibid.*, p. 6086. Willett & Gray's *Sugar Trade Journal*, noting that an oversupply of refined sugar had resulted in soft prices, reported on August 6, 1891, that "the attempt of one or two refiners to dispose of this surplus by a slight underselling of competitors had led suddenly to a general underselling all around, and a collapse of the good and satisfactory situation of the refined market, throwing it into demoralization, with prices at as low a point as they have

Claus, Jr., had reduced the price of refined sugar in order to make a sale in Richmond, Virginia, Searles wrote young Spreckels: "This may be good business management, but I do not believe it. I think you are simply throwing away money."[62]

When it became clear that the younger Spreckels had no intention of co-operating with the American—except when it suited his own purposes—Searles and Henry Havemeyer went over his head, appealing directly to his father. Pointing out that they were then deferring to the older Spreckels' wishes on the West Coast, they insisted that he do something to bring his son into line, and Spreckels promised to speak to the young man. Angered by what he thought was an intrusion on his authority, Claus, Jr., promptly handed in his resignation. "I had a conversation with my father," he later testified. ". . . The trust was complaining they could not control me, it was not to the best interest that I was managing the affairs of the company. . . . I finally concluded if the minority was going to rule the majority my father had no use for me in the management of the concern. . . ."[63]

Claus Spreckels, Sr., then made preparations to come east and take charge of the Philadelphia refinery himself.[64] But it was clear that this was no more than a temporary expedient. The sugar king was already heavily involved elsewhere, not only with the plantation in Hawaii and the refinery in San Francisco, but also with his experiments in trying to grow beet sugar in the western United States. Because of these other commitments, he could not give the Philadelphia refinery the attention it required on a long-term basis. Unless Claus, Jr., could

touched since free sugar came into operation [i.e., since enactment of the McKinley Tariff the year before]." A week later the *Journal* reported: "One notable fact seems to have been brought out by the recent course of the refined sugar market, and that is, that whenever the Spreckels refinery have [*sic*] accumulated a large surplus of production, the other Philadelphia refiners must stand aside until it is disposed of at a cut of 1/16¢ under the market, or else suffer the consequences of a sharp decline in prices. The American Sugar Refining Company therefore appears to be a supporter of the Spreckels Company, although evidently under some peculiar arrangement which is very difficult to explain intelligently." On several other occasions that fall, the *Journal* recorded similar price cuttings by the Spreckels refinery (*ibid.*, October 22 and 29 and November 19, 1891).

62 *United States* v. *American Sugar Refining Co. et al.*, pretrial testimony, 1912, p. 5997.

63 *Ibid.*, p. 5999. The break between father and son was actually part of a much larger family conflict arising out of the elder Spreckels' attempts to dominate and obtain complete obedience from his children. See Cordray, "Claus Spreckels of California," *passim.*

64 *United States* v. *American Sugar Refining Co. et al.*, pretrial testimony, 1912, p. 6010.

be persuaded to return to the family enterprises, the elder Spreckels would eventually be forced to liquidate his investments in the East.

::

Anticipating this possibility, the American Sugar Refining Company had already begun sounding out the elder Spreckels as to how much he would be willing to accept for his Philadelphia refinery.[65] However, before anything definite came of these feelers, officials of the American wanted to be sure that they did not miss the opportunity which had presented itself for completing, at long last, the consolidation of the sugar refining industry. For they realized that the other Philadelphia firms would be more receptive to an offer if they thought Spreckels was going to continue as an active competitor.[66] If they knew that he himself was about to sell out, they might well refuse to come to terms, hoping that once Spreckels' competition had been eliminated their own businesses would again become profitable. It was for this reason that Searles conducted his negotiations with the various Philadelphia refiners in great secrecy, being careful not to let any of them know that the American already owned a minority interest in the Spreckels firm and that it was hoping to increase that interest to a majority.[67]

Next to Spreckels, the American's most important rival in Philadelphia was still the firm of Harrison, Frazier & Company, which had been reorganized and incorporated as the Franklin Sugar Refining Company only the year before.[68] Its head, Charles G. Harrison, was sounded out by John E. Parsons late in 1891 as to whether his firm would be willing to enter into a working arrangement with the American. Harrison, by opening up his company's books to representatives of American and showing them the amount of business controlled by his firm, was able to convince them that it was no use trying to reach an agreement on prices or output; but he said nothing to discourage them from thinking that he and the rest of his family might be willing to sell out entirely.

[65] *United States* v. *E. C. Knight et al.: Transcript of Record*, p. 161.

[66] See, for example, the testimony of Charles C. Harrison in regard to Spreckels' character as a competitor, *ibid.*, p. 133.

[67] Even after the other Philadelphia refiners had sold out to the American, they were not told of the American's previous interest in the Spreckels firm. Charles C. Harrison, for example, who later testified in the *E. C. Knight* case, apparently was unaware of that fact (*ibid.*, pp. 121ff). Actually, the information seems not to have been disclosed until the dissolution suit in 1912.

[68] Willett & Gray's *Weekly Statistical Sugar Trade Journal*, February 20, 1890.

Meanwhile, officials of the American had begun sounding out the other, smaller refiners in Philadelphia. Henry K. Kelly, a raw-sugar broker from that city who also did business with the American, asked E. C. Knight, Sr., if he would be receptive to a merger.[69] Kelly also spoke to George Bunker, the active head of the Delaware Sugar House.[70] From Kelly, officials of the American learned that both the E. C. Knight and Delaware firms were interested in selling out.[71]

The next move came at the first annual stockholders meeting of the American Sugar Refining Company on January 13, 1892. The directors, after reporting net earnings for the year of over $5 million, asked for approval to increase the company's capitalization by $25 million for the purpose of "acquiring other refineries." This request was readily agreed to by the stockholders.[72]

Armed with this new authority, the officials of the American were ready to begin the delicate task of negotiating directly with the various independent refineries. It was Parsons who, following up his previous inquiries, went to see Charles C. Harrison.[73] Their meeting took place on February 6,[74] and this time Parsons' approach was direct. "I want to come immediately to a question with you," he said. "We have, we think, the power to increase our capital stock. We would like to buy your stock. Will you sell it?"[75] Harrison's reply was that he would have to speak with the other members of his family associated with him in the firm.

The head of the Franklin Sugar Refining Company was no less

[69] *United States* v. *American Sugar Refining Co. et al.*, pretrial testimony, 1912, pp. 7444–49.

[70] *Ibid.* This had originally been a molasses factory, but in 1890, when the new sugar tariff made it no longer possible to produce molasses at a profit, the company had switched to the production of sugar, just in time to take advantage of the high prices resulting from the formation of the trust. Like the other sugar firms, however, it had been losing money ever since the completion of the Spreckels refinery in Philadelphia (*United States* v. *E. C. Knight et al.: Transcript of Record*, pp. 141–42).

[71] *United States* v. *American Sugar Refining Co. et al.*, pretrial testimony, 1912, pp. 7444–49.

[72] Willett & Gray's *Weekly Statistical Sugar Trade Journal*, January 14, 1892; *New York Times*, January 14, 1892.

[73] *United States* v. *E. C. Knight et al.: Transcript of Record*, pp. 124–25. Later, during the 1912 dissolution suit, Harrison testified that it was Searles who next approached him (*United States* v. *American Sugar Refining Co. et al.*, pretrial testimony, 1912, pp. 5940–41). Harrison was apparently unaware that he was contradicting his previous testimony. The earlier version has been accepted because it was given when events were much more recent in Harrison's mind.

[74] *United States* v. *E. C. Knight et al.: Transcript of Record*, p. 94.

[75] *Ibid.*, pp. 124–25.

determined than ever to remain his own boss. But he was advancing in years and growing tired of the daily business routine. While still relatively young, he had thought he might like to indulge some of his other interests, especially if it should prove possible to quit sugar refining on advantageous terms. After talking with his brother Alfred and his brother-in-law, William W. Frazier, he realized that they felt the same way, even though some of the younger members of the family "were desirous of remaining in business and continuing as they had done in the past."[76] When Parsons returned three weeks later for his answer, Harrison told him that the members of his family were willing to sell out, but that the amount the American had offered to pay for the property was unsatisfactory. Two years earlier, Harrison noted, a British syndicate had tried to purchase the Franklin refinery, and at that time the members of his family had held out for $10 million.[77] The American, he told Parsons, would have to meet that price now if it wished to obtain control. Parsons promptly agreed to Harrison's terms. The owners of the Franklin refinery, it was stipulated, would receive half of the $10 million in preferred American shares and half in common shares—with an option to sell back immediately for cash as much of the common stock as they wished for thirty cents on the dollar.[78]

Searles, meanwhile, had been carrying on negotiations with the other independent refiners. Following Kelly's lead, he went to see E. C. Knight, Sr., in Philadelphia and after several meetings settled on a price of $2,050,000—again half in American preferred shares and half in common stock.[79] While in Philadelphia, Searles also talked with George Bunker, the active head of the Delaware Sugar House. The negotiations with Bunker followed virtually the same course as those with the other independent refiners, and after two or three meetings they agreed on a price of $472,000. In the case of the Delaware company, however, the motivation for selling out was somewhat different. As one of its stockholders later explained: "The refinery was a small one . . . not located favorably for the manufacture of sugar. . . . When, therefore, the opportunity arose by which stock in a concern which had a very risky future might be exchanged for a marketable [one], I . . . determined that I would sell my stock."[80]

[76] *Ibid.*

[77] *Ibid.*, pp. 131–33.

[78] *Ibid.*, p. 125; *United States* v. *American Sugar Refining Co. et al.*, pretrial testimony, 1912, p. 5942.

[79] *United States* v. *E. C. Knight et al.: Transcript of Record*, pp. 102, 159–60.

[80] *Ibid.*, p. 141; *United States* v. *American Sugar Refining Co. et al.*, pretrial testimony, 1912, pp. 6123–24; Lexow committee investigation, 1897, p. 671.

The Delaware company's coming to terms left only Spreckels to be dealt with. Soon after the latter returned from a European trip in mid-February, Searles made an appointment to see him at his Philadelphia residence. Negotiations for control of the Spreckels refinery then began in earnest, and within three weeks Searles succeeded in persuading the sugar king to dispose of his remaining interest in the Philadelphia refinery for $5.5 million.[81] On March 4, 1892, formal agreements were entered into by the American, not only with Spreckels, but with each of the other Philadelphia firms as well. Six days later, the American's directors voted to increase the company's stock by $25 million, half in preferred shares and half in common stock.[82] Soon thereafter the new stock was formally listed on the New York exchange.

Besides the increased refining capacity that it obtained, the American Sugar Refining Company was infused with new managerial talent. Charles and Alfred Harrison promptly retired from active business life, as they had planned. So did William W. Frazier and E. C. Knight, Sr. But Mitchell and William F. Harrison remained on in the employ of the American, the former continuing to run the Franklin refinery and the latter taking charge of the Spreckels firm. Without sugar men as knowledgeable and experienced as they, the American would have found it difficult to operate the newly purchased refineries.[83]

Still, the most important aspect of the Philadelphia acquisitions was the control that they gave the American Sugar Refining Company over the domestic industry. For of all the sugar refineries still in operation throughout the country, there were now only three that the American did not own outright—the Revere refinery in Boston, the California refinery in San Francisco, and a recently completed refinery just outside Baltimore. And of these three, there was only one in which the American did not own a significant interest.

The refinery outside Baltimore had been built by a group of local businessmen, together with persons formerly associated with the

[81] *United States* v. *E. C. Knight et al.: Transcript of Record*, p. 161; Lexow committee investigation, 1897, p. 671. The American agreed to turn over $10 million of its own securities for the outstanding stock of the Spreckels company, the latter having a par value of $5 million. Spreckels, as the holder of a 55 per cent interest in the firm, therefore received $5.5 million. The remainder went to Searles and the Havemeyers as owners of the minority interest.

[82] *United States* v. *E. C. Knight et al.: Brief for the United States*, pp. 14–15; Lexow committee investigation, 1897, p. 671.

[83] *United States* v. *E. C. Knight et al.: Transcript of Record*, pp. 90–91, 95; *United States* v. *American Sugar Refining Co. et al.*, pretrial testimony, 1912, pp. 5946–47.

Moller & Sierck firm in New York. Soon after it was opened in 1891, Searles had begun secretly to buy up its capital stock, offering through a local broker to purchase all outstanding shares at 50 per cent above their par value. Since the refinery had encountered certain operating difficulties, he had no trouble finding takers for his offer. By March 1, when the purchase of the Philadelphia refineries was all but complete, Searles had succeeded in obtaining two-thirds of the Baltimore Refining Company's outstanding stock. Satisfied that this was sufficient for control, he then withdrew his purchase offer.[84]

The California refinery, meanwhile, remained under lease to the Western Sugar Refining Company. Although Spreckels' was still the predominant voice in the Western's affairs, the American continued to retain its 50 per cent interest. This was to make certain that the sale of refined sugar in the common, overlapping market along the Missouri River was carried out to the mutual interest of both parties.

Thus, only the Revere refinery in Boston was completely independent of the American. But the Revere was capable of supplying only 2 per cent of the total U.S. market, an amount hardly sufficient to affect sugar prices to any significant degree.[85] Moreover, it had been forced to pledge that it would not expand beyond its current capacity.[86]

The acquisition of the Philadelphia refineries meant, therefore, that the American Sugar Refining Company had achieved a virtual monopoly of the sugar refining industry—that no firm then existed which could challenge its power to fix the price of refined sugar in the United States. The consolidation of the American sugar refining industry had, at long last, been completed. All that remained were the inevitable political and legal repercussions.

::

It was not until the latter part of March, 1892, that the acquisition of the four Philadelphia refineries became generally known. Although rumors of the sale, originating on Wall Street, began to circulate early

[84] *United States* v. *E. C. Knight et al.: Transcript of Record*, p. 163; *United States* v. *E. C. Knight et al.: Brief for the United States*, pp. 20–21. The Baltimore refinery was subsequently damaged by fire, and although it was rebuilt, it never opened again; see pp. 285–86 below.

[85] *United States* v. *E. C. Knight et al.: Brief for the United States*, pp. 14–15.

[86] See p. 80 above. Interestingly, the Revere, through the brokerage firm of Nash, Spalding & Company, which handled all purchases and sales for it, was the largest minority holder of American Sugar Refining stock. However, the Revere had no influence whatsoever on the American's management.

in the month, leading to considerable speculation in the American Sugar Refining Company's stock,[87] the rumors could not at once be confirmed. As usual, officials of the American had been unavailable for comment, though Claus Spreckels, Sr., was finally persuaded to answer reporters' questions. Asked on March 12 if he were about to join the "trust," the Hawaiian sugar king replied: "Not while I am on top of the earth. I don't favor trusts and never did. My refinery is now and always will be conducted independently of every other interest."[88] Two weeks later, however, when Spreckels departed for California, turning over the management of his Philadelphia refinery to officials of the American, the truth could no longer be concealed.[89]

Newspapers throughout the country began immediately to raise a hue and cry, pointing with alarm to the excessive economic power that the American Sugar Refining Company now commanded. "Competition being removed," declared the *St. Louis Globe-Democrat*, "the 'combine' has producers and consumers at its mercy. It is enabled to get its raw material at a lower price than it paid when the independent refineries were in operation, and it takes the liberty to put a higher price on the finished product."[90] Said the *New York Times*, "Never has competition been more completely suppressed by a combination in a prominent industry." It demanded that the American Sugar Refining Company be prosecuted under the recently enacted Sherman antitrust law.[91]

This hue and cry was then taken up in Congress. On April 16, 1892, Congressman Owen Scott, a Democrat from Illinois, introduced a resolution which, in effect, called on Republican Attorney General William H. Miller to explain why he had not yet brought suit against the American. It soon became apparent that the resolution, if brought to a vote in the Democratic-controlled House, would pass with strong Republican support.[92] Later, speaking in behalf of his resolution, Congressman Scott remarked with more than just a trace of sarcasm: "It certainly should be the policy of the Administration which claims credit for the enactment of the antitrust law to give it a fair test. It owes it to the people of the country to protect them from the exactions of such great monopolies as the sugar trust." Moreover, he

[87] It was rumored among American Sugar Refining Company employees that Havemeyer himself profited handsomely from the speculation. This information comes from Ernest P. Lorfonfont, of the American's Legal Department.

[88] *New York Times*, March 13, 1892. [89] *Ibid.*, March 29 and 30, 1892.

[90] Quoted in *ibid.*, April 15, 1892. [91] *Ibid.*, April 13, 1892.

[92] U.S., Congress, House of Representatives, *Congressional Record*, 52d Cong., 1st sess., 1892, 23, pt. 4: 3366, 3927–29.

added, "it surpasses comprehension that with all the evidence that is easily accessible, not only to the Government but to individuals, this prodigious extortioner should have been permitted for all this time to levy its tribute upon the people."[93]

Scott had good reason to take the Harrison administration to task. For the truth was that neither the president nor the attorney general had been particularly zealous in his efforts to enforce the Sherman antitrust law. Given their background and sources of political support, this was not surprising. Harrison, before becoming president, had been a lawyer for various corporate interests; Miller had been his law partner. Both men owed their offices to the support of certain segments of the business community, most particularly, the high tariff manufacturers; and both men held firmly to the view that government should play only a limited role in economic affairs. Since the Republican party platform in 1888 had included an antitrust plank, Harrison had been willing to sign the Sherman bill into law. But he had done nothing to advance its passage through Congress, and once the measure received his signature, he showed no further interest in the subject. Miller, taking his cue from the president, viewed the Sherman Act as merely one of the many federal laws he was sworn to uphold.[94] As a result, very little was accomplished in the field of antitrust. In the nearly two years following the passage of the Sherman Act, only one major combination—the whiskey trust—was even indicted for violating the new law's provisions.[95] And the whiskey trust, reorganized as the Distilling and Cattle Feeding Company of Illinois, would not have been indicted had it not been for the personal initiative of the U.S. district attorney in Boston.[96]

[93] *Ibid.*, p. 3928.

[94] Hans B. Thorelli, *The Federal Anti-Trust Policy*, pp. 371–73.

[95] Aside from the case against the whiskey trust, the only antitrust actions taken under the Harrison administration prior to March, 1892, were a suit to enjoin a cartel-like arrangement among certain coal mining companies in Kentucky and Tennessee (*United States* v. *Jellico Mountain Coal Co.*, 43 Fed. Rep. 898; 46 Fed. Rep. 432); a criminal action against a combination of lumber dealers in Wisconsin, Minnesota, Iowa, and Missouri (*U.S.* v. *Nelson et al.*, 52 Fed. Rep. 646); a criminal action against the American Bobbin, Spool Company (the so-called bobbin trust); and a similar action against the oleomargarine trust. The latter two, like the case against the whiskey trust (see note 96) were never brought to trial. See Albert W. Walker, *History of the Sherman Act*, pp. 63–72; Thorelli, *Federal Anti-Trust Policy*, p. 376.

[96] Thorelli, *Federal Anti-Trust Policy*, pp. 376–78. The case against the whiskey trust was eventually thrown out of court because of a faulty indictment. This result reflected not only the haphazard manner in which the case was prepared but also the temper of the courts at the time toward antitrust prosecutions.

Still, in the Harrison administration's behalf it must be pointed out that Congress, after passing the Sherman Act, then failed to provide any funds for its enforcement. (On the other hand, the Harrison administration had not asked for additional funds.) Moreover, the Sherman Act was a difficult law to enforce, calling on the government, as it did, to venture into previously unexplored fields of law, fields in which competence in economic as well as legal matters was essential. Faced with these formidable obstacles, the attorney general was disposed to act with circumspection. "The law is new, and its enforcement not free from difficulty," he had written to one of his district attorneys. "It is, of course, desirable to proceed with caution."[97]

But caution, at least with respect to the sugar combination, was no longer possible. Now that the American Sugar Refining Company's purchase of the four Philadelphia refineries was generally known, the failure of the Harrison administration to take action was threatening to become an issue in the upcoming presidential campaign. His hand forced by the Democrats, Miller ordered the district attorney in Philadelphia, Ellery P. Ingham, to bring suit against the American Sugar Refining Company and its alleged fellow conspirators.[98]

On May 2, 1892, just as the House of Representatives was preparing to vote unanimously in favor of the Scott resolution, a bill of equity was filed in the U.S. district court in Philadelphia, asking that the defendants, E. C. Knight *et al.*, be enjoined from carrying out their proposed merger. The government's complaint charged "that the American Sugar Refining Company, which may be considered as the principal defendant, has monopolized the manufacture of refined sugar, and also the interstate commerce therein, within the United States; and that the other defendants have combined, conspired, &c., with it for this purpose."[99]

The Harrison administration, having weathered the immediate political storm, appeared to be in no particular hurry to bring the case to trial—a fact which the *New York Times* and other newspapers complained of bitterly.[100] But then, after the Republicans lost the

[97] Miller to Frank D. Allen, February 11, 1892, in Department of Justice (JD) File No. 8247, quoted in Thorelli, *Federal Anti-Trust Policy*, p. 375.

[98] Matilda Gresham, *Life of Walter Q. Gresham*, 2:651; Ingham to the Attorney General, March 27, 1893, in JD File No. 8247.

[99] *United States* v. *E. C. Knight et al.: Brief for the United States*, pp. 3–4; House of Representatives, *Congressional Record*, 52d Cong., 1st sess., 23, pt. 4:3926. The resolution was actually passed two days later on May 4.

[100] *New York Times,* July 19 and November 25 and 26, 1892. There is some evidence that political influence may have been brought to bear to prevent the case from proceeding further. On May 19, 1892, Henry Havemeyer

November election, there were no further political repercussions to fear. As was the attorney general's custom, he left the matter to the district attorney to prosecute as he saw fit.

Toward the end of July, each of the defendants had filed separate answers to the government's complaint, in effect denying the charge that they had engaged in a conspiracy to monopolize the manufacture of refined sugar.[101] Then, early in October, a special examiner appointed by the Philadelphia court had begun taking testimony. Aside from eliciting some of the details of how the four Philadelphia firms had been acquired, this testimony brought out the fact that, in agreeing to sell out to the American, none of the major parties connected with the four refineries had been required to promise not to re-enter the business of sugar refining at some later date. These pretrial proceedings had continued in a desultory manner through election day and on into February when suddenly they were brought to an abrupt halt. Searles, the first official of the American called to testify, refused to answer any questions pertaining to the period before 1891 when the sugar trust proper was still in existence, and though Ingham asked the federal district court judge sitting in the case to compel Searles to answer, the judge declined to do so. Discouraged by this hostile ruling, Ingham was reluctant to proceed further until he had had a chance to consult with the new, incoming attorney general.[102] Thus the suit against E. C. Knight *et al.* became one of several such actions under the Sherman Act left up in the air when the Democrats, under Grover Cleveland, assumed office in the spring of 1893.

::

In his inaugural address, the new president spoke out forcefully on the subject of antitrust. Calling attention to the "existence of immense aggregations of kindred enterprises and combinations of business interests formed for the purpose of limiting production and fixing

wrote to Charles C. Harrison: "I hear of nothing adverse to our interest from Washington, but am not easy in my mind on the subject. I was informed that if the Pennsylvania road and Mr. Johnson were to use their influence, Mr. McPherson would consider their version of it very thoroughly." John R. McPherson, the senior senator from New Jersey and one of the most influential Democrats in Congress, was later one of those who made a substantial profit on speculation in American Sugar Refining stock as a result of inside information (see p. 184 below).

[101] *New York Times,* July 29 and August 2 and 6, 1892.

[102] Ingham to the Attorney General, March 27, 1893; *United States* v. *E. C. Knight et al.: Transcript of Record,* p. 155.

prices," Cleveland declared: "These aggregations and combinations frequently constitute conspiracies against the interests of the people. . . . To the extent that they can be reached and restrained by Federal power, the General Government should relieve our citizens from their interferences and exactions."[103] But as it turned out, the key words in this statement were "to the extent that they can be reached by Federal power."

To give his cabinet geographical balance, Cleveland chose as his attorney general a Boston lawyer, Richard Olney, whom he had met only once before and then only briefly.[104] Olney's strong, forceful personality and deep, probing intellect were soon to make him one of the dominant figures in the Cleveland administration. But those, such as Joseph Pulitzer, editor of the *New York World*, who wished to see the antitrust laws enforced more vigorously had good reason to oppose the appointment. As a noted corporate lawyer, Olney had been part of the counsel that successfully defended the Distilling and Cattle Feeding Company against the government's antitrust suit. Like many of the distinguished members of the bar, he felt that the Sherman Act had only a limited application, that it had been enacted to deal only with the problem of trusts proper, and that it could not be used to prosecute corporations duly chartered by one of the states.[105] As Olney subsequently declared in his first annual report as attorney general, "the cases popularly supposed to be covered by the statute are almost without exception not within its provisions, since to make them applicable not merely must capital be brought together and applied in large masses, but the accumulation must be made by means which impose a legal disability upon others from engaging in the same trade or industry."[106] In other words, it was not enough that virtually all the firms in an industry, having joined together in an industrial combination, were legally prevented from ever again acting as independent producers. To fall within the provisions of the Sherman Act, as Olney saw it, it was also necessary that new firms be legally barred from entering the industry. Clearly, the great majority of industrial combinations, especially those formed under the corporate laws of the various states, did not meet that requirement.

[103] Albert E. Bergh, ed., *Addresses, State Papers and Letters of Grover Cleveland*, p. 350.

[104] Thorelli, *Federal Anti-Trust Policy*, p. 383.

[105] *Ibid.;* Henry James, *Richard Olney and His Public Service;* Allan Nevins, *Grover Cleveland*, pp. 512–13.

[106] U.S., Attorney General, *Annual Report*, 1893, p. xxvii.

In setting forth this narrow interpretation of the law, one which all but vitiated the Sherman Act, Olney was merely echoing the view of Judge Howell B. Jackson, one of the jurists in the whiskey-trust prosecutions who, after enunciating the doctrine, had been elevated to the Supreme Court by President Harrison.[107] Still, Olney was aware that others would interpret the Sherman Act differently. "I have, therefore, deemed it my duty," he said, "to push for immediate hearing a case involving these questions, and unless prevented by some unforeseen obstacle, shall endeavor to have it advanced for argument at the present term of the Supreme Court."[108] That case was *United States* v. *E. C. Knight et al.*

On January 19, 1894, nearly two years after the purchase of the Philadelphia refineries, U.S. District Attorney Ellery P. Ingham opened the government's case against the American Sugar Refining Company and its fellow defendants before Judge William Butler of the district court in Philadelphia.[109] No further evidence had been taken since Searles' refusal to answer certain questions the year before, and the government, in its civil suit, still sought to prevent the merger from being completed. Of course, the E. C. Knight plant had long since been incorporated into the larger Franklin refinery, while the Delaware Sugar House had been absorbed by the Spreckels company.

On January 30, Judge Butler announced his decision.[110] The government's suit was dismissed, on the face of it because no attempt to monopolize interstate commerce had been revealed. "The contracts and acts of the defendants," Butler declared in his written opinion, "relate exclusively to the acquisition of sugar refineries and the business of sugar refining, in Pennsylvania. They have no reference and bear no relation to commerce between the states. . . ." Conceding that a monopoly in sugar refining might exist, Butler nonetheless rejected the government's contention that this necessarily demonstrated that a monopoly in commerce also existed. "The most that can be said is that it tends to such a result; that it might possibly enable the defendants to secure it, should they desire to do so." But that, Butler quickly added, had not happened. "At present," he said, "the defendants neither have, nor have attempted to secure, such commercial

[107] *In re Greene,* 52 Fed. Rep. 104; Thorelli, *Federal Anti-Trust Policy,* p. 385.

[108] U.S., Attorney General, *Annual Report,* 1893, p. xxvii.

[109] *New York Times,* January 20, 1894.

[110] *Ibid.,* January 31, 1894.

monopoly. As before stated, if they have a monopoly, it is in refineries and refining alone—over which the plaintiff has no jurisdiction."[111]

Although Butler based his decision on the narrow grounds that manufacturing was separate and distinct from commerce, it was clear that he had been greatly influenced by the view which Justice Jackson had expressed earlier, in the whiskey trust prosecution. ". . . The question is not new," Butler said, in turning to the basic issue of the powers granted the federal government under the Sherman Act. "It was fully considered in a case which arose under the statute . . . and the opinion of [Judge] Jackson (now of the supreme court) is so clear and satisfactory that I am restrained from quoting what he says only by the desire to be brief."[112]

As soon as Butler's decision was made known, Attorney General Olney announced that the government would appeal. "The Administration intends to prosecute this case with vigor," he said, "for the purpose of getting the highest judicial determination of the legality and binding effect of the antitrust law."[113] The Circuit Court of Appeals, in rendering its own decision on March 26, 1894, upheld Butler on every point, including his flattering reference to Justice Jackson's earlier opinion.[114] Both sides then prepared for the final test, an appeal to the U.S. Supreme Court.

::

Before that test could take place, however, officials of the American Sugar Refining Company suddenly found themselves the center of another controversy, this one involving charges that they had used improper influence to secure favorable tariff legislation. "Shameful pledges," "Trust now holds the whip," "Speculative Senators enrich themselves," and "Cleveland et al. to the bar," declared the headlines in the *Philadelphia Press* on May 14. An accompanying story told of a meeting on a private yacht between representatives of the American Sugar Refining Company and the Democratic presidential candidate in 1892, of large campaign contributions coming just in time to rescue several doubtful states, of administration officials intervening to push through the Senate Finance Committee a tariff schedule acceptable to the "trust," and of U.S. senators speculating wildly in sugar stocks. The next day this story was reprinted in the *New York*

[111] *United States* v. *E. C. Knight et al.*, 60 Fed. Rep. 309 (1894).
[112] *Ibid.*, p. 310.
[113] *New York Times*, February 1, 1894.
[114] *United States* v. *E. C. Knight et al.*, 60 Fed. Rep. 934 (1894).

Sun, causing a stir in Washington where the Senate was in the midst of debate over the tariff.[115]

These newspaper accounts, as a subsequent Senate investigation brought out, were greatly exaggerated.[116] The Democrats had been elected in 1892 largely on their promise to reform the tariff. But in order to reduce the duties on manufactured goods, as the Democrats proposed, it had been necessary to find some other source of government revenue. It was only natural, in this situation, that the Democrats should have turned to a tariff on imported raw sugar. Such a tariff had been at the heart of the federal revenue system since the beginning of the Republic. It had finally been eliminated in 1890, but only so the Republicans could justify increasing the duties on manufactured goods. Thus it was with a certain sense of poetic justice that the Democratic members of the Senate Finance Committee decided to re-establish the tariff on imported raw sugar, setting the rates at 40 per cent ad valorem and thus making it possible to reduce or eliminate the duties on other manufactured goods.

This decision, however, drew a strong protest from the two Democratic senators from Louisiana. An ad valorem tariff, they argued, would be difficult to enforce, for there was no way of knowing for certain what prices importers paid for raw sugar. Fraud was unavoidable, they said, with the result that the sugar-cane growers in their state would fail to receive adequate protection.[117] Since the Democrats controlled the Senate by only two votes, the support of both Louisiana senators was essential for passage of any tariff reform bill. Bowing to political necessity, the Democratic members of the Senate Finance Committee amended the tariff on raw sugar to read one cent a pound for all grades instead of 40 per cent ad valorem.[118]

[115] The *Philadelphia Press* article was reprinted in U.S. Senate Committee to Investigate Attempts at Bribery, *Report*, pp. 77–84.

[116] *Ibid.* The supposed meeting between Cleveland and representatives of the American Sugar Refining Company, for example, was clearly shown never to have taken place.

[117] See the testimony of Searles, *ibid.*, p. 369. In lieu of tariff protection, Louisiana's sugar-cane growers had been made eligible, under the McKinley Tariff of 1890, to receive bounties designed to offset their higher costs in comparison with Cuban sugar growers. Since the Louisiana producers accounted for less than a third of the sugar consumed in the United States, this, from a consumer's point of view, was a much less costly way of providing the Louisiana sugar growers with protection. The bounties, however, had been enacted over the opposition of the Louisianians, who considered them a much less certain form of protection than a tariff.

[118] Nevins, *Grover Cleveland*, pp. 572–76; speeches of Senators Newton C. Blanchard and Donelson Coffery, Democrats of Louisiana, U.S., Congress, Senate, *Congressional Record*, 53d Cong., 2d sess., 1894, 26, pt. 8:7745–48, 7823–27.

In the meantime, Searles and Henry Havemeyer had been in Washington lobbying for retention of at least half of the ½-cent-a-pound protection the sugar refining segment of the industry then enjoyed. But as soon as they learned of the change that had been made in the schedule for imported raw sugar, they turned their attention to what they considered the much greater threat to the American Sugar Refining Company's interests. For the 1-cent-a-pound, across-the-board duty on raw sugar, being a specific tariff, discriminated against the lower grades of imported raw sugar. And it was precisely these lower grades which the American Sugar Refining Company could most advantageously process. If the choice had been theirs alone, Searles and Havemeyer would have preferred no tariff at all on imported raw sugar, for the resulting lower prices led to increased consumption. But since some sort of tariff seemed unavoidable, Searles and Havemeyer were determined that it be levied on an ad valorem basis so that the various grades would be taxed according to their value.[119]

Largely as a result of Searles and Havemeyer's unrelenting opposition, the Democratic members of the Senate Finance Committee agreed to change the tariff on imported raw sugar once more, this time to duties which, though specific, nonetheless varied according to the value of the different grades. These duties ranged from 1.0 cent a pound for sugars testing 80° purity to 1.26 cents a pound for sugars testing 98° purity. But Searles and Havemeyer still were not placated. The 0.26-cent spread in duties was not sufficient to produce true ad valorem rates. Moreover, since the price of raw sugar was bound to vary over time, these specific duties would inevitably depart even further from the principle of ad valorem rates. And so, at Searles and Havemeyer's insistence, the tariff on imported raw sugar was changed one more time—back to the original 40 per cent ad valorem duties.[120]

It seemed strange that Searles and Havemeyer had been able to wield such great influence. As to the source of that influence, the article in the *Philadelphia Press* which had touched off the Senate investigation offered one suggestion. "Upon one occasion, some time in February," the article related,

[119] See the testimony of Searles and Havemeyer, U.S. Senate Committee to Investigate Attempts at Bribery, *Report*, pp. 311–54, 357–66, 368–404.

[120] Speech of Senator Coffery, Senate, *Congressional Record*, 53d Cong., 2d sess., 1894, 26, pt. 8: 7824–25; U.S. Senate Committee to Investigate Attempts at Bribery, *Report*, pp. 378–79.

when the Finance Committee, or the Democratic members of it, were in informal session, there came into the room, unexpectedly . . . , none other than the Secretary of the Treasury, [John G.] Carlisle. . . . He said: "Gentlemen, there is one thing I am bound to say to you as earnestly and impressively as I can do it, and I speak to you as a Democrat to Democrats. No party or the representatives of no party can afford to ignore honorable obligations. I want to say to you that there seems to be a danger that this is going to be done. Gentlemen associated with the sugar-refining interests (I may tell you what perhaps you do not know) subscribed to the campaign fund of the Democrat party in 1892 a very large sum of money. They contributed several hundred thousand dollars, and at a time when money was urgently needed. I tell you that it would be wrong, it would be infamous, after having accepted that important contribution, given at a time when it was imperatively needed, for the Democratic party now to turn around and strike down the men who gave it. It must not be done. I trust that you will prepare an amendment to the bill which will be reasonable and in some measure satisfactory to those interests.[121]

It is difficult to say how much weight should be given to this account. Its author, Elisha Edwards, later admitted that it was based primarily on second-hand information and conjecture. Those alleged to have been present at the meeting with the secretary of the treasury all denied that any such confrontation had taken place, and many other details of the *Press* account were clearly shown to be false.[122]

Still, the fact remained that Searles and Havemeyer had prevailed over the powerful opposition of the two Democratic senators from Louisiana. Later, during the floor debate over the tariff bill, those two senators gave their version of what had occurred within the Senate Finance Committee. Searles and Havemeyer, they said, controlled enough Democratic votes in the Senate to prevent any tariff bill to which they were opposed from becoming law. And so, in the interest of party unity—to enable the Democrats to redeem their election pledge—the two Louisiana senators had finally acceded to Searles and Havemeyer's position.[123]

Havemeyer, of course, stoutly maintained that in lobbying for ad valorem rates he and Searles had merely sought to protect a legitimate business interest. And it was true that in this instance the public welfare had not been affected in any substantial way. The conflict was really between groups within the industry, not between

[121] U.S. Senate Committee to Investigate Attempts at Bribery, *Report*, pp. 80–81.

[122] *Ibid.*, especially the testimony of Edwards, pp. 85–113.

[123] Speeches of Senators Blanchard and Coffery, Senate, *Congressional Record*, 53d Cong., 2d sess., 1894, 26, pt. 8:7745–48, 7823–27.

the industry and the public. In that sense it was a throwback to the controversy which had raged twenty-five years earlier over specific versus ad valorem duties.[124] Moreover, on the important issue of tariff protection for the sugar refining industry (to be distinguished from the issue of how the tariff on raw sugar should be levied), Havemeyer and Searles were noticeably less successful. The amount of protection for the refining industry was reduced from ½ to ⅛ of a cent a pound, a decline of 75 per cent.[125]

Nonetheless, the whole train of events, including the confirmed reports of Searles and Havemeyer at one end of the capitol building, the Louisiana senators at the other end, and members of the Senate Finance Committee shuttling back and forth trying to work out some compromise acceptable to both sides, seemed to confirm the fears of many Americans that the nation was evolving from a system of democracy toward a system of plutocracy. The impression was not improved by the disclosure that during the period of behind-the-scenes maneuvering a number of senators had profited handsomely from speculating in American Sugar Refining stock.[126] And so this incident became one of a series of events that was to lead eventually to the political reaction known as the Progressive movement.

The American Sugar Refining Company's alleged bribery of U.S. senators brought renewed demands in Congress that the corporation be prosecuted under the antitrust laws, especially after Havemeyer himself, in testifying before the special committee appointed to investigate the charges, openly acknowledged that the American had been formed to control the price of refined sugar throughout the United States.[127] Quite properly, however, these charges seemed to have little effect on the Supreme Court, which was then about to take up the *E. C. Knight* case.

::

The Supreme Court, after hearing oral arguments during October, 1894, handed down its decision in January of the following year. Chief Justice Melville W. Fuller, speaking for all of his fellow justices except one, declared that Congress had the right to prohibit monopoly in commerce but not monopoly in manufacture. "Doubtless the power

[124] See pp. 55ff.

[125] *United States* v. *American Sugar Refining Co. et al.*, pretrial testimony, 1912, p. 195; for the specific statutes, see p. 97, note 11, above.

[126] U.S. Senate Committee to Investigate Attempts at Bribery, *Report, passim.*

[127] See the resolution passed by the U.S. Senate, May 18, 1894, in JD File No. 8247.

to control the manufacture of a given thing involves in a certain sense the control of its disposition," the chief justice wrote in his majority opinion, "but this is a secondary and not the primary sense; and although the exercise of that power may result in bringing the operation of commerce into play, it does not control it, and affects it only incidentally and indirectly." He then added, "Commerce succeeds to manufacture, and is not a part of it."[128] The federal government might regulate the first, according to Fuller, but not the second. Thus the Supreme Court upheld in full the decision of the two lower courts.

Some persons have criticized Ingham and the attorney general for their failure to make a better case for the fact that refined sugar was an article of interstate commerce.[129] Whatever the merits of this criticism,[130] it is quite beside the point. The disposition of the Supreme Court at this time was such that probably no amount of evidence could have convinced the majority to rule other than the way it did. This was a court deeply committed to preserving state powers, as the subsequent income tax and racial segregation decisions were to prove even more conclusively. The ruling in the *E. C. Knight* case was merely part of a larger pattern.[131] The truth of this can be seen in Justice John M. Harlan's lengthy, clearly reasoned dissent, for Harlan had no trouble seeing where interstate commerce had been

[128] *United States* v. *E. C. Knight et al.*, 156 U.S. 12 (1895).

[129] See William Howard Taft, *The Anti-Trust Law and the Supreme Court*, p. 59; Nevins, *Grover Cleveland*, p. 722; Henry D. Lloyd, letter to the editor, *New York Post*, March 3, 1903, quoted in Thorelli, *Federal Anti-Trust Policy*, p. 387.

[130] In its brief the government did seek to deal with the question of whether sugar was an article of interstate commerce by pointing out that the nature of the business required the movement of sixty pounds of sugar every second in interstate commerce "to satisfy the wants of consumers within those States which do not produce it." The brief then added "that inasmuch as refined sugar necessarily looks mainly to interstate commerce for means to enable it to fulfill its function as necessary American food, it is—so long as upon the market and undistributed among the various States—a subject-matter of interstate commerce so far as to render its monopoly at any time in part a monopoly thereof" (*United States* v. *E. C. Knight et al.: Brief for the United States*, pp. 3–4). The question of how diligently the case was prosecuted nonetheless remains an open one. Olney, for example, seemed relieved that the Supreme Court had ruled as it did. "You will observe," he wrote to a friend, "that the government has been defeated in the Supreme Court on the trust question. I always supposed it would be, and have taken the responsibility of not prosecuting under a law I believed to be no good–much to the rage of the New York *World*" (Olney to A.M.S., Olney Papers, quoted in Nevins, *Grover Cleveland*, p. 671). Olney subsequently used what influence he had in the Cleveland administration to persuade the president that the Sherman Act was unenforceable (Nevins, *Grover Cleveland*, p. 723).

[131] Charles Warren, *The Supreme Court in United States History*, 2: *passim*.

directly affected. "In my judgment," he said, in what was eventually to become the line of argument adopted by the Supreme Court in interpreting the Sherman Act:

> the citizens of the several States composing the Union are entitled, of right, to buy goods in the State where they are manufactured, or in any other State, without being confronted by an illegal combination whose business extends throughout the country. . . . Whatever improperly obstructs the free course of interstate intercourse and trade, as involved in the buying and selling of articles to be carried from one State to another, may be reached by Congress, under its authority to regulate commerce among the States. The exercise of that authority so as to make trade among the States, in all recognized articles of commerce, absolutely free from unreasonable or illegal restrictions imposed by combinations, is justified by an express grant of power to Congress and would redound to the welfare of the whole country. I am unable to perceive that any such result would imperil the autonomy of the States, especially as that result cannot be attained through the action of any one State.[132]

The majority, in handing down its decision in the *Knight* case, had not expressly endorsed Justice Jackson's earlier view of the Sherman Act. As is the court's custom, it preferred to decide the case on narrower grounds. But the immediate effect was the same as if the Supreme Court had endorsed that interpretation. As Harlan noted in his dissent, "While the opinion of the court in this case does not declare the act of 1890 to be unconstitutional, it defeats the main object for which it was passed."[133]

No one was more conscious of this fact than Henry O. Havemeyer. Testifying before a joint New York legislative committee two years after the Supreme Court's decision, Havemeyer retorted sharply when the committee's counsel referred to the American Sugar Refining Company as a monopoly. "Well, fortunately," Havemeyer said, "the term 'monopoly' has been decided by the Supreme Court, and under that decision there can be no monopoly in the sugar business; they have held that there can be no monopoly without restrictions. I do not care to put my personal judgment against that of the Court on this particular word. We do not restrict anybody from going into business; so that we may control ninety-nine per cent and yet not be a monopoly."[134]

By its decision in the *E. C. Knight* case, the Supreme Court had declared that a combination in manufacturing which took the form of

[132] *United States* v. *E. C. Knight et al.*, 156 U.S. 37 (1895).
[133] *Ibid.*, pp. 24, 42.
[134] Lexow committee investigation, 1897, p. 115.

a corporation duly chartered by one of the states was beyond the jurisdiction of federal authority. In so doing, it had given this device for consolidating an industry implicit legal sanction, for a corporation duly chartered by one of the states was also beyond the jurisdiction of all other states. In effect, what the Supreme Court had done was to chart the path that, for the next nine years, industrial consolidations could safely follow.

This became even clearer after the Supreme Court's ruling in the *Addyston Pipe & Steel* case, for in that decision the Court held that all cartel-type devices were illegal under the Sherman Act.[135] This principle of law left consolidation under a single corporation—generally a holding company chartered by the state of New Jersey—as the only legal recourse for businessmen confronted by falling demand and large overhead costs, except the recourse of continuing to absorb heavy losses.

The *E. C. Knight* case came at a most propitious moment. The American economy was just emerging from the Depression of 1893, while the stock market was at last beginning to recover from the shock it suffered when the National Cordage Company failed. This coincidence of events helped to launch the first and more spectacular phase of the American Corporate Revolution; it was a time marked by consolidations in one major industry after another and lasted until the so-called Rich Man's Panic of 1907. The unprecedented wave of merger activity, which has never since been equaled, was to radically transform the rest of American industry in much the same way that the sugar refining industry had already been transformed. And the Supreme Court's decisions in the *E. C. Knight* and *Addyston Pipe & Steel* cases, together with the earlier state-court rulings in regard to trusts proper, established the legal milieu in which that revolution would be carried out.[136]

[135] *United States* v. *Addyston Pipe & Steel Co.*, 175 U.S. 211 (1899). In this decision the Supreme Court held that a market-sharing agreement among manufacturers of sanitary pipes was a violation of the Sherman Act.

[136] The important role played by the courts in determining the direction in which the American economic system has evolved was stressed by John R. Commons in his book *Legal Foundations of Capitalism.*

8 :: THE PROBLEM OF ENTRY

THE decade following 1895—a period during which the consolidation of many other industries was just beginning—saw the American Sugar Refining Company forced to grapple with the problem of how to prevent the entry of new firms into that industry, a problem which was later to destroy more than one combination. In sugar refining, two major barriers were erected to discourage potential entrants: (1) a working arrangement with the wholesale grocers under which the latter refused to handle the sugars of any proscribed company; and (2) the receipt of rebates and other concessions from the railroads which provided the American with a substantial advantage in shipping costs. Despite these and other obstacles, however, a small number of firms nonetheless managed to invade the sugar refining industry, the most serious threat to the American's hegemony coming from the entry of Arbuckle Brothers.

Arbuckle was not only the nation's largest coffee grinder but also the holder of a patent on a machine capable of packaging sugar in two-pound paper containers. While previous interlopers had been willing to accept a minimum share of the market, tacitly agreeing to follow the American's lead in pricing, Arbuckle's entry was marked by animosity from the very beginning and quickly touched off price wars in both the coffee and sugar industries. After several years of unprofitable conflict, the two parties finally reached a *modus vivendi,* Henry O. Havemeyer in the meantime having promoted a merger among three other rival refineries to create the industry's second-largest firm. Through the dynamism of these competitive forces, the sugar refining industry was transformed from a monopoly into an oligopoly—with the American Sugar Refining Company still in control.

::

With the *E. C. Knight* case settled entirely to Henry Havemeyer's satisfaction, the only major problem still confronting the American was the threat of new firms entering the industry. Andrew Carnegie had warned of the danger. "There is no possibility of maintaining a trust," he declared. "It is bound to go to pieces, sooner or later, and generally to involve in ruin those foolish enough to embark on it. If successful for a time and undue profits accrue, competition is courted which must be bought out, and this leads to fresh competition. And so on until the bubble bursts. And then the article which was proposed to enhance in price is made for years without profit and the consumer has his ample revenge."[1]

Underscoring Carnegie's caveat was the recent experience of the National Cordage Company. Like the American Sugar Refining Company, it had originally been a trust which was reorganized as a New Jersey holding company following the *North River* decision; and again like the American, it had succeeded in gaining control of approximately 90 per cent of its industry. No sooner was this control accomplished, however, than new cordage mills were erected to replace those which had been bought out. The officers of the National Cordage Company had tried, by various means, to block the entry of these new firms. They sought to corner the supply of raw hemp. They attempted to purchase exclusive rights to the machinery used in the manufacture of rope and twine. But for one reason or another, all these efforts failed, and on May 4, 1893, unable to continue supporting the price of its stock on the American exchange, National Cordage was forced into receivership, dragging to ruin with it three brokerage houses and many individual investors.[2]

For a while, following the American Sugar Refining Company's acquisition of the four Philadelphia refineries, it had seemed that the history of the National Cordage Company might be repeated in the sugar industry. As soon as the purchase of the four firms had become generally known, plans were laid to create new refining facilities not only in Philadelphia but in other cities as well. In Philadelphia itself, William J. McCahan decided to push ahead with a project that had been in the back of his mind for some time, a scheme to convert his molasses house into a sugar refinery. McCahan had been toying with the idea ever since the passage of the McKinley Tariff Act had made the manufacture of molasses unremunerative, but he had been de-

[1] *New York Times*, October 9, 1888. From his own refusal to have anything to do with the consolidation of the steel industry, it seems clear that Carnegie was sincere in this view.

[2] Arthur S. Dewing, *A History of the National Cordage Company*, pp. 4–32. The company's complete financial collapse not only marked the onset of a severe depression throughout the economy but also threw into temporary disrepute, as far as Wall Street investors were concerned, all industrial securities issues.

terred by the severe price competition then raging among the various sugar refiners. However, now that the competition was a thing of the past, McCahan no longer saw any reason to hesitate. Reorganizing the firm which bore his name into a Pennsylvania corporation capitalized at $2 million, he began remodeling the molasses house so that it would eventually be capable of turning out 3,000 barrels of refined sugar daily.[3]

Motivated by much the same considerations, Frederick Mollenhauer and his two brothers, J. Adolph and Henry F. Mollenhauer, decided to convert their father's molasses house in Brooklyn into a refinery capable of producing 3,300 barrels of sugar daily.[4] Meanwhile, George Bunker and several others connected with the former Delaware Sugar House agreed among themselves to organize the National Sugar Refining Company. Purchasing a site on the Hudson River in Yonkers, they began erecting a refinery which would eventually add another 2,300 barrels of refined sugar to the country's daily output.[5] These three new refineries, when finally completed, threatened to reduce the American Sugar Refining Company's share of the eastern sugar market from 98 per cent to 80 per cent.[6] And there were reports of plans to build still other refineries. A Boston group, for example, was said to be waiting only to see what attitude Congress would take toward sugar duties before beginning construction of a refinery in that city.[7]

Officials of the American Sugar Refining Company were well aware of the threat that the entry of new firms posed to their control of the industry. Realizing that the purchase of these firms would merely encourage the formation of others, they began looking around for some more effective means of limiting external competition. As a first step in this direction, they sought to enlist the support and cooperation of the wholesale grocers, the channel through which all sugar had to pass in order to reach the consumer.

::

These wholesale grocers had been alarmed by the news that the

[3] *United States* v. *American Sugar Refining Co. et al.*, pretrial testimony, 1912, pp. 7413–19; *New York Times*, March 24 and October 14, 1892.

[4] *United States* v. *American Sugar Refining Co. et al.*, pretrial testimony, 1912, pp. 6477–79; Lexow committee investigation, 1897, pp. 322–26.

[5] Lexow committee investigation, 1897, pp. 322–26; *United States* v. *American Sugar Refining Co. et al.*, pretrial testimony, 1912, pp. 6169, 6178.

[6] Willett & Gray's *Weekly Statistical Sugar Trade Journal*, December 28, 1893.

[7] *Ibid.*, October 5, 1893.

American had purchased the four Philadelphia refineries, for it meant that the grocers would henceforth have but one source of supply for refined sugar. This prospect had so frightened them that some of their number had seriously considered erecting their own refinery. One New York wholesale grocer, confirming reports that he had made available as the site of the proposed new refinery a tract of land which he owned on Staten Island, told a reporter for the *New York Times*, "I have consented to act as custodian of subscriptions for a company, the stockholders of which would comprise not less than 100 of the chief sugar distributors in the big cities of the country. . . ." Besides New York itself, these cities included Philadelphia, Boston, Baltimore, Chicago, Cincinnati, and St. Paul.[8] Representatives of the American Sugar Refining Company, however, soon reminded the wholesale grocers that the real threat to their continued existence was not the American's monopoly position but rather the severe competition which then prevailed among the wholesale grocers themselves.

The sale of refined sugar constituted approximately 40 per cent of the wholesale grocers' business, but since sugar was an item of uniform quality, the wholesale grocers generally found themselves forced to handle it "without getting back the actual cost of distribut[ion]."[9] It seemed that some jobber was always willing to cut his price in order to make a sale to a new customer, and since the wholesale grocers' costs were almost entirely overhead in nature, the price at which they found themselves forced to sell refined sugar often was no higher than the price at which they had bought the sugar from the refiner. As G. Waldo Smith, president of the New York Wholesale Grocers' Association, later explained: "Under the laws that govern competition the hundredth man—and he may be a very small dealer at that—can make the price at which his 99 competitors must sell all goods of [uniform quality]. . . . Under the laws of modern competition it is impossible to obtain a profit on such goods."[10] The wholesale grocers, like the sugar refiners before them, had found competition to be unbearable the more closely it approximated the conditions underlying the economists' model.

It was for this reason that wholesale grocers from New York and New England had approached officials of the American Sugar Refining Company the year before, in June of 1891, asking for the adoption of a rebate system which would protect them from the severe com-

[8] Erastus Wiman, quoted in the *New York Times*, April 7, 1892.

[9] Lexow committee investigation, 1897, p. 413.

[10] U.S. Industrial Commission, *Reports*, 1, pt. 2:59–60; see also Smith's testimony before the Lexow committee during its 1897 investigation, pp. 830–31.

petition that they seemed unable to control themselves. "We found that ruin stared the jobbers and grocers in the face," Smith subsequently testified. "We went to the American Sugar Refining Company and asked them for relief. We went there six times and spent three hours each time before they would consent."[11]

Specifically, what the representatives of the wholesale grocers wanted was for the American Sugar Refining Company to force all jobbers to adhere to a single price for sugar, a price that would enable the wholesale grocers to handle sugar at a profit. This was to be accomplished through a system of rebates paid only to those wholesale grocers who honored a pledge not to sell refined sugar for less than the prices posted by the American. That way, even though the wholesale grocers might still be forced to sell refined sugar at cost, they would be assured of a profit—a profit equal to the rebate they received from the American Sugar Refining Company. Those wholesale grocers who refused to become a party to the agreement or who, having signed the agreement, refused to live up to its terms were to be penalized by being denied the rebate and hence any chance to earn a profit on refined sugar. Under those circumstances, it was unlikely that any wholesale grocer would remain outside the system for long.[12] It was, in effect, a privately enforced wholesale price maintenance scheme similar to those agreements which today receive public protection under the so-called fair-trade laws.

In agreeing to the rebate system, officials of the American Sugar Refining Company were motivated, at least initially, by the desire to protect their distribution system. ". . . The thing had come to pass," John E. Searles later testified, "that the wholesalers were suffering in credit. We did not know who was safe. . . . We, as a matter of self-protection in the matter of credits more than anything else, were interested in [the rebate system]."[13] Upon ascertaining what it would cost if the American itself were to try to distribute refined sugar to retail grocers throughout the country, officials of that company agreed to set up a rebate system, as the New York and New England wholesale grocers had requested, based on deferred payments of ⅛ of a cent a pound.[14] The Franklin refinery, then in active competition with the American, agreed to do the same.[15]

[11] Lexow committee investigation, 1897, p. 827.

[12] *Ibid.*, pp. 410–19.

[13] *Ibid.*, p. 414.

[14] *Ibid.*, p. 413; *United States* v. *American Sugar Refining Co. et al.: Exhibits*, 4:2174. The American, in fact, insisted that the wholesale grocers themselves decide how large the rebates should be, since they were in the best position to

The original purpose of the rebate system may well have been to protect the wholesale grocers, but it was not long before Searles and Henry O. Havemeyer realized that the system might serve to protect the American Sugar Refining Company as well. For if it was true, as the wholesale grocers claimed, that they could not survive without a rebate system, then it seemed only reasonable that in return for the American's co-operation the wholesale grocers should be willing to agree not to handle the sugars of any other refiner. Such a *quid pro quo* would make business extremely difficult for new firms entering the refining industry, for if the American with its vast resources and large market could not distribute sugar to retail grocers for less than 3/16 of a cent a pound, as it felt it could not, new firms entering the industry would most likely find the cost of distribution even greater. "I do not think," Havemeyer later wrote, "competitors can market their sugar to their retail trade within 1/8 of a cent. If they attempt it . . . they will certainly lose three times as much money as the American Co., and will soon be out of it."[16]

It is not clear exactly when Searles and Havemeyer realized this ulterior advantage of the rebate system, but it was probably not long after the American succeeded in acquiring its four principal rivals in Philadelphia. For soon thereafter, in an effort to calm the fears of sugar distributors over the purchase of those refineries, the American began entering into rebate agreements with other wholesale grocers' associations similar to the one that it had reached with the wholesale grocers from New York and New England.[17] Within a year of the Philadelphia refineries' purchase, it was the American, not the wholesale grocers, that was actively seeking to enlist sugar distributors in the rebate system—now renamed to avoid the unfavorable connotation of the word "rebate," an equality plan.[18] By September, 1894, Havemeyer was able to write a prominent wholesale grocer in

decide what size rebate would be most effective in eliminating price competition among themselves. See the letter of Henry O. Havemeyer to lawyers representing the Philadelphia wholesale grocers, April 5, 1892, reprinted in *United States* v. *American Sugar Refining Co. et al.*, pretrial testimony, 1912, pp. 9636–37.

[15] Lexow committee investigation, 1897, p. 810.

[16] Henry O. Havemeyer to William A. Havemeyer, February 6, 1899, reprinted in *United States* v. *American Sugar Refining Co. et al.*, pretrial testimony, 1912, pp. 7244–46.

[17] *New York Times*, June 28, 1892; Willett & Gray's *Weekly Statistical Sugar Trade Journal*, September 15, 1892.

[18] See Havemeyer's letters to the wholesale grocers in Winchester, Va., February 14, 1893, reprinted in *United States* v. *American Sugar Refining Co. et al.*, pretrial testimony, 1912, pp. 9637–39.

Chicago that the time of the American's chief salesman, W. F. Osborn, "is now almost entirely devoted to winning followers to the plan."[19] In this way, practically every wholesale grocer east of the Missouri River became, in effect, an exclusive selling agent for the American Sugar Refining Company. Those who refused to become a party to the rebate system found it difficult to survive in the business.[20]

This change in the wholesale grocer's status from independent buyer to franchised dealer was given explicit recognition in 1895 when the rebate system was scrapped and a factor plan substituted in its place. Under this new "equality" scheme, the wholesale grocers were no longer to receive rebates. Instead, they were made factors of the American Sugar Refining Company and were paid a commission for handling its sugars.[21] But despite this change in form, again made to soothe the public sensitivity to rebates in any form, the underlying relationship remained the same—the wholesale grocers were to be protected against competition among themselves in return for the American's being protected against competition from new refineries.

Nowhere in the many agreements between the American and the various wholesale grocers' associations was it specifically stated that the latter could handle only the American's sugar. But as Henry O. Havemeyer later wrote to a wholesale grocer in Rochester, "There is no plan . . . that the grocers can submit to me, which presumably involves a reciprocal advantage, which would permit them to buy competitive sugars and sell them under a plan between ourselves and the grocer." He then added, "It is hardly to be presumed that the American Company would be a party to a plan to establish its rivals and make them successful."[22] In private letters to other prominent wholesale grocers, Havemeyer repeatedly stressed the same point.[23]

[19] Henry Havemeyer to Henry B. Steele, September 17, 1894, reprinted in *ibid.*, p. 8649.

[20] See the testimony of Edward J. Duggan, Francis H. Krenning, and the other wholesale grocers who appeared before the Lexow committee during its 1897 investigation, pp. 279–89, 1057–76; see also the story of M. P. Langley, a Lynn, Mass., grocer, in the *Boston Evening Record*, September 29, 1892.

[21] Willett & Gray's *Weekly Statistical Sugar Trade Journal*, October 10, 1895; Lexow committee investigation, 1897, pp. 415–16.

[22] Henry O. Havemeyer to George C. Buell, January 12, 1903, reprinted in *United States* v. *American Sugar Refining Co. et al.*, pretrial testimony, 1912, p. 7312.

[23] See, for example, Petitioner's Exhibits Nos. 1875, 1289, 1290, and 1293, reprinted in *United States* v. *American Sugar Refining Co. et al.*, pretrial testimony, 1912, pp. 9654–55, 7247–48, 7252, 7255–56.

By forcing the wholesale grocers to handle only the American Sugar Refining Company's products, Havemeyer was merely copying a technique which James Duke's American Tobacco Company and several other industrial consolidations had developed to solve the problem of entry in their own industries.[24] But effective as this control over wholesale distribution outlets might be in preventing the emergence of new competition, Havemeyer was determined to erect even more formidable barriers. The Standard Oil Company had been able to buttress its market position against interlopers through preferential railroad rates, and Havemeyer could see no reason why his own American Sugar Refining Company should not do the same.

::

In its own way, sugar was as important to the railroads as petroleum. As an article which moved primarily from the sea inland, it helped offset the railroads' predominantly eastbound traffic. Refined sugar was, in fact, the only major source of through cargo to the trans-Ohioan regions, accounting for slightly more than a third of the tonnage carried in that direction by the major trunk-line railroads serving the port of New York.[25] It was for this reason that the railroads had battled so fiercely for a share of the sugar traffic during the 1870's and 1880's. "Why, the railroads were always in a scrap among themselves," the traffic manager for Havemeyer & Elder later recalled.[26]

The bitter competition among the railroads was in great part a carry-over from the bitter competition among the sugar refiners themselves, for any firm which found itself hard-pressed by a rival from another city—or a rival served by another railroad—would go to the

[24] Richard B. Tennant, *The American Cigarette Industry*, pp. 304–6. Explaining the rebate and later the factor plans adopted by the American Tobacco Company, Tennant declares: ". . . it was regarded by the Trust as an unfriendly act for a jobber to handle competing brands. In the early days, the rebate and commission arrangements, by allowing the Trust to cancel distributors' profits on past sales, gave it enormous leverage to affect jobbers' policy" (*ibid.*, pp. 305–6). There is evidence that other industries might have used the same techniques to control entry. See the testimony of James Post, *United States* v. *American Sugar Refining Co. et al.*, pretrial testimony, 1912, pp. 6896–97; Lexow committee investigation, 1897, pp. 25–26; U.S. Industrial Commission, *Reports*, 1, pt. 2:21.

[25] *United States* v. *American Sugar Refining Co. et al.*, pretrial testimony, 1912, pp. 10140–42.

[26] Testimony of Lowell M. Palmer, Hardwick committee investigation, 1911, p. 301.

railroad with whom it dealt and demand some concession on freight rates, often claiming that the other railroads had already made a similar concession. "... It would have been impossible," Havemeyer & Elder's traffic manager explained, "for a refinery to live prior to the consolidation of these companies in 1887 without the obtaining of rebates. It was a very bitter fight between the sugar refining interests everywhere; Philadelphia against New York and New York against Boston."[27] With the formation of the sugar trust in 1887, this competition—both that between the railroads and that between the refineries themselves—subsided. It flared up again with the opening of the Spreckels refinery in 1890,[28] but then died down when the American finally succeeded in purchasing its four principal rivals in Philadelphia two years later.

Besides bringing to an end the competition within the sugar refining industry, this last move gave the American Sugar Refining Company a preponderance of bargaining strength vis-à-vis the railroads, for it was now in a position to decide which of the various trunk-line railroads would get the valuable sugar traffic. Henry Havemeyer decided to use this advantage to obtain a *quid pro quo* from the railroads similar to the one he had already obtained from the wholesale grocers. As common carriers the railroads could not refuse to carry other refining companies' sugars, but they could force those other refining companies to pay a higher freight rate.

Just as the wholesale grocers had been plagued by competition among themselves, so the railroads were similarly beset. Somewhat like the wholesale grocers, they found that their costs were almost entirely fixed, and one of the railroads, in order to increase its own tonnage, would inevitably try to grab a larger share of the sugar traffic by secretly cutting its rates. This occurred even though the American Sugar Refining Company was now the only customer. What the railroads desired was for some party to act as "evener," dividing the sugar traffic among the various trunk-line railroads according to previously agreed-to precentages. This was the way the problem of railroad competition was dealt with in the case of wheat, petroleum, and certain other commodities.

It was only logical in this situation that, in return for preferential rates, the American Sugar Refining Company should agree to take on the role of "evener," for it not only controlled 98 per cent of all

[27] *Ibid.*, p. 299.
[28] *New York Times*, April 4, 1890.

sugar shipments in the East but also had in Lowell M. Palmer someone ideally suited to manage such a task. Palmer had been associated with Henry O. Havemeyer since 1874, seeing to it that the various companies with which Havemeyer was associated obtained railroad rates at least as favorable as those received by any rival.[29] It was largely through his efforts that Brooklyn shippers were finally able to gain direct access to all the railroads serving the port of New York. Before 1874, Brooklyn's manufacturers—including its sugar refiners—had been forced to use whichever railroad had the nearest siding, and this, besides the restriction it placed on the choice of carrier, involved considerable expense for overland cartage. But then Palmer built what later came to be known as the Brooklyn Eastern District Terminal, a docking facility for railroad lighters which enabled manufacturers to load their goods directly onto railroad cars and have them towed by tug to the terminal of whatever railroad they wished to ship on.[30] Although Havemeyer himself supplied the land and capital for this enterprise, it was Palmer who conceived the idea and saw it through to completion. Largely as an outgrowth of this entrepreneurial endeavor, Palmer came to be placed in charge of all the transportation arrangements for Havemeyer & Elder and later, when the trust was formed, for that organization and its successor, the American Sugar Refining Company, as well.[31] His assistant, and the one who actually handled the everyday details, was Thomas P. Riley, a former employee of the Erie Railroad.[32]

In April, 1893, acting on Havemeyer's instructions, Palmer and Riley met with representatives of the New York Central and Erie railroads, the two trunk lines that handled most of the sugar leaving the port of New York. It was agreed that, in return for dividing the sugar traffic between the two roads according to the percentages they normally carried, the American Sugar Refining Company would receive a secret rebate of two cents a hundredweight on all its trunk-line traffic—that is, on all the sugar it shipped between Buffalo and

[29] Hardwick committee investigation, 1911, p. 296.

[30] Although the Havemeyer & Elder refinery was located on the water's edge, its docking facilities were completely taken up by ocean-going vessels bringing raw sugar to the plant. In fact, the refinery had been so constructed that the processed sugar came out on the landward side.

[31] Hardwick committee investigation, 1911, p. 300; *United States* v. *American Sugar Refining Co. et al.*, pretrial testimony, 1912, pp. 10309–10.

[32] *United States* v. *American Sugar Refining Co. et al.*, pretrial testimony, 1912, p. 9937.

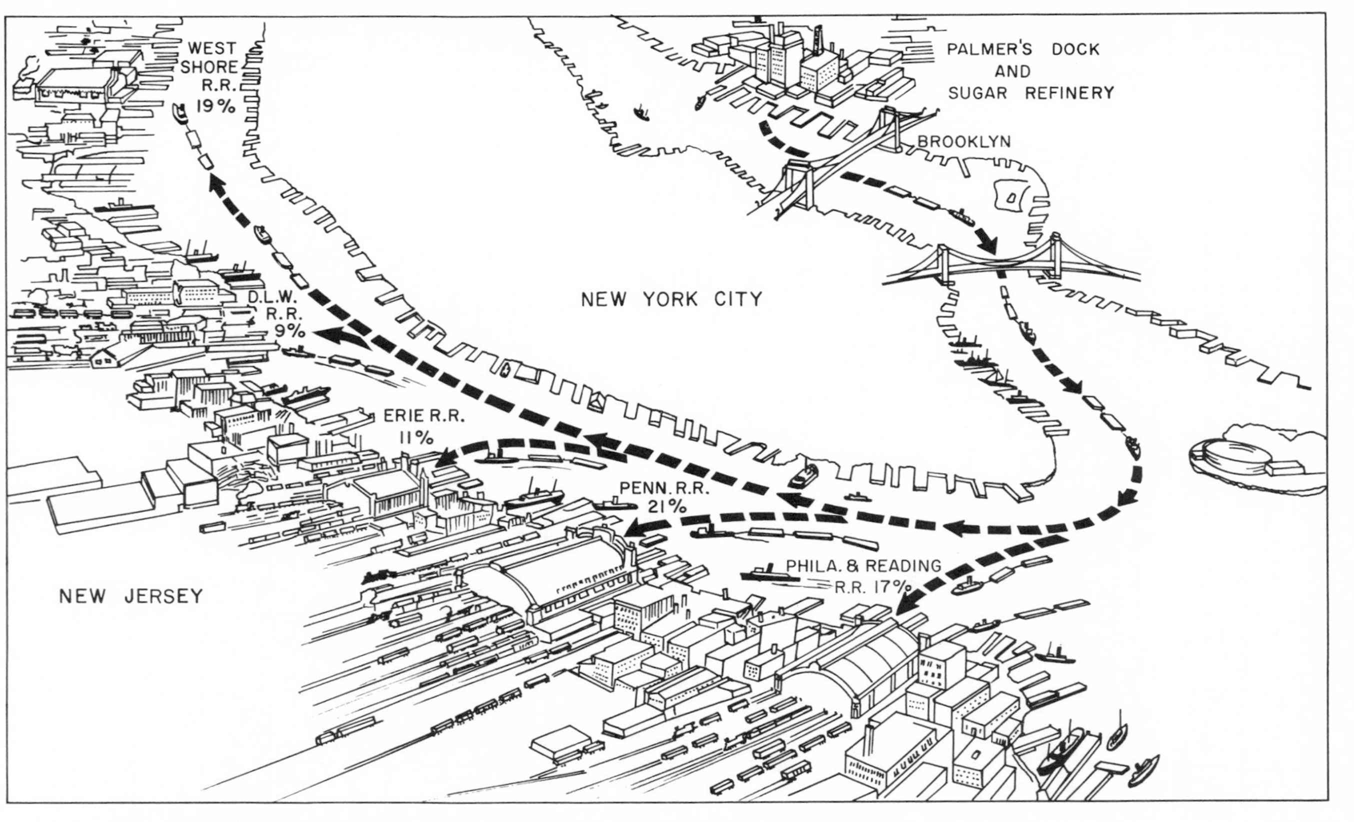

MAP 1. THE AMERICAN SUGAR REFINING COMPANY AND THE RAILROADS, 1906

This map, which is redrawn from that which appeared in the New York American *on March 8, 1906, shows the location of the American Sugar Refining Company's Havemeyer & Elder refinery, Palmer's Dock, and the various railroad terminals located around the New York harbor. It also indicates the percentage of sugar traffic carried by the railroads at that later date.*

Salamanca, New York, on the one hand, and between Chicago and St. Louis on the other.[33]

This initial rebate agreement was soon followed by similar arrangements with other railroads. For example, in return for being assured a certain percentage of the sugar traffic, most of the major railroads serving points beyond the Mississippi River agreed to give the American a further rebate of between 20 and 25 per cent on their prorated share of the joint rate with the trunk lines.[34] Thus, of the forty-four cents a hundredweight which the railroads, according to their published tariffs, supposedly charged for shipping refined sugar from New York to cities along the Missouri River, seven cents was returned to the American Sugar Refining Company by means of secret rebates, two cents by the trunk line that carried the sugar to Chicago, and five cents by the railroad that carried it beyond.[35] Equally favorable rebate agreements were entered into with the railroads serving Boston,[36] as well as with those serving the southeastern states.[37]

Since the money that the railroads were forced to refund under these various agreements represented considerable sums, from time to time the railroads would try to abrogate the agreements unilaterally. However, any such show of independence was usually short-lived, for the American Sugar Refining Company would simply divert its sugar shipments over some other line that was willing to pay a rebate. Under that type of economic pressure, no railroad could hold out against payment of the rebates for long.[38]

As the man in charge of the American Sugar Refining Company's traffic arrangements, Riley had the task of implementing these rebate agreements directly. Each month he would receive waybills from the

[33] Points east of Buffalo (on the New York Central) and Salamanca, N.Y. (on the Erie), were considered to be in the two railroads' home territories and hence were not subject to competition between them. Although no record of the original agreement survives, it was extended *in toto* the following year (*United States* v. *American Sugar Refining Co. et al.*, pretrial testimony, 1912, pp. 10018–21, 10025–26). As to the secret nature of the rebates, Riley later testified, "Yes, these rates and arrangements were all to be regarded as confidential between ourselves and the representatives of the transportation companies" (*ibid.*, p. 10024).

[34] *Ibid.*, pp. 10005–6, 10014–17, 10157. The railroads were the Chicago, Milwaukee & St. Paul, the Chicago, Rock Island & Pacific, and the Chicago, Burlington & Quincy.

[35] *Ibid.*, pp. 10025–26.

[36] *Ibid.*, pp. 10031–32, 10650.

[37] *Ibid.*

[38] *Ibid.*, pp. 10120–32. Riley, for example, testified that "the Burlington road was always in and out; they would be in for a while, and then would drop out, and we would switch the tonnage to the other roads, and they would come back again . . ." (*ibid.*, p. 10157).

railroads with which the American had rebate agreements. These waybills enabled Riley to keep track of how much sugar was being shipped over the various lines, and when he saw that a railroad was receiving more than its full quota, he would reroute traffic over a railroad which was running short of shipments. In this way Riley was able to maintain the percentages to which the railroads themselves had agreed. Periodically, he would submit claims to the railroad companies for the rebates which they owed, and when the sums were received, he would forward them to the American Sugar Refining Company, deducting only the expenses of his own office.[39]

::

The trouble with this arrangement was that the railroads which were not parties to the arrangement became dissatisfied with their failure to obtain any significant share of the sugar traffic, and in an effort to remedy the situation would begin offering lower rates on sugar shipments.[40] While the American Sugar Refining Company would have preferred to ignore these lower rates (being more than satisfied with its rebate arrangement with the other railroads), the wholesale grocers would not let it. As Riley later explained,

> . . . certain grocers that were pretty hard fellows to get into line would say, for instance, "You are charging us a prepaid [freight rate] of 25 cents, and we can get a rate by the Kanawha Despatch [the fast freight line serving the Chesapeake & Ohio Railroad] of 22 cents, and we want to buy our sugar f.o.b. and ship it over the Kanawha Despatch."
>
> Of course that would mean that every pound of sugar that went out f.o.b. over these differential lines [i.e., those lines that were not a party to the rebate arrangement] was interfering not only with our routing of the traffic, but it was disturbing the physical division of the business that I was supposed to look after, to see if the New York Central Railroad was allotted 31 per cent of the sugar traffic that they should get it, and the only way that I could see that they got it was by retaining control of the routing in our own hands.

"Again," Riley added,

> there was about that time the possibility of other sugar refining companies starting around here and we felt that they would undoubtedly take advantage of the differential rate lines if arrangements were not made to put these differential rate lines in a position where, when they were asked what their rate on sugar was, they would say: "The rate is the same as by

[39] *Ibid.*, pp. 9975–78.
[40] *Ibid.*, p. 10053.

any of the standard lines"; that was part of our policy, to look ahead on that matter and even if new refineries did enter the field the question of the division of the sugar traffic and the keeping of the routing in our hands, would still remain effective.[41]

However, the only way that the American could safeguard its rebate agreement was by gradually including more and more railroads in the scheme. Thus, by the middle of 1895, the sugar traffic out of New York was being divided not only between the New York Central and Erie railroads but also among the Lehigh Valley, Chesapeake & Ohio, and Central of Vermont railroads as well.[42] But other carriers, such as the Pennsylvania, Baltimore & Ohio, and Delaware, Lackawanna & Western railroads, which were not as yet included, still remained dissatisfied. And being dissatisfied, they continued trying to undermine the rebate arrangement.

Of these outside railroads, the Pennsylvania was by far the most important sugar carrier. It already handled most of the sugar shipped from Philadelphia, but it wanted a share of the New York traffic as well. This Havemeyer refused to give it—unless it agreed to use Palmer's Dock for the sugar it shipped from New York. The Pennsylvania, however, had its own terminal facilities in Brooklyn and refused to pay Palmer's Dock 4.2 cents a hundredweight for lighterage, such as the other railroads were then paying, when it was capable of performing that service for itself. The fact was that the actual cost of lighterage was considerably less than 4.2 cents per hundredweight. The difference, approximately two cents a hundredweight, represented a payment to Havemeyer personally, made through Palmer's Dock, which he owned, for arranging the division of the sugar traffic among the various railroads. Thus, to give the Pennsylvania a share of the New York traffic when it refused to use Palmer's Dock would have taken money out of Havemeyer's pocket.[43]

Havemeyer tried to get around this impasse by offering to buy the Pennsylvania Railroad's terminal facilities in Brooklyn, but, as Riley later testified, "they [the Pennsylvania's officers] said it was the policy of the Pennsylvania Railroad not to ever sell any piece of real estate

[41] *Ibid.*, p. 10147; see also *ibid.*, pp. 10045–54.

[42] *Ibid.*, p. 10140. The latter two railroads received their share of the sugar shipments only after first having the sugar carried by ocean steamer to their respective eastern terminals, Norfolk, Va., and New London, Conn. The percentages for all the railroads were as follows: New York Central, including the West Shore line, 47.27; Erie, 30.26; Lehigh Valley, 14.78; Chesapeake & Ohio, 3.845; and the Central of Vermont, 3.845.

[43] *Ibid.*, pp. 10075, 10307–8.

they owned."[44] It was not until 1898 that the deadlock was finally resolved, with the Pennsylvania Railroad agreeing to pay Palmer's Dock 4.2 cents for every hundred pounds of sugar it shipped from New York—and an additional two cents per hundredweight when the Pennsylvania performed its own lighterage.[45] This agreement soon led to a more comprehensive rebate arrangement, one that included not only all the railroads omitted from the previous arrangement but also all the sugar shipped from Philadelphia.

According to this new arrangement, entered into by members of the Trunk Line Association and the American Sugar Refining Company in April, 1898, the sugar traffic out of New York and Philadelphia was to be divided among the various railroads according to the following percentages:

New York Central (including its West Shore line)	28.81%
Erie	19.01
Pennsylvania	29.59
Baltimore & Ohio	8.00
Lehigh Valley	10.39
Delaware, Lackawanna & Western	4.00
New York, Ontario & Western	2.10
Central of New Jersey	2.80
Central of Vermont (via New London, Conn.)	2.40
Chesapeake & Ohio (via Norfolk, Va.)	2.50

Palmer and Riley, acting for the American Sugar Refining Company, were once again to be responsible for seeing to it that each railroad received its quota of traffic. In return, the American was to receive, through Palmer and Riley, a rebate of two cents on each one hundred pounds of sugar shipped. Previously, the amount of rebate had fluctuated between two and five cents a hundredweight. To avoid an

[44] *Ibid.*, p. 10078.

[45] *Ibid.*, pp. 10078–79. Why the Pennsylvania should have agreed to pay more when it performed its own lighterage is not exactly clear, unless this charge was meant to discourage it from performing that service for itself. In any case, the amount of sugar carried by the Pennsylvania Railroad from New York was never very great; most of its sugar shipments originated from Philadelphia.

open violation of the Interstate Commerce Act, however, the rebate was to be disguised in the form of a payment for cartage.[46]

According to section 3 of the Interstate Commerce Act, it was unlawful for any common carrier to give undue or unreasonable advantage to any person, concern, locality, or class of traffic.[47] While this prohibition on rebates remained largely unenforced until passage of the Elkins Act in 1903,[48] by 1895 the railroads were becoming increasingly concerned that by charging less than the published freight rates they were leaving themselves open to criminal prosecution. It was for this reason that the rebates were, at various times, disguised as "extra lighterage" and as payments for dunnage.[49] Under the new arrangement with the railroads in 1898, however, Palmer and Riley suggested that the rebates on sugar be called an allowance for cartage, even though only 30 per cent of the sugar shipped by rail was ever carted. (The rest was simply put on boats at the refinery and towed across the harbor.)

To further conceal the nature of these payments, Palmer and Riley suggested that the rebates be paid to the account of the Brooklyn Transportation Company, a subsidiary of the American Sugar Refining Company which handled all its cartage arrangements.[50] As Riley later testified, "We told them [the members of the Trunk Line Association] . . . we would undertake to divide the sugar between the roads as nearly as we possibly could based on those percentages, with the understanding that the [published] rates were to be maintained at all times on sugar through the Trunk Line territory, and that we were to be allowed two cents per hundred pounds for cartage or transfer on all the sugar." He was then asked, "Was anything said on the question of whether or not the allowance of two cents was to be the compensation to you for maintaining the percentages?" "That was our view of the matter," he replied; "we would agree to divide the sugar amongst the roads if they would agree to make us the regular allowance year in and year out of two cents a hundred pounds on the sugar

[46] *Ibid.*, pp. 9985–86; see also, 14 ICC Reports 622 (1908). The Trunk Line Association was the equivalent of a steamship conference or a cartel, to which all the trunk-line railroads belonged.

[47] 25 U.S. Stat. 855 (1887).

[48] I. L. Sharfman, *The Interstate Commerce Commission*, 1: 19–37; see also pp. 274 and 277 below.

[49] *United States* v. *American Sugar Refining Co. et al.*, pretrial testimony, 1912, pp. 10065–66, 10145–49. Dunnage was normally the lumber used in the railroad cars to protect sugar barrels from damage. When the American Sugar Refining Company provided its own dunnage, it normally received an allowance on the freight rate.

[50] *Ibid.*, pp. 9978–82.

for cartage, no matter whether it was carted or not."[51] This agreement with the trunk-line railroads was, of course, supplemented by the rebate arrangements with the various connecting roads.

How much all these rebate arrangements were worth to the American Sugar Refining Company cannot be determined. Palmer and Riley deliberately kept their accounts in such a way that it was impossible to distinguish between legitimate refunds from the railroads (such as for damages, overcharges, etc.) and refunds that were, in fact, illegal rebates.[52] But Riley later estimated that the special rates which the American received on its shipments to the Midwest alone represented a savings to the company of approximately $150,000 a year.[53] While this might not appear to be a large sum of money, it should be remembered that the rebates served a strategic purpose which transcended their size alone. For the special rates that the American obtained from the railroads enabled it to quote prices in distant markets which, to a potential competitor, seemed to offer far less of a margin for profit than was in fact the case. The effect was to remove some of the incentive that new firms might otherwise have had to enter the industry. Thus, the true measure of how important the rebates were to the American was less the sums themselves than the extent to which they protected the company from the rise of rival refineries.

::

Rebates were not the only form of preferential treatment which the American Sugar Refining Company received from the railroads. Almost as important was the fact that the railroads provided free storage of sugar at key points throughout the country.[54] According to Riley, the roads "gave [our company] storage here in New York Harbor, and at lake ports, and at other places, wherever we wanted it, and in such quantities as we wanted it. . . . They gave us the room, and we put the sugar in there and ordered it out as we wanted it to be shipped." "Did you pay, or did they collect storage from you?" he was asked. "Storage, no, sir," Riley replied. "The arrangement always definitely provided that free storage should be given." And when the

[51] *Ibid.*, p. 12166.

[52] *Ibid.*, pp. 12276–80.

[53] Midwestern shipments generally involved the areas surrounding Cleveland, Chicago, Milwaukee, and Peoria (*ibid.*, p. 12177).

[54] These key points included, among others, New York harbor, West Albany, Buffalo, Cleveland, Chicago, Detroit, Milwaukee, Duluth, West Superior, Peoria, Norfolk, Newport News, and Toledo (*ibid.*, p. 12169).

railroads' own facilities were already occupied, the sugar was stored in public warehouses at the railroads' expense.[55]

This provision for free storage enabled the American not only to meet the needs of wholesalers quickly and efficiently but also to take advantage of favorable seasonal rates. It could, for example, ship its sugar in the summer when the competition of the canal and lake lines forced down railroad rates, then store the sugar free of charge at the railroads' own warehouses until the winter when the rates were higher.[56] Only the American was afforded this privilege—other companies would have had to pay six cents a barrel in monthly storage charges[57]—and Riley estimated that it saved the company approximately $75,000 a year.[58]

In other ways, too, the American received preferential treatment. Despite a Trunk Line Association resolution to the contrary, the American was permitted to ship less-than-carload lots at the cheaper, full-carload rate. As Riley testified, "We never paid . . . less-than-carload rates."[59] Then, beginning in 1896, the American was permitted to pay only the through rate from New York to local points throughout the Midwest, even though in most cases the sugar was actually being transshipped from some large city nearby, such as Chicago, Cleveland, or Milwaukee. Since the through rate was invariably cheaper than the trunk-line rate plus the local haul, this enabled the American Sugar Refining Company to save additional sums of money.[60]

In implementing these various arrangements with the railroads, Riley worked closely with Osborn, the American's chief salesman. It was important that Osborn know exactly what it cost the American to ship its sugars anywhere in the United States, for it was on the basis of the New York price plus transportation costs that Osborn would quote prices to wholesale grocers throughout the country. For this reason, Riley explained, he and Osborn met almost daily to "go over the reports from our own representatives and from the various brokers, to see what was being done in [the various] markets."[61] When the American found that it was being undercut by some other supplier in a particular area, Osborn would ask Riley if he could possibly obtain a more favorable freight rate from the railroads in order to meet the competition. As Riley later testified, Osborn would come to him

[55] *Ibid.*, pp. 10001–2. [56] *Ibid.*, p. 12187.
[57] *Ibid.*, p. 10181; see also *ibid.*, p. 10229. [58] *Ibid.*, p. 12128.
[59] *Ibid.*, pp. 10133–34. [60] *Ibid.*, pp. 10174–75.
[61] *Ibid.*, pp. 10088–90.

"saying, 'Conditions are such that I cannot sell sugar at the regular prepaid basis, and I want you to get me as low a special rate as you can.' That sort of condition prevailed at all times, you might say. . . . We always had a condition of that kind existing in some particular part of the country, more or less."[62] Most of the time, Riley was able to obtain the special rate.

As a result of this close co-operation between Osborn and Riley, on the one hand, and between the American (represented by these two men) and the railroads on the other, new refineries would have found it extremely difficult to compete with the American in all except nearby markets. But it was not only in selling the final product that potential rivals were placed at a substantial disadvantage. The American was also able to obtain certain of its inputs at less than published prices.

Lowell M. Palmer, who had charge of the terminal facilities that bore his name, was also president of the Brooklyn Cooperage Company, a subsidiary of the American Sugar Refining Company which had been organized by Searles in 1891 to supply the parent company with barrels. Brooklyn Cooperage had inherited as its manufacturing facilities the three barrel factories included in the original consolidation—the factory in Boston previously owned by the Boston Cooperage Company, the one in Brooklyn owned by Havemeyer & Elder, and the one in Jersey City owned by Matthiessen & Wiechers. Palmer himself had been largely responsible for establishing the cooperage plants in Brooklyn and Boston, and in return for his help in bringing the principal Boston refinery into the combination, he had been placed in charge of all three barrel factories when the original trust was formed.[63]

As president of the Brooklyn Cooperage Company, Palmer was able to obtain from the railroads the same type of rate concessions on barrel staves that he was able to obtain on refined sugar. The barrel staves came from timberlands located in Missouri, Arkansas, Ohio, Indiana, and Michigan, among other places, and in return for dividing

[62] *Ibid.*, pp. 12172–73.

[63] This was, of course, three and a half years before the Brooklyn Cooperage Company was organized. Palmer, although the active manager of the Havemeyer & Elder cooperage plant and its nominal owner, actually held no proprietary interest in the enterprise, just as he held no proprietary interest in Palmer's Dock. He did, however, hold a one-third interest in the Boston Cooperage Company, in partnership with the Standard and Continental refineries, and as such received one-third of the $180,000 in cash which the Sugar Refineries Company (i.e., the sugar trust) paid for the Boston Cooperage Company at the time the trust was organized (*ibid.*, pp. 7108–17; Hardwick committee investigation, 1911, pp. 296, 316–23; see also p. 74 above).

the traffic among the railroads according to certain percentages, Palmer's company received a special rebate. "We had general arrangements with the various railroads," Riley testified, "continuing along month after month and year after year for an allowance out of the [published] tariff rate on shipments for cooperage, generally two cents a hundred pounds."[64] The rebate applied not only to shipments made by the Brooklyn Cooperage Company but also to those made by its competitors—for example, the rival cooperage firms that supplied barrels to the Franklin and Spreckels refineries before they were acquired by the American.[65] This arrangement with the railroads meant that no rival refinery could hope to obtain its barrels as cheaply as did the American.

Palmer, as part of his manifold business activities, also dealt in anthracite coal, another important item in sugar refining; here, too, he handled all of the American's purchases.[66] Although in this situation he was dealing with an equally powerful seller—the combination of anthracite-coal carriers—he still was able to obtain a better bargain for all of the American's refineries together than any potential rival could hope to obtain for itself alone.[67]

In addition to the barrier of special advantages enjoyed by the American Sugar Refining Company, there were other, more conventional barriers that any firm hoping to enter the sugar refining industry had to overcome. There was, for example, the relatively high cost of a plant of efficient size, or in more formal terminology, the scale-economies barrier.[68] By 1892 a refinery capable of producing 3,000 barrels of sugar daily (the minimum size for optimum efficiency) could not be built for less than $1.5 million.[69] This was a considerable sum to risk in an industry where one firm already had the capacity to supply 120 per cent of the demand.[70]

Then there was the difficulty of obtaining qualified persons to over-

[64] *United States* v. *American Sugar Refining Co. et al.*, pretrial testimony, 1912, pp. 9939, 9959.

[65] *Ibid.*, pp. 9961–62, 12254–62.

[66] *Ibid.*, p. 7112.

[67] This barrier to the entry of new firms, like all the others cited so far in this chapter, was a reflection of the pecuniary economies of scale discussed in Chapter 5 above (see pp. 102, 107–10). As for the evidence of the American Sugar Refining Company's bargaining power, see the minutes of its executive committee, Hardwick committee investigation, 1911, pp. 2997–3062, esp. p. 2998 (in regard to beer) and p. 3003 (in regard to coal).

[68] This terminology is taken from Joe S. Bain, *Industrial Organization*, pp. 239ff.

[69] U.S. Industrial Commission, *Reports*, 1 pt. 2: 551.

[70] *Ibid.*, p. 107.

see the manufacturing and mercantile ends of the business. Both were specialized activities, and most of those with the necessary skill and experience were connected—either as officers, employees, or stockholders—with the American Sugar Refining Company. This placed the potential new entrant at an absolute cost disadvantage, for it either had to pay large salaries and bonuses to entice the men it needed from the American, or else incur the extra cost that went with inexperienced management. It is not surprising, therefore, that the only new refineries ever built were organized and promoted by persons active in the sugar industry before the trust was formed. But this meant that as time went by and these persons died off, the lack of skilled and experienced sugar men became an even greater barrier to entry.

Finally, there was the inevitable disadvantage that any new firm has in marketing its product against the competition of established brands. This product-differentiation barrier was a formidable one for the potential new entrant into sugar refining, for while sugar was essentially a homogeneous product, the manufacturer of an unknown brand generally found that until he was able to establish a reputation for purity and quality, the only way he could obtain a share of the market was by selling sugar for ⅛–¼ of a cent a pound less than did his rivals.[71]

::

In view of these barriers, particularly the American's special advantages, it would seem that any firm would have found it extremely difficult to enter the sugar refining industry. And, in fact, the three firms that did enter the industry in the years immediately following 1892 were able to survive and prosper only because Henry Havemeyer extended to them the same preferential arrangements which the American enjoyed. All three of these firms—the McCahan refinery in Philadelphia, the Mollenhauer refinery in Brooklyn, and the National refinery in Yonkers—were in one way or another linked to the American in an over-all community of interests.

The Mollenhauers, for example, were related by marriage to the Dicks, one of whom, William Dick, was a director of the American Sugar Refining Company. Members of the Dick family were among the original investors in the Mollenhauer refinery, and William Dick himself held a small interest. This tie to American was made even stronger when, in the fall of 1892, just as their refinery was nearing

[71] Willett & Gray's *Weekly Statistical Sugar Trade Journal*, January 5, 1899.

completion, the Mollenhauers sold 3,000 shares in their company to Charles Senff, Henry and Theodore Havemeyer's cousin and another of the American's directors.[72] Several months later Senff exchanged these shares for stock in the American, and in this way the American came to own an interest in the Mollenhauer refinery which amounted to 30 per cent of the company's outstanding shares.[73] As Frederick Mollenhauer later testified when explaining why the stock was sold to Senff, he and his brother "felt some [larger] interest ought to be associated with us."[74]

It was through the Mollenhauer Sugar Refining Company that the National was tied to the American, for the Mollenhauer and National refineries relied on the same firm of commission merchants—B. H. Howell, Son & Company—to handle their purchases of raw sugar and their sales of refined. James H. Post, one of the senior partners in B. H. Howell, was, in fact, directly responsible for the establishment of both enterprises. It was at his urging that the principals in the two companies decided to undertake the construction of their respective sugar refineries; and in the first few years, when they might have had trouble obtaining credit through normal banking channels, Post saw to it that they were provided, out of B. H. Howell's own funds, with all the working capital they needed.[75]

Post's motives in this respect were not difficult to discern. B. H. Howell, Son & Company had been the commission merchant for a number of small refineries and molasses houses, including Oxnard Brothers, the old Mollenhauer molasses company, and the Delaware Sugar House, but one by one these had all disappeared, either going out of business entirely or being absorbed by the American Sugar Refining Company.[76] If B. H. Howell was to avoid being forced out of business, it would have to find new refineries for which it could act as commission merchant. And so it promoted the formation of the Mollenhauer and National refineries, agreeing to handle all purchases of raw sugar and the sale of refined for a 1 per cent commission.[77]

Having accomplished its primary objective—to retain a foothold in the industry—the B. H. Howell firm had no desire to provoke a price war with the American. Post therefore conducted his mercan-

[72] *United States* v. *American Sugar Refining Co. et al.*, pretrial testimony, 1912, pp. 6479–82.

[73] Hardwick committee investigation, 1911, pp. 193–94.

[74] *United States* v. *American Sugar Refining Co. et al.*, pretrial testimony, 1912, p. 6481.

[75] *Ibid.*, pp. 6160–61, 6170–71.

[76] *Ibid.*, pp. 6151–54.

[77] *Ibid.*, pp. 6160–67.

tile activities in the same spirit of harmony that the Mollenhauers had displayed earlier in selling a 30 per cent interest in their company to Senff. Post was perfectly willing to take as the selling price for refined sugar the price that the American posted outside its offices at 10 A.M. each day, and he deviated from this price only occasionally, when it became imperative to dispose of an excessive accumulation of unsold sugar.[78] To the extent that there was competition between the American and its two rivals in the New York area, it was predominantly non-price in nature—the pitting of one brand against another.[79]

In Philadelphia a similar harmonious relationship existed between the McCahan refinery and the American Sugar Refining Company's principal subsidiary in that city, the Franklin Sugar Refining Company. Soon after the McCahan refinery was built, George Frazier, the Franklin company's chief salesman, met with the owners of the new plant to suggest that they limit their output each month according to the demand, as all the other refineries were then doing. "We told him," William J. McCahan later testified, "we would take it under consideration."[80] Not long after that, McCahan agreed to limit his company's output as requested. Each month Frazier would notify McCahan as to how many pounds of raw sugar he should melt that month; it was then up to McCahan to arrange his production accordingly. Often this presented considerable difficulty. ". . . Sometimes," McCahan was to testify, "they would not tell us the melt for the month until possibly the 20th of the month and we had already melted more sugar than we were entitled to melt for that month, [but] we could not stop our house, because we had to supply our customers. . . ."[81] Thus it was not uncommon for the McCahan refinery to exceed its allotted output.[82] Despite these lapses, however, McCahan was careful to carry on his business in tune with the desires of the American Sugar Refining Company.

To make sure that all the refineries quoted identical prices for re-

[78] U.S. Industrial Commission, *Reports*, 1, pt. 2: 57, 149.

[79] Lexow committee investigation, 1897, p. 317.

[80] *United States* v. *American Sugar Refining Co. et al.*, pretrial testimony, 1912, pp. 7413–19, 7437–39.

[81] *Ibid.*, p. 7422.

[82] In his testimony McCahan hinted that his producing more sugar than he was assigned was a relatively frequent occurrence. He said he followed Frazier's suggestion as to output only "when it suited our convenience. . . . I think very seldom it suited our convenience" (*ibid.*, p. 7440). But McCahan was testifying as a defendant in an antitrust suit and hence was undoubtedly eager to minimize the extent to which he might appear guilty of conspiring to monopolize trade.

fined sugar, especially in the trans-Ohioan regions, Riley agreed to furnish Post and McCahan with the same lists of prepaid freight rates that he made available to the American's own salesmen. ". . . Once in a while," Riley said, explaining why he had met for that purpose with Post, McCahan, Osborn, and Frazier in May, 1895, "some of them would get out and use different rates, so the idea was to get them together, and make an arrangement whereby they would all use the same basis, we to furnish the prepaid figures to all of them. In the case of the Philadelphia refineries, I was to furnish the figures to Mr. Frazier, and he in turn was to see that Mr. McCahan was advised."[83] In this way the American was protected against its smaller rivals' inadvertent or deliberate undercutting of the price of refined sugar.

In return for this co-operative spirit, Henry Havemeyer saw to it that all three smaller refineries enjoyed the same special advantages with respect to the wholesale grocers and the railroads that his own American Sugar Refining Company enjoyed. They were each made parties to the various factor agreements; and grocers were no more penalized for handling their sugars than they would have been for handling the American's own brands.[84] In addition, the three refineries received—through Palmer's office—the same rebates from the railroads that the American received.[85]

Havemeyer chose to live at peace with these independent refineries—rather than try to destroy them through a price war—for several reasons. For one thing, at the time the three smaller refineries were getting started, the American still faced the prospect of prosecution under the Sherman Act, and a concerted campaign to eliminate its smaller rivals would not have helped its case in court. The existence of competition, however feeble, would provide an answer to those critics who charged that the American had a monopoly of the sugar refining business. For another thing, once the independent refineries had established themselves, it would have taken a long and costly battle to drive them from the industry. The American could easily have forced prices below a profitable level, but since it supplied approximately 80 per cent of the market, the resulting losses in revenue would have appeared most prominently on its own ledgers. The

[83] *Ibid.*, pp. 10081–82.

[84] *Ibid.*, pp. 6850, 7001–2, 7007.

[85] *Ibid.*, pp. 12195–96. These special advantages were less important to the McCahan firm than to the other refineries. The McCahan was smaller and its product was marketed primarily in Philadelphia and the nearby surrounding areas.

independent companies could suspend production whenever they wished, and wait for prices to return to a more reasonable level, but the American Sugar Refining Company, as a permanent institution with long-run interests to defend, did not have that option. Under these circumstances, as James Post subsequently pointed out to the U.S. Industrial Commission, it might have required from fifteen to twenty years for American to force the independent firms out of business.[86]

But perhaps the most important reason that Havemeyer chose to live at peace with the three smaller firms was that once they agreed to follow the American's prices, they no longer posed a threat to his company's control of the industry. On the one hand, he could be certain that whatever price the American posted for refined sugar would stand up in the market. On the other hand, he knew that the independent refineries, having eschewed price competition, were not likely to increase their share of the market. While the sugar that these independent companies refined was sugar which the American itself could have produced just as easily—the American was capable of supplying the entire eastern market and then some—this was not a matter which in any way threatened the American Sugar Refining Company's continued existence.

In sum, then, the close working relationship with the three smaller refineries represented a second-best solution with which Havemeyer felt he could live.

Having acquiesced to the entry of the Mollenhauer, National, and McCahan refineries, but having closed the door to all other comers, Havemeyer was for the next several years in firm control of the sugar refining industry. As a matter of policy he sought to maintain an average margin between raw and refined sugar of approximately 7/8 of a cent a pound. And for the years between 1893 and 1898 he was more than successful. The lowest average annual margin during that time was 0.88 of a cent a pound; this occurred in 1894. In 1896 the margin increased slightly to 0.908 of a cent a pound and in the following year the figure was 0.946.[87] As Havemeyer later testified before the U.S. Industrial Commission, the intention was "to keep the prices so low as to defy competition." "As I understand [your] testimony," he was then asked, ". . . you try to hold your prices at a figure that will be profitable to you by reason of your economical methods of concentration, and at the same time at a figure that would not be very profitable

[86] U.S. Industrial Commission, *Reports,* 1, pt. 2: 163.
[87] See Appendix D of this volume.

to others who are not so concentrated?" "Precisely," Havemeyer replied.[88] It was partly because the margin had been 1.035 cents a pound in 1892 and 1.153 cents a pound in 1893 that the Mollenhauers and the parties connected with the National and McCahan firms had been encouraged to erect their refineries. Consequently, Havemeyer had become convinced that 1.0 cent a pound was too high a margin.

Since the American's direct refining costs were only sixty cents a pound,[89] even a margin of ⅞ of a cent left considerable room for profit. From 1892 to 1897 this amounted to approximately $10 million annually, enough to pay a 7 per cent dividend on the American's preferred shares, a 12 per cent dividend on its common stock, and to add approximately $2 million each year to its reserves.[90] By all indications, the consolidation that the American represented seemed to have solved the problem of entry which had once brought ruin to the National Cordage Company. The fact that Wall Street investors so agreed was shown by the price of the American's common stock: by late 1897 it was selling for between 126 and 143 per cent of par.[91] This auspicious state of affairs might have continued indefinitely had not Havemeyer allowed the American to be drawn into a debilitating struggle with a powerful and resourceful customer.

::

Arbuckle & Company was one of Pittsburgh's largest wholesale grocers and an important purchaser of sugar from the American. Through a companion firm, Arbuckle Brothers, owned by the same partners and located in New York, it was also the leading roaster of coffee in the United States. It had reached this position of dominance in large part because of a patent which it held on a special packaging machine. This machine was capable of measuring out sixteen ounces of ground coffee, filling a container with the prescribed quantity, and then sealing the package. Because of the convenience it offered over the normal method of selling coffee in bulk form, this marketing innovation had found ready acceptance among consumers, and by 1892 Arbuckle Brothers accounted for a larger share of the coffee market than its two closest competitors combined. Encouraged by its success in selling coffee in that manner, the company had then adapted the

[88] U.S. Industrial Commission, *Reports*, 1, pt. 2:110, 120.
[89] Hardwick committee investigation, 1911, pp. 1149–51.
[90] Lexow committee investigation, 1897, p. 119.
[91] *Commercial and Financial Chronicle* (Supplement), 65 (December, 1897): 17. These figures were the low and high for November.

same machine for use in packaging sugar, buying the refined product by the barrel from the American and repacking it in two-pound paper containers. This experiment had continued for four years with marked success. From packaging 100 barrels of sugar a week, the business had grown to 250 barrels a week.[92]

Still, the partners in Arbuckle Brothers had found the results, in terms of profit, disappointing. "We . . . found we could not make any money," James N. Jarvie, a member of the firm, later testified, ". . . buying sugar from the refineries and putting it up in that way and then selling again to the wholesale grocers . . ."[93] The trouble was that the American Sugar Refining Company, and with it the National and Mollenhauer refineries, refused to allow Arbuckle Brothers any special discount. It had to buy its refined sugar at the same wholesale price that any ordinary jobber paid, and this made it difficult for the firm to earn a profit on its sales of packaged sugar. The partners in Arbuckle Brothers began to think seriously of building their own refinery.

If the latter were unhappy over their failure to earn a larger profit on the sale of individually packaged sugar, Havemeyer and the other officials of the American Sugar Refining Company were even more unhappy over the inroads that were being made in what they considered to be their own special bailiwick. Determined to put a stop to the business, they threatened not to sell Arbuckle Brothers any more sugar if it continued to package the refined product and resell it under the Arbuckle brand.[94]

Then, in September, 1896, F. O. Matthiessen, one of the American's directors and chairman of its manufacturing committee, paid a visit to John Arbuckle, the senior partner in Arbuckle Brothers. Matthiessen asked Arbuckle if his firm would be willing to sell the patent rights to its packaging machine. In that way, he explained, the source of friction between the two companies would be eliminated. Arbuckle said he would like to discuss the matter with his partners. When Matthiessen returned several days later, "we told him," Arbuckle subsequently recalled, "that we had decided not to sell the machine and that we were going to build a refinery ourselves. . . ." The interview ended with Matthiessen's threat that, if Arbuckle Brothers went into

[92] Hardwick committee investigation, 1911, pp. 1185–86; *United States* v. *American Sugar Refining Co. et al.*, pretrial testimony, 1912, pp. 6916–25; U.S. Industrial Commission, *Reports*, 1, pt. 2: 141.

[93] U.S. Industrial Commission, *Reports*, 1, pt. 2: 141.

[94] *United States* v. *American Sugar Refining Co. et al.*, pretrial testimony, 1912, pp. 6920–23; Hardwick committee investigation, 1911, p. 1187.

sugar refining, the American Sugar Refining Company might well decide to go into coffee roasting.[95]

In the weeks that followed, Havemeyer tried in various ways to persuade the members of Arbuckle Brothers to reconsider their decision. At his suggestion Lowell M. Palmer dropped by to see Jarvie and repeated to him the same warning which Mathiessen had given Arbuckle earlier.[96] In November, Havemeyer himself wrote to Arbuckle, this time in a conciliatory manner. Taking note of the continuing reports that Arbuckle's firm intended to build a sugar refinery, Havemeyer wrote: "Permit me to inquire whether you have any cause of complaint about your business relations with the American Sugar Refining Co. Our wish is, in the conduct of our business, to meet any reasonable requirements on the part of our customers."[97] John Arbuckle replied that it was not unsatisfactory business relations which had led his firm to decide to build a sugar refinery. "Commercial reasons, and prospects of commercial profits have alone controlled our decision," he wrote. "Having large investments in machinery and real estate particularly well adapted and located for the sugar business, we have thought to turn them to profitable account by contracting for the erection of a Refinery."[98]

Those familiar with the market strength and financial power of the two parties were certain they would eventually compromise their differences.[99] It seemed that both had too much to lose to allow a long and bitter struggle to develop. But the truth was that each of the parties felt it had a vital interest to protect. Arbuckle Brothers was persuaded that, if it was ever going to make money on its sugar packaging machine, it had to have a source of refined sugar which it alone controlled. Havemeyer, on the other hand, was convinced that, should Arbuckle Brothers be permitted to enter the sugar refining industry unopposed, not only would his control of the industry be jeopardized, but other firms might be encouraged to follow suit. No matter what it cost, he was determined to prevent either eventuality.

Realizing that warnings alone would not suffice, Havemeyer de-

[95] Lexow committee investigation, 1897, pp. 133–34, 136–37.

[96] *Ibid.*, p. 136.

[97] *United States* v. *American Sugar Refining Co. et al.*, pretrial testimony, 1912, p. 9833.

[98] *Ibid.*, p. 9834.

[99] *New York Times*, December 19, 1896. The American Sugar Refining Company's assets at the time were estimated to be $120 million, including $15 million in cash reserves. (Since Havemeyer refused to issue precise financial statements, no one could be certain of the exact figures.) Arbuckle Brothers was said to be worth $20 million (*ibid.*, December 22, 1896).

cided to translate his threats into positive deeds quickly and decisively. On November 25, 1896, the Executive Committee of the American Sugar Refining Company voted to use one of the abandoned Brooklyn properties as the site for a coffee-roasting plant. At the same time, it voted to set up a special corporation to carry on a coffee business.[100] But these steps were not quick enough for Havemeyer. On his own initiative and with his own funds he went out and purchased a controlling interest in the Woolson Spice Company of Toledo, Ohio, Arbuckle Brothers' leading competitor in the coffee-roasting business.[101] Shortly thereafter, on December 17, the Woolson company announced a one-cent-a-pound reduction in the price of coffee, despite what appeared to be a rising market. In this way Arbuckle Brothers came to discover that its chief rival had been purchased by Havemeyer, and that the president of the American Sugar Refining Company was making good on his threats.[102] When Arbuckle Brothers tried to match the price reduction, the Woolson company simply lowered its price further. As John Arbuckle later remarked, "No matter at what price we might put our coffee they would put a lower price; they intended to drive us out of the market."[103]

But these tactics, instead of deterring Arbuckle Brothers, only made it more determined than ever to press on with its plans. As one member of the firm remarked, after the Woolson Spice Company an-

[100] Hardwick committee investigation, 1911, p. 3009. On February 4, 1897, the American Coffee Company was formally organized under the corporate statutes of New Jersey (*New York Times*, February 5, 1897).

[101] Lexow committee investigation, 1897, pp. 80–81; *United States* v. *American Sugar Refining Co. et al.*, pretrial testimony, 1912, p. 6929. Havemeyer was able to purchase 1,100 shares of the Woolson Company stock, representing 11⁄18 of its outstanding stock, at $1,150 a share. Initially, the holders of this stock had asked $1,500 a share, pointing to the book value of $1,200 a share as well as the company's strong market position. But Havemeyer warned that, if he went ahead and built his own coffee roasting plant, as he planned to do if the Woolson people refused to sell out to him, the resulting price war would greatly reduce the value of the stock. As a result, the majority stockholders agreed to a price of $1,150 a share (*New York Times*, December 21, 1896). Later, when the remaining stockholders in the Woolson Spice Company threatened to sue if they were not also bought out, Havemeyer saw to it that their stock also was purchased (Hardwick committee investigation, 1911, p. 3010). Havemeyer had already had one unpleasant experience with minority stockholders in the case of the Baltimore Sugar Refining Company; see pp. 285–86 below, as well as Hardwick committee investigation, 1911, pp. 3007–12, and *New York Times*, November 26, 1896. It was because of these and other legal difficulties that the Woolson stock was not immediately transferred from Havemeyer to the American Coffee Company, the corporation specifically set up by the American Sugar Refining Company to engage in the coffee business; see note 100 above.

[102] *New York Times*, December 19, 1896.

[103] Lexow committee investigation, 1897, pp. 147–48.

nounced a further price cut, "If they think this price cutting is going to change the decision of Arbuckle Brothers to go into the sugar refining business, they are mistaken."[104] In John Arbuckle, Henry Havemeyer had encountered someone who was just as strong willed, independent of mind, and fiercely competitive as he—and who had the financial resources with which to stand up to him, blow for blow.[105]

::

Initially, Henry Havemeyer had the advantage, for it took Arbuckle Brothers nearly two years to complete its refinery, even working at top speed.[106] During that time Havemeyer was able to inflict heavy financial losses on his opponent, by using the Woolson Spice Company as a weapon. At first Arbuckle Brothers simply allowed the Woolson Spice Company to undercut it by half a cent a pound, preferring to hold its own price at the higher level. Since its market share was ten times greater and its roasting capacity twice that of the Woolson company, this seemed the more advantageous policy.[107] But as the Woolson Spice Company gradually succeeded in capturing a larger and larger share of the packaged-coffee market, Arbuckle Brothers found that it really had no choice but to match its competitor's price, no matter how low that price might be.[108] Eventually roasted coffee sold for only 8.5 cents a pound, leaving virtually no price difference between green coffee and roasted coffee.[109] As a result, Arbuckle Brothers found itself operating at an absolute loss, failing even to cover its average variable costs.[110] Of course, the Woolson Spice Company also operated at a loss, especially since it was more often than not an aggressive price cutter while at the same time spending

[104] *New York Times*, August 29, 1897.

[105] See the sketch of Arbuckle in the *Dictionary of American Biography*, as well as the article in *Cosmopolitan*, 33 (September, 1902): 543.

[106] Willett & Gray's *Weekly Statistical Sugar Trade Journal*, August 25, 1898; Hardwick committee investigation, 1911, p. 1119.

[107] Lexow committee investigation, 1897, p. 155; *New York Times*, December 19, 1896.

[108] *New York Times*, August 29, 1897. Although the facts are not entirely clear, it appears that while Arbuckle Brothers alone controlled a patent for a sugar packaging machine, both it and the Woolson Spice Company controlled patents on coffee packaging machines. Apparently the latter were sufficiently different to be covered by separate patents.

[109] *Ibid.*, February 17, 1898; Hardwick committee investigation, 1911, p. 1147.

[110] *United States* v. *American Sugar Refining Co. et al.*, pretrial testimony, 1912, p. 6946.

heavily on advertising and other forms of sales promotion.[111] But Havemeyer was able to make up for the Woolson losses from his profits in the sugar refining industry, as yet untouched by the war with Arbuckle Brothers.

In the fall of 1898, however, when Arbuckle Brothers finally succeeded in getting its 3,000-barrels-a-day refinery into full-scale production, this state of affairs changed drastically. Arbuckle Brothers began cutting the price of refined sugar, and in the six weeks following the new refinery's opening, the margin between raw and refined sugar fell to 0.41 of a cent a pound, less than half of what it had been before.[112] The war between Havemeyer and Arbuckle entered a new and deadlier phase, for now the two rivals were more evenly matched.

The ensuing competition was made all the more severe when, as Havemeyer had feared, the completion of the Arbuckle refinery was followed by the entry of yet another new firm into the sugar refining industry. Claus Doscher had formerly been one of the principal owners of the Brooklyn Sugar Refining Company. When that company was merged with the other New York refineries to form the sugar trust, Doscher had retired from the industry to become a banker, his oldest son, Henry, remaining in the employ of first the trust and later the American Sugar Refining Company.[113] Early in 1897, however, soon after Arbuckle Brothers announced its intention of building a refinery, Claus Doscher decided to re-enter the sugar refining business.[114] In part he may have been attracted by what he thought was an unusually large margin between raw and refined sugar. In part, too, he probably hoped to provide his several sons with a going business concern, a property which they might one day inherit and which, in the meantime, would provide them with practical experience as independent businessmen. Whatever the reasons, Havemeyer felt betrayed. Calling Henry Doscher, who by then was superintendent of the Havemeyer & Elder refinery, into his office,

[111] Hardwick committee investigation, 1911, p. 1134; *United States* v. *American Sugar Refining Co. et al.*, pretrial testimony, 1912, pp. 6931–48. Later, an accountant for the Justice Department's Bureau of Investigation went over the books of the American Coffee Company and reported that its losses through the end of 1898 were $2,843.31, not counting the $1,200,000.00 which had been paid for the Woolson Spice Company's stock (*ibid.*, p. 7398). There is reason to believe that the American Coffee Company's actual losses were much greater.

[112] *New York Times*, October 6, 1898; Willett & Gray's *Weekly Statistical Sugar Trade Journal*, December 22, 1898.

[113] *United States* v. *American Sugar Refining Co. et al.*, pretrial testimony, 1912, pp. 6621–22.

[114] Willett & Gray's *Weekly Statistical Sugar Trade Journal*, February 18, 1897.

Havemeyer in a fit of anger ordered him off the premises and told him never to set foot on the refinery grounds again.[115]

On March 31, 1897, the New York Sugar Refining Company of Long Island City was incorporated, with the Doscher family controlling two-thirds of the $600,000 in stock issued.[116] Soon thereafter, construction of a refinery capable of producing 3,000 barrels of sugar daily was begun. This refinery was ready for operation in November, 1898, several months after the Arbuckle refinery was completed.[117] While this new entrant served to further aggravate the severe price competition then so much in evidence in the sugar refining industry, the main conflict was still that between Henry O. Havemeyer and the firm of Arbuckle Brothers.

In this conflict, both sides fought with every means they could command. To protect his company's long-standing position within the sugar refining industry, Henry Havemeyer sought to bring to bear the special advantages he enjoyed with respect to the wholesale grocers and the railroads. He warned the wholesale grocers that if they handled either the Arbuckles' or the Doschers' sugar, the price maintenance agreement with his company would be jeopardized.[118]

As a result of this pressure, Arbuckle Brothers had a difficult time finding wholesale grocers willing to handle its sugar. In order to break through this barrier, it was forced to resort to drastic measures. When wholesale grocers refused to carry its brand in Boston, Arbuckle Brothers went over their heads by selling directly to retailers.[119] It then threatened to follow the same tactic if wholesale grocers in the South and Midwest did not open up their channels of distribution to its sugar products. Informed of this maneuver by his competitor, Havemeyer dismissed it as a "bluff," warning that "it is better to meet the competition representing 5 per cent of the output of refined sugars than it is that of 100 per cent."[120] When wholesale grocers in the South went ahead and agreed to handle Arbuckle Brothers' sugar

[115] *United States* v. *American Sugar Refining Co. et al.*, pretrial testimony, 1912, p. 6621.

[116] Willett & Gray's *Weekly Statistical Sugar Trade Journal*, April 1, 1897.

[117] U.S. Industrial Commission, *Reports*, 1, pt. 2: 87–92. The refinery actually cost $1,800,000, not counting working capital.

[118] See, for example, his letters to Francis H. Leggett, Smith & Sills, and William Havemeyer early in 1899, reprinted in *United States* v. *American Sugar Refining Co. et al.*, pretrial testimony, 1912, pp. 7244–52; see also the letter to J. T. Witherspoon, manager of the New Orleans refinery, February 27, 1899, *ibid.*, pp. 9405–6.

[119] Hardwick committee investigation, 1911, p. 1127.

[120] *United States* v. *American Sugar Refining Co. et al.*, pretrial testimony, 1912, pp. 7244–46.

anyway, Havemeyer countered by threatening to have his company open its own retail outlets and thus bypass the grocery trade in that region.[121]

In addition to dealing with retailers directly, Arbuckle Brothers tried offering large discounts to those wholesale grocers who would handle its sugar. Several of the smaller jobbers, finding these discounts attractive, agreed to brave the American Sugar Refining Company's blacklist. To meet this situation, Havemeyer gave permission to the other wholesale grocers to sell below the posted price, even though this tended to subvert the price maintenance agreement.[122] At the same time, he warned that his company would throw cheap sugar on the market to make up for any of its normal sales displaced by either Arbuckle Brothers or the New York Sugar Refining Company. When the wholesale grocers complained that they could not be responsible for what some of the smaller firms did, Havemeyer replied that it was up to them to control the members of their trade or suffer the consequences.[123]

In the meantime, of course, the American Sugar Refining Company continued to receive rebates from the railroads, not only on the sugar that it shipped, but also on the sugar shipped by its new rivals, Arbuckle Brothers and the New York Sugar Refining Company.[124] In addition, to enable the Woolson coffee-roasting plant in Toledo to compete with the Arbuckle Brothers plant in Brooklyn, Havemeyer obtained special rebates on all his company's coffee shipments. On February 10, 1897, the New York Central agreed to make a special allowance of 2.0 cents a hundred pounds on all the Woolson company's green coffee carried west from New York to Toledo and another 2.5 cents on all the roasted coffee carried back east from Toledo to New York. Later, other railroads agreed to make similar allowances. The Woolson company shipped from fifteen to twenty carloads of coffee each day, and the rebates continued until early in 1899 when the American Coffee Company, the subsidiary of the American Sugar Refining Company which had been organized to conduct its coffee business, finally completed its own plant in Brooklyn.[125]

[121] Henry O. Havemeyer to Judson Lounsberry, the American's chief salesman, February 24, 1899, *ibid.*, p. 7249.

[122] Henry O. Havemeyer to William Havemeyer, January 3, 1899, *ibid.*, pp. 7242–43.

[123] Henry O. Havemeyer to J. W. Cooper, October 2, 1900, *ibid.*, p. 9683.

[124] *Ibid.*, pp. 12229–30.

[125] *Ibid.*, pp. 10213–15, 10266; Willett & Gray's *Weekly Statistical Sugar Trade Journal*, March 30, 1899.

In other ways, too, the railroads lent Havemeyer assistance in his battle with John Arbuckle. The western lines, for example, agreed to give a special rebate on shipments to F. Letts, the largest wholesale grocer in the Missouri River valley, an area of particularly intensive competition between the American and Arbuckle Brothers. The rebate enabled the American to sell Letts sugar at a lower figure than the prevailing market price and thereby to obtain his exclusive patronage without giving the appearance of having cut prices to do so.[126] This tactic of tying the largest wholesale grocers to his company through secret rebates was one which Henry Havemeyer frequently followed in his efforts to deny competitors an outlet for their sugar.[127]

But although Havemeyer enjoyed many advantages, he found it impossible to dislodge Arbuckle Brothers from the sugar refining business. For one thing, the Arbuckle refinery was not very large. Its capacity was only 3,000 barrels a day,[128] and a significant portion of this output found a ready market through Arbuckle & Company's own wholesale grocery business in Pittsburgh and the surrounding Ohio valley. Then, too, only Arbuckle Brothers was able to offer sugar in paper containers, and this further assured it of a ready market for its output. In an effort to offset its disadvantage in this respect, the American Sugar Refining Company began selling refined sugar in small cotton bags, at first in five-pound sizes and later in two-pound sizes, but the cotton bags were not as popular as Arbuckle Brothers' paper containers.[129]

With Havemeyer unable to dislodge his chief adversary from the sugar refining industry, the war between the American and Arbuckle Brothers continued unabated. In 1899 the margin between raw and refined sugar fell to ½ of a cent a pound, the lowest it had ever been in the history of sugar refining in the United States.[130] Although the American continued to pay a 7 per cent dividend on its preferred shares and a 12 per cent dividend on its common stock, for the first time since it had been organized it was forced to dip into its reserves to meet those payments.[131] Meanwhile, Arbuckle Brothers privately

[126] *United States* v. *American Sugar Refining Co. et al.*, pretrial testimony, 1912, p. 10267.

[127] See, for example, the testimony of John Arbuckle, Hardwick committee investigation, 1911, pp. 2319–21.

[128] Willett & Gray's *Weekly Statistical Sugar Trade Journal*, October 6, 1898.

[129] *Ibid.*, April 6, 1899.

[130] See Appendix D of this volume.

[131] Hardwick committee investigation, 1911, pp. 1930, 2008.

put its losses in the sugar refining business at $1.25 million.[132] But while both Havemeyer and Arbuckle may have found their war somewhat expensive, it was the older and smaller independent refineries which suffered most severely.

Stuck with plants that were somewhat more costly to operate, the Mollenhauer and National refineries found it increasingly difficult to meet the competition. Quite often, James Post later said, sugar was sold "at less than cost, and the loss in refining at times was quite large." In 1899 the National finally decided to shut down completely, while the Mollenhauer firm was forced to cut back its production to only a fraction of what it had been.[133]

::

For James Post and the firm of B. H. Howell, Son & Company, this decline in the business of the two older independent firms was a matter of great concern, for it directly affected their own profits as well. At first, Post tried to obtain an agreement among the various refiners to limit production, especially during the winter months when the competition was the most severe, but these efforts failed.[134] Then Post began to explore the possibility of a consolidation, one that would bring together all the independent refineries in one large company. The idea for such a consolidation had first been suggested by Joseph A. Auerbach, a Wall Street lawyer active in organizing mergers in several other industries, but it was Post who now carried the idea forward. "The first negotiations," Post later testified, "were with Mr. Mollenhauer and the owners of the National, and very probably with Mr. Doscher who lived next door to me . . . [for] we often met and talked about conditions [in the sugar refining industry]." Doscher's New York Sugar Refining Company, although it too was losing money, was not in the same desperate straits as the Mollenhauer and National refineries, "and it took him [Doscher] some time to get into a mood to discuss the plans of consolidation."[135]

Post was convinced that a merger of the three companies—the Mollenhauer, the National, and the New York—would offer considerable advantages to all concerned. "I knew," he subsequently said, "that the consolidation of three important refineries into one company would greatly economize the conducting of the business in many

[132] *Ibid.*, p. 1131.

[133] *United States* v. *American Sugar Refining Co. et al.*, pretrial testimony, 1912, p. 6570.

[134] *Ibid.*, p. 6547.

[135] *Ibid.*, pp. 6191–94, 6606–8.

ways . . . that the buying and selling . . . by one group of men could not help but save the company a great deal of money. . . ."[136] But Post also knew that the new company's chances of success would be much greater if the president of the American Sugar Refining Company could be persuaded to take an active role in its formation. With Henry Havemeyer personally involved, the new company would almost certainly start off on friendly terms with the American—and thus stand a better chance of earning a dividend.[137]

For this reason Post approached Havemeyer early in 1900 and asked if he would be interested in helping to arrange a consolidation of the independent refineries. Havemeyer said no, he was not interested. Nevertheless, Post persisted in his efforts to bring about a merger of the Mollenhauer, National, and New York refineries, and finally succeeded in obtaining options to purchase the stock of all three companies. Then, late in April, when it appeared that the consolidation would take place even without his help, Havemeyer agreed to take a role in the negotiations. Soon the president of the American Sugar Refining Company was actually calling the shots, Post having readily given way to his leadership.[138]

Under Havemeyer's direction, the details of the consolidation scheme were speedily concluded. A new corporation, the National Sugar Refining Company of New Jersey, was to be organized with $10 million in 6 per cent preferred stock. This preferred stock was then to be exchanged for the outstanding shares in the three refineries. (When the owners of the refineries were unable to agree on the division of the preferred shares among their respective interests, it was Havemeyer who intervened to settle the matter.) In addition to the preferred shares, a certain amount of common stock was to be issued. How much was not immediately decided, but whatever the amount, it was to go almost entirely to Havemeyer. In this way, his interests—and those of the company that he headed—were to be inextricably linked to the interests of the preferred shareholders, for ownership of the common stock would give Havemeyer absolute control over the new company's affairs, thereby enabling him to determine the conduct of its operations. But Havemeyer would be able to exercise this control only as long as the new company continued to pay its preferred shareholders the dividends guaranteed them. If the company failed to pay those dividends, control would revert to the original refinery owners.[139]

[136] *Ibid.*, p. 6223. [137] *Ibid.*, pp. 6224, 6403, 6815.
[138] *Ibid.*, pp. 6194–6200. [139] *Ibid.*, pp. 6202, 6235.

Individual agreements embodying these provisions were drawn up by John E. Parsons and signed by all parties concerned—except Havemeyer himself—on May 28, 1900.[140] Five days later, on June 2, the National Sugar Refining Company of New Jersey was formally organized, and its preferred shares were exchanged for the stock in the three refineries.[141] By this time it had been decided that, in addition to the $10 million in preferred stock, $10 million in common stock would be issued. At the moment it seemed a point of minor consequence, since the common stock was intended merely to give Havemeyer control over the company. It was not expected that dividends would be paid on the stock, and, in fact, Havemeyer never even took the trouble to exercise his stock warrants.[142]

Immediately after the National Sugar Refining Company's formation, Post was able to bring another refinery into the consolidation—at least partially. Following the agreements of May 28, he had turned his attention to the McCahan refinery in Philadelphia, hoping to interest its owner in his merger scheme. McCahan proved unreceptive to the suggestion, however, and though Post continued to press him to change his mind, it appeared that the McCahan refinery would remain outside the new company. Then, on the day after the National was formally organized, McCahan let it be known that he was willing to sell a quarter interest in his refinery. While this would not give the National control of the McCahan refinery, it would at least establish a closer working arrangement between the two companies. Post informed Havemeyer of McCahan's limited concession, and Havemeyer told him to proceed with the purchase. Thus the National Sugar Refining Company started out with a full interest in three previously independent refineries and a quarter interest in still another.[143]

As the owner of 3,000 shares in the Mollenhauer refinery, the American Sugar Refining Company automatically became a preferred stockholder in the National Sugar Refining Company. In addition, Havemeyer had agreed to buy back, from those who wished to sell, a

[140] *Ibid.*, p. 6199.

[141] *Ibid.*, p. 6244. As far as can be ascertained, the owners of the New York refinery received $3,125,000 in preferred stock, the owners of the National, $2,250,000 in preferred stock, and the owners of the Mollenhauer, $2,875,000 in preferred stock for their respective properties (*ibid.*, pp. 6608, 6648).

[142] *Ibid.*, pp. 6235, 6282–86. Stock warrants are certificates which indicate that the persons named in them are entitled to a stated number of shares in a company.

[143] *Ibid.*, pp. 6537–40. The National paid $1,470,000 for 5,000 shares in the McCahan refinery, or $294 a share (*ibid.*, pp. 6543–44). This increased the amount of preferred shares issued by the National to $9,720,000. The remaining $280,000 in preferred stock was then sold at par to the general public and the money most probably was used for working capital (*ibid.*, pp. 6553–54).

limited amount of preferred shares in the new company. Several of the stockholders in the original refineries decided to accept Havemeyer's offer, and Havemeyer in turn arranged for his own company to put up the money. In this way the American, as distinct from Havemeyer personally, came to own 12 per cent of the preferred stock in the National Sugar Refining Company soon after it was organized.[144] Through subsequent purchases this share was increased to slightly more than 50 per cent.[145]

At Havemeyer's insistence, three of the directors originally elected by the National Sugar Refining Company's preferred stockholders were replaced by directors of Havemeyer's choosing, namely, by three of the American's directors.[146] Moreover, Havemeyer had Post report to him each month the amount of sugar melted by the National. From time to time the two men would also meet to discuss market conditions. Post later denied that Havemeyer ever gave specific instructions for National to reduce its output, but the fact was that through these meetings Havemeyer was able to regulate the supply of refined sugar to the over-all demand.[147]

To the outside world, the National Sugar Refining Company was simply following the price posted by its larger competitor each morning, just as its predecessors had done before 1898. Occasionally there would be complaints from the American's salesmen that the National was undercutting the price of refined sugar, but actual incidents of that sort occurred infrequently, and when they did occur they were quickly dealt with through a meeting between Havemeyer and Post.[148] In return, Havemeyer saw to it that the National earned the required dividend on its preferred stock. All the special advantages that the American enjoyed were made available to the National, and those types of sugar which the National did not have the machinery to produce were supplied to it by the American at from five to ten points below the market price.[149]

[144] *Ibid.*, pp. 6211–13. In the case of the purchase of the Woolson Spice Company's stock, as well as in other such incidents, it was difficult to distinguish between those actions taken by Havemeyer as president of the American Sugar Refining Company and those taken by him as an individual. Havemeyer himself was not always careful about the distinction, and in the case of the National Sugar Refining Company stock, this carelessness was to lead to a troublesome law suit (see pp. 310–11 below).

[145] See p. 311 below.

[146] *United States* v. *American Sugar Refining Co. et al.*, pretrial testimony, 1911, pp. 6562–63. These three were Carl Meyer, Arthur Donner, and George H. Frazier.

[147] *Ibid.*, pp. 6586, 6594.

[148] *Ibid.*, pp. 6586, 6591–92.

[149] *Ibid.*, pp. 6596–97, 6849–50, 6864–66.

It was the same community of interests which had existed before 1898, but it was now more tightly drawn together. As a matter of fact, the American Sugar Refining Company had come as close to absorbing its smaller competitors as it could without purchasing them outright. It had brought three (and part of a fourth) previously independent refineries under a single management, making them not only better able to survive in the face of outside competition but also more susceptible to the American's control. Yet, because the National Sugar Refining Company retained the façade of a separate enterprise, the American escaped the public criticism that surely would have come its way had it been known that, through its president, it actually controlled its largest competitor, one capable of supplying 10 per cent of the refined sugar in the United States.[150]

By helping to organize the National Sugar Refining Company, Henry Havemeyer succeeded in eliminating a troublesome competitor, who was personally objectionable to him. As George Bunker later explained, one of the purposes of the consolidation was to neutralize the effect of Claus Doscher on the industry. "He was the newest refiner," Bunker said; "he was cutting prices in order to get business, and consequently with him eliminated, competition with the whole trade was largely eliminated."[151] Once the National was organized, Doscher and his sons were forced to retire from the industry. The Mollenhauers were given management of the New York refinery, while their own plant in Brooklyn was shut down and used thereafter only as a reserve facility.[152]

::

Shortly after the National Sugar Refining Company was organized, the price war between the American Sugar Refining Company and Arbuckle Brothers ended. Perhaps Havemeyer now realized that he could not drive Arbuckle Brothers from the industry. Perhaps, too, he was eager for a respite in order to replenish the American's nearly depleted treasury. In any case, the severe competition between the two parties ceased.[153] This easing of the rivalry in sugar refining coincided with a similar easing of the rivalry in the coffee business.[154]

[150] *Ibid.*, p. 6434.

[151] *Ibid.*, pp. 6384–88; see also the corroborating statement of Frederick Mollenhauer, *ibid.*, pp. 6503–4.

[152] *Ibid.*, p. 6820.

[153] Willett & Gray's *Weekly Statistical Sugar Trade Journal*, June 7 and 14, 1900.

[154] *Ibid.*, June 14, 1900.

The precise means by which the price wars were brought to a halt is not known. What probably happened, as Henry O. Havemeyer, Jr., has suggested,[155] was that his father and John Arbuckle simply agreed to call an end to their destructive price war, but fearing prosecution under the Sherman Act,[156] they must have decided merely to enter into an informal understanding, especially since a written agreement would not have been enforceable anyway. Such a loose arrangement, however, seems to have led to misunderstanding and conflict, with Havemeyer insisting that all refineries share equally in any reduction of output made necessary by seasonal fluctuations, and Arbuckle in turn insisting that his refinery be allowed to operate at full capacity. After a brief period during which Havemeyer and Arbuckle each tried to impose his will on the other through market pressure—in a manner reminiscent of classical Cournot and Edgeworth duopoly behavior—a compromise seems to have been worked out. The Arbuckle refinery began reducing its output during the winter slack months, but not to the same extent that the American did.[157]

However uncertain the means by which the price war was brought to an end, the results were clear enough: control over sugar prices was once more established. Although Havemeyer had not been entirely successful in his efforts to prevent the entry of new competitors, he had at least demonstrated that any group invading the sugar refining industry would have to be prepared to face substantial losses. This in itself had a certain deterrent value and reinforced the barriers already in existence. Moreover, Havemeyer's American Sugar Refining Company still retained its dominant position within the industry. Although it could no longer impose its policies at will, it could usually count on Arbuckle Brothers to follow the moves that it, as price leader, initiated. In effect, the American Sugar Refining Company and Arbuckle Brothers had learned to behave in the interdependent manner typical of oligopolistic firms, with the American, of course, *primus inter pares*. If this represented less than the full control Havemeyer had once exercised as the head of a monopolistic enterprise, it was at least a tolerable substitute.

Thus it was that after June, 1900, following Havemeyer's design, the margin between raw and refined sugar returned to the level that had prevailed before the price war with Arbuckle Brothers, averaging

[155] Henry O. Havemeyer, Jr., *Biographical Record of the Havemeyer Family, 1606–1943*, p. 69.

[156] Hardwick committee investigation, 1911, p. 2311.

[157] Willett & Gray's *Weekly Statistical Sugar Trade Journal*, October 4, 1900, and January 2, 1902.

approximately 9/10 of a cent a pound for the last six months of that year. In 1901 the margin rose even higher, averaging slightly more than one cent a pound for the first time in eight years.[158] Havemeyer's policy, however, proved a mistake, for the large margin encouraged the entry of still another new refinery, this one built by Claus Spreckels, Jr., under the name of the Federal Sugar Refining Company of Yonkers.[159] While it was only a small refinery, capable of producing no more than 3,000 barrels daily, Havemeyer realized that he had miscalculated; thereafter he saw to it that the margin was held somewhat lower.

Before the new century was a year old, then, the sugar refining industry had evolved from monopoly into oligopoly—even though one firm, the American, was still clearly dominant. The change occurred because a firm with a strong position in another industry and a marketing innovation which it wished to exploit more fully was able to breach the barriers to entry which Havemeyer had so carefully erected. This, in turn, persuaded Havemeyer to sponsor the consolidation of the various firms that had managed to survive at the fringe of the industry, a sponsorship which made it easier for him to control them. Thus it was a unique set of circumstances which made possible the emergence of two powerful rivals to the American, not any general breakdown of the barriers to entry. The building of the Federal refinery merely demonstrated that the barriers were not absolute. On the other hand, while Havemeyer originally had been convinced that nothing less than virtual monopoly would suffice to give his company the necessary freedom from price competition, he gradually had come to learn—as the moving spirits behind other consolidations would also come to learn—that he could live with an oligopolistic situation in which his firm was the recognized price setter. This educational process was itself an important development, for it meant that monopoly no longer had to be the minimum goal.

Yet, despite the period of price stability which Havemeyer's acceptance of oligopoly ushered in, the American Sugar Refining Company found its share of the national market continuing to shrink.[160] Only in part was this due to the enlargement of the Arbuckle refinery and the entry of the Federal. Far more important was the sudden emergence of a new source of supply, the sugar beet. It was to this threat that Havemeyer turned his attention, late in 1901.

[158] See Appendix D of this volume.

[159] Willett & Gray's *Weekly Statistical Sugar Trade Journal*, June 5 and July 3 and 10, 1902.

[160] See Appendix E of this volume.

9 :: THE EXERCISE OF CONTROL

THE control over prices achieved by consolidation could just as easily have been jeopardized by the emergence of a substitute product as by the entry of new firms into the industry itself. The only protection against this first danger was entrepreneurial vigilance and resourcefulness, two traits Henry Havemeyer displayed in abundance in meeting the challenge which arose from sugar beets. By judiciously supplying critically needed capital funds—approximately half the amount invested in sugar beet factories—Havemeyer and the American Sugar Refining Company were able to turn what might have been an antagonistic interest into a docile appendage of their own industrial empire. This feat, in turn, made possible their continued exercise of effective control over domestic sugar prices. Through the leverage that their 70 per cent interest in all domestic beet factories and their 90 per cent control of the sugarcane market provided, Havemeyer and the American were able to perform the delicate task of adjusting supply to demand in numerous local markets simultaneously, and in this way see to it that the prices set by the American were the prices that prevailed throughout the United States.

::

". . . In capitalist reality, as distinguished from its textbook picture," Joseph Schumpeter has written,

> it is not the competition [between firms in the same industry] which counts but the competition from the new commodity, the new technology, the new source of supply, the new type of organization. . . . This kind of competition is . . . so much more important that it becomes a matter of comparative indifference whether competition in the ordinary sense [exists. For the other type of competition] revolutionizes the economic structure *from within*, incessantly destroying the old one, incessantly creating a new one. This process of Creative Destruction is the essential fact about capitalism. It is what capitalism consists of and what every capitalist concern has got to live with.[1]

[1] Joseph Schumpeter, *Capitalism, Socialism and Democracy*, pp. 84–85, 83.

So it was for Henry Havemeyer in 1901, for in that year his control of the sugar refining industry was threatened by the development of a new source of sugar, the sugar beet.

Although sugar beets had been grown successfully in Europe since the Napoleonic Wars, efforts to transplant the crop to the soil, climate, and economic milieu of the United States were for many years unsuccessful. Despite bounties offered by many of the individual states, one after another of the early efforts to grow sugar beets failed.[2] In part, this failure reflected the inability of Americans to develop the technical skill that the cultivation and processing of sugar beets required. But equally important was the fact that sugar cane could be obtained more cheaply from the world's tropical islands. Beginning in the late 1880's, however, these two obstacles to the development of a native sugar beet industry were gradually overcome.

In 1887, Claus Spreckels, Sr., made one of his frequent trips to Europe, this time on his doctor's advice to get away from business pressures. However, the energetic Mr. Spreckels was not one to let time pass idly and he used the occasion to catch up on the latest developments in the sugar beet industry of his native Germany. On earlier visits he had made similar studies, but now he became convinced for the first time that the crop might profitably be introduced into the United States. Returning to California, he made preparations to erect a beet sugar factory at Watsonville, in the Pajaro Valley, using machinery imported from Germany. At the same time, he encouraged the farmers in the surrounding area to grow sugar beets, offering practical advice as to the best methods of cultivation. The Watsonville factory, completed in 1888, was an immediate success, processing three million pounds of sugar in its first season of operation.[3]

In 1887 Henry T. Oxnard also made a trip to Europe. Unlike his brothers, Robert and James, he had decided not to remain an employee of the sugar trust after the family refinery was sold.[4] While in Europe he investigated various aspects of the beet sugar industry, even working for a short time in one of the factories to gain firsthand practical experience. On his return to the United States a year later he organized the Oxnard Sugar Refining Company, with his two brothers and the Cutting family of New York as principal stockholders. Attracted by the bounties that Nebraska then offered, the

[2] Roy G. Blakey, *The United States Beet-Sugar Industry and the Tariff*, pp. 14–34; William W. Cordray, "Claus Spreckels of California," pp. 101–2.

[3] Cordray, "Claus Spreckels of California," pp. 104–8.

[4] A fourth brother, Benjamin, purchased a sugar plantation in Louisiana.

MAP 2. Beet Factory Sites in California, 1907

new company decided to build a beet factory in that state at Grand Island. When this first plant was completed, two other factories were constructed, one at Norfolk, Nebraska, and the other at Chino, California. Like the Spreckels plant at Watsonville, all three factories proved successful from a technical standpoint.[5]

While the Spreckels and Oxnard ventures demonstrated that sugar beets could be grown satisfactorily in the United States, large-scale expansion of the industry was still hindered by the fact that sugar cane could be imported more cheaply from other parts of the world. In 1890 Congress unwittingly acted to offset this disadvantage. As part of the Republican party's maneuvering to devise a tariff that would protect American industry without producing an uncomfortably large revenue surplus, members of that party in Congress eliminated the duty on raw sugar and substituted instead a bounty of two cents a pound on sugar produced in this country. Although it was intended primarily to protect the sugar-cane growers of Louisiana, this bounty also had the effect of stimulating the domestic sugar beet industry.

In 1895 the Democrats eliminated the bounty provision in the tariff, but three years later, with the Republicans again in control of Congress, passage of the Dingley tariff, with its 1.35- to-1.685-cents-a-pound duty on imported raw sugar, again gave the domestic sugar beet industry the protection it needed.[6] Given this stimulus, beet factories were constructed on a large scale for the first time in Michigan, Colorado, Utah, and California, among other states. The output of these factories increased steadily until by 1899 they were producing 3.1 per cent of all sugar consumed in the United States. What was significant, however, was not the figure itself but rather the rate at which it was growing, for by 1901 the sugar beet's share of the domestic market had increased by another 50 per cent, to 4.7 per cent of all sugar consumed in the United States.[7] If this fact were not enough to force Henry Havemeyer to take precautionary measures, the news which Wallace Willett brought him in the fall of 1901 was.

Since the passage of the Dingley tariff, Willett had used the pages of his *Weekly Statistical Sugar Trade Journal* to promote and proclaim the advantages of sugar beet cultivation. Extensive articles were published on how to grow the crop, and each new development in the

[5] Hardwick committee investigation, 1911, pp. 372–77.

[6] Blakey, *The United States Beet-Sugar Industry*, pp. 35–38; Hardwick committee investigation, 1911, p. 176. The 1.35-cent figure is based on the 40 per cent ad valorem duty of 3.378 cents a pound applied to the average price of raw sugar during the three years (30 U.S. Stat. 151 [July 21, 1897]).

[7] See Appendix E of this volume.

industry was duly heralded. As a result, Willett had become known as one of the most knowledgeable men on the subject in the United States. One day in October, 1901, he went to see Lowell M. Palmer, by then one of the directors of the American Sugar Refining Company and still a close confidant of Havemeyer—to the extent that Havemeyer had close confidants. Having recently returned from a trip through the West during which he had visited various sugar beet factories, Willett was able to tell Palmer of the latest developments in that industry. "He told me," Palmer later recalled, "that the [beet] companies were making sugar [for between 3¾ and 4 cents a pound,] less than we had supposed they could make it at; and that he thought it would be a wise thing for us to have an investment in those companies."[8]

Realizing that Havemeyer would probably want to hear this news from Willett himself, Palmer arranged for a meeting between the two men. Havemeyer listened with interest to what Willett had to say, for sugar beets were providing ever-increasing competition for the American Sugar Refining Company's own cane products, especially in the various Midwestern markets.[9] For this reason, Havemeyer and the other officers of the American had been giving serious consideration to entering the beet sugar field themselves. They had hesitated to commit themselves only because of doubts as to the essential soundness of such an investment. These doubts, however, were at last removed by the news which Willett now brought Havemeyer. When the editor of the *Weekly Statistical Sugar Trade Journal* was finished, Havemeyer said: "Mr. Willett, we have decided to go into the beet sugar industry. What are the best States and who are the best people?"[10]

In reply to Havemeyer's question Willett said that "Colorado was a good State for sunshine, but that it could not control its farmers as well as Utah. . . ." The latter state was particularly attractive, Willett said, not only because "the Mormons could control their people," but also because the factory at Lehi was run by a man named Thomas R. Cutler, who had succeeded in growing beets for the lowest cost yet, 3¾ cents a pound. "Go out and see him," Havemeyer told Willett. He then added, "You understand, Mr. Willett, that this is not the American Sugar Refining Company, but you can say it is parties interested in that company, and that they wish to purchase one half, [though] not

[8] Hardwick committee investigation, 1911, p. 329.
[9] See pp. 244–45 below.
[10] *United States* v. *American Sugar Refining Co. et al.*, pretrial testimony, 1912, p. 4693.

exceeding one half, the stock of beet sugar factories, and that they are also ready to join in building other beet sugar factories. . . ."[11]

: :

It was largely due to Cutler's efforts that the Mormons, after a number of failures, were finally able to establish a viable sugar beet industry in Utah.[12] A merchant aware of the high price of sugar in his home town of Lehi, Cutler had traveled to France and Germany in 1891 to study the most advanced methods of beet cultivation and processing. Upon his return to this country he had helped reorganize the floundering Utah Sugar Company and had then directed the construction of a new beet factory in Lehi.[13] Once some initial financial difficulties were overcome—with the strategic intervention of the Mormon church—the company prospered. Its shares, at one time worth only 50 cents on the dollar, were selling for considerably above par when, in November, 1901, Cutler was unexpectedly visited by the editor of the *Weekly Statistical Sugar Trade Journal.* Willett conveyed to Cutler the message he had been told to deliver, that certain "parties" in New York "had made up their minds to go into the beet sugar business if they could get into it, [that] they believed it was going to grow, and [that] they would like to invest money in it. . . ." Specifically, Willett said, the persons he represented wished to obtain a half interest in the Utah Sugar Company and any other beet factories that might be built, provided they were sound investments. When Cutler seemed interested, Willett suggested that he travel to New York and discuss the matter further with the "parties" themselves.[14] Although Willett did not identify these "parties," Cutler suspected that they were connected with the American Sugar Refining Company.[15]

As far as Cutler was concerned, Willett's message was virtually an answer to a prayer. As the Utah sugar man later testified, "I had been in New York hunting capital for years"—though always without success.[16] After consulting with his fellow directors and certain of the large stockholders in the Utah Sugar Company, Cutler agreed to

[11] *Ibid.*

[12] Hardwick committee investigation, 1911, pp. 765–87.

[13] See the sketch of Cutler in the *National Cyclopedia of American Biography.*

[14] *United States* v. *American Sugar Refining Co. et al.*, pretrial testimony, 1912, pp. 2228–29.

[15] Hardwick committee investigation, 1911, p. 820.

[16] *Ibid.*, pp. 773–74; *United States* v. *American Sugar Refining Co. et al.*, pretrial testimony, 1912, pp. 2244–45.

make the trip east. It was only after he had actually boarded the train for New York that Willett told him who it was that he represented.[17]

Thus it was that late in November Cutler found himself in Henry O. Havemeyer's office on Wall Street. The president of the American Sugar Refining Company confirmed what Willett had already said, that the American had a surplus of capital and intended to enter the beet sugar industry. "We have heard of you, Mr. Cutler," Havemeyer said, "and have heard, also, that you have been fairly successful in building up the beet sugar industry in Utah, and I have sent for you to know if you would take hold and help us establish the industry in any good location in the United States."[18]

"I told him," Cutler subsequently testified, "that I was not at liberty to accept a position of that sort; that my position was with my people, my home was in Utah; but that I wanted capital, my company wanted capital, and if he would entertain a proposition to supply us with one-half the capital that we required at any time, I would then agree to act in concert with him. . . ." As a beginning, Cutler said he would try to arrange for the American Sugar Refining Company to obtain a half interest in the Utah Sugar Company.[19]

The new alliance was formally sealed on March 2, 1902, when the American Sugar Refining Company acquired 74,000 shares in the Utah Sugar Company, half of its outstanding stock, for $18.00 a share. This was $8.00 a share more than the par value, but Havemeyer's own audit had confirmed that the stock was worth the price.[20] Assured now of adequate capital backing, Cutler was ready to proceed with his plans for expanding the beet sugar industry in Utah and nearby Idaho. Communities throughout those Mormon areas had long been clamoring for sugar beet factories, and Cutler was now in a position to supply them.[21]

The Utah Sugar Company had previously taken over a bankrupt irrigation company near Garland, Utah, hoping eventually to develop the surrounding area as a beet sugar center. Now, with Havemeyer's support, Cutler was able to move ahead with that project. The irrigation company's drainage systems were repaired and work on a beet factory was begun, the latter being finished in time for the 1903 sugar

[17] *United States* v. *American Sugar Refining Co. et al.*, pretrial testimony, 1912, pp. 2230–31.

[18] Hardwick committee investigation, 1911, pp. 773–74.

[19] *Ibid.*

[20] *Ibid.*, pp. 774–76; *United States* v. *American Sugar Refining Co. et al.*, pretrial testimony, 1912, p. 2235.

[21] *United States* v. *American Sugar Refining Co. et al.*, pretrial testimony, 1912, pp. 2612–13.

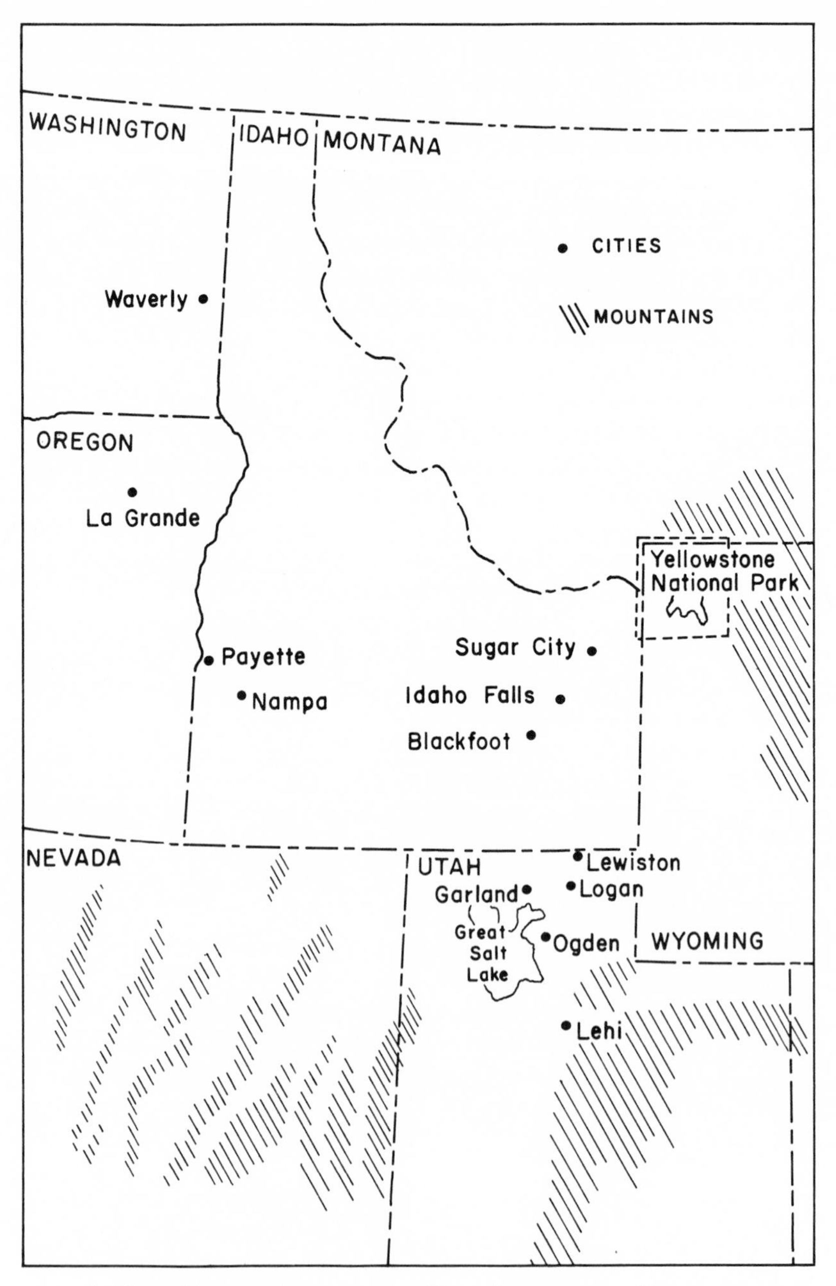

MAP 3. BEET FACTORY SITES IN THE UTAH-IDAHO AREA (INTERMOUNTAIN REGION), 1907

beet season.[22] (Sugar beets were generally harvested in the fall just before the first frost.)

Meanwhile, a new company had been organized, the Idaho Sugar Company, to construct a beet factory near Idaho Falls. This third plant also was completed in time for the 1903 season.[23] In successive years other companies were organized and other beet factories constructed, the Fremont Sugar Company's plant at Sugar City, Idaho, being completed in time for the 1904 season and the Western Idaho Sugar Company's plant at Nampa opening in time for the 1905 season. As he had promised, Havemeyer saw to it that the American Sugar Refining Company purchased a half interest in each of these enterprises.[24]

As vice president and general manager of all four companies,[25] Cutler sought to encourage orderly expansion of the industry in the Utah-Idaho area. Before a beet factory was even considered for a particular locality, an agricultural agent from one of Cutler's companies would survey the soil, water, and climatic conditions to make sure they were suitable. Even then, before the factory was built, the farmers in that locale had to demonstrate that they were capable of growing a sufficient number of beets.

At the same time, Cutler sought to prevent other groups from invading his companies' territory with beet factories of their own. While some of the sugar which Cutler's companies produced had to find an outlet in Colorado and the Missouri River valley, the primary market was at home in the intermountain region. It was in this market that Cutler's companies actually earned their dividends, and he did not want competition from other beet factories to force up the price his own companies had to pay for their sugar beets or force down the price they were able to command for their processed

[22] Hardwick committee investigation, 1911, pp. 775–76; *United States* v. *American Sugar Refining Co. et al.*, pretrial testimony, 1912, pp. 2308–10. A new company, the Utah Sugar Company, was organized to take over the properties of both the beet factory and the irrigation company. To calm fears that the American's purchase of half interest might lead to the loss of local control, Havemeyer agreed to allow the directors of the new company to serve for a term of five years. He also agreed to the appointment of Joseph Smith, president of the Mormon church, as the seventh member of the board of directors. This gave the Utah interests four of the seven votes on the board and thus assured them of control for at least five years (*ibid.*, pp. 2276, 2302–5).

[23] Hardwick committee investigation, 1911, p. 771; *United States* v. *American Sugar Refining Co. et al.*, pretrial testimony, 1912, pp. 2310–30.

[24] Hardwick committee investigation, 1911, pp. 775–82.

[25] *Ibid.*, p. 771. Smith was nominally president of the various companies; see *United States* v. *American Sugar Refining Co. et al.*, pretrial testimony, 1912, p. 2443.

sugar.[26] By a combination of persuasive reasoning and forceful action, Cutler was notably successful in accomplishing both his aims. In 1903, for example, when an enterprising egg merchant from Utah sought to promote a beet sugar factory in Blackfoot, Idaho, only 25 miles from Idaho Falls, Cutler was able to convince him to abandon the attempt and join as a major stockholder in the Idaho Falls company.[27] Then, several years later, when the citizens of San Pete and Sevier counties, Utah, seemed on the verge of inviting an outside party to build a beet factory in their area after being turned down by Cutler, the latter was able to take over the project himself by promising to build a beet factory within a year's time. In fact, the San Pete and Sevier Sugar Company, organized in 1905, became the fifth member of the Cutler group of companies.[28] By similar strategic moves, Cutler was able to forestall the building of several other projected beet factories.[29]

In only one instance did he fail to head off an invasion of his own companies' territory. In 1904 a group of Binghamton, New York, businessmen agreed to move a beet factory from their own city where it had proved unsuccessful to Blackfoot, Idaho, provided the citizens of Blackfoot raised $100,000 locally for the project and guaranteed the availability of 3,000 acres of beets. Although Cutler tried to dissuade the townspeople from going through with the arrangement, they refused to heed his warnings. Thus the Snake River Valley Sugar Company, Limited, was organized and the New York beet factory was relocated in Blackfoot independently of Cutler and the American Sugar Refining Company. It was not long, however, before Cutler succeeded in gaining control of the company anyway. By threatening to build a competing factory in Blackfoot, he was able to persuade a majority of the Snake River company's stockholders to sell out their holdings, especially when he offered to buy the stock at slightly better than par. In this way, even the Snake River enterprise came to be included among the Cutler companies.[30]

Cutler's success in preventing outside groups from gaining a foothold in the Utah-Idaho region may well have been due, as some per-

[26] *United States* v. *American Sugar Refining Co. et al.*, pretrial testimony, 1912, pp. 2400–402; Hardwick committee investigation, 1911, pp. 791–93.

[27] *United States* v. *American Sugar Refining Co. et al.*, pretrial testimony, 1912, pp. 2310–30; Hardwick committee investigation, 1911, pp. 779–80.

[28] *United States* v. *American Sugar Refining Co. et al.*, pretrial testimony, 1912, pp. 2427–39. However, due to serious loss from the blight, a factory was not built until 1911, and then it was built by another Cutler-directed company. The San Pete and Sevier company was, in fact, dissolved in 1907.

[29] *Ibid.*, pp. 2395–426.

[30] *Ibid.*, pp. 2373–94, 4012–32.

sons later charged, to the close ties between the companies he headed and the Mormon church.[31] Aside from the fact that the president of that religious body also served as president of the various beet sugar companies with which Cutler was connected, the Church of Jesus Christ of Latter-day Saints was a substantial stockholder in all of the enterprises. Also, Cutler was a bishop in the Mormon church.[32] No less important than this alliance between the secular and the religious, however, was the fact that the prestige and resources of the American Sugar Refining Company stood behind whatever actions Cutler might take.

As time went by, it became increasingly clear that if the various companies which Cutler headed were combined into a single organization, substantial economies would result. It would no longer be necessary, for example, to have a complete set of spare equipment for each of the individual companies; they could all draw from the same stock. Agricultural agents could be assigned where they were needed, instead of being limited to the area in which the particular company they worked for had contracts with the farmers. Perhaps most important of all, at least insofar as Cutler himself was concerned, a consolidation would end the complaints that certain of the companies were being favored over others, for the fact was that the stockholders in the various companies were not all the same.[33]

This very diversity of ownership, however, was the main obstacle to consolidation.[34] Those holding shares in one of the newer, more efficient factories did not want to see their plant merged with one that was considerably older. To overcome this objection it was finally agreed that in exchanging their stock for shares in a new, combined enterprise, those with an interest in one of the more recently built, more efficient factories would receive a premium on the par value of their holdings.[35] In this way the path was cleared for the formation in 1907 of the Utah-Idaho Sugar Company as a vehicle for consolidating all the Cutler-managed beet factories. Henry O. Havemeyer and the American Sugar Refining Company received $5,681,740 of the

[31] See, for example, the testimony of Barlow Ferguson, *ibid.*, pp. 4121–23, 4129–30.

[32] Hardwick committee investigation, 1911, pp. 765–66.

[33] *United States* v. *American Sugar Refining Co. et al.*, pretrial testimony, 1912, pp. 2453–55.

[34] *Ibid.*, p. 2350.

[35] *Ibid.*, p. 782. Stockholders in the Utah Sugar Company were to receive par value for their shares; stockholders in the Idaho Sugar Company, the result of a previous merger of the Idaho and Fremont companies, were to receive a 10 per cent premium; and stockholders in the Western Idaho Company were to be given a 25 per cent premium.

$11,102,180 in common and preferred shares that were issued, or slightly more than 51 per cent of the outstanding stock.[36] This, however, represented only a minor portion of the interest that, by then, Havemeyer and the American had come to hold in various beet sugar enterprises.

The Evolution of the Utah-Idaho Sugar Company

1. Utah Sugar Company, with a factory at Lehi, Utah, built in 1891
2. Bear River Water Company

The Utah Sugar Company, organized in 1902, with a second factory at Garland, Utah

3. Idaho Sugar Company, with a factory at Idaho Falls, Idaho, built in 1903
4. Fremont Sugar Company, with a factory at Sugar City, Idaho, built in 1903

The Idaho Sugar Company, organized in 1905

5. Snake River Valley Sugar Company, Limited, with a factory at Blackfoot, Idaho, built in 1905
6. Western Idaho Sugar Company, with a factory at Nampa, Idaho, built in 1905

The Utah-Idaho Sugar Company, organized in 1907

7. San Pete and Sevier Sugar Company. No factory was built, however, and the company was dissolved in 1907. Later, the Utah-Idaho Sugar Company itself built a factory in Sevier County.

Note: Brackets indicate companies that were merged to form larger companies. Boxes indicate companies organized by groups other than Cutler and his associates. Arrows point to companies acquiring control of other companies through the purchase of their stock.

Source: *United States* v. *American Sugar Refining Company et al.: Testimony Taken Before William B. Brice, Special Examiner,* pp. 2479–2502.

[36] *Ibid.,* pp. 2501–5. The Havemeyer and American Sugar Refining Company stock was held in the names of C. R. Heike, Arthur Donner, and H. C. Mott, all

::

The same process by which Havemeyer and the American Sugar Refining Company emerged as the principal stockholder in Utah and Idaho's leading sugar beet enterprise was simultaneously being repeated in Colorado and in Michigan. In those states, too, Havemeyer chose to work through a single individual, someone with deep roots in the area. In Colorado the individual selected was Chester A. Morey, a wholesale grocer who had helped organize one of that state's first beet sugar factories; in Michigan, it was Charles B. Warren, a Detroit lawyer.[37]

Like Cutler, Morey and Warren were responsible for seeing to it that, in each of their areas, no beet factories were built in which Havemeyer and the American did not have a controlling interest. Toward that end they could count on the vast resources of the American Sugar Refining Company in support of whatever measures they might have to take. As Havemeyer's personal representatives, Morey and Warren each came to preside over a small but substantial beet sugar empire. In Morey's case it consisted of six factories, with four others in various stages of construction, plus a railroad. In 1905 these separate enterprises were taken over by the Great Western Sugar Company of New Jersey, a holding company organized as the Utah-Idaho company had been to end the rivalry between individual factories and to assure uniformly efficient management. Of the $10 million in preferred shares and the $10 million in common shares that were issued by the Great Western, Havemeyer and the American Sugar Refining Company, as a result of their previous investment in Colorado beet factories, received all but about a third. In Warren's case the empire consisted of eight plants, two of which were subsequently dismantled because they duplicated existing facilities. All eight enterprises were merged in 1906 to form the Michigan Sugar Company. Initially the American Sugar Refining Company held

---

either directors or officers of the American. Of this amount, $231,740, the stock held in Mott's name, belonged to Havemeyer personally. Once again, however, for purposes of control, it made little difference whether the stock actually belonged to Havemeyer personally or to the American Sugar Refining Company. It was only after Havemeyer's death that this became an important matter, though not, as it turned out, a critical one as it was to be in the case of the National Sugar Refining Company stock (see pp. 308–11 below).

[37] *United States* v. *American Sugar Refining Co. et al.*, pretrial testimony, 1912, pp. 624–30, 681–82.

slightly more than a third of the $9,161,000 in stock issued, but as additional shares were sold in order to finance capital improvements, the American came to own well over half of the Michigan Sugar Company's common stock.[38]

While the Utah-Idaho, Great Western, and Michigan companies were the predominant beet sugar enterprises in each of their respective areas, they were by no means the only such enterprises—or even the only ones in which Havemeyer and the American were financially interested. Together, Havemeyer and the American owned half of the stock in the Amalgamated Sugar Company, a corporation formed in 1902 to assume control of the three factories that David Eccles, an Ogden, Utah, businessman, had built in his home state and in Oregon.[39] In addition, they held a 50 per cent interest in the Menominee River Sugar Company on Michigan's upper peninsula and an almost two-thirds interest in the Continental Sugar Company with its two factories straddling either side of the Michigan-Ohio border.[40] The American also became interested in beet factories in other parts of the country—in Chaska, Minnesota,[41] in Waverly, Iowa,[42] and in Billings, Montana.[43]

All the same, there were quite a few factories in Michigan and its surrounding states in which Havemeyer and the American Sugar Refining Company did not have an interest. The same was true in Colorado, especially in the southern part of the state.[44] But for the most part these independent factories were the more poorly located and the less successful sugar beet enterprises. From Utah to Michigan, with only a few exceptions, Havemeyer was able to acquire a decisive

[38] *Ibid.*, pp. 660–933, 7968–9028; Hardwick committee investigation, 1911, pp. 100. 631–41, 874–75. A more complete description of the evolution of these companies can be found in the dissertation from which the present monograph developed.

[39] *United States* v. *American Sugar Refining Co. et al.*, pretrial testimony, 1912, pp. 22–24, 2260, 2299–2301, 2864–67.

[40] *Ibid.*, pp. 8626–34, 9038–51; see also p. 309 below.

[41] *Ibid.*, pp. 8434–85.

[42] *Ibid.*, pp. 7986, 8772.

[43] *Ibid.*, pp. 903–20.

[44] Besides those already cited, the American Sugar Refining Company may possibly have been interested in one other Michigan sugar beet company. The executive committee minutes for March 10, 1903, record a resolution calling for the purchase of $400,000 of the $750,000 in outstanding shares in the German-American Beet Sugar Company of Salzburg, Michigan (Hardwick committee investigation, 1911, p. 3027). Except for this notation, however, there is no evidence that the American Sugar Refining Company was interested in the company, and a later compilation of the American's beet holdings does not include the German-American company (*ibid.*, p. 100).

vote in the affairs of those companies which he felt represented the greatest potential threat to his control of the domestic sugar industry. And this was true in California as well.

::

Through the half interest it held in the Western Sugar Refining Company, the American was heavily involved in the California sugar beet situation even before it was decided that it would take an active role in the development of the industry nationally. The factory at Watsonville had been built by Claus Spreckels entirely on his own, without outside assistance, but in 1897, following passage of the new, more favorable tariff, Spreckels had concluded that, even though the Watsonville factory had been greatly enlarged, it was no longer adequate for his purposes.[45] Deciding to build an entirely new plant, one that would have an even greater slicing capacity, he had called upon the American Sugar Refining Company for help in financing the project.[46] This the directors of the American had finally acceded to, as part of an agreement extending the working arrangement between Spreckels and the American on the West Coast for another ten years.[47]

For $1,500,000 the American Sugar Refining Company had acquired a half interest in the factory at Watsonville, and for another $500,000 it had acquired a half interest in the Pajaro Valley Railroad, a narrow-gauge road used to bring beets to the factory. In addition, the American had pledged to supply half of whatever funds were needed to build a new beet factory on a site Spreckels had selected five miles south of Salinas, California.[48] It was understood, however, that while the American would have an equal interest in the combined enterprises (to be known as the Spreckels Sugar Company), its role was to be primarily that of a passive investor.[49] Two years later, in 1899, the new factory, with a slicing capacity of 3,000 tons of beets daily, was completed in the midst of what had become an entirely new town, appropriately named Spreckels, California. The town's leading citizen

[45] The equipment was outmoded, and it proved difficult to obtain adequate supplies of sugar beets, since the surrounding area was equally well suited for growing other crops (*ibid.*, p. 952).

[46] Spreckels was, at the time, involved in building a competing railroad in an effort to end the Southern Pacific Railroad's dominant position in northern California, and so he may have found himself temporarily strapped for funds; see Cordray, "Claus Spreckels of California," pp. 132ff.

[47] See p. 166 above.

[48] Hardwick committee investigation, 1911, p. 2934.

[49] Cordray, "Claus Spreckels of California," p. 122.

took great pride in the fact that this was the largest sugar beet factory in the world.

The Spreckels factory, however, had a close rival in terms of size. For in the same year that the new Spreckels plant was built, Henry T. Oxnard and his associates completed construction of a beet factory of their own, one capable of slicing close to 2,500 tons of beets daily, on a site approximately halfway between Los Angeles and Santa Barbara. The Southern Pacific Railroad, along whose right-of-way the factory lay, had, following custom, named the site after the family responsible for founding the new community.[50] The plant at Oxnard was a new addition to the factories that the same group of individuals already owned, those at Chino, California, and at Grand Island and Norfolk, Nebraska. Later that same year, all four plants were brought under the control of a single corporation, the recently formed American Beet Sugar Company. Organized under the laws of New Jersey, this new company was capitalized at $20 million, three-fourths in preferred stock and one-fourth in common shares. Although the company was listed on the New York Stock Exchange, its shares were still held for the most part by a small number of persons consisting primarily of the several Oxnard brothers and the Cutting family of New York.[51]

The output of the new factory at Oxnard, together with the output of the factory at Chino, proved to be far greater than the local California market could absorb at the current level of prices, and as a result the American Beet Sugar Company found itself increasingly forced to dispose of its surplus sugar in the various population centers along the Missouri River at whatever price could be obtained.[52] Its need to dispose of surplus sugar in this manner became all the greater when, in 1900, it finished building a fifth beet factory at Rocky Ford, Colorado, in the southeastern portion of the state. This latest plant was capable of slicing 1,100 tons of beets daily, more than any other factory constructed so far outside of California.[53] It was not long, however, before this dumping policy brought a sharp response from Havemeyer, for the various Missouri River points were an important market for the American Sugar Refining Company's own products.

The custom of the American Beet Sugar Company, in marketing its

[50] Hardwick committee investigation, 1911, pp. 376–77.

[51] *Ibid.*, pp. 378–81.

[52] *United States* v. *American Sugar Refining Co. et al.*, pretrial testimony, 1912, pp. 3608–9.

[53] Hardwick committee investigation, 1911, p. 378; *United States* v. *American Sugar Refining Co. et al.*, pretrial testimony, 1912, pp. 278–79.

surplus sugar at the various Missouri River points, was to sell at a fixed differential below the American Sugar Refining Company's price on the day the sugar was actually delivered. In this way, wholesale grocers were willing to sign contracts to purchase the American Beet Sugar Company's product even before the season's first beets had been harvested, knowing that they would be protected against any possible decline in cane sugar prices. In the meantime, the American Beet Sugar Company was assured of a ready market for its product once the actual season began.[54] These benefits were, of course, enjoyed primarily at the American Sugar Refining Company's expense, but Havemeyer quickly saw in the system a means of inflicting financial losses on the American Beet Sugar Company.

Havemeyer waited until the late summer of 1901, by which time the American Beet Sugar Company had already entered into contracts for the forthcoming season. Then he dispatched Judson Lounsbery, the American Sugar Refining Company's chief salesman, to Kansas City with instructions to sell 7,500 barrels of refined sugar a week at 3.5 cents a pound f.o.b. New Orleans—a full cent below the normal price. Once these instructions were carried out, wholesale grocers began demanding that the American Beet Sugar Company deliver on its contracts by selling them beet sugar on the basis of 3.4 cents a pound f.o.b. New Orleans.[55]

If the American Beet Sugar Company had complied, it would have incurred substantial losses, for even at the prices that generally prevailed, it was unable to recover the full costs of production on the sugar that was sold in the Missouri River markets. This was because the expense of transporting sugar was so much greater from California than from New Orleans; the only reason that the beet sugar was sold at the Missouri River points was that it was the most economical way of disposing of surplus California beet sugar. Claiming that the American Sugar Refining Company's prices were not true prices, the American Beet Sugar Company challenged the wholesale grocers with whom it had contracts to purchase cane sugar from the American Sugar Refining Company at the 3.5-cent figure. Since Lounsbery had made only a limited amount of cane sugar available at the 3.5-cent f.o.b. New Orleans price, the wholesale grocers were forced to admit that the American Beet Sugar Company's contention was true.[56]

Recognizing that his scheme would fail unless he made more cane

[54] *United States* v. *American Sugar Refining Co. et al.*, pretrial testimony, 1912, pp. 7218–20.
[55] *Ibid.*, pp. 3613–14.
[56] *Ibid.*, pp. 3614–15.

sugar available, Havemeyer increased the weekly allotment at Lounsbery's request to 10,000 barrels and, in an effort to dampen the demand somewhat, raised the price to 4 cents a pound f.o.b. New Orleans. Even so, it proved impossible to supply all the sugar the wholesale grocers were willing to buy, and within three weeks Havemeyer was forced to raise the price once again, this time to 4¾ cents a pound f.o.b. New Orleans.[57] There it remained throughout the rest of the sugar beet season, still sufficiently low to cause the American Beet Sugar Company substantial losses.

If it had not been for the affluence of its stockholders, the American Beet Sugar Company might well have gone under.[58] Although the company did survive, Bayard Cutting for one was ready to call an end to the struggle. Contacting Havemeyer in New York, he initiated a series of discussions as to how the conflict between the two companies might be peacefully resolved. Gradually the basis for a settlement emerged. "The negotiations were two-fold," Oxnard subsequently testified. "On the one hand, they [the lawyers for the American Sugar Refining Company] were to draw up a contract by which the American Sugar Refining Company should act as the supervising selling agents for the American Beet Sugar Company. That was one part of the negotiation. The other part was to fix a price on one half of the common stock of the [American Beet Sugar] company that the American Sugar Refining Company . . . should . . . pay." The first point was raised at Havemeyer's insistence, the second at Cutting's.[59]

Although the basis for a settlement had been reached, the two parties found themselves unable to agree on one important detail: how much the American Sugar Refining Company should pay for its half interest in the American Beet Sugar Company. When by April the two parties still found themselves deadlocked on this point, they decided to refer the matter to third parties for arbitration.[60] The arbitrators suggested a price which they thought should be paid for the American Beet Sugar Company stock, but Havemeyer refused to be bound by their recommendation.[61] The negotiations dragged on inconclusively through the summer and into the late fall. By then the American Beet Sugar Company had experienced a second season of strong competition from the American Sugar Refining Company, and its officers had lost whatever determination they once might have had to hold out against Havemeyer's terms. At the latter's insistence it was agreed that the American Sugar Refining Company would receive

[57] *Ibid.*, pp. 7224–26. [58] *Ibid.*, pp. 3615–18. [59] *Ibid.*, p. 3619.
[60] *Ibid.*, pp. 3620–29. [61] *Ibid.*, pp. 3628–33.

¼ of a cent for every pound of sugar marketed by the American Beet Sugar Company during the next five years and that, in addition, it would acquire 75,000 American Beet Sugar Company preferred shares for $1,875,000, a figure which represented only one-fourth of the stock's par value. A formal agreement embodying these provisions was signed by the two parties on December 16, 1902.[62]

Havemeyer then suggested that other California beet sugar companies might be willing to enter into similar arrangements with the American Sugar Refining Company. In response to this suggestion, Oxnard contacted the officers and directors of the Alameda Sugar Company and the Union Sugar Company, the first being located across the bay from San Francisco at Alvarado, the second just outside Santa Barbara.[63] Edmund C. Burr, one of the principal figures in both companies, was immediately receptive to Havemeyer's suggestion. As he later explained, "I thought this way, that if the controlling interests in the manufacture of sugar in the United States, as I judged them to be, were associated with us in business, they would not be apt to try and crush us and, at the same time, hurt themselves,"[64] Burr won his fellow directors over to the same view, and on February 10, 1903, an agreement was signed between the American Sugar Refining Company and the Alameda Sugar Company which was virtually identical to the one previously entered into by the American Sugar Refining Company and the American Beet Sugar Company.[65] Although the Union Sugar Company was not a party to this agreement, it was clear that the marketing of its output was indirectly affected as well.

Other beet sugar companies in California were approached by Oxnard, but since they were able to sell most of their relatively small output in nearby markets, they could see little value in paying the American Sugar Refining Company a ¼-of-a-cent-a-pound commission to supervise their sales. Without exception, they refused to enter into any agreement with the American.

Its alliance with the American Sugar Refining Company enabling it once more to earn a return on its invested capital, the American Beet Sugar Company decided to proceed with plans to establish itself even more firmly in Colorado's Arkansas River valley. In 1905 it

[62] *Ibid.*, pp. 3634–44; a copy of the contract is reprinted in *ibid.*, pp. 7160–63.
[63] *Ibid.*, pp. 3137–39, 3647. The men connected with the two enterprises had formerly been shareholders in the old American Sugar Refinery before its acquisition by the trust.
[64] *Ibid.*, p. 3158.
[65] *Ibid.*, pp. 3151–59.

closed its plant at Norfolk, Nebraska, and moved the machinery to a new site at Lamar, Colorado, sixty-seven miles from the existing factory at Rocky Ford.[66] A year later the company's officials decided to build still another beet factory in the area—the company's sixth—at Las Animas, Colorado. In this instance the factory was to be erected by an entirely new company, thus enabling local investors to join in the venture. Once built, however, the new factory was to be leased and operated by the American Beet Sugar Company.[67]

The American Sugar Refining Company was asked if it would like to subscribe to a portion of the new company's stock, but the American's executive committee, fearing the company was already too heavily involved in other beet-growing areas, declined the offer. It did, however, agree to exempt the output of the Las Animas factory from the commission agreement with the American Beet Sugar Company.[68]

::

As preparations were made for the 1907 sugar beet season, Henry O. Havemeyer could take satisfaction in the fact that he and the American Sugar Refining Company together held a commanding interest in almost every important sugar beet company in the United States. In the Utah-Idaho area the companies in which they were interested accounted for 100 per cent of the beet-slicing capacity; the same was true in the northern Colorado area. In the lower Michigan area the companies that were under Havemeyer and the American's control accounted for 52 per cent of the capacity; in California the figure was 81 per cent, and in the southern Colorado area it was 42 per cent. Of the various other companies scattered throughout the country, those in which Havemeyer and the American were interested accounted for 47 per cent of the slicing capacity. On an over-all basis, 70 per cent of the beet sugar processed in this country was handled by companies that were, in one way or another, under the control of Havemeyer and the American Sugar Refining Company.[69]

While it was true that beet sugar still accounted for only 13 per cent of all the sugar consumed by Americans, it was also true that this

[66] *Ibid.*, pp. 283–84.

[67] Hardwick committee investigation, 1911, pp. 3047–48.

[68] The American Sugar Refining Company had previously turned down an opportunity to subscribe to the stock of the Holly Sugar Company, an enterprise which then erected beet factories at Holly and Swink, Colorado, for substantially the same reason (*ibid.*, p. 3036).

[69] See Appendix F of this volume.

percentage represented a fourfold increase since 1900.[70] Moreover, in certain parts of the country at certain times of the year—most specifically, in the region between the Sierra Mountains and the Ohio River during the fall and early winter—beet sugar dominated the market, its share of total sugar sales then greatly exceeding the yearly national average. But aside from these considerations, the important point, at least as far as the American Sugar Refining Company was concerned, was that beet sugar was a home-grown product. This meant that, regardless of the attitude Congress might later adopt toward sugar duties, the American's control of the domestic industry would remain intact.

From the point of view of the beet companies themselves, this outside interest brought many important benefits. The most apparent, of course, was the large infusion of capital. The direct investment by Havemeyer and the American Sugar Refining Company in the beet sugar industry totaled close to $30 million.[71] Not counting those companies which failed, this represented well over half the funds invested in the industry.[72] While not all of this sum represented an original investment in beet sugar processing facilities—a significant part was used merely to acquire title to already existing facilities—it is nonetheless true that a great many of the factories in existence in 1907 would not have been built had it not been for the availability of these outside funds. Even when Havemeyer and the American Sugar Refining Company purchased the shares of other stockholders, the money was often used to finance additional beet factories.

The American Sugar Refining Company was also an important source of short-term capital. On October 20, 1903, Havemeyer was authorized to loan the company's funds "to the various sugar-beet companies, in which the company is interested,"[73] and this he proceeded to do on a continuing basis, making available at 6 per cent interest whatever funds were needed for working capital while the sugar beet season was in progress. These loans averaged between $6 million and $7 million a year.[74]

Less apparent, but perhaps even more important, than the infusion of capital was the stimulus provided to greater efficiency. The

[70] See Appendix E of this volume.

[71] This is a rough estimate based on the par value of Havemeyer's and the American's holdings in 1911; see Hardwick committee investigation, 1911, pp. 100, 559.

[72] *Ibid.*, p. 100.

[73] *Ibid.*, p. 3030.

[74] This can be seen from an examination of the minutes of the American Sugar Refining Company's executive committee, *ibid.*, pp. 3030ff.

American Sugar Refining Company had its own staff, men thoroughly familiar with various aspects of the sugar beet industry, both the agricultural end of the business and the manufacturing end. These experts regularly visited the various sugar beet factories in which Havemeyer and the American were interested, advising the local management as to what new methods might best be adopted.[75] In this way, under the over-all supervision of Cutler, Morey, and Warren, all the factories were brought to a uniformly higher level of technical performance.

Each company maintained a separate set of books, showing not only its profits and losses but also in detailed form its costs. When a company consistently failed to report any net earnings and the American Sugar Refining Company's sugar beet experts could see no extenuating circumstances, Havemeyer would then seek a change in management. In 1905, for example, he insisted that Robert Oxnard take over as president of the American Beet Sugar Company. Pointing out that the average cost of manufacturing sugar at a typical factory controlled by the American Sugar Refining Company was 3.211 cents a pound while the average cost at the various factories owned by the American Beet Sugar Company was 3.985 cents a pound, he wrote, "I invite your attention to the differences [in costs, a detailed breakdown of which he included,] and hope during your administration that the cost of producing 100 lbs. of Granulated will not exceed 3¼ cents a pound."[76] Similarly, just before the start of the 1907 season, Havemeyer forced a change in the Continental Sugar Company's management because of its repeated failure to earn a profit. Typically, however, he replaced the old set of officers with a new set recruited from among the local stockholders.[77]

These benefits—the infusion of capital and the stimulus to greater efficiency—were social as well as private in nature. But they were incidental to the primary purpose for which Havemeyer and the American had acquired an interest in the various sugar beet companies. That primary purpose was to maintain and reinforce Havemeyer's control over the domestic sugar industry.

::

The American Sugar Refining Company's predominant interest in the domestic beet industry would, by itself, have been insufficient to assure price stability. There was also the need to co-ordinate the

[75] *United States* v. *American Sugar Refining Co. et al.*, pretrial testimony, 1912, pp. 2653, 2683–85, 2779–81, 3347, 3476, 9145.
[76] *Ibid.*, p. 3689.
[77] *Ibid.*, pp. 9078–80, 9144–54.

marketing activities of the various refineries controlled by or allied with the American in each of the several cane-refining centers. In the 1900's, these refining centers were, as they had been for over half a century, the Atlantic seaboard cities of New York, Philadelphia, and Boston, the Gulf coast city of New Orleans, and the West Coast city of San Francisco.

The pattern of railroad freight rates defined for each of these cane-refining centers a "natural" market territory, that is, an area in which it enjoyed lower transportation costs than did any other refining center. For the refineries located in the Atlantic seaboard cities of New York, Philadelphia, and Boston, the natural market territory included all the states and portions thereof to the east and north of a line extending from Charleston, South Carolina, on one side to Fargo, North Dakota, on the other (see Map 4). The natural market territory for the refineries located in San Francisco included all the states and portions thereof between the Pacific slopes and the Continental Divide. The remaining areas of the United States comprised the natural market territory of the refineries located in New Orleans.[78]

For the most part a refinery would try to limit its sales to its own natural market territory, for to sell outside that territory meant that it had to absorb part of the transportation costs. Still, there were times when a company from one refining center found that it was to its advantage to sell sugar in the market territory of another refining center.

The Western Sugar Refining Company, for example, under Spreckels' direction, had for many years followed a policy of selling no more sugar in its home territory than the market would take at a predetermined price level, this level being based on a profit margin sufficient to enable the company to earn what Spreckels felt was a "satisfactory" level of profit.[79] The Western was able to follow such a

[78] *Ibid.*, pp. 3079–80, 3459–62; Hardwick committee investigation, 1911, p. 1426.

[79] *United States* v. *American Sugar Refining Co. et al.*, pretrial testimony, 1912, p. 3459. If it can be assumed that Spreckels was a short-run profit maximizer, this "satisfactory" profit would then have been determined by the principles underlying traditional price theory. Otherwise, his actions would fall into the category of "cost-plus" pricing. For a discussion of differences between the two types of pricing behavior, as well as an argument that they are actually the same, see Fritz Machlup, "Marginal Analysis and Empirical Research," pp. 519–54. It is the present author's contention, however, that the two types of pricing behavior are, in fact, quite different, the "cost-plus" type being based on long-run rather than short-run profit maximization; see his *The Theory of Oligopoly* (in preparation). One of the theoretically significant aspects of the Corporate Revolution was that it marked the beginning of the shift in emphasis from short-run profit maximization to long-run profit maximization for the megacorps which emerged during the period.

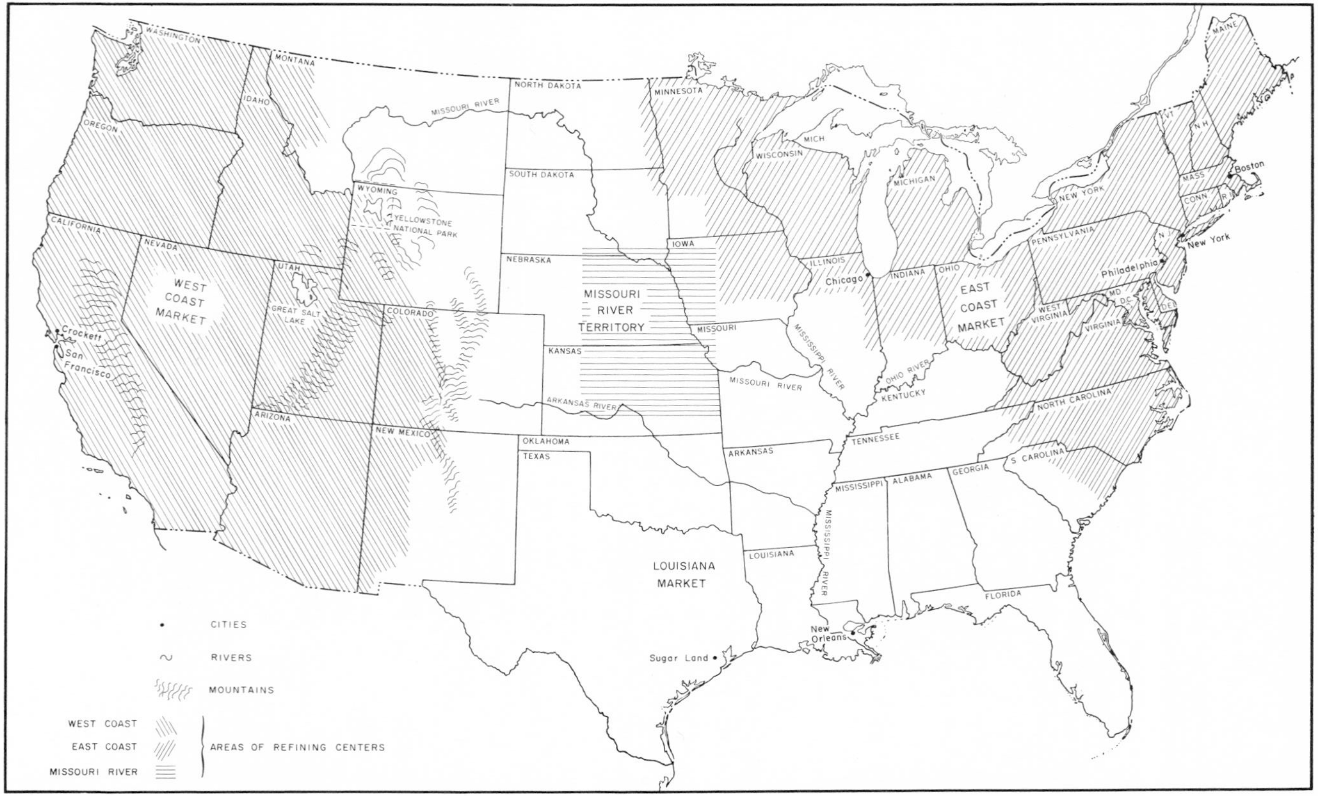

WEST COAST MARKET

EAST COAST MARKET

MISSOURI RIVER TERRITORY

LOUISIANA MARKET

• CITIES

RIVERS

MOUNTAINS

WEST COAST / EAST COAST / MISSOURI RIVER — AREAS OF REFINING CENTERS

MAP 4. PRINCIPAL CANE-REFINING CENTERS AND "NATURAL" MARKET TERRITORIES, 1907

policy because, from the time it had been organized by Spreckels and the American Sugar Refining Company in 1891 until 1898, it had enjoyed an almost absolute monopoly of the refining business on the West Coast. In 1898 a group of Hawaiian planters long opposed to Spreckels' hold on the industry[80] attempted to operate a converted flour mill in competition with the Western; but they were forced to give up the struggle in 1902 after the annual loss reached $600,000.[81] It was agreed that their plant, located at Crockett, California, would be leased to the Western for $200,000 annually, the arrangement to last until at least 1906. For the next three years, the Western Sugar Refining Company again enjoyed a monopoly on the West Coast.[82]

However, Spreckels' policy of limiting his company's sales in the home territory to the amount the local market could take at predetermined price levels had one potential disadvantage. If that were all the sugar produced, he would be unable to operate his California refinery, the one refinery still in use, at its most efficient level of production.[83] To avoid this result Spreckels allowed the actual output to exceed the needs of the local market, disposing of the surplus sugar by selling it for whatever it would bring in the various cities along the Missouri River. As long as the price obtained in that market was greater than the direct cost of refining plus the expense of transportation, this policy made sense, for then the Western Sugar Refining Company would be able to spread its overhead costs over a larger volume of production.[84] For much the same reason the American and National sugar refining companies also used the various Missouri River points as a "dumping" ground for their surplus sugar.

These Missouri River points, however, were in the natural market territory of the New Orleans refineries—specifically, that of the one remaining plant still operated in that city by the American Sugar Refining Company. The old Planters Sugar Refinery had been

[80] See pp. 88–90 above.

[81] Hardwick committee investigation, 1911, p. 976; *United States* v. *American Sugar Refining Co. et al.*, pretrial testimony, 1912, p. 3891. Because the Crockett plant was formerly a flour mill and had not been intended to serve as a refinery, it proved to be expensive to run. For this reason, before its purchase by the Hawaiian group, it had not been a significant factor on the West Coast.

[82] *United States* v. *American Sugar Refining Co. et al.*, pretrial testimony, 1912, pp. 3892–907. This condition lasted until 1907; see pp. 270–71 below.

[83] The old American refinery, immediately after being leased to the Western Sugar Refining Company, had been closed down and held as a reserve facility. It never again operated, for it was destroyed in the 1906 San Francisco earthquake.

[84] *United States* v. *American Sugar Refining Co. et al.*, pretrial testimony, 1912, p. 3459.

combined with the Louisiana Sugar Company's plant at the time the trust was formed, and all production had been concentrated in the enlarged facility.[85] While two other sugar refineries had subsequently started up in competition with the American in New Orleans, they were both quite small, their combined output being only about 1,100 barrels of sugar daily.[86] There was also a refinery at Sugar Lands, Texas, just outside of Galveston, but its output was only 400–600 barrels a day.[87] In comparison, the American Sugar Refining Company's plant at New Orleans was capable of producing 12,000 barrels of refined sugar daily. Moreover, while the other refineries depended almost entirely on the local Louisiana crop for their raw-sugar supplies, the American imported cane sugar from Cuba to keep its New Orleans plant going during the late spring, summer, and early fall months when the local product was not available.

Thus, the invasion of the natural market territory of the New Orleans refineries was made primarily at the expense of the American Sugar Refining Company's plant in that city. If the policy of dumping surplus sugar at the Missouri River points was not to lead to a price war between the several cane-refining centers and result in such a demoralization of prices that the original reason for the dumping would be obviated, co-ordination among these refining centers was essential. Havemeyer was able to provide this co-ordination, implicitly by his interlocking interests if not explicitly through direct control.[88]

Co-ordination was made somewhat easier by the timing of the various cane-sugar seasons. The Louisiana crop, which supplied the New Orleans refineries with most of their raw sugar, was first harvested toward the end of September. By late October the season was at its height, the quantities going to market being in excess of what the local refineries could process. Some of the surplus was stored; the rest was sold in a semifinished state as "plantation sugars."[89] The Louisiana season ended around the first of January,

[85] See p. 115 above.

[86] *Ibid.*, pp. 7486–87, 7614–16. The Henderson refinery was erected in 1887, the year the trust was formed; the Cogswell refinery was built five years later by a former employee of the Henderson refinery.

[87] Hardwick committee investigation, 1911, p. 1502.

[88] See pp. 229 and 248 above.

[89] Plantation sugars were those that had been refined to the extent possible on one of the Louisiana plantations. Since the methods available for processing the raw sugar on a plantation were crude compared to those available at a refinery, the end product was usually some shade of yellow rather than white, and it generally contained certain impurities. For this reason it sold at a differential substantially below that of refined sugar.

just as the initial shipments of Cuban cane began reaching North American ports. The Cuban product continued to pour into this country throughout the spring and summer, not only supplying the eastern seaboard refining centers with the great bulk of their raw sugar but also supplementing the stocks of the American Sugar Refining Company's New Orleans plant. For the remaining months of the year, the eastern seaboard refineries obtained whatever additional raw sugar they needed by importing it from the Dutch East Indies.[90] The Hawaiian crop, on which the San Francisco refineries depended for their raw-sugar supplies, was also harvested at about the first of the year, but since it took approximately sixty days in transit, the initial shipments did not reach San Francisco until March. By July the importations were at a peak, the quantities reaching San Francisco also exceeding what the local refineries were capable of processing. This situation usually lasted until the end of September, when the large importations from Hawaii fell off.[91]

Thus it was that at certain times of the year the several refining centers, especially New Orleans and San Francisco, found themselves burdened with surplus supplies of raw sugar. In San Francisco, the Western Sugar Refining Company was under long-term contract to purchase a certain portion of the sugar cane produced in the Hawaiian Islands, so that even though its large warehouses might be filled to capacity, it could not stop its importations. To avoid excessive storage costs, the Western had no choice but to sell its refined sugar as expeditiously as possible. The American Sugar Refining Company's plant at New Orleans was in a somewhat similar position, for though it was not contractually obligated to purchase the entire Louisiana crop, it realized that what it did not purchase would nonetheless find its way back into the market through other means, either as plantation sugar or as a competing brand of refined sugar.

Since this surplus occurred in the two refining centers at different times of the year, it was possible to co-ordinate the marketing of the surplus in such a way as to minimize the losses between centers.[92] For example, in July of 1891 Havemeyer wrote as follows to Robert Oxnard, who was then the American Sugar Refining Company's repre-

[90] It was this sugar imported from Java which the domestic beet sugar largely displaced. Because of the great distance it had to travel, Dutch East Indies raw sugar was often in poor condition by the time it reached the eastern seaboard cities, and the losses from deterioration were usually significant; see p. 292, n. 3, below.

[91] *United States* v. *American Sugar Refining Co. et al.*, pretrial testimony, 1912, pp. 191, 3726–30.

[92] *Ibid.*, pp. 3731–34.

sentative on the Western Sugar Refining Company's board of directors and also secretary of the company:

> . . . I think, in view of the probable decline in prices after October 1st, say ¼ of a cent, that the [California] refinery should increase its meltings at once to the maximum, and work up all the raw sugar possible so that on October 1st, with the stock of raw sugar on hand then and the anticipated supplies thenceforth, the output of the refinery will be lessened for the three final months of the year to what the local markets only may require.
>
> The New Orleans sugars must be marketed, and the stock of San Francisco sugars should be so low at that time as not to bring the refined product within the competition of the New Orleans product.

Havemeyer explained to Oxnard the basis on which the Atlantic seaboard refineries were then quoting prices on sugar sold at Missouri River points, suggesting that the Western Sugar Refining Company quote identical prices in that territory. He then concluded, "I hope you will carefully consider what I have written, and bring it to the attention of Messrs. Spreckels. . . ."[93]

Even after the emergence of an economically viable sugar beet industry, this co-ordination of marketing policies among the several refining centers continued.[94] But as time went on, it became increasingly clear that unless the marketing of beet sugar was also co-ordinated, these other efforts would be for naught. It was for this reason that Havemeyer arranged for his own company to acquire a major interest in almost every important beet sugar factory. Once this was accomplished, Havemeyer was able to provide the needed co-ordination.

::

The beet sugar season began first in California, the initial beets usually being harvested at the end of August, just as the importations of cane sugar from Hawaii were coming to an end. A month later, the season began in the interior parts of the country, with production reaching a peak during the first week in November. By then the output of sugar was usually greater than the local markets could absorb without depressing prices, and so it became necessary to dispose of the surplus in other markets. This state of affairs generally lasted until the end of December, by which time the beet season was usually over.[95] Not only the timing of the seasons but also the structure of rail-

[93] *Ibid.*, pp. 3571–72.
[94] *Ibid.*, pp. 3481–83, 3283, 3296–98.
[95] *Ibid.*, pp. 191–92, 673, 3089–94, 3777–79.

road freight rates forced the shipment of surplus beet sugar from west to east, for the rates were prohibitive on sugar moving in the opposite direction.[96] The problem was to avoid having the surplus beet sugar from the producing areas farther west undercut prices in the natural market territories of the beet-producing areas to the east, while at the same time avoiding interference with the normal distribution of refined sugar cane.

It was to find a solution to this problem that officials of three of the companies in which the American Sugar Refining Company was interested met, with Havemeyer's blessing, during the week of June 8, 1903.[97] These gentlemen within the week reached agreement on the broad outlines of a plan. Each company was to sell as much of its sugar as it could in its own home territory where it enjoyed the advantage of favorable railroad freight rates. The California companies were then to dispose of their surplus in the Missouri River market, bypassing the Utah-Idaho and the Colorado territories. The Utah and Idaho companies were also to dispose of their surplus in the Missouri River market, bypassing the Colorado territory. The Colorado companies, meanwhile, were to dispose of their surplus in the Chicago market. In this way, no company would have to face the competition of outside sugar in its home territory.[98]

If the plan had involved nothing further, it probably would have been unacceptable to certain of the companies involved. Due to the vagaries of railroad freight rates, it cost the same to ship sugar from California and from the intermountain region of Utah and Idaho to the Missouri River territory as it did to ship sugar from Colorado to the same destination, despite the different distances involved.[99] On the other hand, it cost ten cents a hundredweight more to ship sugar from Colorado to Chicago than from Colorado to the Missouri River territory.[100] Thus, adoption of the simple division-of-markets scheme would have meant an increase in the transportation costs of the Colorado companies. Offsetting this disadvantage was the fact that the Colorado companies would probably suffer most heavily from outside competition in the absence of such a scheme. But how was one to weigh these considerations?

Again, due to the vagaries of railroad freight rates, it cost 75 cents a hundredweight to ship sugar from California to the Utah-Idaho region, but only 50 cents a hundredweight to ship it from California to the Missouri River territory. Thus, for the California companies,

[96] *Ibid.*, p. 2693. [97] *Ibid.*, p. 3319. [98] *Ibid.*, pp. 3650–55, 3660.
[99] *Ibid.*, pp. 3777–78. [100] *Ibid.*, pp. 1398–99.

adoption of the division-of-markets plan would mean a certain savings in transportation costs, since the plan would limit the sales of their surplus sugar to the Missouri River territory. But while the California companies would save on their transportation costs, they would be forced to sell in a market where sugar prices were generally lower than they were in Utah and Idaho. The Utah-Idaho companies, meanwhile, would be able to sell in the home market, incurring only local transportation costs, at a price no longer affected by outside competition. Again, how was one to measure the benefits to be received as opposed to the sacrifices that would have to be borne if the division-of-markets plan were actually adopted?[101]

To avoid the issue it was decided to include as part of the plan a provision for equalizing revenues. Each company was to supply detailed information on the prices it received for its output, and at the end of the season this information was to be used to compute the average price received by each company. This figure was then to be compared with the average price received by all of the companies together. Finally, those companies whose average price was greater than the over-all figure would be required to pay the difference into a common pool which would then be distributed among those companies whose average price was less than the over-all figure.[102]

Once the details of this plan had been transmitted to Havemeyer and his approval obtained, the next step was to win the support of those companies which had not been represented at the meetings in San Francisco.[103] This task was begun at once. On July 21, two weeks after Havemeyer had indicated his approval, William Hannan wrote to the head of the American Sugar Refining Company in New York, telling him that "the details of the plan have been under discussion, and the beet producers located in San Francisco believe that it can be very successfully operated." Eventually, with but a single exception—a small, strategically unimportant factory in Waverly, Washington—all the beet sugar factories west of the Missouri River agreed to give the plan a try.[104]

::

The division-of-markets plan was put into effect on a one-year trial basis only, but it was found to work so well that when the year was up, the plan was extended for another two years.[105] Although the

[101] *Ibid.*, pp. 2533–39.
[102] *Ibid.*, 1398–99, 3651–57, 3776–77.
[103] *Ibid.*, pp. 3323–24.
[104] *Ibid.*, pp. 3006, 3326, 3651.
[105] *Ibid.*, p. 2545.

mechanics of the plan, including the equalization of revenues, was by now fairly well established, Havemeyer's constant intervention was still essential. He was, in fact, the focus of an elaborate intelligence network. Each week he received reports from the refineries in which the American Sugar Refining Company was interested, informing him of the amount of raw sugar on hand, the amount of raw sugar newly purchased, and the amount of raw sugar melted that week, together with the prices paid for the raw cane and the prices received for the final refined product.[106] Since the refineries in which the American was interested supplied approximately 90 per cent of all the refined sugar consumed in the United States,[107] Havemeyer was able to obtain a fairly accurate picture of the flow of cane sugar to the consumer.

During the sugar beet season Havemeyer also received weekly reports from the beet factories in which American was interested, and these provided him with the same sort of information supplied by the refineries; at other times of the year, he received weekly reports on how the sugar beet crop was progressing.[108] Again, since the factories in which the American was interested represented 70 per cent of the nation's beet-slicing capacity,[109] these reports enabled Havemeyer to gauge fairly accurately the amount of beet sugar that was likely to find is way to market in any given year.

Both the reports from the several refineries and those from the various beet factories were supplemented by frequent intelligence from raw-sugar brokers throughout the world and large wholesale grocers across the United States, describing local market conditions. These reports enabled Havemeyer, drawing on his many years of experience, to make a reasonable estimate of what trends were likely to prevail in the months ahead. His judgment in such matters, communicated to the officers of the various companies in which the American was interested, was an important part of the direction that Havemeyer exercised over the domestic sugar industry.

[106] *Ibid.*, pp. 3296–98.

[107] Hardwick committee investigation, 1911, p. 43. The figure is based on the year 1906 and has been revised to include the production of the refineries in which the American was interested, namely, the McCahan, the National, and the Western. Figures for the McCahan and the National are based on their given capacities, 600,000 barrels and 2,000,000 barrels respectively; the figure for the Western was arrived at through the following formula: Listed production for the American included half of the Western's output (*ibid.*, p. 57). Since the Western's production in 1906 was 120,000 tons, 60,000 tons, or 4.14 million barrels, were added to the American's total.

[108] *United States* v. *American Sugar Refining Co. et al.*, pretrial testimony, 1912, pp. 1345–46, 1515–17, 3251–52.

[109] See p. 248 above.

These reports not only benefited the companies individually but also, and perhaps most important, helped to make sure that prices were co-ordinated among them. As Havemeyer wrote on November 1, 1904, to F. R. Hathaway, the person newly appointed to take charge of all sales for the six Michigan beet sugar companies:

> I have sent you a wire recommending that the business be done not exceeding 5¢ [a pound]. I would disregard in every way what any competitor of the American Sugar Refining Company is doing. . . . The outside refineries in the winter time do not represent over 30% [of the market]. . . . Do as all the other beet companies do, hold your sugars on the basis of the American Sugar Refining Company's net prices—f.o.b. New York, plus the freight, and allow not less than 10¢. . . . Stick to the American Sugar Company's prices as a basis. Besides all of which there is no need of hurrying the sale of the sugar as I doubt if the price will be any lower in view of the beet market.[110]

Havemeyer continually reiterated the advice that the various other companies in which the American was interested should adhere to its posted prices. "Business all over the United States in Refined sugar is absolutely dull," he wrote to Hannan on March 21, 1905. "Grocers do not take their orders. You have a large stock; so has New Orleans. Nothing will be gained by lowering the price except to increase the demoralization. As soon as the trade resumes, you will undoubtedly get your fair share of it."[111] The extent to which companies followed the American Sugar Refining Company's prices—both those companies in which the American was interested and those in which it was not—was the extent to which Havemeyer was able to exercise control over the domestic sugar industry.

::

Perhaps it should be more clearly specified what is meant by "control." It does not mean that Havemeyer or the American Sugar Refining Company was able simply to dictate, unilaterally, the price at which refined or processed sugar was sold to the public. The price of raw sugar, the size of the beet crop, and the current seasonal demand for granulated sugar were all constraints that had to be taken into consideration. Other factors also had to be weighed, such as the possibility of refined sugar's being imported from abroad, the likelihood of new firms being encouraged to enter the industry, and the effect of a change in price on future consumption. But given these

[110] *United States* v. *American Sugar Refining Co. et al.*, pretrial testimony, 1912, p. 8345.

[111] *Ibid.*, p. 3288.

parameters, "control" did mean that Havemeyer, acting through the American Sugar Refining Company in New York, was able to set a price which, calculated to maximize industry profits in the long run, was then adopted as their own by virtually every other producer of refined cane and processed beet sugar. The price set by Havemeyer was, in effect, the industry price.[112]

The mechanism by which this price was effectuated throughout the industry was as follows: Each morning at 10 o'clock the price set by Havemeyer was posted outside the American Sugar Refining Company's offices on Wall Street. Meanwhile, the heads of the refineries in Boston, Philadelphia, and New Orleans, as well as Havemeyer's representative in San Francisco, had been informed by telegraph what the New York price would be that day, and taking into account local conditions, they adjusted their own refineries' price to whatever change, if any, had been made by Havemeyer.[113] This price was then posted outside each of their offices. The independent refineries in each of the refining centers, if they so chose, had only to follow the price posted by the American.[114]

Any change in the posted price of cane sugar was telegraphed immediately to the major beet sugar companies in which the American was interested, for the price of beet sugar was based on the price of refined cane in either New York, New Orleans, or San Francisco (depending on which city was cheapest to reach by rail) plus the cost of transportation, less the customary differential. Thus a change in the price of cane led automatically to a change in the price of beet sugar. Of course, if local conditions warranted, that is, if the beet companies found themselves becoming overstocked with sugar, they might decide to increase the differential between cane and beet. But this was done infrequently and usually only after consultation with Havemeyer. In general, the price of beet sugar simply followed the price of cane.[115]

[112] There was, of course, more than one price for refined sugar, depending on the grade desired. But the price of granulated sugar was the basis for all other prices, the other grades usually selling for a fixed differential below granulated.

[113] Obviously the American's quoted price in Boston and Philadelphia was most clearly related to the price in New York, the price in New Orleans being somewhat less so, and the price in San Francisco being least clearly related to that in New York. Still, all the prices tended to move together.

[114] It will be remembered that there were no independent refineries in San Francisco at this time, the Crockett refinery still being under lease to the Western. In Boston the only independent refinery was the Revere; in New York, besides the National, the only independent refineries were the Arbuckle and the Federal; in Philadelphia, there were no independent refineries except the McCahan.

[115] *United States* v. *American Sugar Refining Co. et al.*, pretrial testimony, 1912, pp. 3072–73.

Each of the major beet sugar companies—the Spreckels in northern California, the American Beet Sugar in southern California and southern Colorado, the Utah-Idaho in the intermountain region, the Great Western in northern Colorado, and the Michigan in Michigan—was the price leader for beet sugar in its particular area. The other, independent factories located in those beet-growing areas based their own prices on the price quoted by the majors.[116] At the same time, in those markets, such as the Missouri River valley and Chicago, where more than one major beet sugar company sold its product, prices were co-ordinated by having a single broker handle all sales, whether of beet sugar or of cane.[117]

Thus, as a general rule, there existed in each community, regardless of how distant it was from a refinery or beet factory, a single wholesale price for refined cane sugar and, based on the price of cane, a single wholesale price for processed beet sugar; and both these prices were governed by the price set by Havemeyer in New York each morning.

One would expect that the companies in which the American was interested would not deviate from the single price, both because of the division-of-markets plan and because of the fact of the American's partial ownership. The other, independent companies, however, were another matter. One might think that the temptation to cut the price, even slightly, and thereby gain a larger share of the market would have been irresistible. From time to time, the independent refineries did, of course, succumb to that urge. But when they did, one of the companies allied with the American was usually quick to retaliate, for the very success of a price cut in siphoning off its customary trade was a sure tip-off that the single price was not being maintained. "We have had instances here in the east," Havemeyer wrote to Hannan in San Francisco on an occasion when the Western Sugar Refining Company was being plagued by price competition, "where some of our competitors would make a cut of 10 to 25 cents [a hundredweight] for trade; lately in West Virginia and Ohio. To meet the competition in that particular territory we allowed loyal customers to make corresponding prices and settle with them at the end of the month on sugars sold in that prescribed territory. Our competitors soon got tired of the business and withdrew. . . ."[118] Havemeyer urged that the Western adopt the same tactic.

For the most part, the knowledge that one of the companies

[116] *Ibid.*, pp. 3959–60.
[117] *Ibid.*, pp. 1291–93, 1309–19, 3061–65, 3665–66.
[118] *Ibid.*, p. 3365.

affiliated with the American would retaliate was sufficient to dissuade an independent refinery from cutting below the industry price. As the head of the Los Alamitos Sugar Company later testified when explaining why his company always followed the price set by the Western, ". . . if we would cut the price ten cents they would meet it probably, and cut it ten cents more, so it would mean a price war, and being a small producer we could not afford to fight a big concern like the Western Sugar Refining Company. . . ."[119] Thus it was the economic power of the American Sugar Refining Company and its various affiliates which enforced the maintenance of the single industry price, both for refined cane and for processed beet sugar.

The ability to enforce this single industry price was, in turn, the key to Havemeyer's control of the domestic sugar industry. It was with this purpose in mind—the establishment of a single industry price and the corresponding elimination of price competition—that the original sugar trust had been formed and the American Sugar Refining Company organized to take its place. It was, moreover, the underlying motive for Havemeyer's efforts to prevent the entry of new firms into the industry and his endeavors to gain a commanding interest in the various beet sugar companies. It was, finally, the explanation for his constant intervention to see that sales were co-ordinated among the various companies in which the American had invested.

Thus, by 1907, when the more general Corporate Revolution was about to enter its second phase, Havemeyer as the head of the American Sugar Refining Company had succeeded in countering whatever economic threats had arisen to challenge his control over domestic sugar prices. The problem of entry had largely been solved, although not before several breaches occurred. The danger of sugar beet competition had for the most part been allayed through subvention. The only remaining threats to Havemeyer's control lay outside the economic system.

[119] *Ibid.*, pp. 3959–60.

10 :: THE OLD ORDER PASSETH

IT was not only the Rich Man's Panic of 1907, making it temporarily difficult to float further industrial securities, that brought an end to the Great Merger movement as the first phase of the Corporate Revolution. It was also the changing legal climate—the demonstrated willingness of the Roosevelt administration to enforce both the Sherman antitrust law and the prohibition of railroad rebates. The sugar refining industry, although its consolidation had long been completed, was not immune from these larger political and social influences. Henry Havemeyer, as president of the American Sugar Refining Company, found his efforts to regulate the industry increasingly hampered by fears of antitrust prosecution. Far more serious, the American was forced to plead guilty to charges of receiving illegal payments from the railroads. And this prosecution was only the beginning of the company's legal troubles. Havemeyer, if he had been more sensitive to the newer trends, might have been able to better protect the empire he had so carefully built up. But he was just about the last member of his generation still active in the American's affairs, and in the area of government relations he proved less adaptable than he had been when faced with the sugar beet threat.

::

By the fall of 1907 Henry Havemeyer, almost alone among those who had helped to organize the original sugar trust, was still associated with the successor to that consolidation—the American Sugar Refining Company. His older brother, Theodore, had died in 1897 at the age of sixty-three while serving as vice-president of the American. Although less forceful and less well known than his younger brother, Theodore had nonetheless exerted considerable influence in the company's councils and, perhaps most important, on the company's strong-willed president. His death deprived Henry Havemeyer of his closest and most trusted business associate.[1]

[1] *New York Times*, April 27, 1897.

Also gone was F. O. Matthiessen who, along with Theodore Havemeyer, had directed the manufacturing end of the business since the original consolidation. In 1900 Matthiessen had become so bitterly opposed to the continuing price war with Arbuckle Brothers that he had resigned his various posts in the company. A year later he had died in Paris at the age of sixty-eight.[2] Eight years earlier, in 1893, death had also overtaken Joseph B. Thomas, his place in the American Sugar Refining Company then being taken by his son, Washington B. Thomas.[3] The ties of John E. Searles, Jr., and Lowell M. Palmer to the American had been severed also, but for different reasons. Searles had been forced to resign his various positions in the company in 1898 when his outside financial losses proved embarrassing to the American;[4] Palmer had been forced to do the same in 1902 after questioning the propriety of Henry Havemeyer's personal interest in the National Sugar Refining Company.[5] Thus, of those involved in the original formation of the sugar trust, only Charles Senff, Havemeyer's cousin, John E. Persons, his trusted legal counselor, and Arthur Donner, an old business associate and a partner in the formerly Havemeyer-controlled DeCastro & Donner refinery, were still connected with the American Sugar Refining Company, sharing the burdens of management.

But Henry Havemeyer still preferred to shoulder most of those burdens himself. He was justly famous for his quick temper and his insistence on having things done his own way. This autocratic temperament was conspicuous in his management of the American Sugar Refining Company. As Charles R. Heike, who succeeded Searles as secretary of the company, later testified, "It was really a one-man concern. . . ."[6] Then, as an afterthought, he added: "There were some . . . strong men on [the board of directors]. Perhaps it was an exaggeration to call it a one-man concern. But, nevertheless, he [Havemeyer] was the dominating figure."[7] The testimony of others connected with the American painted a similar portrait.[8]

The American had, by 1907, already taken on certain of the characteristics of what has since been described as the "modern" corporation or the "megacorp."[9] From the point of view of size alone, it was

[2] *Ibid.*, March 10, 1901.
[3] Hardwick committee investigation, 1911, p. 1911.
[4] *New York Times*, October 25, 1908.
[5] Hardwick committee investigation, 1911, pp. 332–33, 340–42.
[6] *Ibid.*, p. 203. [7] *Ibid.*, p. 212. [8] *Ibid.*, p. 1914.
[9] See Adolph A. Berle and Gardener C. Means, *The Modern Corporation and Private Property*; Alfred S. Eichner, "Business Concentration and Its Significance."

the sixth-largest industrial corporation in the United States. Only the United States Steel Company, the International Harvester Company, the International Mercantile Marine Company—all three being consolidations of other industries which J. P. Morgan or his partners had arranged—the American Tobacco Company, and the Standard Oil Company could claim more than the $140 million in assets which the American Sugar Refining Company held.[10] Moreover, the American's stock had become widely dispersed among a large number of shareholders. There were over 9,200 separate owners of the company's preferred shares and 9,800 separate owners of the common stock, the average holding being no more than forty-nine and forty-six shares respectively.[11] The largest single block of stock owned by any one family represented less than 2.5 per cent of all the stock outstanding.[12]

Strangely enough, Henry Havemeyer and the members of his family owned very few shares in the American Sugar Refining Company. Shortly after the original sugar trust was formed, Henry had disposed of most of his trust certificates on the open market. Because it was not at all certain that the consolidation would prove successful, or even that it would be able to withstand legal attack, he had preferred to realize whatever he could from the sale of the trust certificates and put the money into a more secure form of investment. His brother Theodore had done the same.[13] This decision to dispose of the trust certificates led to an early separation of management from ownership—though few persons, even within the company itself, were aware that this had happened. By 1907, Henry Havemeyer held only 822

[10] This has been determined by comparing Gardiner C. Means's list of the largest industrial corporations in 1919 with *Moody's Manual* for 1907. The Means list can be found in his "The Large Corporation," pp. 38–39.

[11] Hardwick committee investigation, 1911, pp. 2973–74.

[12] This was a block of from 18,000 to 23,000 shares, held by Washington B. Thomas and other members of his family, out of 900,000 shares, both common and preferred, outstanding (*ibid.*, pp. 2054–55).

[13] This, however, did not preclude speculation in the American Sugar Refining Company's stock from time to time (see pp. 98 and 173–74 above). The decision to transfer the family wealth out of the sugar refining industry (an attempt to emulate the successful examples of John Jacob Astor and Cornelius Vanderbilt) was later to be a source of great disappointment to the heirs of the two Havemeyers. "Both brothers," the family biographer has written, "invested heavily in New York City real estate, which turned out badly, and they and their respective families would have been better off if they had retained their ownership of the stock of the American Sugar Refining Company" (Henry O. Havemeyer, Jr., *Biographical Record of the Havemeyer Family, 1606–1943*, p. 68). It was only in comparison with what the shares of American Sugar Refining Company stock were ultimately worth that the Havemeyer investment in real estate turned out badly.

shares of preferred stock and 137 shares of common stock in the company he headed, a merely nominal amount.[14]

But though the American Sugar Refining Company was beginning to display the characteristics of a more modern type of enterprise, Havemeyer continued to run it as if it were still a typical nineteenth-century proprietorship. In 1905, for example, he arranged for his son Horace to join him as an unpaid assistant, obviously with the intention of preparing him to take over one day as head of the company. Although he was only nineteen at the time, Horace had already spent two years in an unsalaried position learning the business.[15] This attempt to assure a dynastic succession was not the only throwback to an earlier way of doing things.[16] The elder Havemeyer also consistently refused to divulge any information as to the financial condition of the company—except what was required to obtain listing on the New York Stock Exchange—on the grounds that it was not in the interests of the company to do so. "In my report of a year ago," he told the annual meeting of stockholders in 1904, "I made the point that a business corporation is an aggregation of individuals, and that there were obvious objections to giving to competitors information about corporate affairs, that is to say, the affairs of a union of individuals, which a partnership or individual is not compelled to make public in respect of its or his own affairs. . . . I repeat the statement as applicable to the present situation."[17]

This refusal to disclose any information as to the financial condition of the American Sugar Refining Company was part of a more general policy of ignoring all public criticism. But perhaps the most significant instance of Havemeyer's failure to adapt to the changing nature of the company he headed was the single-handed manner in which he attended to all important matters. For example, in 1902, the American's board of directors had appointed Havemeyer, Washington B. Thomas, Palmer, and Donner as a committee "to take charge of the purchase and management of beet sugar companies."[18] The committee never met. Havemeyer simply went ahead and arranged for the purchase of the various beet sugar companies himself, returning to the

[14] Hardwick committee investigation, 1911, pp. 220–21, 553–54.

[15] *Ibid.*, pp. 563, 3038.

[16] One of the outstanding characteristics of the modern corporation, or megacorp, is that the management is chosen for its technical competence and previous service with the company rather than on the basis of family connections. This change in the selection of corporate management has significantly altered the nature of inheritance.

[17] Hardwick committee investigation, 1911, p. 2957.

[18] *Ibid.*, p. 2952.

full board of directors for its approval only after the terms of a sale had already been worked out. ". . . [H]aving confidence in his judgment and sagacity," Thomas later testified in regard to his and his fellow directors' role in the beet factory acquisitions, "we all agreed to follow [Havemeyer's] suggestions."[19] Other committees had been appointed in the past—such as the 1898 committee "to fix the price of refined sugars"—but most had met a similar fate, usurpation of their function by Havemeyer.[20]

While at times Havemeyer's fellow directors were troubled by the high-handed manner in which he ran the American Sugar Refining Company—though in general they deferred to his judgment—the stockholders themselves seemed not at all concerned. As long as the American continued to pay its customary dividend of 7 per cent on the preferred and common stock,[21] they were content to leave the stewardship of the company to the elected officers. At least that was the impression created by the lack of opposition to the company's policies at the annual stockholders' meetings.[22] In any case, the American seemed to have little difficulty in meeting its dividends once the price war with Arbuckle Brothers ended.[23] Its market position seemed impregnable, its long-term prospects favorable. Then, quite suddenly, the sugar empire that Havemeyer had struggled so long to create began to show signs of too great a strain.

::

The first sign of trouble appeared in the West. Beginning in 1898, the American Sugar Refining Company had entered into a series of long-term contracts to purchase that part of the Hawaiian crop not otherwise committed to the Western Sugar Refining Company. This

[19] *Ibid.*, p. 1939.

[20] *Ibid.*, p. 1926.

[21] *Ibid.*, p. 2522–23. The preferred stock of the American had received dividends of 7 per cent annually ever since the company was formed. The common stock had received dividends of 8 per cent in 1891, 9 per cent in 1892, 22 per cent in 1893, 12 per cent from 1894 to 1899, 6.5 per cent in 1900, and 7 per cent from 1901 to 1907.

[22] However, it should be noted that the meetings were seldom attended by more than a handful of persons (see the record of the annual meetings, *ibid.*, pp. 2904ff). At least one major stockholder, Edward F. Atkins, did sell most of his stock in the American when he learned that the company intended to invest in the beet sugar industry. Atkins objected to the policy on the grounds that it would "compete with and injure the refining interests" (*ibid.*, pp. 79–80). For more on Atkins, see pp. 307–8 below.

[23] The fact was that the American Sugar Refining Company's shares had become a "widows and orphans" stock, its steady earnings recommending it to the managers of trusts and estates. This same characteristic was reflected in

had been done to take the edge off complaints from the independent Hawaiian planters that the Western, by limiting its meltings to 120,000 tons annually, was denying them the natural market for their product.[24] While this arrangement provided the independent planters with an outlet for their sugar, the prices they received from the American were lower than what they thought they would have obtained had they been able to dispose of the sugar on the West Coast closer to home. Unhappy over this situation, the Hawaiian planters resolved to do something about it. When the contract with the American was renewed in 1905, they insisted on exempting from the terms of the agreement a total of 150,000 tons.[25]

By withholding this amount the planters hoped to force Claus Spreckels to give them more favorable treatment, that is, to take a larger share of their sugar cane on more advantageous terms. They realized that the only chance of accomplishing this objective lay in confronting Spreckels with a concrete threat to his company's position. Thus, after the contract with the American was renewed, the attention of the Hawaiian planters centered at first on the possibility of using the 150,000 tons of uncommitted cane to produce "washed sugars—the Hawaiian equivalent of the semirefined Louisiana "plantation" sugars—which could then be sold in competition with the Western Sugar Refining Company's product.

One enterprise, the Honolulu Plantation Company had, in fact, already gone ahead with its plans to install a centrifugal machine on its property and was beginning, in January of 1905, to make the first shipments of semirefined sugar to the mainland. It was not long before the Honolulu company was joined by at least one other large cane grower.[26] Still, selective price cuts made by the Western, together with the differential below refined sugar which the washed sugars had to be sold for, took most of the profit out of this type of operation.

---

the trading of the American's shares on the New York Stock Exchange, the price of both the common and preferred stock showing only steady growth and seldom fluctuating violently. From a low-high of 113.0–135.0 in 1902, the common stock had risen to a low-high of 127.5—157.0 in 1906, while from a low-high of 115.0–122.0 in 1902, the preferred shares had reached a low-high of 128.5–140.0 in 1906. See *Commercial and Financial Chronicle*, 1902—6.

[24] *United States* v. *American Sugar Refining Co. et al.*, pretrial investigation, 1912, pp. 3328–53, 3500–3501; Hardwick committee investigation, 1911, pp. 1127, 2948.

[25] *United States* v. *American Sugar Refining Co. et al.*, pretrial investigation, 1912, pp. 3359–60.

[26] *Ibid.*, pp. 3386–78.

The other independent Hawaiian planters, members of a previously formed Sugar Factors Association, turned their attention to the possibility of resuming operation of the converted flour mill at Crockett, California, once the lease to the Western Sugar Refining Company expired in 1906. Fully a year before that date, in March of 1905, the Sugar Factors Association formally acquired title to the property, then levied an assessment of $3 a ton on the sugar grown by all of its members to finance the enlargement and expansion of the refinery.[27] The reorganized enterprise was known as the California & Hawaiian Sugar Company.

In the face of this double onslaught—the importation of washed sugars and the threatened reopening of the Crockett refinery—officials of the Western Sugar Refining Company became increasingly disposed to try to reach a settlement with the Hawaiian cane growers. But although negotiations between the two parties continued over the next nine months, an agreement proved impossible because of differences over three points—the specific mechanism for bringing the two refining interests together, the share of the market each group was to have, and the problem of controlling the influx af washed sugars to the mainland.[28] On December 8, 1905, Havemeyer wired William Hannan, announcing that negotiations had broken off. A month later he wrote to J. T. Witherspoon in New Orleans, warning: "There will be a row on, on the Pacific Coast beginning about March 1st, between the sugar refining interests there. The Crockett refinery will open and refined prices will be low and will be reflected on the Missouri River."[29] Others in the industry also expected that when the California & Hawaiian's refinery opened, western sugar prices would fall.[30]

Late in March, 1906, the Crockett refinery turned out its first sugars, but the anticipated price war with the Western failed to materialize. As the California & Hawaiian's general manager later testified: ". . . we were in rather bad shape. The pipes in the refinery had corroded and rusted to such an extent that they were held together largely by the paint."[31] The small quantity of granulated sugar the

[27] *Ibid.*, pp. 3374–78.

[28] From a reading of the correspondence it is questionable how eager the members of the Sugar Factors Association were to reach an understanding. Hannan, for example, complained that the association had been "dilatory about bringing the matter to any final conclusion," and he questioned whether its members "really mean business" (*ibid.*, pp. 3406, 3409).

[29] *Ibid.*, p. 3412.

[30] See Willett & Gray's *Weekly Statistical Sugar Trade Journal*, March 15, 1906.

[31] George M. Rolph, *United States* v. *American Sugar Refining Co. et al.*, pretrial testimony, 1912, p. 3926.

company was able to produce had almost no noticeable effect on prices in the face of the normally large spring demand for sugar.[32] Both sides were glad for the respite; the California & Hawaiian's people wanted to get their refinery into better shape, while the Western's officials planned to continue the negotiations. Throughout that spring, before the competition grew more intense, Hannan tried to reach an agreement with representatives of the Sugar Factors Association but without success.[33] Then Havemeyer decided to have a go at it himself.

He suggested a way of resolving the issues, but found his efforts to bring about a peaceful settlement stymied by two factors. One was the bitter hatred which members of the Factors Association felt toward the Spreckels family. The other was the question of how in detail the harmony of interests should be arranged. Havemeyer proposed that a new company be formed to handle the sales of both the Western and California & Hawaiian plants.[34] But when representatives of the two companies met to consider the specific details of such an arrangement, they decided instead merely to divide the West Coast cane market between them according to fixed percentages, leaving each company free to market its own sugars as it wished.

When Havemeyer learned of this he became quite disturbed. "I have gone hurriedly over what you have written in reference to the negotiations," he wrote in reply to Hannan in February, 1907, "and it only leaves an unpleasant impression in my mind—not as to any percentage the Crockett people may be entitled to and which the Messrs. Spreckels may grant—but there is a legal way as well as an illegal way of bringing these things about." Unless the matter can be arranged in strict conformity with the law, Havemeyer continued, "we are entirely out of it and disavow any responsibility whatever."[35]

Although Havemeyer refused to have anything further to do with this output-limiting arrangement, on the grounds that it violated the Sherman antitrust law, the agreement appears to have been put into effect anyway. Early in October, 1907, just as the California sugar beet crop was being harvested, Willett & Gray's *Weekly Statistical Sugar Trade Journal* reported that the San Francisco market was "unsettled," with prices being cut ten cents a hundredweight.[36] A week

[32] Willett & Gray's *Weekly Statistical Sugar Trade Journal,* March 22, 1906, and subsequent issues.

[33] *United States* v. *American Sugar Refining Co. et al.*, pretrial *testimony,* 1912, p. 3926.

[34] *Ibid.*, pp. 3414, 3419–20.

[35] *Ibid.*, p. 3421.

[36] October 3, 1907.

later, however, it reported an advance in prices of twenty cents a hundredweight, an unusually large jump for that time of year. "This is a full recovery of the recent declines in that market," the journal noted, "and indicates a renewal of harmonious actions on a normal basis."[37]

Meanwhile, the American Beet Sugar Company had itself cited fears of antitrust prosecution to justify its unilateral abrogation of the commission agreement with the American Sugar Refining Company. One of the American Beet Sugar Company's influential stockholders, Henry R. Duval, had been questioning for some time the legality and desirability of paying the American Sugar Refining Company ¼ of a cent a pound to "supervise" the sale of its sugar.[38] Although Cutting, who had negotiated the agreement, continued to insist on its value to the company, Duval was finally able to persuade the American Beet Sugar Company's directors to submit the commission agreement to special counsel for an opinion. The special counsel, Wayne McVeigh, U.S. attorney general under President Garfield and a distinguished member of the New York bar,[39] agreed with Duval that the contract was of doubtful legality. On December 18, 1906, the American Beet Sugar Company's board of directors informed the American Sugar Refining Company that in light of McVeigh's opinion it would make no further payments under the commission agreement.[40]

Havemeyer replied that it was hardly fair for the American Beet Sugar Company, having benefited from the agreement for four years, to terminate it arbitrarily without even compensating the American Sugar Refining Company.[41] But, having appealed to the good faith of the American Beet Sugar Company's directors and found it wanting, Havemeyer preferred to let the matter drop rather than risk litigation.[42] As it was, the only change in the relationship of the two companies was that the ¼ of a cent a pound which had previously flowed

[37] Willett & Gray's *Weekly Statistical Sugar Trade Journal*, October 10, 1907; see also Havemeyer to Hannan, March 5, 1907, reprinted in *United States* v. *American Sugar Refining Co. et al.*, pretrial testimony, 1912, p. 3422.

[38] *United States* v. *American Sugar Refining Co. et al.*, pretrial testimony, 1912, pp. 7170–71. For biographical data on Duval see *National Cyclopedia of American Biography*, as well as *Who's Who* for 1906–7.

[39] For biographical data on McVeigh see *National Cyclopedia of American Biography*, as well as *Who's Who* for 1906–7, and p. 294, n. 8, below.

[40] *United States* v. *American Sugar Refining Co. et al.*, pretrial testimony, 1912, pp. 7171–73.

[41] *Ibid.*, pp. 7174–76.

[42] At Havemeyer's request, the directors of the American Beet Sugar Company had McVeigh's law partner meet with Parsons, but nothing came of the conference (*ibid.*, p. 7177); see also Hardwick committee investigation, 1911, pp. 2113–14.

into the treasury of the American Sugar Refining Company now remained in the coffers of the American Beet Sugar Company.[43] Insofar as the marketing of the American Beet Sugar Company's product was concerned, nothing changed; the division-of-markets arrangement remained in effect.[44]

Far more serious than Havemeyer's difficulties in controlling his burgeoning empire, however, were the threats by various groups independent of the American Sugar Refining Company to erect refineries in Baltimore and New Orleans.[45] Already, one such independent plant, known as the Knickerbocker, had been built at Edgewater, New Jersey, across the Hudson River from New York City—although its financial backing was so weak that the refinery had as yet been unable to operate for more than one or two weeks during a sixteen-month period.[46] But most serious of all were the increasing legal difficulties in which the American Sugar Refining Company and its officers found themselves.

::

A significant change had come over the federal government. In part, it simply reflected the youthfulness of President Theodore Roosevelt, who had been only forty-three years old when he succeeded William McKinley in 1901. But the change in Washington's mood also reflected the chief executive's views as to the proper role of government, views that differed sharply from those of his predeces-

[43] *United States* v. *American Sugar Refining Co. et al.*, pretrial testimony, 1912, p. 7171.

[44] Willett & Gray's *Weekly Statistical Sugar Trade Journal*, October 17, 1907, and subsequent issues.

[45] *Ibid.*, April 19, May 17, and August 30, 1906. In Baltimore the Chesapeake Sugar Refining Company was incorporated on May 15, 1906, with an authorized capital of $1.5 million. Organized by a group of Baltimore businessmen interested in expanding the industry of their port, the company announced plans to erect a refinery that would produce 1,500 barrels of refined sugar daily.

[46] This refinery, originally owned by the Knickerbocker Sugar Refining Company, had been started by a group of western wholesale grocers in 1901 and later had been taken over by an individual promoter (see p. 288 below). However, it had remained unfinished, with its outer shell in place but without machinery, until it was taken over by the Warner Sugar Refining Company in 1906. The refinery had then been fully equipped, and it sold its first sugar on June 28, 1906. Following these initial sales, however, the desperate financial condition of the Warner company's owners had forced the refinery to discontinue production. Incidentally, those owners, members of the Warner family, had obtained the money for their sugar refining venture from the sale of a glucose factory at Waukegan, Illinois, to the Corn Products Company. See Willett & Gray's *Weekly Statistical Sugar Trade Journal*, April 19, June 28, and October 4, 1906. For one reason why the Warner family may have been unable to operate their refinery profitably, see p. 294 below.

sors. Roosevelt came into office committed to the belief that government should play a positive role in regulating the economic life of the nation.[47] Believing as he did that large aggregations of capital were a concomitant of social progress, he refused to condemn all such combinations outright. ". . . Nothing of importance is gained," he said, "by breaking up a huge interstate and international industrial organization *which has not offended otherwise than by its size*. . . . Those who would seek to restore the days of unlimited and controlled competition . . . are attempting not only the impossible, but what, if possible, would be undesirable."[48] A moralist at heart, Roosevelt was inclined to draw a distinction between "good" and "bad" trusts. To deal with the latter, he believed that two measures were required, publicity for corporate activities and elimination of railroad rebates. Thus it was that during his first term of office Theodore Roosevelt concentrated his efforts on securing from a somewhat reluctant Congress passage of the Elkins Act, which for the first time provided stiff criminal penalties for railroad rebating, and of the Department of Commerce Act, which included a provision for the establishment of a Bureau of Corporations to collect and publish information on companies engaged in interstate commerce.[49]

Roosevelt recognized, however, that new laws were of little value unless they were backed by officials willing and able to enforce them. He therefore made a conscious effort to appoint men of dedication, intelligence, and ability to positions with responsibility for dealing with business activities, and his success in this respect was one of his administration's more significant accomplishments.[50] Among the many bright young men whom the president attracted to federal office was Henry L. Stimson, a thirty-eight-year-old corporation lawyer. Although New York's senior Republican senator had favored someone else for the post, Stimson was named by Roosevelt in January, 1906, as U.S. attorney for the Southern District of New York.[51]

Stimson was, in terms of social and class background, cut from the same cloth as the president himself. It was significant that he had

[47] John M. Blum, *The Republican Roosevelt*, pp. 107–8; George E. Mowry, *The Era of Theodore Roosevelt*, p. 112; see also Henry Steele Commager and Richard B. Morris' introduction to the latter book, pp. x–xi.

[48] Blum, *The Republican Roosevelt*, pp. 116–17.

[49] Theodore Roosevelt, *The Letters of Theodore Roosevelt*, ed. Elting E. Morison, 3: 591–92; Mowry, *The Era of Theodore Roosevelt*, pp. 123–24.

[50] Roosevelt, *Letters of Theodore Roosevelt*, 5: 328; Blum, *The Republican Roosevelt*, pp. 49–50.

[51] Henry L. Stimson and McGeorge Bundy, *On Active Service in Peace and War*, pp. 3–4; Elting E. Morison, *Turmoil and Tradition*, pp. 94–95.

first come to Roosevelt's attention in 1897 when he successfully staged a revolt against the old-line Republican leadership on New York City's East Side (though the two men soon discovered that they also shared a love of outdoor camping).[52] Stimson had not asked for the appointment as U.S. attorney, nor had he expected it; but when he traveled to Washington soon after the nomination was announced to discuss his new duties with Attorney General William H. Moody, he learned that the president had good reason for insisting on the appointment of someone other than the usual political sycophant.[53]

Moody first told Stimson how important he considered the New York U.S. attorney's office, calling it and the Chicago office "the right and left arms of the Attorney General."[54] He then explained that under Stimson's predecessor the New York office had fallen into a state of laxness and ineffectuality. Moody told Stimson that he wanted the office completely reorganized, that he expected the New York office to take a major role in attacking corporate abuses. The attorney general pointed out that as yet not a single prosecution under either the Sherman Act or the Elkins Act had been initiated in the Southern District of New York, although that was where the offices of most large corporations were located.

Moody then explained why an immediate reorganization of the U.S. attorney's office in New York was of such crucial importance. The administration, he told Stimson, had in its possession evidence that the American Sugar Refining Company was receiving illegal rebates from the major trunk-line railroads. Moreover, the evidence had come from William Randolph Hearst's *New York American*.[55]

At the time of Moody's conversation with Stimson it seemed that Hearst might be the next Democratic candidate for president. Having used his inherited wealth to build a nationwide chain of widely read newspapers, Hearst was in the process of using that journalistic empire to drum his way into the White House. Through the personal publicity that these various papers afforded him, Hearst was able to portray himself as an unrelenting "foe of the trusts," while the editorial pages of his newspapers pilloried virtually every other politician, from President Theodore Roosevelt on down, for failing to take action against "the corporations."[56]

Trading on his reputation as a "foe of the trusts," Hearst easily won

[52] John D. Viener, "A Sense of Obligation," pp. 4–8.
[53] *Ibid.*, pp. 3–4; Roosevelt, *Letters of Theodore Roosevelt*, 5: 127.
[54] Stimson Diaries, bk. 1, Stimson Papers.
[55] *Ibid.*; Morison, *Turmoil and Tradition*, pp. 100–101.
[56] W. A. Swanberg, *Citizen Hearst*, pp. 187–89, 200–203, 241–42.

election to Congress in 1902, and on his arrival in Washington he promptly introduced bills to strengthen the Sherman antitrust law and to increase the power of the Interstate Commerce Commission.[57] Three years later, having bolted the Democratic party, he narrowly missed being elected mayor of New York City while running as the candidate of the independent Municipal Ownership League. Hearst may well have been the demagogue his enemies thought him to be, but there was no doubting that his appeal to extreme national pride and fear of corporate power were winning him the support of many small businessmen and skilled laborers—precisely the groups whose loyalty Theodore Roosevelt hoped to win with his own "Square Deal" program.[58] It was probably because of this reputation which Hearst and his newspapers enjoyed that Thomas P. Riley, after a falling out with Lowell M. Palmer in the fall of 1905, decided to go to the *New York American* with evidence he hoped would put his former employer in jail.

Realizing that the factor plans with the various wholesale grocers associations were of little value as a barrier to new competition, the American Sugar Refining Company had scrapped those agreements early in 1903.[59] Then, following the example of the Standard Oil and American Tobacco companies,[60] it had experimented with other devices designed to discourage entry. For a while it tried acquiring its own chain of retail outlets, as well as increasing its advertising expenditures, but neither expedient proved suited to the particular circumstances of the sugar trade.[61] The most important competitive advantage which the American Sugar Refining Company had over potential rivals was still the combination of special concessions it received from the railroads.

[57] *Ibid.*, pp. 209–10. Hearst was soon criticized, not only for his frequent absences from Congress, but also for his failure to push actively for the enactment of the bills he had introduced.

[58] *Ibid.*, pp. 202–3; Oliver Carlson and Ernest E. Bates, *Hearst, Lord of San Simeon*, pp. 132–37; Blum, *The Republican Roosevelt*, pp. 55–57.

[59] The factor plans were abandoned, according to Willett & Gray's *Sugar Trade Journal*, "because the grocers themselves have not adhered to the terms they themselves made. . . . The South has never, from its initiation years ago, abided by [the arrangement]. The West generally have [*sic*] been in and out of it. New England alone has adhered strictly to its terms, with New York and New Jersey following it closely" (January 8, 1903). Apparently the factor plan was retained only in Philadelphia; see *United States* v. *American Sugar Refining Co. et al.*, pretrial testimony, 1912, pp. 12724–25.

[60] Allen Nevins, *Study in Power*, 2: 37–53; Richard B. Tennant, *The American Cigarette Industry*, pp. 54–55.

[61] *United States* v. *American Sugar Refining Co. et al.*, pretrial testimony, 1912, pp. 12707, 12769–70.

Following the passage of the Elkins Act in 1903, the railroads had attempted to cancel the two-cents-a-hundredweight special allowance for "cartage" on the grounds that it was illegal. But after two months, during which time the American Sugar Refining Company refused to continue dividing the sugar traffic among the various lines according to the usual percentages, the railroads backed down and promptly paid the claims for refunds submitted to them through Palmer's office. Still, to protect themselves from possible prosecution, they insisted on publishing the two-cents-a-hundredweight allowance in their tariff schedules, referring to it as a "transfer" allowance and making it available to any sugar refining company capable of supplying its own lighterage services.[62] Arbuckle Brothers qualified for this special allowance by shortly thereafter building its own terminal facilities,[63] but for prospective new firms to do the same would have meant an additional capital expense. While it was true that the two-cents-a-hundredweight allowance now went to the Havemeyer-owned Eastern District Terminal, not the American Sugar Refining Company, the latter did continue to receive special rebates from the railroads whenever it found itself faced with an unusually competitive situation in one of its distant markets. It was the evidence of these special rebates—the correspondence between Palmer's office and the railroads—together with the records of the financial transactions which Riley turned over to the *New York American* and which the representatives of that newspaper then turned over to the U.S. Attorney general.[64]

::

For the next several months Stimson was completely absorbed in reorganizing his office and in going through the documents received from Riley. Helping him sift through the evidence was Henry A. Wise, one of the few assistants under the previous U.S. attorney retained by Stimson.[65] Because of the large number of documents and the cryptic manner in which the records of payment had been kept, this was a slow, difficult task; and only because Riley was available to explain the various notations were Stimson and Wise able to make any progress. Finally, however, the U.S. attorney and his assistant

[62] 14 ICC Reports 621, 623–24.

[63] Hardwick committee investigation, 1911, p. 2310.

[64] Stimson Diaries, bk. 1, Stimson Papers. On February 1, 1907, an hour after he took the oath of office, Stimson met with Moody in New York, at which time he was introduced to Riley and two representatives of the *New York American*. A transcript of that meeting can be found in Department of Justice (JD) File No. 59–8–13, sec. 4.

[65] Stimson Diaries, bk. 1, Stimson Papers.

felt they understood the facts in the case well enough to begin presenting evidence to a grand jury. On March 6, 1906, subpoenas were issued directing officials of the major trunk-line railroads, the American Sugar Refining Company, and several leading wholesale grocery firms to appear in court to answer questions in regard to railroad rebates, thus for the first time revealing publicly the investigation by Stimson's office. The *New York American* used the occasion to trumpet its own role in initiating the inquiry by printing on its front page a "complaint" signed by William Randolph Hearst accusing the railroads of granting secret rebates under the guise of an allowance for lighterage.[66] Eighteen days later, indictments were handed down against the American Sugar Refining Company and the New York Central Railroad, the first of twenty-one such indictments to be issued by federal grand juries during the next twelve months.[67]

In preparing his cases Stimson had made a crucial strategic decision. Rather than seek the conviction of any company for broadly violating the Elkins Act, he had decided to prosecute each individual instance of rebating separately. This decision was dictated in part by the complicated nature of the alleged offenses, the difficulty of tracing even for a single transaction the payment of rebates through the maze of corporate structures which had been erected. Although this method of procedure was considerably more time-consuming and tended to obscure the over-all pattern of rebating, it had one important advantage. It meant that the American Sugar Refining Company and the railroads accused of granting it special concessions would remain continually in the public spotlight as they were forced to defend themselves against first one and then another charge of illegal practices. In the eyes of the U. S. attorney general and his "right arm" in New York, it was this glare of unfavorable publicity which offered the most effective weapon against corporate abuses. As Moody had remarked earlier to Stimson, alluding to the recent state investigation of insurance companies, "We have had the lesson here in New York that, after

[66] *New York American*, March 8, 1906. Needless to say, the "complaint" by Hearst had no legal significance. Moreover, the special allowance for "transfer," since it was openly published, was less clearly a violation of the law than were the secret concessions the American Sugar Refining Company received to meet competition in selected areas. Only after lengthy proceedings did the Interstate Commerce Commission order an end to the special allowance for "transfer," although the same payment (two cents a hundredweight) was reinstated as an allowance for lighterage when this was actually performed. See 14 ICC Reports 621; Hardwick committee investigation, 1911, pp. 1424ff.

[67] Report, Stimson to Attorney General Charles J. Bonaparte, July 15, 1907, Stimson Papers, pp. 9–12. The indictments can be found in *United States* v. *American Sugar Refining Co. et al.: Exhibits*, pp. 2592ff.

all, publicity . . . is about the best remedy that modern conditions afford. We have seen this tremendous insurance power pulled down like a house of straw—not by any prosecution, but by public opinion."[68] Although Stimson subsequently sought to broaden his line of attack by bringing a charge of conspiracy to violate the Elkins Act against the American Sugar Refining Company and the various railroad companies, Southern District Court Judge George C. Holt refused to sustain the indictment.[69]

Thus it was that the first case to come to trial involved a seemingly minor episode in the over-all scheme of special concessions, the granting of a rebate by the New York Central Railroad to the Detroit wholesale grocery firm of W. H. Edgar & Sons on 1,840,000 pounds of the American's sugar shipped from New York between December 2, 1902, and January 11, 1903. The rebate, which amounted to five cents off the published freight rate of twenty-three cents a hundred pounds, had been arranged for and handled by Palmer's office and was intended to enable the Edgar firm, one of the American's principal distribution outlets in the Midwest, to meet the local competition of beet sugar companies.[70] But while the focus of the case had narrowed greatly, several major legal questions remained. These were the issues of whether or not, under the Elkins Act, a corporation could be held criminally liable for the acts of its officers; whether or not a payment made by a railroad, even if the payment could not be shown to have reached the shipper, was nonetheless a rebate; whether or not a rebate paid on goods shipped before the Elkins Act went into effect was illegal; and, finally, whether or not the shipper receiving a rebate, as well as the carrier paying the rebate, could be convicted under the law. It was because of this last question that the charge against the New York Central was tried first, beginning October 18, 1906.[71] Stimson and Wise had prepared the government's case carefully, and after a two-day hearing the railroad was found guilty on all counts. After imposing an $18,000 fine, Judge Holt declared:

The case was a flagrant one. The transactions which took place under this illegal contract were very large; the amounts of rebates returned were considerable . . . amounting to more than one-fifth of the entire tariff charge

[68] Transcript of meeting between Moody, Stimson, and Riley on February 1, 1907, JD File No. 59–8–13, sec. 4, pp. 42–43.

[69] Report, Stimson to Bonaparte, July 15, 1907, Stimson Papers, p. 13; Stimson Diaries, bk. 1, Stimson Papers.

[70] Decision of Judge Holt in *United States* v. *New York Central Railroad,* JD File No. 59–8–13, sec. 1.

[71] Report, Stimson to Bonaparte, July 15, 1907, Stimson Papers, p. 13; Morison, *Turmoil and Tradition,* p. 105.

for the transportation of merchandise from this city to Detroit. . . . Such a violation of the law, in my opinion, is a very much more heinous act than the ordinary common, vulgar crimes which come before criminal courts constantly for punishment. This crime was committed by men of education and of large business experience and whose standing in the community was such that they might have been expected to set an example of obedience to law, upon the maintenance of which alone in this country the security of their property depends. It was committed on behalf of a great railroad corporation, which, like other railroad corporations, has received gratuitously from the state large and valuable privileges . . . and which is charged with the highest obligation . . . not to carry on its business with unjust discrimination.[72]

To Elihu Root's letter congratulating him for his successful prosecution, Stimson replied, "Ever since I began this work it has seemed to me that if we could stop rebating and keep the railroads open on equal terms to all shippers, and so prevent the large corporations from strengthening themselves behind illegal transportation favors, the most serious of our trust difficulties would be solved." In line with Root's advice to "press, press, press after the first conviction and to follow, follow that up by rapid and strong blows," Stimson announced his intention to proceed next against the American Sugar Refining Company.[73]

Stimson, however, was not the only one who was receiving credit for the outcome of the case. William Randolph Hearst, in the midst of an election campaign to become the governor of New York on the Democratic ticket, was capitalizing on the news of the New York Central's conviction to proclaim his own role in the affair—to the embarrassment of the Republican party chairman in New York.[74] That official, Herbert Parsons, brother of the American Sugar Refining Company's counsel, wrote to Stimson asking if it might not be possible to delay further action in the rebate matters until after the election. "I do not suggest that anything improper be done," Parsons continued, "but if Government officers have any discretion therein,

[72] *United States* v. *New York Central Railroad*, JD File No. 59–8–13, sec. 1. The quotation has been edited slightly for greater readability.

[73] Root to Stimson, October 14, 1906; Stimson to Root, October 22, 1906; and Stimson to Moody, October 27, 1906; all in Stimson Papers.

[74] Hearst, after making his peace with Tammany Hall, had secured the Democratic nomination for governor. His opponent in the bitterly fought contest was Charles Evans Hughes, who had been picked by Roosevelt to oppose Hearst because of his role in the New York insurance companies investigation. Roosevelt's decision to send Elihu Root to Utica to deliver an election-eve speech denouncing Hearst as a demagogue is believed by some to have made the difference in Hughes's narrow margin of victory, 58,000 votes of the 1.5 million cast (Swanberg, *Citizen Hearst*, pp. 242–52).

it seems to me it is their duty, in the public interest, to avoid a course which will play into the hands of a liar and which he will distort to his own selfish advantage."[75] Although Stimson had earlier rejected a similar suggestion from Root with the comment that, "if I should once begin to allow my official conduct to be swayed by considerations such as those, I feel it would end by eventually leading me wholly astray,"[76] the fact was that the first case against the American Sugar Refining Company did not come to trial until the middle of November, 1906.

This case involved an incident of rebating that differed from the one considered in the trial of the New York Central. The American was charged with receiving a rebate of six cents off the published freight rate of twenty-one cents a hundred pounds on shipments over the New York Central's lines to Cleveland for reconsignment to points beyond and one of four cents off the published rate on shipments to Cleveland itself. Although the total amount of such rebates was unknown, it was charged that at least one payment of $26,141.81 had been made on April 2, 1903, as part of the illegal arrangement. The specific instance of alleged rebating was different, but the outcome of the trial was the same. The American was found guilty and fined $18,000.[77] Stimson then made preparations to begin trying the next case.

At this point the attorneys for the American realized that it was pointless to continue contesting the government's charges. Approaching Stimson, they asked if it would be possible to arrange a deal. "I told them," Stimson reported to Moody, "that in case they should abandon their defiant attitude and plead guilty, thereby saving the Government the expense of prosecution, and affording to the public the example of this great corporation admitting its guilt, and naturally promising to avoid such practices in the future, my own disposition would be to treat them much more leniently than if they continued to force me to try out the cases." But he warned the lawyers for the

[75] Parsons to Stimson, October 20, 1906, Stimson Papers. There is no evidence that the fraternal relationship ever had any bearing on the prosecution of the rebate cases. In his Diaries, bk. 1 (*ibid.*), Stimson does mention that when he was in Washington immediately after his appointment as U.S. attorney, he attended a social gathering at the White House and that "in the course of the evening T.R. very nearly made an ominous break by beginning to talk to me about the proposed prosecution of the Sugar Trust—in the presence of Parsons who was counsel for the company." It is not entirely clear from the diary entry whether it was John or Herbert Parsons to whom Stimson was referring.

[76] Root to Stimson, October 4, 1906, and Stimson to Root, October, 8, 1906, Stimson Papers.

[77] *United States* v. *American Sugar Refining Co. et al.: Exhibits*, pp. 2656–61.

American that "the fine must be of sufficient magnitude to avoid any possible criticism on the part of the public."[78] The attorney general agreed with Stimson's decision to end the pending cases without further litigation, although he realized that "every single case which is tried hurts the company altogether out of proportion to any punishment which can be inflicted upon it."[79]

After several conferences between Stimson and attorneys for the American, it was agreed that the company would plead guilty to the remaining indictments against it, and be fined an additional $150,000. On December 11, 1906, this arrangement was carried out, thus bringing to an end the prosecution of the American Sugar Refining Company for receiving illegal rebates.[80] While certain of the other defendants continued to fight the government's charges, Stimson had for the most part accomplished his objectives. In addition to resolving certain unsettled questions in regard to the Elkins Act in a way that was most favorable to the government, he had taught the railroads and one of their large industrial customers a painful lesson. Although the fine levied against the Standard Oil Company four months earlier by Judge Kenesaw Mountain Landis for illegal rebating had been spectacularly larger (the penalty on being found guilty on 1,461 counts having been set at $29,240,000), everyone expected—correctly, as it turned out—that the fine would be declared excessive by a higher court.[81] Stimson, while obtaining a more modest penalty, had secured the "sugar trust's" complete surrender, without even the possibility of an appeal. Now it would be possible to test whether publicity of wrongdoing and elimination of rebating were sufficient to remedy the alleged abuses of large corporations. Meanwhile, the American Sugar Refining Company and its officers found themselves confronted by legal prosecution of another sort.

: :

Adolph Segel was an Austrian immigrant who had made a career of promoting industrial enterprises, then selling them to others. He had already built a match factory and a soap-rendering plant and had succeeded in selling them at a profit to other firms in those industries when, in 1894, he decided to promote a sugar refinery. Organizing the United States Sugar Refining Company, he purchased a tract of land

[78] Stimson to Moody, November 28, 1906, Stimson Papers.
[79] Moody to Stimson, November 29, 1906, *ibid.*
[80] Stimson to Moody, December 11, 1906, *ibid.*
[81] Nevins, *Study in Power*, 2: 365–67.

in Camden, New Jersey, and proceeded to erect a plant capable of turning out 1,500 barrels of sugar daily. When the refinery was completed, Segel sat back to wait for an offer from the American Sugar Refining Company.[82]

He did not wait long. In the fall of 1895, shortly after the Camden refinery was completed, Segel received a call from John Dos Passos representing the American Sugar Refining Company. Dos Passos asked Segel how much he wanted for his plant, and Segel mentioned a figure of $1.4 million. Later, however, following the financial panic of 1896, Segel agreed to settle for half that sum, but even this amount provided him with a profit of between $50,000 and $100,000 on the transaction. After this successful venture, Segel went on to organize companies and build plants which he successfully unloaded on the steel, shipbuilding, and asphalt combinations. Then, in 1901, he decided to have another go at the American Sugar Refining Company.[83]

This time Segel made plans to build a plant capable of turning out 3,000 barrels of sugar daily. Choosing a site across the river from the Camden refinery, he organized the Pennsylvania Sugar Refining Company in Philadelphia to undertake the project. This second refinery was completed in the fall of 1903 at a cost of $1,075,000 (exclusive of the land) and was then stocked with nominal quantities of bone black, anthracite coal, and raw sugar, all with the purpose of making it appear that the plant was about to begin operating. Once more Segel sat back to wait for an offer from the sugar "trust."[84]

An offer, however, failed to materialize. Officials of the American Sugar Refining Company had, for some time, been following the progress of the Pennsylvania refinery, and they knew from their informants that Segel was having trouble raising sufficient working capital to get his plant into operation. They decided to bide their time, having been told that if they waited long enough they probably would be able to acquire the property through foreclosure proceedings. The fact was that Segel, at a time of financial stringency, had overextended himself. He was in the midst of several projects, including the construction of a 600-room apartment house in Philadelphia, none of which could be completed without the funds he hoped to receive from the sale of the Pennsylvania refinery.[85] And as time went

[82] Hardwick committee investigation, 1911, p. 1328; *United States* v. *American Sugar Refining Co. et al.*, pretrial testimony, 1912, p. 5534.

[83] *United States* v. *American Sugar Refining Co. et al.*, pretrial testimony, 1912, p. 5202.

[84] *Ibid.*, pp. 5397, 5525–34.

[85] *Ibid.*, pp. 12719–20, 5187–89, 5193–203.

by, and not even the hint of an offer came from the American, Segel became increasingly desperate.

Finally he turned to George Kissel, a financier of sorts, for assistance. Examining Segel's business affairs, Kissel concluded that his client needed at least $1.25 million to avoid immediate bankruptcy.[86] It is not clear from the record whether the idea originated with Kissel or with Segel, but, in any case, they decided to go to the American to ask for a loan of that amount.[87] Meeting with Havemeyer, and later with Parsons in New York, Kissel was able to work out the following arrangement: The American Sugar Refining Company would lend Segel the sum he requested for one year at 6 per cent interest. In return, Segel would turn over to the American as collateral $1 million in bonds which had been issued to finance construction of the Philadelphia apartment house and, in addition, $500,000 in bonds and 26,000 shares of common stock in the Pennsylvania Sugar Refining Company. The common shares, tendered in the form of a trust arrangement, were sufficient to give the American control of the company, and it was agreed, moreover, that Havemeyer would have the right to appoint four men of his own choice to the seven-member board of directors. Finally, until the loan was repaid, the Pennsylvania refinery was not to be operated except with the consent of the lender. To avoid the latter's direct involvement, the entire arrangement was to be made through Kissel, who would act as agent for the American Sugar Refining Company.[88]

[86] *Ibid.*, pp. 5348–49, 5413.

[87] On July 6, 1905, Parsons wrote to Havemeyer as follows: "Mr. Kissel was Segel's broker, on Segel's behalf made the proposal . . ." (*ibid.*, pp. 5651–52). It may have been that the idea to go to the American Sugar Refining Company for the loan was Kissel's alone. Segel's lawyer in the matter, Thomas B. Harned, later testified that in return for agreeing to help Segel in his financial plight, Kissel had stipulated that Segel should not object to the source from which the funds were obtained (*ibid.*, pp. 5348–49). On the other hand, it is quite clear that Kissel and Segel later worked hand in hand to try to get American to buy out Segal's interest in the Pennsylvania refinery (see p. 287 below). As a seasonal greeting, Kissel wrote the following to Segel in December of 1905: "I send you this little pencil merely to enable you to write checks at all times of the day and night, which you can do if you hang it on your watch chain. With it accept my best wishes for a good Christmas and the best of New Years. May you succeed in making the Bellevue Stratford look like 30 cents, make sugar cane grow in North Broad Street and smash the U.S. Steel Trust with small briquettes . . ." (*United States* v. *American Sugar Refining Co. et al.*, pretrial testimony, 1912, pp. 5689–90). Given Segel's way of doing business, the secretiveness with which he carried on his affairs and the instinctive habit he had of disclosing less than the full truth even to his closest business associates, it was possible that he had first suggested the plan of going to the American Sugar Refining Company to borrow money and then failed to tell Harned of this fact.

[88] *Ibid.*, pp. 5211–16.

When Kissel had worked out the preliminary details of this agreement, he had Segel join him in New York, insisting that he bring an attorney with him. When informed of the clause requiring the refinery be kept idle until the loan was repaid, the lawyer, Thomas B. Harned, advised his client to turn down the proposition. "Suppose this money were being advanced by the Sugar Trust," Harned was asked, "could you not then understand the objection to allowing you to open the refinery?"[89] Later, just before Segel committed himself to the arrangement Kissel had worked out, his lawyer took him aside and asked, "Mr. Segel, are you borrowing this money from the American Sugar Refining Company?" "It is not a matter of any importance where I am getting the money," Segel replied, pointing out that he had a note for $250,000 coming due that very day.[90] On December 30, 1903, a formal contract embodying the above provisions was entered into, the loan from the American coming through a week later.[91]

Havemeyer's motive in agreeing to this arrangement was not to ruin Segel, even though the latter had proved himself to be quite a nuisance. If such had been his objective, he could have accomplished it far more easily by refusing to make the loan to Segel. What had induced Havemeyer to go along with the proposition was the fear that, if Segel failed, the Pennsylvania refinery—a completely new plant equipped with the latest machinery—might fall into the hands of some other group with the financial resources to operate it successfully. By making the loan and stipulating that the refinery was not to be run until the principal and interest had been repaid, Havemeyer could be certain that the American would not be faced with competition from the Pennsylvania refinery for at least another year and a half.[92]

Havemeyer's actions in this respect were no different from the other efforts he had made through the years to discourage the establishment of additional sugar refineries. The motive had been the same when he and the other officials of the American agreed to buy the first Segel refinery, knowing at the time they purchased it that it would never be used. For, at that time, the American already owned one

[89] *Ibid.*, p. 5309.
[90] *Ibid.*, pp. 5350–52, 5389–90.
[91] *Ibid.*, pp. 5211, 5310–12.
[92] Parsons later wrote to Havemeyer as follows: "The [American Sugar Refining] Co. did not think then, it does not believe now, that Segel or any one else can run the present refinery to a profit. Similar attempts have been tried before and have failed. But the attempt could do harm. To the extent of making the loan, the Co. yielded" (*ibid.*, pp. 5651–52). In addition to the year that the loan was due to run, another six months would have been required—coinciding with the peak summer demand—to get the idle refinery in shape for high rates of production.

newly built refinery which it was forced to keep idle. Under pressure from the minority stockholders in the Baltimore Sugar Refining Company, the American had agreed in 1893 (soon after it acquired its two-thirds interest in the Baltimore company) to share in the cost of rebuilding its refinery, which only recently had been destroyed by fire.[93] However, since its own plants were capable of meeting the current demand at lower per-unit costs, the American refused to allow the Baltimore refinery to operate once it was rebuilt. This led to considerable friction with the minority stockholders, and the American was able to avoid a legal suit only by buying them all out.[94] The desire to prevent the installation of a redundant refining capacity was also the reason why, shortly after the loan was made to Segel, Havemeyer and his associates did their best to dissuade certain of the Louisiana planters from erecting an independent refinery in the New Orleans area, threatening that, if the planters went through with their plans, the American would cease to buy raw sugar from them.[95]

None of these actions were, in themselves, clearly illegal—especially not as the law was then generally interpreted. But to ease any doubts in this regard, John E. Parsons cited the case of the Mogul Steamship Company.[96] "The highest court in England," he wrote to Havemeyer, "decided in that case that shippers in the Chinese trade could combine to freeze out a competitor, and without responsibility [under the law], as long as they did not resort to means which in themselves were criminal."[97]

As for Segel, even the $1.25 million loan from the American Sugar Refining Company failed to bail him out of his financial difficulties. Despite a boast that he would be able to repay the money in ten days with income from his other investments, he barely succeeded in mak-

[93] See pp. 172–73 above.

[94] *United States* v. *American Sugar Refining Co. et al.*, pretrial testimony, 1912, pp. 9202–15, 9228. After 1903 the refinery was dismantled, having been operated for less than two months in all the time since its completion, and its parts were distributed among the American's other plants (*ibid.*, pp. 9217–27).

[95] *Ibid.*, pp. 7486–949.

[96] *Mogul Steamship Co.* v. *McGregor, Gow & Co.* (1892), A.C. 25 (H.L.).

[97] *United States* v. *American Sugar Refining Co. et al.*, pretrial testimony, 1912, p. 5676. The Mogul Steamship line, after being driven out of the Far Eastern trade by means of a "fighting ship"—i.e., a ship competing in the same trade and offering to carry cargo at greatly reduced rates, the losses from which were shared by those seeking to drive the intruder out of business—had sued the members of the shipping conference that sponsored the "fighting ship" but failed to collect damages in a civil suit ultimately decided by Great Britain's House of Lords; see Donald Dewey, *Monopoly in Economics and Law*, p. 136.

ing the first three quarterly installments on the interest.[98] Realizing that he would never be able to pay the full note when it came due, Segel began to connive with Kissel to force the American to buy the Pennsylvania refinery from him outright.

First he tried to bluff, offering in June, 1904, to repay the loan in its entirety, hoping that by so doing he might induce the American to make an offer for the plant.[99] When this stratagem failed, he took a different tack. Claiming that he had not known the source of the funds he borrowed, that he had been tricked into agreeing not to operate his refinery until the loan was repaid, Segel threatened to bring suit against the American. He even retained Samuel Untermyer, already noted for his role in the New York insurance companies investigation, to represent him in the matter.[100]

On Segel's behalf, Untermyer urged the American Sugar Refining Company to allow the Pennsylvania refinery to operate so that the $1.25 million loan could be repaid out of revenues. "Mr. Segel and his personal counsel feel, and I agree with them," Untermyer wrote to Parsons, "that Segel should not be forced by the fact of the refinery being closed, to sacrifice the property. . . ."[101] But Parsons, on behalf of the American, refused, pointing out that to allow the refinery to operate would endanger the value of the security being held against the loan. For it was true that, if the refinery was operated and thereby went into debt to the suppliers of raw materials, these obligations would take precedence over the American's outstanding claims. However, the more important reason (although Parsons did not mention it) was that allowing the Pennsylvania refinery to operate was tantamount to the American's taking money out of one pocket and putting it into another, for any sugar sold by the Pennsylvania refinery would be sold primarily at the American's expense. Untermyer subsequently proposed that the Pennsylvania refinery be allowed to operate, but with the American Sugar Refining Company itself supervising production and with output limited to 1,000 barrels a day, or one-third of the refinery's capacity. Parsons turned down this suggestion also, whereupon Untermyer withdrew from the case.[102]

In the meantime, to put additional pressure on his creditor, Segel had invested in two sugar refining properties located across the

[98] *United States* v. *American Sugar Refining Co. et al.*, pretrial testimony, 1912, pp. 5350–52, 5577–600.

[99] *Ibid.*, pp. 5552–61, 5563–64.

[100] *Ibid.*, pp. 5647–51.

[101] *Ibid.*, pp. 5654–55.

[102] *Ibid.*, pp. 5631–33, 5651–52, 5654–55.

Hudson River from New York City. One was the Knickerbocker Sugar Refining Company's plant, which he had been able to pick up from its bankrupt promoters for approximately $350,000. Spending another $100,000 to install a vacuum pan and several bone-black filters, Segel made it appear that the newly built refinery was ready to begin operations. The other property in which Segel invested was a proposed Metropolitan Sugar Refining Company plant, to be located just south of the Knickerbocker refinery; he spent $20,000 to have plans drawn up and the site prepared for construction. In the back of Segel's mind there supposedly was a scheme to link both refineries with the Federal Sugar Refining Company in order to confront the American with a major rival.[103]

By this time it was June, 1905, and both the final interest payment and the principal on the $1.25-million loan were six months overdue. Although Havemeyer was disposed to sell the Pennsylvania company bonds and common shares being held as security, he was dissuaded from doing so by several considerations. For one thing, he still wished to avoid having some outside group take over and operate the refinery. For another, if the American itself were to assume control, it undoubtedly would come under pressure from the Pennsylvania company's minority stockholders, just as it had earlier been challenged by the Baltimore Sugar Refining Company's minority stockholders, to allow the refinery to run.[104] Faced with this dilemma, Havemeyer preferred to let the matter ride, with Segel continuing to owe the principal and final interest payment on his loan and with the Pennsylvania refinery continuing to remain idle.[105]

Then, a year later, in the summer of 1906, the "bubble" burst. It turned out that the bonds pledged as security for the $1.25 million loan had belonged, not to Segel, but to the Real Estate Trust Company of Philadelphia. Segel had merely "borrowed" them temporarily. Moreover, the Pennsylvania refinery was but one of several losing ventures in which the Real Estate Trust Company and its president, Frank K. Hipple, had been involved with Segel. Realizing that his company faced imminent ruin and that he himself would be held criminally responsible, Hipple on the night of August 27 placed a pistol in his mouth and pulled the trigger. The next day, following a

[103] *Ibid.*, pp. 5546–51, 5668.

[104] *Ibid.*, pp. 5600–607; see also p. 216, n. 101, above and n. 94 of this chapter.

[105] The fact that the loan had been made in the name of Kissel, who acted for unnamed parties (i.e., the American), was a further complication persuading officials of American not to press for sale of the security (*ibid.*, pp. 5606–7).

rush of depositors to withdraw their funds, the Real Estate Trust Company was forced into bankruptcy.[106]

George H. Earle, Jr., a Philadelphia lawyer with extensive experience in reorganizing companies, was subsequently appointed as receiver for the bankrupt firm. Examining the books of the ruined company, Earle quickly spotted the large loans to the Pennsylvania Sugar Refining Company and various other of the Segel-run enterprises. Later, after being appointed receiver for the Pennsylvania company as well, he uncovered the arrangement between Segel and the American whereby the Pennsylvania refinery had been prohibited from running.[107] When questioned by Earle, Segel claimed that he had not known when he borrowed the money that the funds came from the American Sugar Refining Company; and Harned, at Segel's request, supported this story.[108] Earle then came to the conclusion that the ruin of the Real Estate Trust Company of Philadelphia had been caused by the sugar "trust"; and after trying unsuccessfully to persuade the president and attorney general of the United States to bring suit under the Sherman Act, he initiated his own civil action under that law to collect treble damages from the American Sugar Refining Company.[109]

::

In his annual report to the stockholders on January 9, 1907, Henry Havemeyer mentioned both the rebate cases and the civil suit by Earle. The officers of the American, although still convinced of their company's innocence, had agreed to settle with the government in the matter of rebates, he said, "in the interest of the stockholders," who were the ones hurt by such proceedings. He then added: "The officers of the company will continue to do what they can to prevent in the future any claim that the company does not comply with the interstate-commerce act. Whether it will be able in every case to anticipate just what about doubtful points will be ultimately decided by a court remains to be seen." As for the suit by Earle—"a receiver of the Pennsylvania Sugar Refining Company, one of the schemes of Adolph

[106] *Ibid.*, pp. 5204–5; Hardwick committee investigation, 1911, pp. 1217–21, 1237.

[107] Hardwick committee investigation, 1911, pp. 1217–23.

[108] *United States* v. *American Sugar Refining Co. et al.*, pretrial testimony, 1912, p. 5504. Harned subsequently revealed the truth, but by then Earle had become convinced that the original story was the more accurate one.

[109] Hardwick committee investigation, 1911, pp. 1224–31; *New York Times*, November 20, 1907.

Segel"—Havemeyer told the stockholders that he had been advised "that there is no legal foundation for any such proceedings."[110]

Despite these various legal difficulties, the American Sugar Refining Company's vital interests had not yet been significantly affected. The fines paid to the government in the rebate cases, although quite large in the context of the times, had done little to impair the company's basic financial strength. As for the private antitrust suit initiated by Earle, company officials had no reason to revise their opinion that it would ultimately be defeated.[111] Then, a far more serious legal problem arose. Federal agents, making a surprise visit to the Brooklyn docks of the Havemeyer & Elder refinery on November 20, 1907, uncovered evidence of widespread fraud in the collection of sugar customs.[112] Stunned by the news, officials of the American immediately offered their full co-operation to the government in its investigation.[113] Eight days later, while having Thanksgiving Day dinner with his family, Henry Havemeyer became ill, complaining of acute indigestion. Within the week he died of a heart attack.[114]

[110] Hardwick committee investigation, 1911, pp. 2967–68.

[111] Earle was at first reluctant to push his suit, for he hoped that he would still be able to persuade the federal government to bring action against the American Sugar Refining Company (see pp. 300–301 below). Finally, giving up that hope, he went ahead on his own, and the trial was set for November 19, 1907. On that date, however, the case was postponed when Earle decided to amend his complaint. See *New York Times*, November 20, 1907.

[112] Harold J. Howland, "The Case of the Seventeen Holes." This is one of the most complete accounts of the sugar frauds. For the history of the article itself, see p. 297 below.

[113] William Youngs, U.S. attorney for the Eastern District of New York, to Bonaparte, November 27, 1907, Department of Justice (JD) File No. 121616, pt. 1.

[114] *New York Times*, December 5, 1907.

11 :: THE ACCEPTANCE OF OLIGOPOLY

LIKE a number of other consolidations, the American Sugar Refining Company found itself facing dissolution in 1910 for having violated the Sherman Antitrust Act. The subsequent history of the suit against the American closely reflected the changing attitudes toward industrial combination during the Progressive and post-Progressive periods. It also reflected the difficulty of taking effective legal action against the "trusts," given insufficient enforcement funds and the need to proceed slowly in order to build up a solid body of case law. While the executive branch tended to take an increasingly less tolerant view of the consolidations as time went on, the courts, concerned about the possible loss of scale economies and stockholders' equity rights, were predisposed to move more cautiously. Whatever reservations of this sort judges may have had about ordering dissolution were greatly reinforced by the wartime experience when many of the same corporations being prosecuted proved invaluable to the military effort. This was particularly true of the American Sugar Refining Company, without whose co-operation it would have been impossible to stabilize the domestic price of sugar during the war years. After the Supreme Court ruled in the *United States Steel* case in 1920 that mere size alone did not offend the antitrust laws, the American Sugar Refining Company was among those defendants whose cases were settled by a consent decree leaving the oligopolistic structure of their industries unchanged. Thus oligopoly in sugar refining, as well as in other industries, came to be the accepted norm.

::

In November, 1907, acting on a tip from a former employee of the American Sugar Refining Company, federal agents raided the Havemeyer & Elder private dock in Brooklyn and uncovered an ingenious device by which the government was being systematically defrauded of revenue. The dock contained seventeen scales that were used to weigh incoming cargoes and to determine the duties owed the U.S. Treasury. These scales, located at intervals along the open wharf, were each operated from inside a wooden enclosure by a government weigher and a company checker. On the side of the scales where the latter normally sat, federal agents found that holes had been drilled and a spring attached to the weighing mechanism. By applying a single ounce of pressure to the spring, it was found, the company weigher was able to make the scale read forty-eight pounds less than the actual weight of the load resting on the platform outside.[1]

On the day that the federal agents made their unannounced visit to the Havemeyer & Elder dock, they were able to intercept two drafts of sugar shortly after they came off the scale; then, having them reweighed, they found that the government had been short-tallied by 14 and 18 pounds respectively.[2] While these two intercepted drafts, together with the scales and their "seventeen holes," provided dramatic evidence of fraud against the government, they still gave no clue as to how extensive the cheating was or who in the company bore the ultimate responsibility for it. But then, taking advantage of the offer by the American to examine its books, federal officials found that two sets of records had been kept. One showed the weights of imported sugars as recorded by customs officials; the other showed the weights as determined by "city weighers." The latter were private individuals who acted in behalf of overseas sellers in ascertaining the actual weight of the sugar upon landing, and it was on the basis of the second reading, made only minutes after the drafts came off the government scales, that the sellers of certain raw sugar—that which was imported from Java—were paid.[3] Comparison of the two sets of figures revealed a considerable discrepancy, and indicated that the

[1] Harold J. Howland, "The Case of the Seventeen Holes," pp. 25–29.

[2] A third load was also intercepted, but apparently not before the company weigher's suspicions were aroused, for the third load when re-weighed showed no undercharge.

[3] Raw sugar imported from Cuba and other nearby lands was generally purchased on the basis of "invoice weight," i.e., the weight at the time the sugar was loaded aboard ship for the journey to the United States. However, the sugar imported from Java tended to deteriorate during the long ocean voyage to this country, and for this reason it was customarily purchased on the basis of "landed weight." It was this second type of commercial arrangement which afforded an opportunity for fraud not present in the case of "invoice weight" sugar, since the invoices themselves were checked by American consuls at the ports of embarkation. Incidentally, the decision to develop a domestic beet sugar industry had the effect of reducing the quantities of raw cane imported from Java and hence the extent of fraud, since it was this source of supply which the domestic beet sugar displaced.

federal government had been underpaid on raw sugar imported from the Dutch East Indies since at least 1895.[4]

Stimson, into whose hands the prosecution of the frauds eventually devolved,[5] had more than sufficient evidence to convict the superintendent of the Havemeyer & Elder dock, as well as many of the men who worked under him. But again, as in the case of the railroad rebates, he hoped to accomplish a larger objective. First, he wished to establish the fact of corporate responsibility, and thereby enable the federal government to recover its lost custom duties while at the same time publicly exposing the American Sugar Refining Company once more as a wrongdoer. Then, going beyond what had been accomplished in the rebate cases, he hoped to establish the culpability and criminal liability, not only of the subordinates involved but also, more important, of the company's highest officials.[6]

In the family biography, Henry O. Havemeyer, Jr., denies that his father was, in any way, connected with the customs frauds.[7] Yet there is circumstantial evidence—the two sets of records kept in Havemeyer's own office, the extra compensation secretly paid the company checkers who operated the hidden springs, the political pressure used to remove troublesome customs officials[8]—that Havemeyer did know of the customs frauds personally.

[4] Howland, "The Case of the Seventeen Holes," pp. 29–38.

[5] Since the frauds were discovered in Brooklyn, the cases were initially handled by U.S. Attorney for the Eastern District of New York William Youngs. It was he who actually discovered the two sets of books when he took up the American Sugar Refining Company's offer to examine its records. But Youngs made the tactical error of choosing to try first a subsidiary case involving charges of attempted bribery of a federal officer by the superintendent of the Havemeyer & Elder dock, Oliver Spitzer, arising out of the initial investigation of the customs frauds. When Youngs lost this case, largely because the federal agent who had allegedly been bribed reversed the testimony he had given before a grand jury, the government was put on the defensive. Moreover, Youngs seemed not to understand the strategy required to win a case of such magnitude; this was apparent particularly in his feeling that the evidence was insufficient to convict anyone higher in the company hierarchy than Spitzer. For this reason Justice Department officials contrived to have Stimson switched to the case in the summer of 1908 by pointing out that the main offices of the American Sugar Refining Company lay in the Southern District. This face-saving gesture was necessary because Youngs was a close friend of Stimson and the latter had no wish to injure his feelings. See Department of Justice (JD) File No. 121616, especially the correspondence prior to August 15, 1908.

[6] Report, Stimson to President William H. Taft, April 20, 1910, pp. 8–9, Stimson Papers; Stimson to Attorney General Charles J. Bonaparte, March 18, 1908, JD File No. 121616.

[7] Henry O. Havemeyer, Jr., *Biographical Record of the Havemeyer Family, 1606–1943*, pp. 69–70.

[8] These were the two sets of records found by federal officials. In regard to the second point, the five company checkers handling dutiable importations of

It was clear that the frauds had begun long before 1895, probably as far back as 1879 if not earlier.[9] They were, in fact, part of the way in which the sugar refining business had been conducted through the years, at least in the port of New York. For the frauds, as it turned out, were not confined merely to the American Sugar Refining Company; they were prevalent among all the refiners operating in that locale—except the apparently naïve Warner Sugar Refining Company.[10] Still, the American was to bear the brunt of the resulting prosecution.

---

sugar were paid $20.00 a week, while all other company checkers were paid only $13.50 a week. The pay envelopes of all the men, however, were marked the same amount, and the only evidence of the additional payment was to be found in the company's books (Youngs to Bonaparte, March 21, 1908, JD File No. 121616). As for the removal of troublesome customs officials, Secretary of the Treasury Wayne McVeigh (the same individual who had advised that the commission agreement between the American Sugar Refining Company and the American Beet Sugar Company violated the Sherman Act) and Attorney General George W. Wickersham later reported to President Taft: "The evidence at the trial [of those involved in the customs frauds] indicated that the company's superintendents exercised a large amount of influence in the New York Customs House, and they often procured the removal of obnoxious weighers and Government laborers from their docks. Whether this influence was purely political or was exercised by means of payments to higher Government officers had not been ascertained." It was brought out that small, regular payments were made to customs-house officials by the American Sugar Refining Company, but they were so small in amount as to seem to be no more than mere gratuities. As for Havemeyer's personal involvement, the report by McVeigh and Wickersham to Taft declared, "The evidence adduced indicates that this company, down to minute details, was virtually run by one man, and that its executive management during the period of the frauds was in the hands of the president, Henry O. Havemeyer." The report is dated May 5, 1910, and can be found in JD File No. 121616. It closely follows the earlier report of Stimson to Taft, April 20, 1910, Stimson Papers.

[9] Report, Stimson to Taft, April 20, 1910, pp. 19–20, Stimson Papers; U.S., Congress, House of Representatives, Committee on Expenditures in the Treasury Department, *Hearings on Sugar Frauds,* p. 21; see also Chapter 3 above.

[10] U.S. House Committee on Expenditures in the Treasury Department, *Hearings on Sugar Frauds,* p. 30; Report, Stimson to Taft, April 20, 1910, pp. 10–14, Stimson Papers. At a later congressional hearing it was suggested that Havemeyer had continued to countenance the underweighing of the Java sugars because the Havemeyer & Elder refinery had become a high-cost plant, and that for sentimental as well as pecuniary reasons he wished to make it appear that the refinery was able to operate more economically than it actually did so it would not be forced to shut down in favor of one of the other plants owned by the American (U.S. House Committee on Expenditures in the Treasury Department, *Hearings on Sugar Frauds,* pp. 24–27).

It was testified that from 1901 to 1908 the average profit per 100 pounds at the Havemeyer & Elder refinery was 8.8. cents, compared with 22.8 cents at the Matthiessen & Wiechers refinery in Jersey City, 24.4 cents at the Standard refinery in Boston, 17.0 cents at the Louisiana refinery in New Orleans, and 18.0 cents at the Spreckels refinery in Philadelphia. The sentimental reason for Havemeyer's wanting to keep the Havemeyer & Elder refinery going was that

Pursuing the line of attack that he had outlined to the attorney general before taking over the case,[11] Stimson first brought a penalty suit (which was a quasi-criminal action under the customs law) to recover the back duties owed to the government plus a punitive sum. Because the evidence of underweighing was most conclusive for the year 1907, this initial suit sought to recover the government's losses for that twelve-month period alone.[12] On March 5, 1909, the case came to trial, and after an hour's deliberation the jury ordered the American Sugar Refining Company to pay full penalties of $135,486.32. "I regard the case of very great importance," Stimson wrote after the jury had delivered its verdict, "not only for itself, but because it is the first successful breach in what I believe will be a wall of corruption connecting the defendant sugar company with certain branches of the Treasury Department."[13]

Having established in court the American's criminal liability, Stimson was now prepared to push on with a civil suit to collect the back duties owed to the government from earlier years. But the American had lost its will to fight. Once again suing for peace, it agreed to pay an additional $2 million in estimated back duties, provided the

---

this was the plant most closely identified with his family and name, the one he had brought into the trust and the one with whose work force he was most intimately connected. The pecuniary reason was that Palmer's Dock, which the Havemeyer family owned, received the two-cents-a-hundredweight allowance for "transfer" only on the sugar produced by the plant. It was to protect this traffic that Havemeyer had earlier refused to give the Pennsylvania Railroad a share of the sugar business out of New York. See pp. 201–2 above.

[11] Stimson to Bonaparte, March 18, 1909, JD File No. 121616. This letter was written five months before Stimson took over the management of the case, at which time Bonaparte, concerned over the way Youngs was handling the prosecution, asked Stimson for an advisory opinion on the strategy to be followed.

[12] Report, Stimson to Taft, April 20, 1910, p. 8, Stimson Papers. A criminal suit would have permitted a maximum penalty of $5,000 for each offense.

[13] Stimson to Wickersham, March 5, 1909, JD File No. 121616. Stimson's hopes in this respect were somewhat premature. Asking for the services of a secret agent only two months later, Stimson wrote to Wickersham: "From the reports which I am getting from the men now at work, I find that the bulwark existing around the corrupt agents of the Company and the corrupt representatives of the Government has not yet been penetrated. The Assistant Weighers (themselves officials of the Government) are still more afraid of the Sugar Company's influence than they are of our prosecution, and will not talk freely with my agents. From these, as well as other circumstances, I am convinced that men, very high in the Customs Service, are still exerting their influence to prevent me from getting at the real facts" (Stimson to Wickersham, July 6, 1909, *ibid.*). Although minor customs-house officials were ultimately convicted and the service itself was drastically overhauled, proof of collusion between high customs-house officials and high sugar-company executives was never uncovered; see the report of McVeigh and Wickersham to Taft, May 5, 1910, *ibid.*

government would accept this sum as full restitution. While the terms of this settlement were acceptable to Stimson as far as the civil suit was concerned, he refused to call off further criminal prosecution of individual officers of the American. On this matter he had the full support and backing of the attorney general. "What I am really more concerned with than the collection of the monies due the Government," Attorney General George W. Wickersham wrote to Stimson when the American's lawyers first indicated their client's willingness to surrender without a court fight, "is to bring to justice those who are responsible for the frauds, if they can be discovered and convicted."[14] This hope was to be only partially realized.[15]

[14] Wickersham to Stimson, April 26, 1909, *ibid.* Although officials of the American had begun to sue for peace immediately after losing the penalty suit in March, a final settlement in the civil cases was not reached until two months later on May 19, 1909.

[15] Stimson's plan in regard to the criminal prosecutions was first to indict the less important subordinates involved in the sugar frauds, in the hope that with the threat of jail hanging over their heads they could be persuaded to give evidence against those higher up in the company. Accordingly, the first indictments obtained were against Spitzer, the superintendent of the Havemeyer & Elder dock, and five of the company checkers. Stimson's hopes that these underlings would provide evidence against their superiors proved wrong, however, and on December 10, 1909, a week before all six were found guilty by a federal jury, a criminal indictment was obtained against Ernest Gerbracht, the superintendent of the entire Havemeyer & Elder refinery. See the report of Stimson to Taft, April 20, 1910, pp. 16–18, Stimson Papers.

Havemeyer himself, of course, had died in the meantime, leaving as the only other official of the American in any way connected with the customs frauds Charles R. Heike, the company's secretary. His link to the frauds was the fact that he had initialed the entries which comprised the two sets of records found by federal officials. On January 14, 1910, Heike, too, was indicted; he was the last person connected with the American to be indicted (*ibid.*, p. 17; U.S. House Committee on Expenditures in the Treasury Department, pp. 36–37).

Heike vehemently proclaimed his innocence, contending that the difference in weights shown in the two sets of records merely reflected the more "liberal" tally made by the city weighers on behalf of their foreign clients and that, in any case, he had been entirely ignorant of any frauds perpetrated on the government. In fact, he said, it was he who enabled federal officials to make sense of the two sets of figures (*ibid.*, pp. 37–38). But Stimson as well as other government officials connected with the case (all except Youngs) were convinced that Heike's involvement in the frauds was more direct than he was prepared to concede, and the jury which decided the case on June 10, 1910, agreed. That same jury also convicted Gerbracht, sentencing both men to pay a $5,000 fine and to serve eight months and two years in jail respectively (Memorandum prepared June 14, 1911, for Congressman Coxe, JD File No. 121616).

Heike, meanwhile, had appealed his indictment on the grounds that he was entitled to immunity for turning certain of the American Sugar Refining Company's records over to the U.S. attorney during the latter's investigation into violations of the Sherman Act. The Supreme Court did not finally rule on the issue until 1913, at which time it rejected Heike's claim to immunity (*Heike* v.

Stimson could take justifiable pride in the fact that the back duties and penalties collected from the American were the largest such amounts ever recovered by the federal government from a single party.[16] They were, moreover, only the first of the large sums that the various sugar refining companies were to pay back into the treasury.[17] Still, there was one important respect in which Stimson was disappointed by the results. The most effective weapon against corporate transgressions, he now believed more than ever, was unfavorable publicity.[18] Yet, despite the seriousness of the charges brought against the American, and the company's almost complete confession of guilt, none of the New York newspapers had given the case what Stimson felt was adequate coverage. For this reason he arranged through Theodore Roosevelt to have *Outlook*, the former president's own political organ, do an extensive article on the sugar-fraud cases.[19]

The article in *Outlook* had its intended effect, leading to renewed interest in and criticism of the "sugar trust" in the New York press.

United States). By this time Heike was in failing health, and for that reason President Taft, despite considerable criticism, commuted his prison sentence to the time already served. Gerbracht, meanwhile, had been pardoned after serving thirty days of his sentence, on the condition that he assist in recovering certain back duties from the American. With his help the government succeeded in collecting a further $700,000 for excessive drawback payments (Wise to Wickersham, May 3, 1912, JD File No. 121616). The other company employees convicted were also pardoned after serving only a small portion of their sentences, the five company weighers, on Stimson's recommendation, as soon as the conviction of Heike and Gerbracht had been obtained in June, 1910 (Stimson to Wickersham, June 13, 1910, *ibid.*).

16 Elting E. Morison, *Turmoil and Tradition*, p. 103.

17 The full amounts recovered by the government from the various sugar refining companies were as follows:

American S. R. Co.	$2,959,872.61
Arbuckle Brothers	695,573.19
National S. R. Co.	604,304.37
McCahan S. R. Co.	124,386.29

Winfred T. Dennison, Assistant Attorney General, to Representative Joseph W. Fordney, February 21, 1913, JD File No. 121616.

18 Report, Stimson to Taft, April 20, 1910, p. 21, Stimson Papers.

19 Stimson to Theodore Roosevelt, March 8, 1909, *ibid.* The article was Howland's "The Case of the Seventeen Holes." Later, when the terms of the civil settlement were criticized by several New York newspapers, Stimson wrote: ". . . I should be mighty well pleased to see some of these light-tongued gentlemen of the press try to do any better in a similar situation. At the time when we needed help—namely, in February of last winter, when we were trying the critical case against the Sugar Trust, the gentlemen of the press, instead of giving us their aid, were doing their best to suppress the real facts; and their over-zeal now, after the battle has been won, has always struck me as being a little bit ludicrous."

But, in turn, this unfavorable publicity put pressure on the new Republican administration to bring suit against the American Sugar Refining Company under the Sherman Act—especially after George H. Earle, Jr., claiming that he had been forced to proceed on his own because the government refused to take action, succeeded in June, 1909, in obtaining a $2 million out-of-court settlement in his private suit against the company.[20]

::

Roosevelt, by ordering his attorney general in 1903 to bring the eventually successful suit against the Northern Securities Company,[21] had rescued the Sherman Act from the state of virtual disuse into which it had fallen after the Supreme Court's decision in the *E. C. Knight* case.[22] Although it was a surprise even to his closest advisers, this decision to proceed against the Northern Securities Company—a holding company organized by the Hill-Morgan and the Harriman-Rockefeller interests to resolve their struggle for control of the Pacific Northwest railroads—was in keeping with Roosevelt's determination to assert the ultimate authority of the national government over private business.[23] But while the president subsequently spoke forcefully of the need to apply "The Big Stick" to industrial consolidations, he was inclined to proceed cautiously against any

[20] *New York Times,* June 15 and 19, 1909; *New York World,* June 9, 1909. Of the $2 million settlement, $1.25 million represented the cancellation of the loan made by the American through Kissel.

[21] *Northern Securities Co.* v. *United States.*

[22] See pp. 186–87 above.

[23] George E. Mowry, *The Era of Theodore Roosevelt,* pp. 130–31; John M. Blum, *The Republican Roosevelt,* pp. 119–20. In his autobiography, Roosevelt pointed out that the Supreme Court's decision in the *E. C. Knight* case had implied that the federal government lacked the power to deal with industrial combinations which took the form of holding companies chartered by one of the states. "This decision," he said, "I caused to be annulled . . ." (*An Autobiography,* p. 426). Roosevelt seems to have been reinforced in his determination to proceed against the Northern Securities Company when, after the suit was announced, Morgan suggested that Roosevelt send his "man" to see Morgan's "man" to see if a compromise acceptable to both parties could be worked out (Blum, *The Republican Roosevelt,* p. 121). Earlier, Roosevelt had been irked when Morgan talked to him as though he were a rival businessman "who either intended to ruin his interests or else could be induced to come to an agreement to ruin none . . ." (Joseph B. Bishop, *Theodore Roosevelt and His Times, Shown in His Own Letters,* quoted in Mowry, *The Era of Theodore Roosevelt,* p. 133). The *Northern Securities* case itself has a rich and dramatic background; see William Letwin, *Law and Economic Policy in America,* pp. 182–237; Hans B. Thorelli, *The Federal Anti-Trust Policy,* pp. 421–25, 470–75; John A. Garraty, *Right-Hand Man,* pp. 90–91; Donald Dewey, *Monopoly in Economics and Law,* pp. 214–15.

particular one of these combinations. In addition to the lack of precedent in such matters, this caution reflected the distinction Roosevelt customarily made between "good" and "bad" trusts and his consequent preference for regulation rather than prosecution, for publicity rather than dissolution.[24] Nevertheless, the Roosevelt administration did institute suits against the beef, oil, tobacco, and blasting-powder combinations under the Sherman Act—the companies involved seeming to be rather clear examples of "bad" trusts—though the president had little faith in the efficacy of the basic antitrust approach.[25]

After inauguration day in 1909 William Howard Taft occupied the White House, and although he was Roosevelt's hand-picked successor, he had his own distinctive views on certain issues, antitrust policy included. On this question he took a more optimistic position than Roosevelt had. While sitting on the U.S. Court of Appeals for the Sixth Circuit he had written the unanimous opinion, later upheld by the U.S. Supreme Court, in the *Addyston Pipe & Steel* case.[26] That decision, relying heavily on common-law precedents, asserted the right of the federal government under the Sherman Act to deal with *all* combinations in restraint of trade, not simply those which were in *unreasonable* restraint of trade.[27] This same unwillingness to differentiate between "good" and "bad" trusts remained with Taft when he became president. The former law professor, with his scholarly, judicial frame of mind, preferred to make a distinction of a different sort: between those combinations which had been organized primarily to restrict competition and those which, having been organized with other objectives in view, restricted competition incidentally. He believed that the Sherman Act offered the most effective remedy for consolidations of the former type.[28]

[24] Letwin, *Law and Economic Policy*, pp. 244–47; Blum, *The Republican Roosevelt*, pp. 116–19.

[25] Mowry, *The Era of Theodore Roosevelt*, pp. 131–32, 134.

[26] *United States* v. *Addyston Pipe & Steel Co.*, 1 F.A.D. 631 (1898); see also p. 187 above.

[27] Although the emphasis earlier was on the *Addyston Pipe & Steel* case's prohibition of cartel-type combinations, what is now being stressed is its legal jurisdictional implications. It and the later *Northern Securities case* both widened the scope of federal authority under the Sherman Act, the *Addyston Pipe & Steel* case eliminating the need for the government to prove "unreasonable" restraint—that is, "unfair competition"—and the *Northern Securities* case bringing holding companies under the purview of the law.

[28] Letwin, *Law and Economic Policy*, p. 252; Henry F. Pringle, *The Life and Times of William Howard Taft*, 2: 654–59. To force the courts to choose between "reasonable" and "unreasonable" competition, Taft later declared, "is to force upon the courts a burden they have no precedents to enable them to carry, and to give them a power approaching the arbitrary, the abuse of which might

The American Sugar Refining Company seemed to be such a combination. In agreeing to settle out of court the suit brought against it by George H. Earle, Jr., the American appeared to have admitted the truth of the charge leveled against it—that it had conspired through illegal means to suppress a rival. Moreover, Earle's victory in that suit removed whatever valid reasons the executive branch may have had previously for refusing to initiate actions of its own against the American.

On September 21, 1906, shortly after being appointed receiver for the Real Estate Trust and Pennsylvania Sugar Refining companies, Earle had written a letter to Roosevelt, asking that the American Sugar Refining Company be prosecuted by the government for its role in "destroying" the two bankrupt enterprises that had been placed in his charge. This letter was followed by others, all repeating the request.[29] Earle was then instructed to present his facts to the attorney general, but shortly thereafter that official, William H. Moody, was nominated to the Supreme Court. Since Earle expected that any case initiated by the government might eventually reach that judicial body, and because he did not want Moody to have to disqualify himself, he decided to wait until Moody's successor, Charles J. Bonaparte, could be sworn into office. On March 13, 1907, the change in personnel having been effected, Earle renewed his request that the government take action against the "sugar trust." "I have come upon evidence," he wrote to Bonaparte six months before federal agents made their surprise visit to the Havemeyer & Elder dock, "that justifies the suspicion that they [the officers of the American] are strengthening their monopoly, not merely by rebating and like infractions of the law, but by the most serious frauds upon the customs of the Government."[30]

In reply Bonaparte wrote that he could see no difference between the charges now levied against the American Sugar Refining Com-

involve our whole judicial system in disaster" (Special Message to Congress, January 7, 1910, reprinted in William H. Taft, *Presidential Addresses and State Papers*, pp. 524–32). Taft twice seemed to shift in this view, first when he was serving in the Roosevelt administration, and later as president when he refused to criticize the Supreme Court's decision in the *Standard Oil* case, in which the rule of reason was first enunciated (see note 47 below). But both instances were essentially examples of Taft's loyalty to institutions—to Roosevelt as chief executive and to the Supreme Court as the highest judical body—which overrode his own views with regard to the Sherman Act.

[29] George H. Earle, Jr., to Roosevelt, September 21, 1906, Department of Justice (JD) File No. 60–104–0, pt. 1; Hardwick committee investigation, 1911, pp. 1227–28. The correspondence can also be found in S. Doc. 687, 60th Cong. 2d sess., 1908.

[30] Earle to Bonaparte, March 13, 1907, JD File No. 60–104–0, pt. 1.

pany and those dismissed by the Supreme Court in the *E. C. Knight* decision. In both cases, Bonaparte pointed out, the American was charged with the same offense, namely, obtaining control over a competing refinery. Taking note of Earle's pending private suit, the attorney general expressed an unwillingness to have the government, in effect, intervene in behalf of one of the contending parties to that litigation.

Although Earle tried to overcome Bonaparte's objections in a special brief prepared for the attorney general, Bonaparte could not be moved from his previously stated position.[31] Undaunted, Earle proceeded to press his own suit. When, after a six-day trial beginning in January, 1908, the New Jersey Court of Chancery refused to sustain his claim against the American Sugar Refining Company for civil wrongs, Earle next proceeded to file suit in the District Court for the Southern District of New York, asking treble damages under the Sherman Act. Here, too, the court ruled against him, dismissing the complaint by citing the Supreme Court's decision in the *E. C. Knight* case. But, taking the matter on appeal to the circuit court, Earle finally found partial vindication. In a unanimous decision ordering the lower court to rehear the suit on its merits, the U.S. Court of Appeals for the Second Circuit upheld Earle's contention that the *Knight* case was not relevant to the present situation, pointing out not only the interstate ramifications but also the conspiratorial nature of the alleged acts. "A comparison of the Knight case with the case at bar," the court's opinion declared,

> shows some striking superficial resemblances. Both relate to the actions of the American Sugar Refining Company in obtaining control of independent sugar refining companies in Philadelphia. But there is this fundamental

[31] Bonaparte to Earle, March 19, 1907, and Earle to Bonaparte, March 20, 1907, JD File No. 60–104–0, pt. 1. The refusal of the Roosevelt administration to prosecute the American Sugar Refining Company for its role in the Segel transaction was later to become a political issue, this being one of the matters covered by the Hardwick committee investigation in 1911 (see p. 308 below). Earle himself cited this alleged failure of the Roosevelt administration in urging support for Taft over Roosevelt for the 1912 Republican presidential nomination. In retrospect, however, it appears that the Roosevelt administration probably was correct to proceed first against combinations in other industries, where the precedent of the *E. C. Knight* case would be a less immediate factor. This appears especially true in light of the limited resources then available for antitrust prosecution. Even Wickersham subsequently agreed with Roosevelt, after the latter had borrowed the Justice Department's files to review the correspondence in the case, that Bonaparte had been correct in refusing to bring suit against the American Sugar Refining Company at the time. For the correspondence between Roosevelt and Wickersham, as well as that between Earle and Wickersham, see JD File No. 60–104–0, pts. 4 and 5.

distinction between them: The one was an agreement for the restriction of competition which related directly to manufacture and only indirectly to interstate commerce. The other was a conspiracy to prevent a manufacturer from engaging in business which necessarily directly restrained interstate commerce.[32]

It was because of this opinion, reopening what was thought to be a closed question, that the American Sugar Refining Company decided to reach an out-of-court settlement with Earle. But if officials of the American thought that this concession would put an end to the matter, they soon realized their mistake. For the circuit court's opinion, removing as it did the haunting specter of the *E. C. Knight* decision, promptly led to action against the company by the Taft administration. In mid-June of 1909, Attorney General George W. Wickersham, President Taft's personal choice to lead the fight against the "trusts," called Henry A. Wise to Washington. Wise, who had succeeded Stimson as U.S. attorney for the Southern District of New York,[33] was instructed to proceed as soon as possible against the American Sugar Refining Company under the provisions of the Sherman Act.[34]

::

Taking advantage of the facts brought out in Earle's private suit, Wise obtained criminal indictments against the American Sugar Refining Company, its directors, and others connected with the Segel loan within two days of his return from Washington. Those named as defendants included Washington B. Thomas, Arthur Donner, Charles Senff, George Frazier, John E. Parsons, Thomas Harned, and Gustav Kissel.[35] After being informed of the grand jury's action, Wickersham wrote to Wise, "I feel great personal regret that men of the prominence of these gentlemen should be indicted, but the facts under the law, as laid down by the Circuit Court of Appeals, seem to justify no other course."[36]

Despite this promising start, the government's case soon ran into a legal snag. Under federal law, criminal prosecution was barred three

[32] JD File No. 60–104–0, pt. 1; *Pennsylvania Sugar Refining Co.* v. *American Sugar Refining Co.*, reprinted in S. Doc. 718, 60th Cong. 2d sess., 1908. The quotation can be found on p. 2 of the printed document.

[33] Stimson had resigned as U.S. attorney in the fall of 1908; however, in order that he might continue to direct the prosecution of the sugar-fraud cases, he had received an appointment as special assistant U.S. attorney.

[34] Wise to Wickersham, June 24, 1909, JD File No. 60–104–0, pt. 2.

[35] *Ibid.*

[36] Wickersham to Wise, June 25, 1909, *ibid.* Wickersham was referring, of course, to *Pennsylvania Sugar Refining Co.* v. *American Sugar Refining Co.*

years after the alleged offense by the statute of limitations; the loan to Segel, the act forming the basis for the indictments, had occurred in 1903, six years before the government decided to initiate its own suit in the matter. To get around this difficulty, Wise alleged that the loan to Segel was part of a larger, continuing conspiracy to suppress the competition of the Pennsylvania Sugar Refining Company. But Judge Holt, before whom arguments to quash the indictments were heard in October, 1909, was no more willing to sustain a charge of conspiracy in this instance than he had been in the railroad rebate cases.[37] Wise, in behalf of the government, appealed Judge Holt's decision dismissing the conspiracy charge, but until this and other issues could be resolved by a higher judicial body, the criminal case against the American Sugar Refining Company and its chief officers would be left hanging.[38]

The government having been stymied in its efforts to obtain a quick criminal conviction, Wickersham ordered Wise to begin gathering evidence for a civil suit against the American. In line with these instructions, Wise issued subpoenas to Heike and other officials of the American to appear before a federal grand jury beginning December 1, 1909. This investigation continued through December into the new year; and as more of the facts were revealed, Wise began to realize the extent of the American Sugar Refining Company's influence over the domestic sugar industry. Deciding that it was necessary to gather evidence outside New York, he arranged for one of his assistants, James R. Knapp, to go to Colorado and California to question witnesses before grand juries in those states.[39] Meanwhile, the grand jury investigation in New York had run into a legal difficulty of its own.

A 1903 appropriations measure, which incidentally had provided the first specific funds for antitrust enforcement, stipulated that persons testifying or producing evidence in cases involving the Sherman Act were to be granted immunity from prosecution, except when guilty of perjury.[40] As part of his inquiry into the American Sugar

[37] Wickersham to Wise, June 27, 1909, and Wise to Wickersham, October 28, 1909, JD File No. 60–104–0, pt. 2. Judicial reluctance to sustain indictments for conspiracy is a reflection of the historical use of such charges to get around constitutional and similar prohibitions on the right of the state to prosecute.

[38] Memorandum, Wise to Wickersham, April 5, 1910, *ibid.*, pt. 3.

[39] Wise to Wickersham, December 1, 1909, and January 5 and February 17, 1910, and Memorandum, Wise to Wickersham, April 5, 1910, *ibid.*, pts. 2 and 3.

[40] 32 U.S. Stat. 903 (1903). The amount authorized was $500,000 and led to the creation of the Antitrust Division of the Justice Department; see Thorelli, *Federal Anti-Trust Policy*, pp. 534–37.

Refining Company's affairs, Wise sought to obtain copies of the company's correspondence and other pertinent records. Officials of the American refused to produce these records, however, without first being sworn in as witnesses and thereby qualifying for immunity—a protection Wise did not want to grant. On the other hand, they refused in the name of the company itself to turn over the records, claiming that the American was entitled to protection against self-incrimination under the Fifth Amendment of the Constitution. Thus the matter stood for several weeks until finally a federal circuit court judge ordered the American Sugar Refining Company to pay a fine of $500 for contempt of court. Through this and parallel decisions at the same time there was established the important principle that a corporation—as distinguished from its officers—could be compelled to produce records for inspection by a federal grand jury.[41]

Once this issue had been resolved, Wise was able to proceed with his investigation. By summer's approach he had largely completed the examination of witnesses and had begun the task of preparing the government's bill of complaint. Despite Wickersham's frequently expressed hope that the matter be expedited, Wise insisted on taking time to prepare his petition thoroughly, receiving assistance in these labors from J. C. Reynolds, an eminent corporate lawyer who had been retained as special counsel. Thus it was not until September, 1910, that the draft of the bill was finally completed.

For the next three months the petition was gone over carefully by Justice Department officials in Washington to remove possible legal flaws and strengthen the line of argument. Then the 220-page document was printed. Finally, on November 28, 1910, a full year after Wise had initiated the inquiry into the affairs of the American Sugar Refining Company, a bill of complaint was filed in the U.S. District Court for the Southern District of New York.

The petition outlined in exhaustive, if not always accurate, detail the history of the sugar refining industry's consolidation, charging "derogation of the common rights of all the people of the United States" and violation specifically of the Sherman antitrust law. As equity relief, it called on the court to order the dissolution of the sugar empire which Havemeyer, with the help of others, had worked so hard to erect.[42] Before proceeding any further in the matter, how-

[41] Memorandum, Wise to Wickersham, April 5, 1910, and Wise to Wickersham, April 11, 1910, JD File No. 60–104–0, pt. 3. The American Sugar Refining Company appealed the circuit court judge's ruling to the Supreme Court, but the appeal was dismissed without a hearing (*American Sugar Refining Co.* v. *United States*).

[42] *United States* v. *American Sugar Refining Company et al.: Plaintiff's Petition.*

ever, Justice Department officials decided to await the Supreme Court's decision in the cases still pending against the Standard Oil and American Tobacco companies.

Both of those companies had long been favorite targets of would-be "trust-busters" because of the well-publicized methods they had employed to suppress competition. In November, 1906, responding to the growing public clamor for government action, the Roosevelt administration had finally filed suit under the Sherman Act against the first of the two companies, and then, two years later, against the other. In both cases the relief asked was quite broad—dismemberment of the offending consolidation into several parts.[43]

While the *Northern Securities* case seemed to afford a precedent for such recourse, it was clear that a victory for the government in its dissolution suits against the Standard Oil and American Tobacco companies would establish an important new precedent. For the *Northern Securities* decision merely indicated that a holding company organized to bring an end to competition between two competing railroad systems could be enjoined from carrying out that purpose; it said nothing of breaking up large industrial corporations that had been allowed to operate unchallenged for many years while continuing to sell its shares to the public at large.

The courts were heard from first in the case against the American Tobacco Company. In December of 1908 a four-judge panel specially convened in the Southern District of New York under the 1903 Expediting Act upheld, by a three-to-one margin, the gist of the government's complaint against the defendant, finding that the American Tobacco Company had violated the Sherman Act and ordering that it be barred from interstate commerce "until the conditions existing before the illegal contracts or combinations were entered into are restored."[44] However, the court exempted from the terms of this decree certain important affiliates of the American Tobacco Company, and since neither of the parties to the suit was entirely satisfied with the decision, both appealed to the Supreme Court.[45] A year later, on November 20, 1909, another specially convened four-judge panel in Missouri upheld the government's charges in full against the Standard Oil Company, ordering it to divest itself of all subsidiaries within

[43] Allan Nevins, *Study in Power*, 2: 356–62; Richard B. Tennant, *The American Cigarette Industry*, pp. 57–59.

[44] *United States* v. *American Tobacco Co.*, 164 Fed. 700, 704 (1908). Because of the crowded calendars of the federal courts, the provision for the expeditious handling of antitrust cases was as important to the effective enforcement of the Sherman Act as the special appropriation for antitrust passed by Congress that same year (see note 40 above).

[45] Tennant, *American Cigarette Industry*, p. 59.

thirty days. This decision was also appealed to the Supreme Court, but by the defendants alone.[46]

In May of 1911 the Supreme Court delivered its verdict. Chief Justice Edward D. White, speaking for all but one of his fellow justices, affirmed, in most of its details, the lower court's decision ordering divestiture of the Standard Oil Company's various subsidiaries. In so doing, however, he apparently narrowed the scope of the Sherman Act, declaring, in an opinion so tortuously written that its exact intent will never be known, that the act's prohibition on contracts in restraint of trade referred only to restraints that were "unreasonable" in nature.[47] Two weeks later the Supreme Court affirmed the dissolution of the American Tobacco Company, including under the terms of its decree the various affiliates exempted by the lower court.[48]

The power of the courts to break up a large industrial consolidation having been established, Wise could now proceed with his prosecution of the American Sugar Refining Company. His next move was to have a special examiner appointed, as had been done in the Standard Oil case, to take pretrial testimony. Due to the congestion of the federal court calendars, this could not be arranged until the end of April, 1912.[49] Then began what turned out to be 140 days of hearings, extending well over a year, to present the government's case alone. During this time 12,000 pages of testimony were taken and 2,800 exhibits were introduced into the record.[50] Altogether, the nineteen volumes of typewritten pretrial testimony provided an incomparable insight into the evolution of the sugar refining industry's industrial organization; and even before all testimony had been taken,

[46] *United States* v. *Standard Oil Co. of New Jersey*, 173 Fed. 177 (1909); Nevins, *Study in Power*, 2: 378.

[47] *United States* v. *Standard Oil Co. of New Jersey*, 221 U.S. 1 (1911). For two interpretations (largely in agreement) of what White did mean, see Letwin, *Law and Economic Policy*, pp. 256–64, and Dewey, *Monopoly in Economics and Law*, pp. 181–82. Their view is that White meant only to point out that the Sherman Act did not apply to *all* combinations which might incidentally result in restraint of trade. Nevertheless, this was not the interpretation placed on the decision at the time, although Harlan's dissent may well have been responsible for part of the confusion. It is interesting to note in this connection that President Taft himself described the decision as a "good opinion," thereby disappointing those who had expected him to attack the rule of reason enunciated by the court's majority (Pringle, *William Howard Taft*, pp. 664–67; see also note 28 above).

[48] *United States* v. *American Tobacco Company*, 221 U.S. 106, 184 (1911).

[49] Wise to Wickersham, April 30, 1912, JD File No. 60–104–0, pt. 6.

[50] *United States* v. *American Sugar Refining Co. et al.*, pretrial testimony, 1912; Wise to Attorney General James C. McReynolds, May 7, 1913, JD File No. 60–104–0, pt. 7.

attorneys for the defendants indicated that they might accept settlement rather than have the case go to trial.[51]

::

The government's objectives in the suit had, to a certain extent, already been accomplished through the death in 1907 of the American Sugar Refining Company's first president. Although Henry Havemeyer had hoped that his son would succeed him as head of the American and its related companies, Horace—twenty-one years old at the time—obviously was too young and inexperienced for the position. Instead, he had to be content with being elected a director of the company, while Washington B. Thomas succeeded to the presidency.[52] Later, when it was realized how few shares the Havemeyer family actually held in the company, Horace's influence dwindled to insignificant proportions.[53] Thomas, who together with his family turned out to be the American's largest single stockholder, became the dominant figure in the company; but although he was an experienced sugar man, coming from an old sugar family, he lacked the personality and standing that had enabled Havemeyer to dominate his colleagues. Thus, one of the principal unifying forces in the industry had been lost.

By his own choice, Thomas inaugurated a less personal and at the same time less secretive rule. In recognition of the fact that a majority of the American Sugar Refining Company's shares was now held by residents of New England, two additional directors were added to give that region greater representation on the board. Among the new directors was Edward F. Atkins, who had been connected with the old Bay State Refinery before its absorption into the trust and who was now asked by Thomas to help him with the active day-to-day management of the American.[54]

These changes constituted a virtual revolution in control—a fact which was then cited in urging that the government call a halt to its dissolution suit. "The old gang has been cleaned out," Henry Lee Higginson, head of a Boston banking firm, wrote to Charles D. Norton, President Taft's secretary and a fellow New Englander, in August of 1910, "and the present directors are good, honest and able. . . . They are thoroughly ashamed of the conduct of affairs under

[51] Wise to Wickersham, November 14, 1912, JD File No. 60–104–0, pt. 6. There were twenty-eight volumes altogether, but only nineteen of them dealt with the government's original presentation.

[52] Hardwick committee investigation, 1911, pp. 2971–75.

[53] *United States* v. *American Sugar Refining Co. et al.*, pretrial testimony, 1912, pp. 6683–89.

[54] Hardwick committee investigation, 1911, pp. 35, 2040–41, 2983–93.

Mr. Havemeyer, and astonished at it. . . . They have pushed the reorganization of this company most energetically, and have got it pretty well done. These directors have the confidence of the public and, as it seems to me, are entitled to a chance to show themselves for what they are."[55]

This same theme was later repeated by Thomas and Atkins when they were called to testify before a congressional investigating committee. The House of Representatives, which had gone Democratic in the 1910 election, had become impatient with the administration's delay in prosecuting the American Sugar Refining Company, among other alleged "monopolies," and appointed a special committee under the chairmanship of Congressman Thomas B. Hardwick to look into the company's affairs, especially its relations with various beet sugar companies. This investigation of the American Sugar Refining Company was paralleled by a similar inquiry into the affairs of the United States Steel Corporation by a second special committee under the chairmanship of Congressman Augustus O. Stanley—sugar and steel, in the eyes of the Democrats, being the two outstanding examples of protected industries in which "trusts" had arisen.[56]

In their testimony before the Hardwick committee, Thomas and Atkins both emphasized the change in management which had occurred, arguing that the present officers and stockholders should not be penalized for the sins of the old regime.[57] In effect, they hoped to convince Congress that the American Sugar Refining Company had been transformed from a "bad" trust into a "good" one. But the time had passed when simply "cleaning house" was sufficient to satisfy the government's demands for reform. In the course of his year-long investigation into the affairs of the American, Wise had discovered that the dominant position of that company was predicated not only on the personal qualities of its first president and on the obtaining of railroad rebates but also, and more important, on the web of interlocking corporate relationships which Havemeyer had created. It was the destruction of that web—and nothing less—which Wise and his superiors in the Justice Department insisted upon.

Again, Henry O. Havemeyer's death had, to a certain extent, accomplished this objective. In some instances, control of another company

[55] Henry Lee Higginson to Charles D. Norton, August 8, 1910, JD File No. 60–104–0, pt. 3.

[56] U.S., Congress, House of Representatives, *Congressional Record*, 62d Cong., 1st sess., 1911, 47: 1142–47.

[57] Atkins' and Thomas' testimony can be found in the Hardwick committee investigation, 1911, pp. 3–176 and 1911–2061 respectively.

rested not with the American Sugar Refining Company alone but with the American and the Henry O. Havemeyer family jointly. This was true in the case of the Utah-Idaho, the Great Western, and the Continental Sugar companies.[58] Moreover, in certain related enterprises it was the Havemeyer family alone and not the American Sugar Refining Company which held an interest. This was true of Palmer's Dock, now renamed the Brooklyn Eastern District Terminal, and it was true also of the Cuban-American Sugar Company.

The latter company had been organized in 1906 to consolidate various cane-growing properties in Cuba acquired in the years following the Spanish-American War. The purchases had been arranged by the partners in B. H. Howell, Sons & Company, with James Post persuading Henry Havemeyer personally to join in the venture. In 1906, when the properties were consolidated under the name of the Cuban-American company, Havemeyer emerged as the owner of 9,783 shares of common stock and 8,275 preferred shares, slightly less than 12 per cent of the value of all the shares issued in the new company.[59] These holdings marked the first, small beginnings of direct investment by U.S. sugar refining interests in cane-growing lands in Cuba. But the greater significance of the Cuban-American Sugar

[58] The following table shows the par value of the shares held in the three companies by the American Sugar Refining Company and by the Havemeyer family:

	Utah-Idaho	Great Western	Continental
Value of Total Shares Outstanding (Common and Preferred)	$9,450,560[a]	$23,674,000[c]	$1,200,000[a]
Value of Shares Held by American S. R. Co.	4,650,500[a]	9,224,100[c]	415,440[a]
Percentage	49.2	38.9	34.6
Value of Shares Held by Havemeyer and Members of His Family	2,317,400[b]	8,494,000[c]	360,000[b]
Percentage	24.5	35.8	30.0

Sources: (a) Hardwick committee investigation, 1911, p. 100; (b) *United States* v. *American Sugar Refining Co. et al.*, pretrial testimony, 1912, pp. 6658–62; (c) *United States* v. *American Sugar Refining Co. et al: Final Decree,* p. 2.

[59] *United States* v. *American Sugar Refining Co. et al.*, pretrial testimony, 1912, pp. 6662, 6696–909. Although the Cuban-American company's authorized capital was $20 million, only $15,119,400 in common and preferred shares was issued (*ibid.*, pp. 6697–98).

Company, at least for the moment, lay in the fact that two years after its formation it had acquired control of the Colonial Sugars Company with a refinery just outside of New Orleans at Gramercy, Louisiana —potentially the most important competitor of the American Sugar Refining Company's new refinery being built at nearby Chalmette.[60]

The split nature of these holdings in various other companies had not mattered as long as Henry O. Havemeyer was alive, for as president of the American Sugar Refining Company he was able to exercise a unified direction over the jointly owned enterprises. But after his death, and especially after his son Horace found himself shunted to one side, this divided control began to take on an important dimension. It meant that, much as the American Sugar Refining Company's new management might have preferred to sever the last link with the old regime, for the sake of public appearance, if for no other reason, Horace Havemeyer's continued association with the company was essential for the maintenance of the over-all community of interests. Finally, however, in December of 1910, growing restive over his relatively minor voice in the company's affairs, Horace decided to resign from the American and seek an independent role for himself in the industry.[61]

Horace's announced plan was to have the common stock of the National Sugar Refining Company which had been set aside for his father, but never actually claimed, transferred to his own name. These 95,000 shares, together with the 2,623 preferred shares which the Havemeyer family held, would have been sufficient to give him, if not an actual majority interest, at least effective working control of the National. Horace also indicated his desire to cancel the commission agreement between the firm of B. H. Howell, Sons & Company and the National and take over the management of the mercantile end of the business himself.[62]

These moves, if successful, would have confronted the American with a powerful rival. For in addition to the National's several refineries in the New York area, Horace would have controlled the lighterage facilities on which the American was dependent, the largest

[60] *Ibid.*, pp. 6760–65. The refinery at Chalmette, completed in 1909, was being built to replace the older refinery in New Orleans, which had become outmoded (Hardwick committee investigation, 1911, p. 394). It, incidentally, was the first refinery built by other than outside interests since the original trust was formed.

[61] *Norman B. Tooker et al.* v. *National Sugar Refining Co.: Answer and Cross-bill of Louisine W. Havemeyer et al.*, p. 117.

[62] *Ibid.*, pp. 103–4; *United States* v. *American Sugar Refining Co. et al.*, pretrial testimony, 1912, p. 6662.

single block of stock in the Great Western Sugar Company,[63] and other significant holdings in the Utah-Idaho Sugar Company, the Continental Sugar Company, and the Cuban-American Sugar Company. And behind these properties would be the wealth of the Havemeyer family itself. Perhaps most important for the American Sugar Refining Company, Horace Havemeyer's actions, particularly his announced intention to cancel the Howell contract, threatened to upset the community of interests which ruled the sugar industry.

At the instigation of the American Sugar Refining Company's officials, other owners of preferred stock in the National Sugar Refining Company brought suit to cancel the company's common stock, charging on the basis of the evidence uncovered by Wise's own investigation that the stock had been issued "without consideration"—that is, without anything of value being given up in exchange.[64] In dispute was the question of what, if anything, Havemeyer had contributed to the formation of the National Sugar Refining Company that would warrant his receiving almost half the company's authorized capital stock. The case, which dragged on in the New Jersey Chancery Court for nearly two years, was finally decided on August 1, 1912, with a ruling upholding the complainants and ordering cancellation of the entire common-stock issue.[65]

While this decision temporarily ended the threat of a rival Havemeyer interest challenging the American Sugar Refining Company's leadership, it further complicated that company's relations with the government. For the cancellation of the National Sugar Refining Company's original common-stock issue left outstanding only the preferred shares, now converted to common stock, of which the American Sugar Refining Company had by now come to own slightly more than half.[66] For some time, in order to be able to present their company in a more favorable light, officials of the American had been trying to sell off their company's holdings in other enterprises, particularly its holdings in the various beet sugar companies. This effort presented certain problems because it was not easy to find buyers for such large quantities of stock at a price that was reason-

[63] As a result of subsequent sales since the government's complaint in the civil antitrust suit had been filed, the proportion of stock held in the Great Western Sugar Company by American had declined to 32.6 per cent. See Hardwick committee investigation, 1911, p. 100, as well as note 58 above.

[64] *Norman B. Tooker et al.* v. *National Sugar Refining Co.: Bill of Complaint*, pp. 1–19.

[65] *Norman B. Tooker et al.* v. *National Sugar Refining Co.: Final Decree.*

[66] Hardwick committee investigation, 1911, p. 81.

able. Still, by the beginning of 1913, officials of the American had succeeded in selling their entire half-interest in the Western Sugar Refining Company, their holdings in the American Beet Sugar Company, all their stock in the Carver County Sugar Company, $2,758,800 out of $9,224,100 worth of shares in the Great Western Sugar Company, and $2,000,000 of the $4,098,300 in stock held in the Michigan Sugar Company.[67] These efforts toward divestiture, however, were now largely offset by the increased hold that the American Sugar Refining Company had acquired over the National as a result of the New Jersey court's decision.

To avoid this embarrassing situation, officials of the American sought to distribute the shares that the company owned in the National among its own stockholders on a *pro rata* basis. Then, when Wise objected that such a procedure would not sufficiently dilute control, they agreed instead to sell the shares to their stockholders at par value. Under this arrangement the American disposed of slightly more than half of its holdings in the National; but it was still unable to find buyers for the remaining 24 per cent interest.[68]

Meanwhile, the government was reaching the end of its case against the American Sugar Refining Company in the civil dissolution suit. It already had decided to abandon its criminal prosecution of the company and its officers for their actions in regard to the Segel loan. First, the case had been delayed in coming to trial for two years as a result of various appeals to the Supreme Court by certain of the defendants.[69] Then, when the case finally did reach the trial stage in the spring of 1911, Wise had been greatly handicapped in his presentation of evidence by the statute of limitations barring testimony in regard to any events before 1906. The fifteen-day trial had ended in a hung jury, eleven of the twelve members voting for acquittal. Although the government could have sought a retrial, Wise advised against it. Of the principal defendants, he pointed out in a letter to Wickersham on November 23, 1912, Havemeyer and Kissel were both dead; only John Parsons was still alive, and he was eighty-two years old. In view of these circumstances and the severe handicap under which the government would be forced to operate in presenting its case a second time, Wise urged that the criminal prosecution be dropped, and

[67] *New York Times,* January 23, 1914; *United States* v. *American Sugar Refining Co. et al.: Final Decree.*

[68] Wise to Wickersham, February 1, 1913, and Wickersham to Wise, February 5, 1913, JD File No. 60–104–0, pt. 7; *New York Times,* January 21 and 23, 1914.

[69] *United States* v. *Kissel and Harned,* 218 U.S. 601 (1910).

Wickersham agreed.[70] Since the railroad-rebates matter and the customs-fraud cases had been concluded, this left the civil dissolution suit as the only litigation still pending against the American Sugar Refining Company.

::

On July 1, 1913, the government presented the last of its evidence in this case.[71] Wise, however, was not on hand for the occasion. On March 4, the new Democratic administration of Woodrow Wilson had been inaugurated, and Wise had been replaced as U.S. attorney for the Southern District of New York by F. Snowden Marshall, one of the attorneys representing Earle in his treble-damages suit against the American.[72] Wise had taken great care in preparing the government's case. He was, as Stimson remarked, "an even, hard worker." But as Stimson also pointed out, he "did not have a subtle mind."[73] By failing to bring the prosecution to a speedier conclusion, he had forfeited his chance to see the case through to the end—and by so doing had helped contribute to the image of the Taft administration as sluggish in enforcing the Sherman Act.

Control of "trusts" and "monopoly" had been one of the major issues in the previous fall's election. While Wilson was more disposed than others to view the problem in moral terms, he had nonetheless formulated a position during the campaign—largely with the help of Louis D. Brandeis, one of his chief advisers—which sharply differentiated him from either of his two opponents: Taft running as the regular Republican candidate and Roosevelt running as the Bull Mooser. On the one hand, the Taft administration was criticized for its handling of antitrust enforcement, in particular, of the Standard Oil and American Tobacco dissolution suits. Wilson and his supporters charged that the final settlements in those cases, to which the Taft administration had given its approval, were a "sham"; for while both of the consolidations had been ordered broken up into a number of separate parts, the same groups of stockholders previously in control of the over-all combinations were allowed to retain their interest in the several reconstituted companies. On the other hand, Roosevelt's program of federal regulation for large corporations was also attacked.

[70] Wise to Wickersham, November 23, 1912, and Wickersham to Wise, December 4, 1912, JD File No. 60–104–0, pt. 6.

[71] James R. Knapp to James C. McReynolds, Attorney General, July 9, 1913, *ibid.*, pt. 7.

[72] *Pennsylvania Sugar Refining Co.* v. *American Sugar Refining Co.*

[73] Stimson Diaries, bk. 1, Stimson Papers.

This approach, Wilson and his supporters argued, would give legal sanction to clearly illegal monopolies; they called instead for a program of vigorous antitrust enforcement, aided by new laws, to revive and preserve competition.[74] These campaign positions were soon reflected in the new administration's handling of the dissolution suit against the American Sugar Refining Company and its fellow defendants.

When the government finished presenting its evidence in the case, certain of the defendants, most particularly the beet sugar companies, expressed their willingness to accept a consent decree. In return for an end to the government's efforts to dissolve them, they indicated that they would agree to sever all ties with the American and with one another. The Justice Department, while receptive to this plan, insisted that the case against them was inextricably linked to the case against the American, and that it was reluctant to reach an agreement with them for fear of prejudicing its case against the chief target of the suit.[75] In the fall of 1913, counsel for the American Sugar Refining Company, former Judge James M. Beck, indicated that his company also was interested in an out-of-court settlement. He suggested that if the American were allowed to retain its refineries in New York, Boston, Philadelphia, and New Orleans, it would dispose of its holdings in the National Sugar Refining Company and the various beet sugar companies. In effect, he proposed that the American be reduced to its size as of 1895, the time immediately following the *E. C. Knight* decision.[76]

This proposal was strongly opposed by James R. Knapp, Wise's former assistant, who had been retained by the Wilson administration as a special prosecutor in the sugar case. Such an arrangement, he pointed out in a letter to the attorney general, would leave the American Sugar Refining Company as the dominant firm in the industry, for it was still capable of supplying 40 per cent of all the sugar consumed in the United States. In Boston, New Orleans, and Philadelphia its share of the market would be 95, 90, and 85 per cent respectively.

Knapp conceded the truth of the American Sugar Refining Company's contention that competition "is now keener and stronger than it has been" since the company was formed. For example, he said, "the American has not even voted its stock in many of the beet sugar

[74] Ray S. Baker, *Woodrow Wilson*, pp. 353–58; Arthur S. Link, *Wilson*, pp. 241–43, 417–23.

[75] Knapp to McReynolds, July 9 and October 21, 1913, JD File No. 60–104–0, pt. 7.

[76] James R. Beck, General Counsel, American Sugar Refining Company, to McReynolds, October 21 and 23, 1913, *ibid.*

companies since the beginning of the action and these beet sugar companies are selling their products in wider markets and at comparatively lower prices than ever before." But he warned that this state of affairs might not endure once the government's antitrust suit was ended. "These conditions," he declared, "are to a great extent the result of the moral pressure which exists while the action is pending, and if it should be terminated it would be necessary in order to continue or improve them that the American be placed in a position where it would be unable to accomplish a return to the old condition of universal domination."

In addition to the terms proposed by Beck, Knapp argued that the government should at the very least insist that the American divest itself of either the Spreckels or the Franklin properties in Philadelphia. "The company which owns both the American refineries in New York and the Spreckels and Franklin in Philadelphia is certain to be the dominating factor in the United States in the fixing of the price of sugar," he said. Since sufficient competition already seemed to exist in New York—and was likely to become even greater after the American disposed of its holdings in the National Sugar Refining Company—Knapp preferred that one of the Philadelphia refineries be sold off. Since the Spreckels plant was the more efficient, while the Franklin trade-mark was more valuable, it did not seem to matter which of the two properties was relinquished.

Knapp recognized that the Boston area could not support more than one refinery, but, that being the case, he felt that at least this one should not be controlled by the American. He also believed that an independent company should take over and operate one of the two refineries owned by the American in the New Orleans area. These last two suggestions, Knapp indicated, were less important than the divestiture of one of the Philadelphia refineries and might even be dropped in the interests of a speedy settlement. He recognized that, in light of the earlier *E. C. Knight* ruling, a court might be reluctant to go along with his recommendations.[77]

In effect, Knapp advocated that the government seek a radical restructuring of the industry, creating the maximum degree of competition compatible with technical economies of scale. And his superior, Attorney General James C. McReynolds, who had resigned as a special prosecutor during the previous administration in protest against what he felt was the ineffectual dissolution of the American Tobacco Company, was inclined to support him.

Knapp's proposed terms of settlement, however, were hardly de-

[77] Knapp to McReynolds, December 29, 1913, *ibid.*, pt. 8.

signed to appeal to officials of the American Sugar Refining Company; and rather than accept them, these men proposed to fight the case to the end. On March 20, 1914, two months after the breakdown in negotiations and three years after the institution of the suit, attorneys for the American Sugar Refining Company finally began presenting testimony, a process which, together with the evidence presented by the other defendants, was to last another year.[78]

During this period, the various defendants continued their efforts to cast themselves in a more favorable light. Leaders of the Mormon church, for example, began to buy out the American Sugar Refining Company's interest in both the Utah-Idaho and Amalgamated Sugar companies.[79] Officials of the National Sugar Refining Company announced their intention to purchase the American's remaining shares in their own company—although they subsequently found that they lacked the funds to do so.[80] Even the American Sugar Refining Company made a conciliatory gesture, with Beck arranging for a company to be formed in Louisiana to take over one of the refineries in that state. But McReynolds informed the American's counsel that the case had already progressed so far that he believed it was best to let the matter go to trial and be decided by the courts.[81]

On April 3, 1915, the pretrial testimony in the case of *United States v. American Sugar Refining Company et al.* was finally brought to an end, and oral arguments were scheduled for the first Monday in October. When fall came, however, it was decided to postpone these arguments until after the Supreme Court announced its decision in the case against the International Harvester Company.[82]

: :

[78] McReynolds to Beck, January 7, 1914, *ibid.*; *New York Times*, March 17 and 21, 1914. In an effort to bring pressure on the government to agree to a settlement on more favorable terms, the American Sugar Refining Company had its stockholders write to various federal officials, including the president, asking that the suit against their company be dropped. See JD File No. 60–104–0, pt. 8, for a copy of the circular sent to the American's stockholders and some of the letters it brought forth.

[79] *New York Times*, June 15, October 9, and December 11, 1914. By the end of the year the American had disposed of its entire interest in the Amalgamated and $2,325,250, or half, of its remaining interest in the Utah-Idaho company, the latter stock being sold for approximately $2 million.

[80] F. Snowden Marshall to McReynolds, July 13, 1914, JD File No. 60–104–0, pt. 8.

[81] Beck to Carroll G. Todd, Assistant Attorney General, October 23, 1914, and Todd to Beck, November 2, 1914, *ibid.*

[82] Marshall to McReynolds, April 21, 1915, and Marshall to Todd, November 23, 1915, *ibid.*

International Harvester was one of several large consolidations promoted by the firm of J. P. Morgan & Company. Organized in 1902 with a total capitalization of $120 million, International Harvester brought together under one management five previously independent companies that accounted for more than 80 per cent of the farm implements produced in the United States. The heart of the combination was the union of the rival McCormick and Deering interests. The former represented the descendants of the reaper's inventor, the latter a family which had entered the business relatively recently but which had succeeded in establishing itself as a close rival to the McCormicks. The bitter competition between the companies owned by the two families had greatly depressed the price of farm implements; and it was this competition which the formation of International Harvester was designed to eliminate. Soon after its organization the consolidated enterprise had purchased a sixth firm, thereby bringing its total market share to more than 85 per cent. It had then pursued a policy of tying up local dealers through exclusive distributorship arrangements, acquiring control of important patents, and buying out potential competitors, all with the purpose of maintaining its market dominance.[83]

In April, 1912, just as he was preparing to do battle with Roosevelt for the Republican presidential nomination, Taft ordered the Justice Department to bring suit against the International Harvester Company for violation of the Sherman Act.[84] Two years later, after testimony and evidence in the case (running to nearly 10,000 printed pages) had been compiled, a federal district court in Minnesota handed down its decision. A majority of the court said it could find no evidence of "unfair" competition, that is, of direct suppression of competition. Nonetheless, on the basis of the large share of the market controlled by the company, as well as the various methods used to maintain its dominance, the court held that the International Harvester Company had been a combination in restraint of trade ever since its formation in 1902. It therefore ordered that the company's business and assets "be divided in such manner and into such number of parts of separate and distinct ownership as may be necessary to restore competitive conditions and bring about a new situation in harmony with the law."[85]

[83] Garraty, *Right-Hand Man*, pp. 126–27; *United States* v. *International Harvester Co.*, 214 Fed. 988 (1914).

[84] Garraty, *Right-Hand Man*, pp. 257–58.

[85] *United States* v. *International Harvester Co.*, 274 U.S. 696 (1927). The court at first ordered the company split into three equal parts (*ibid.*, 214 Fed. 988 [1914]), but then modified the decree as noted in the 1927 case.

This decision was appealed to the Supreme Court, the defendant taking hope from the lone dissent to the lower court's ruling. "The evidence in this case seems to me," Judge Sanborn wrote in his minority opinion,

> to present a new case under the Anti-Trust Law. No case has been found in the books, and none has come under my observation, in which the absence of all the evils against which that law was directed at the time the suit was brought, and for seven years before, was so conclusively proved as in this suit, the absence of unfair or oppressive treatment of competitors, of unjust or oppressive methods of competition, the absence of the drawing of an undue share of the business away from competitors and to the defendants, the absence of the raising of prices of the articles affected to their consumers, the absence of the limiting of the product, the absence of the deterioration of the quality, the absence of the decrease of the wages of the laborers and of the price of the materials, the absence, in short, of all the elements of undue injury to the public and undue restraint of trade, together with the presence of free competition which increased the share of the competitors in the interstate trade and decreased the share of the defendants.[86]

The case did, in fact, break new ground, which was why the parties to the suit against the American Sugar Refining Company wished to wait until the Supreme Court had a chance to review the district court's decision. For the American undoubtedly would plead that, at least since 1907, it had not engaged in unfair competition and that over that same period its share of the market had fallen.

Before the Supreme Court could rule in the matter, however, the United States found itself at war in Europe, the possibility of which had for some time been drawing attention away from domestic problems such as antitrust. To get on with what it felt was the more important business of prosecuting the war, the Wilson administration agreed to accept a consent decree in its suit against the International Harvester Company. Under the terms of that settlement, the company was to sell off three of its trade lines to independent companies. (Despite the many years since the merging of the rival interests, the

[86] *Ibid.*, 214 Fed. 1010–11 (1914). Sanborn, incidentally, gave vent to the thought that must have been on the minds of many judges when they hesitated to order a drastic dismemberment of an industrial consolidation. ". . . It is not improbable," he said, "that many parties hold stock of the International Harvester Company which they purchased during these ten years in reliance upon these facts, the value of which a decree against the defendants will greatly depreciate. So it is that in any event this suit does not appeal to the conscience of a chancellor with the force it might have had in 1903 or 1904 before the actual conduct of the business of the defendants had demonstrated its innocuous effect and no parties had been induced to act in reliance upon its freedom from attack."

various product lines of the previously independent firms had never been fully integrated. Thus International Harvester's dealers were forced to carry several different models of the same farm implement.) In addition, the company agreed to locate no more than one dealer or distributor in any one town. In case the government's objective in the suit—"to restore competitive conditions in the United States in the interstate business in harvesting machines and other agricultural implements"—was not achieved within eighteen months after the end of the war, the government was to have the right to seek further relief.[87] While the terms of this decree amounted to a substantial retreat from the previous insistence on a drastic breakup of the International Harvester Company, they could be interpreted as a partial victory for the government since the accused was technically forced to admit having violated the Sherman Act.[88]

Some officials in the Wilson administration hoped to dispose of the suit against the American Sugar Refining Company in a similar manner. But Henry E. Colton, the latest of the special prosecutors retained by the government in the case, advised against a consent decree. The American, he pointed out, still controlled 50 per cent of the sugar trade in the ten populous northeastern states and 30 to 40 per cent of the trade in the country as a whole. "I think it will embarrass the Government in its argument of the Steel and Can Cases," Colton wrote, "to have already consented to the continued existence of the American Sugar Refining Company, which, under the Government theory of the law, was at the time of its formation clearly an illegal combination, and which, as the result of such illegal combination, still greatly outclasses its competitors and controls such a large percentage of the trade in an important section of the country." He then added: "It seems to me, under the circumstances, that the Executive Department ought to leave it to the courts, especially as the proof has already been taken, to determine whether the American Sugar Refining Company's control over the sugar trade has declined to such an extent as to fully restore competitive conditions in the sugar trade."

Adjudication of the International Harvester case, Colton realized, might well bring a demand from the American Sugar Refining Company that its case also be settled. Moreover, he was aware that a "decision in the Sugar Case at this time, if adverse to the Government, would weaken the force of the Government's victory in the Harvester Case." Nonetheless, Colton wrote, "I am inclined to think . . . that the

[87] *Ibid.*, 274 U.S. 697 (1927); Dewey, *Monopoly in Economics and Law*, p. 201, n. 16.
[88] Garraty, *Right-Hand Man*, p. 388.

Government would be more embarrassed by a settlement which leaves intact such a powerful combination as the American Sugar Refining Company would still be after its so-called investment stocks have been disposed of, than it would be by an adverse decision in the New York Court."[89] Thus the matter was allowed to remain in abeyance until after the war, while Colton went off to join the Field Artillery.

The coming of peace in November, 1918, brought with it a quite different mood toward big business. In the view of many, it was the productive power of the American economy, and especially its large-scale enterprises and giant corporations, which had made victory possible in such a short time.[90] The American Sugar Refining Company shared in this generally favorable attitude toward big business, for its own contribution to the war effort had been significant.

Upon the United States' direct involvement in the conflict, and even before, a serious sugar shortage had seemed likely. The problem was not the lack of raw sugar but rather the difficulty in obtaining adequate shipping to transport the raw sugar from Cuba and other semitropical islands to the United States. Moreover, as the various Allied countries began bidding among themselves for the available sugar supplies, the price rose to extraordinary heights. To deal with this and similar problems, Congress had enacted soon after America's entrance into the war a Food Control bill which established the Food Administration under the direction of Herbert Hoover. In passing this measure, however, Congress failed to give Hoover the power that he had requested either to fix sugar prices or to make purchases of raw sugar abroad.[91]

Without this authority, the Food Administration's Sugar Division was able to carry out its assigned duties only through the voluntary co-operation of the sugar producers, most notably, the American Sugar Refining Company. First, the refiners agreed to buy all their raw sugar through a single committee, known as the American Refiners' Committee, which in turn was to co-ordinate its purchases abroad through the Allied-controlled International Sugar Committee. Representing the United States on the latter were Earl D. Babst, who had become president of the American Sugar Refining Company in 1915, and William A. Jamison of Arbuckle Brothers. Next, the

[89] Memorandum, Special Assistant U.S. Attorney Henry E. Colton to Todd, November 14, 1917, JD File No. 60–104–0, pt. 9.

[90] George E. Mowry, "The First World War and American Democracy," pp. 174–75.

[91] Joshua Bernhardt, *Government Control of the Sugar Industry in the United States*, pp. vii–10.

domestic beet producers agreed to sell their product for a maximum price of 7.25 cents a pound, shipping it only to those localities and in those quantities designated by the director of the Food Administration. Meanwhile, profits in the wholesale and retail trade of sugar were strictly limited by administrative edict. This regulation of the domestic sugar industry was similar in nature but far greater in effectiveness than the control which Henry Havemeyer had at one time established; and when some persons questioned whether these arrangements might not constitute a violation of the Sherman Act, an opinion was obtained from the attorney general attesting to their legality.[92]

In the second year of the war, this system of voluntary agreements was replaced by a Sugar Stabilization Board operating under the legal authority granted it by Congress.[93] Still, there could be no doubting the importance of the co-operation given by the domestic sugar producers both before and after the board was established. This fact was pointed out by, of all persons, George H. Earle, Jr., who urged that the government dismiss its antitrust suit against the American Sugar Refining Company. In a letter to the attorney general, Earle wrote that as an appointee to the American Refiners' Committee he had "had an opportunity of observing Mr. Babst's earnest and complete devotion to the National interests, whilst acting as a member of the International Committee." He then added:

> . . . As I have no connection but one of rivalry with the American Sugar Refining Company, and in the past conducted to a successful issue a serious litigation against it, I felt that it was appropriate, and could not be misunderstood, for me to ask your careful and public-spirited consideration of the question, whether it would not be a gracious thing, and subserve public interest to have the litigations on behalf of the Government, which have been so long held over that company, withdrawn, in view of the fact that they all originated years ago, and against a management that has long since ceased to exist, and of which Mr. Babst was no part.
>
> . . . .
>
> Among the strange results that the War has forced upon us, is the fact that under Government request, if not compulsion, the sugar refiners are very largely doing as a public service, things very nearly approaching those which gave rise at least in great part, to such actions as that against Mr. Babst['s company].[94]

---

[92] *Ibid.*, pp. 10–20.

[93] *Ibid.*, pp. 42–49.

[94] Earle to Attorney General Thomas W. Gregory, November 5, 1917, JD File No. 60–104–0, pt. 8. Although the letter predates the Wilson administration's decision not to accept a consent decree in the suit against American, it nonetheless is indicative of the postwar climate of opinion.

Although the suit against the American Sugar Refining Company was left standing, the ultimate disposition of the matter was soon foreshadowed by the Supreme Court's decision in the *United States Steel* case, delivered in March of 1920. The United States Steel Corporation was perhaps the greatest of the consolidations promoted by J. P. Morgan & Company. Organized in 1901 as the world's first billion-dollar corporation, it had brought under one management 180 previously independent firms, many of which were the result of previous mergers. Together, the combined enterprise controlled from 80 to 90 per cent of the steel produced in the United States.[95]

The antitrust action initiated against the company by the Taft administration in 1911 had not come before the courts until four years later, at which time a four-member district court panel in New Jersey ruled against the government. The judges had been divided as to the original purpose of the consolidation. Two of the court's members held that the formation of the United States Steel Corporation was intended to realize certain economies of vertical integration, that it "was an evolutionary, a natural consummation of the tendencies of the industry."[96] The other two members of the panel took the opposite view, arguing that the consolidation was intended to achieve market control "and thereby monopolize and restrain trade." But whatever its original aims, the latter agreed with their colleagues that the United States Steel Corporation no longer stood in violation of the Sherman Act.[97] They based this conclusion on the fact that the company had "resorted to none of the brutalities or tyrannies that the cases illustrate of other combinations." Then, in a view of the law reminiscent of the dissenting opinion in the International Harvester case, they added:

It did not secure freight rebates; it did not increase its profits by reducing the wages of its employees; it did not increase its profits by lowering the quality of its products, nor create an artificial scarcity of them; it did not oppress or coerce its competitors—its competition, though vigorous, was fair; it did not undersell its competitors in some localities by reducing its prices there below those maintained elsewhere, or require its customers to

---

[95] Garraty, *Right-Hand Man*, p. 93; Ida M. Tarbell, *The Life of Elbert H. Gary*, pp. 72ff.; *United States* v. *United States Steel Corp.*, 223 Fed. 161 (1915).

[96] *United States* v. *United States Steel Corp.*, 223 Fed. 55 (1915); Dewey, *Monopoly in Economics and Law*, pp. 232–33. The summary of the lower court opinions is taken from Justice Joseph McKenna's majority opinion in *United States* v. *United States Steel Corp.*, 251 U.S. 437 (1920).

[97] *United States* v. *United States Steel Corp.*, 223 Fed. 161 (1915) and 251 U.S. 441 (1920).

enter contracts limiting their purchases or restricting them in resale prices; it did not obtain customers by secret rebates or departures from its published prices; there was no evidence that it attempted to crush its competitors or drive them out of the market; nor did it take customers from its competitors by unfair means. . . .[98]

The exemplary behavior cited by the two judges was a result of deliberate policies initiated by the head of the United States Steel Corporation, Elbert H. Gary. A lawyer rather than a practical steel man, Gary had been selected as chairman of the board of directors by Morgan himself to serve as the company's spokesman to the outside world as well as the arbiter of its internal conflicts. Recognizing that a corporation of that size and degree of market control was vulnerable to attack under the Sherman Act, Gary had seen to it that the United States Steel Corporation followed policies least likely to offend public opinion. Acquisition of additional steel companies had been avoided; the purchase of the Tennessee Coal and Iron Company was one of the few exceptions, and in that instance the acquisition had been carefully cleared beforehand with the Roosevelt administration.

Meanwhile, the questionable methods employed by other large industrial consolidations to forestall the entry of new competitors had been eschewed—control of the Mesabi iron-ore lands already provided an effective substitute barrier.[99] As a result of these limitations imposed by Gary, the share of the market controlled by United States Steel had gradually declined over the years. Yet the company's chief executive officer had not been concerned about this reduction in market share, for he had found that he was effectively able to coordinate prices throughout the industry by means of the famous "Gary dinners"—discontinued just before the government's suit was initiated—and the "Pittsburgh-plus" basing-point system. Rather than a cause for criticism, these practices so characteristic of oligopolistic industries became the reason for praise by the two lower-court judges. ". . . Instead of relying on its own power to fix and maintain prices," their concurring opinion declared, "the corporation, at its very beginning, sought and obtained the acceptance of others."[100]

Following its defeat in the lower court, the government had appealed to the Supreme Court, but because of the war the case was not argued for the second and final time until October of 1919. Five

[98] *Ibid.*

[99] Tarbell, *Elbert H. Gary, passim.*

[100] *United States* v. *United States Steel Corp.*, 223 Fed. 161 (1915) and 251 U.S. 441 (1920).

months later, in March, 1920, the Supreme Court handed down its decision. Justice Joseph McKenna, speaking for the four-to-three majority, concurred in the lower court's finding that the United States Steel Corporation, whatever may have been true at the time of its formation, was no longer a monopoly in restraint of trade. The only cause for complaint shown by the government, he said, was the preponderant market position of the defendant. Then, in a passage that was soon seized upon by others, he added:

> The Corporation is undoubtedly of impressive size and it takes an effort of resolution not to be affected by it or to exaggerate its influence. But we must adhere to the law and the law does not make mere size an offense or the existence of unexerted power an offense. It, we repeat, requires overt acts. . . . It does not compel competition nor require all that is possible.[101]

In affirming the lower court's judgment, the Supreme Court not only gave a new twist to White's earlier rule of reason but also, in effect, put the stamp of judicial approval on oligopoly as a form of industrial organization.

Within a year after this decision, the Wilson administration was swept out of office by the Republicans. Having campaigned for a "return to normalcy," Warren G. Harding had no desire to strike out boldly in the field of antitrust; rather, he was content simply to follow the implicit dictates of the Supreme Court in the *United States Steel* opinion. Antitrust actions involving the American Can and Quaker Oats companies already had been abandoned,[102] leaving among the few cases still pending the suit against the American Sugar Refining Company. On May 9, 1922, this case, too, was finally brought to an end through a consent decree, twelve years after it had been formally initiated.

The American Sugar Refining Company, like the International Harvester Company before it, was forced to admit that it had at one time violated the Sherman Act—though the government on its part conceded that the violation no longer existed. Aside from this "confession," however, the decree merely sanctioned the status quo. The American was allowed to retain the interest it still held in other companies—25 per cent of the stock in the National Sugar Refining Company, 31 per cent of the stock in the Great Western Sugar Company, and 34 per cent of the stock in the Michigan Sugar Company—on the condition that it would neither vote nor increase the shares it held in

[101] *Ibid.*, 251 U.S. 451 (1920).
[102] Dewey, *Monopoly in Economics and Law*, p. 236, n. 19.

those companies. These holdings were all that remained of the considerable interest the American had once had in the various other sugar companies. Finally, the American and the other defendants in the case were enjoined from "combining and conspiring among themselves to restrain interstate and foreign trade."[103]

::

While the American Sugar Refining Company thus emerged somewhat scarred but still intact from its protracted legal battle with the government, there were other developments no less critical to its survival and growth. Over the years between 1907 and 1922, the company had undergone a series of changes in its organizational structure which, taken together, were of considerable significance for the future. Like many of the other consolidations, the American had become, in Alfred Chandler's words, an integrated, multi-departmental enterprise.[104]

In September, 1917, an Operating Department had been created as successor to the Manufacturing Committee originally set up during the trust era.[105] Within this department there were seven separate divisions—engineering, refining, packing, delivery, etc.—and the heads of these divisions, together with the vice president in charge of operations, constituted an operating board which oversaw the technical performance of the American's five refineries, offering staff assistance to the individual plant superintendents. This board, consisting of men with a specialized knowledge of some particular aspect of refinery operations, stood in sharp contrast to the original manufacturing committee, the members of which had had only a generalized, though perhaps more intimate, knowledge of the refining end of the business. The Traffic Department, previously comprised solely of Thomas Riley and several clerks, had also become institutionalized and bureaucratized. It now contained four divisions—a rates division, a routing division, a claims division, and a superintendent-of-transportation office—which reported through a traffic manager to the vice president in charge of operations and provided staff assistance to the four district freight agents in New York, New Orleans, Boston, and Chicago.[106]

There had also been changes in organizational structure on the mercantile side of the business. While the buying of raw sugar and

[103] *United States* v. *American Sugar Refining Co. et al.: Final Decree.*
[104] Alfred D. Chandler, Jr., *Strategy and Structure*, chap. 1.
[105] *American Sugar Family*, 1 (February, 1920).
[106] *Ibid.*

ORGANIZATION CHART
American Sugar Refining Company
1922

Board of Directors
Earl D. Babst
President
Joseph E. Freeman
Legal Dept.
Edwin Gibson
Secretary
Robert M. Parker
V.P. Raw Sugar
Customs
Dept.
Raw-Sugar
Dept.
Ralph S. Stubbs
V.P. Operations
Traffic Dept.
Traffic Manager
Rate
Division
Routing
Division
Claim
Division
Supt. of
Trans-
portation
Dist. Freight
Agent
New York
Dist. Freight
Agent
New Orleans
Dist. Freight
Agent
Boston
Dist. Freight
Agent
Chicago
Operating Board
(Division Heads)
Refining
Division
Parking
Division
Delivery
Division
Drafting
Division
Plant
Values
Division
Employ-
ment and
Industrial
Relations
Engineering
Division
Power
Section
Safety
Section
Superintendent
New York
Refinery
Superintendent
Philadelphia
Refinery
Superintendent
Boston
Refinery
Superintendent
Chalmette, La.,
Refinery
Superintendent
Baltimore
Refinery
Purchasing
Dept.
Robert F. Mason
V.P. Sales
Molasses
Dept.
General Sales
Dept.
Manu-
facturers'
Division
Service
Bureau
Export
Division
Advertising
Division
Domino
Division
Sales Offices in Various Cities
E. Edward Foster
V.P. Finance
Arthur B. Woolam
Treasurer
Insurance
Division
Comptroller
Accounting
Dept.
Cashiers
Dept.
Auditing
Dept.
Tax
Dept.
Billing
and
Ledger
Dept.
Statistics
Dept.
Branch
Delivery
and
Stock
Dept.

other essential inputs was still carried out in much the same manner as when the trust was first formed (the reorganization of this activity still lying in the future), the sale of refined products was now handled somewhat differently from Havemeyer's day. Instead of simply waiting passively for orders from the wholesale grocers, the American Sugar Refining Company had moved, beginning in 1917, to establish its own sales force to actively solicit business. The purpose was to give the company greater control over how its products were promoted. In particular, it was hoped that with a sales force to push its own brand—Domino sugar—and a substantial advertising campaign to make that brand well known to the public, American might be better protected against the inroads of competitors. This had been the strategy followed by the National Biscuit Company when Babst, the American's president, had been associated with it, and it was the strategy which the American hoped to emulate successfully. Toward this end a $1 million reserve fund for advertising was set up which, together with the $1 million a year normally spent for that purpose, was intended "to make certain a continuous advertising policy, through good and poor years."[107]

These changes in sales policy were subsequently reflected elsewhere in the company's organizational structure. Within the General Sales Department, headed by a vice president in charge of sales, a Domino division was established to handle the sales of trade-mark products, and a separate advertising division was created to develop consumer loyalty to those products. Although the American subsequently realized that it could not replace the wholesale grocers, because of the heavy cost involved in setting up an alternative distribution system,[108] the separate Domino and advertising divisions were nonetheless retained to supplement the wholesale grocers. Meanwhile, because of the increasing importance of sales to other food processors, a manufacturers' division was formed within the General Sales Department and a service bureau was attached to it to help meet the special needs of industrial customers. An export division,

[107] American Sugar Refining Company, *Annual Report,* 1917.

[108] In this respect, the American Sugar Refining Company had failed to capitalize on its opportunities. When it finally decided to establish its own independent distribution system, it found itself financially handicapped by the losses which it had suffered from fluctuations in the price of raw sugar in the years immediately following World War I. If it had moved along these lines at an earlier date, when competition was weaker and its treasury richer, it might have been more successful in erecting this type of barrier to entry and in creating this form of product differentiation. Of course, in the years after 1911, the fear of antitrust prosecution was an important inhibiting factor.

which grew to substantial size during the war years and immediately thereafter, completed the General Sales Department.[109]

On the financial end, organization had also become more structured. Under a vice president in charge of finance there were a treasurer and a comptroller, the latter directing the activities of several divisions, including accounting, auditing, billing and ledger, and statistics. The Legal Department, however, reported directly to the president of the company, a reflection of the critical importance attached to that department's activities. Babst himself was a lawyer by profession, as was his counterpart in the United States Steel Corporation. The secretary of the American, who was responsible for managing all of the company's vast real estate holdings, also reported directly to Babst. While there were thus several anomalies in the company's organization chart, a rational, bureaucratic structure had nonetheless been created.

Turning from the American's internal organization to the structure of the sugar refining industry as a whole, it can be generally stated that the latter had changed only superficially during the years between 1907 and 1922. Two new refineries had been built, the Godchaux in New Orleans in 1920 and the Savannah in 1922, thus bringing the total number of separate and independent cane-refining enterprises to fifteen; but while the American Sugar Refining Company's share of the cane market had declined from 53 per cent in 1907 to 36 per cent in 1918 and 32 per cent in 1922,[110] the slippage had had little to do with the entry of the new firms. It reflected two other factors: one, the relatively more rapid growth of the West Coast market in which the American did not compete and, two, the inherent disadvantage of being the industry price leader with the government's antitrust lawyers peeking over one's shoulder. Like the dominant firms in other industries, the American Sugar Refining Company found that its rivals continually took advantage of the efforts to maintain uniform prices by granting secret price concessions and thereby enticing away customers. The stake of these smaller firms in price stability was not nearly as great as the American's. The secret price concessions, in turn, reflected the fact that the American Sugar Refining Company was no longer able to exercise the same degree of control over its rivals that it had during Havemeyer's last years.

World War I tended to obscure the true situation in the industry, for with the government itself providing over-all regulation, there had

[109] *American Sugar Family*, 1 (February, 1920).

[110] The information comes from the American Sugar Refining Company's internal records, privately made available by the company.

been no need for any private party to fill that role. When after two years the government's price-control machinery was abruptly dismantled, the American found itself handicapped in trying to reestablish its former hegemony. It was not only that in the interval its own grip on the industry had necessarily been loosened, or even that it was still limited in its freedom of action by the pending antitrust suit. The precipitate termination of wartime control led to wildly fluctuating prices as first the suddenly released, pent-up demand drove prices skyward and then, when this demand was partially satisfied, the war-stimulated overproduction of sugar drove prices downward again, past the original starting point. When prices finally stabilized in 1922, the American Sugar Refining Company found itself forced to absorb substantial inventory losses, to the point where it had to pass the dividend on its common stock for the first time in its history. Moreover, it found itself embroiled in numerous law suits with wholesale grocers and other customers over whether they could be held to the contracts they had entered into before the price of sugar fell so sharply.[111] It was the American's weakened financial condition, the result of these events, which prevented it from dealing more effectively with the secret price concessions, concessions that were to become even more widespread in the years ahead.[112]

But while the American could no longer be said to exercise the same degree of control over sugar prices it once had, its influence on the industry was still considerable. Approximately three times the size of its largest competitor, it remained the undisputed price leader. And when it thought other firms were secretly shading the price, it did not hesitate to match them, concession for concession, until it was convinced that its own announced price list was once again being adhered to. In announcing the final settlement of the antitrust suit against the company, Justice Department officials declared, "It is believed that the consumer of sugar can now rest assured that competitive conditions in the industry have been entirely restored and that the price he pays for his sugar in the future will be the result of natural unrestrained competition."[113] This claim was, of course, greatly exaggerated. The one-time competitive character of the sugar refining industry had not been restored; the government had merely acquiesced to the continued existence of oligopoly.

[111] American Sugar Refining Company, *Annual Report*, 1922.

[112] *United States* v. *Sugar Institute et al.: Transcript of Testimony*, pp. 9190–92.

[113] Justice Department announcement, May 9, 1922, JD File No. 60–104–0, pt. 9.

It had been the hope of some, especially those Progressives associated with the Wilson administration, that the results would be otherwise, that a resolute application of the antitrust laws would bring about a return to the competitive conditions prevailing before the Corporate Revolution. But in the sugar refining industry the most that the efforts in this direction had accomplished was to create a better-balanced oligopolistic situation. The American Sugar Refining Company had, it was true, been forced to surrender its voice in the affairs of other sugar companies. The resulting increase in autonomy was particularly significant in the case of the National Sugar Refining Company, which was soon to grow into the American's most formidable rival. It was also true that the years of facing prosecution at the hands of the government had made the American Sugar Refining Company somewhat circumspect in its behavior—although, insofar as this constrained the company's one-time dynamic role as innovator, it also had its negative aspect. Still, in the final analysis, making it possible for other firms in the industry to exercise their independence was not the same thing as restoring the old competitive order.

Despite the fact that the American Sugar Refining Company emerged from fifteen years of litigation with its control over the industry greatly impaired, the objective of the original consolidation—the elimination of price competition or at least its confinement within certain narrow limits—had not been lost. The American still dominated the industry, especially in the eastern half of the United States. And, even in the case of those companies in which the American had been compelled to relinquish all influence, the many years of close co-operation had established patterns of interdependent behavior which were not readily extinguished—as the prosecution of the Sugar Institute, a trade association formed in 1928 to co-ordinate pricing activities throughout the industry, would subsequently bring out.[114]

The oligopolistic pattern that emerged in sugar refining as well as in other industries was a condition to which the American people, as reflected by their political institutions, seemed to give tacit approval. For neither the executive nor the legislative branch of the federal government made any effort to overrule the principles of law in regard to industrial consolidations which the courts had laid down. Those principles were that while the combining of all the firms in an industry under a single large corporation would no longer be tolerated, the regrouping of the industry under several large corporations was

[114] *United States* v. *Sugar Institute,* 15 Fed. Sup. 817 (1900) and 297 U.S. 553 (1927); Arthur R. Burns, *The Decline of Competition,* pp. 72–73, 322–25.

beyond the reach of the law—as long as no overt effort was made to exclude the entry of new firms. These principles were to apply not only to those industries which already had been consolidated but also to those which, as a result of evolving technology, would be ready for consolidation at some future date.

Thus it was that through the interaction of powerful economic and political forces—the insistence, on the one hand, of those manufacturers for whom fixed costs were a significant portion of their total costs that they be allowed to organize in such a way as to have some degree of control over prices; and the refusal, on the other hand, of the great majority of Americans to countenance what they felt was excessive market power—there came into being a unique social institution, the large corporation, or megacorp, as part of an oligopolistic industry. To create such an institution was not what either the "trust" organizers or the "trust-busters" had intended, but it was, in fact, what emerged as a result of the Corporate Revolution, not only in sugar refining but in many other industries as well.

12 :: HISTORICAL PERSPECTIVES

AT the beginning of this monograph it was suggested that the failure of the economic theorist and national policy-maker to understand the historical processes responsible for the Corporate Revolution has impaired their ability to meet the challenges posed by that traumatic event. In the case of the economic theorist the challenge has been to devise new analytical models; in the case of the national policy-maker it has been to develop new forms of social control. Now that the history not only of the Corporate Revolution but also of the antecedent stages in the evolution of industrial organization in the United States has been recounted—at least with respect to one industry—it might be well to dwell briefly on the lessons of that experience which have relevance to the problems of the theorist and policy-maker today.

The first point to be emphasized is the fundamental motivation behind the consolidation movement, as well as the motivation behind the subsequent maneuverings for position by the giant enterprises thus created. That motivation was the desire to eliminate price competition as a significant factor in business life. Why this should have been the persistent goal has been explained at length: to wit, the desire to avoid the destructive effects that price competition has on capital values when the technology of an industry necessitates a high capital-output ratio and the economy itself is subject to pronounced cyclical fluctuations in aggregate demand, conditions that characterized the United States economy after 1873. What has also been described is the restructuring of American institutions—the change in value orientation, legal principles, and business organization—which had to occur if the elimination of price competition was to be more than just a passing phenomenon. The point that should not be overlooked in all this is that the giant enterprises or megacorps which emerged from the Corporate Revolution were created with precisely that goal in mind, and that while for the most part they have since evolved into more complex forms of organization pursuing considerably broader objectives related to their growth as ongoing concerns, the elimination of price competition still remains a *sine qua non* for whatever else they do. Thus it should occasion little surprise when one of these firms is found to have engaged in an overt price-fixing conspiracy or to have joined with the other members of its industry in announcing simultaneously an identical increase in prices. These more obvious manifestations of interdependent behavior are but a small part of a continuing process, extending from the time of the Corporate Revolution to the present, by which price competition has been severely constrained if not eliminated altogether.

The second point that should be emphasized relates to the first. This is that the competitive structure of the American economy was undone, not simply because men willed it, but, more important, because the competitive structure was unviable. The breakdown of competition was inherent in the very conditions that made competition, as economists have defined the term, a reality. The same technology which enabled items of uniform quality to be mass produced also led to an increase in the capital-output ratio, and this in turn reduced the ability to adjust supply to demand. Since the capital represented primarily fixed plant and equipment rather than inventories of goods (as was true during an earlier period of commercial capitalism), it was no longer possible to liquidate one's losses when the bottom fell out of the market simply by disposing of any unsold stock for whatever price it would bring. Certain costs could be avoided only by going out of business entirely, and if one did that, the plant and equipment would bring as scrap only a small fraction of their value as part of a going concern. Forced as a practical matter to remain in business as long as possible, manufacturing firms were left with little choice but to cut their prices in a vain effort to expand their sales and spread the fixed costs over a larger volume—the high capital-output ratio providing a substantial margin between variable and total costs within which the price cutting could take place.

At the same time that it was becoming more difficult to adjust the supply of manufactured goods to the demand, the very fact that the market structure of the economy was essentially competitive made the demand for those goods more volatile. With private investment and savings decisions effectively decentralized and the federal government committed to playing only an unwitting role in the economy, fluctuations in aggregate demand were all but inevitable, thus aggravating the adjustment problems of individual manufacturers. This state of affairs was untenable because it jeopardized the source of the system's vitality—the willingness of private individuals to commit their wealth to long-term investments in particular industries.

The fact that the competitive structure of the American economy was unviable is an important point to remember because it explains why all attempts to re-create the Golden Age of Competition have been, and continue to be, doomed to failure. The efforts are as quixotic as attempts to revive feudalism. This is not to say that increasing the number of firms in an industry may not be beneficial. The larger the number of independent decision-making units in any given environment, the greater is the probability of useful innovation. Merely increasing the number of firms, however, is not the same as restoring competitive conditions to an industry or assuring the degree of social control implicit in competitive conditions. This leads to the third point that should be emphasized as one of the conclusions of this study.

Any program for re-establishing the social control lost when the competitive structure of the American economy was so dramatically altered at the turn of the century must take into account the real economic forces at work in the system. The failure to do this was one of the fatal shortcomings of the "trust-busting" program launched during the Progressive period, this country's first attempt to re-establish social control over pricing decisions in the manufacturing sector. By seeking a return to an earlier, misperceived Golden Age rather than accepting the impracticality of price competition under modern conditions of production, the Progressives, especially those in the Wilsonian or Brandeisian tradition, made inevitable their own eventual frustration. Their program was too radical in the sense that, if fully implemented, the workability of the economic system would have been too greatly impaired—not because, as their opponents argued, the advantages of large size would have been lost, but rather because the advantages of being able to control prices would have been sacrificed. The latter included more than the mere ability to better regulate production to demand. Investment was also facilitated, both because of the megacorp's power to generate internally virtually all of the investment funds it required and because of the greater security surrounding investment in an industry from which outside competitors were effectively excluded. At least equally important was the fact that it was possible to devote more managerial time and energy to other matters once price competition was eliminated. All of these are factors which can, and in fact subsequently did, contribute to a high rate of capital formation and technological change, and thus to a high rate of economic growth.

In this respect Theodore Roosevelt, for all his naïveté about "good" and "bad" trusts, emerges in retrospect as the political leader during the Progressive period with perhaps the best understanding of what needed to be done. His preference for regulation over "trust-busting" reflected an awareness that the large industrial concern was an institution concomitant with economic progress and that, this being the case, some alternative to the social control provided by competitive markets had to be devised. If it must be pointed out that the forms of regulation which he favored were inadequate to the task, it must also be noted that no subsequent political leader has been able to suggest, let alone implement, more appropriate forms. The most serious attempt to date to apply the regulatory approach to manufacturing, the experiment with government-sanctioned and government-supervised cartels carried out by Franklin Delano Roosevelt's National Recovery Administration, was abandoned after two years with few persons left who were still willing to champion that approach.[1]

Because of the political and economic difficulties raised by any attempt to deal realistically with the problem of social control over business pricing decisions, there has been an understandable tendency simply to ignore the question in the hope that market forces will somehow in the long run serve as a corrective force.[2] Yet the problem of social control cannot be ignored without danger, as the persistent recurrence of non-demand-induced inflation and related maladjustments of the economic system attest.[3] If the problem is ever to be solved, it will be by taking up where Theodore Roosevelt left off, that is, by seeking to establish a form of regulation which, while it recognizes that the large corporation or megacorp is a permanent fixture on the economic landscape, is nonetheless capable of assuring that the megacorp's actions, especially with respect to prices, are consistent with the public interest.[4] This is the most important inference to be drawn from the historical experience of the Corporate Revolution.

[1] Ellis W. Hawley, *The New Deal and the Problem of Monopoly*, pt. 1, esp. chaps. 6–7.

[2] Intellectual support for this position derives primarily from the writings of Joseph Schumpeter and his emphasis on the dynamic characteristics of capitalism, particularly the process of creative destruction; see his *Capitalism, Socialism and Democracy*, pp. 59–110.

[3] These related maladjustments are elaborated on in the present author's "Business Concentration and Its Significance," pp. 193–96.

[4] This problem of social control is discussed in the present author's *The Theory of Oligopoly* (in preparation).

APPENDIXES AND BIBLIOGRAPHY

APPENDIX A

SUGAR REFINERIES LOCATED IN NEW YORK CITY
1868-87*

REFINERY	68	69	70	71	72	73	74	75	76	77	78	79	80	81	82	83	84	85	86	87
Aldama & Fuller						•	•	•												
Atlantic S.R. Co.	•	•																		
Joseph Bensel																			•	•
Birbeck & Howell						•														
Booth & Edgar	•	•	•	•	•	•	•	•	•	•	•	•	•	•	•	•				
Wm. P. Breck (succ'd by	•																			
Breck & Schemerhorn)		•	•	•	•	•														
Brooklyn S. R. Co.										•	•	•	•	•	•	•	•	•	•	•
Brunjes, Ockershausen & Co. (succ'd by	•	•	•	•	•															
Brunjes, Bohde & Doscher)						•														
Peter Brunjes					•															
Burden Control S. R. Co.																	•	○	○	•
Burger, Hurlbut & Livingston	•	•	•	•	•	•	•	•	•	•	•	•	•	•	•	•	•			
Hugh Camp & Co.	•	•																		
Canfield & Benner			•	•	•	•														
Chicago S. R. Co.																			•	
Cunningham, Harris & Co.		•																		
Curtis, Shapter & Co.			•	•																
DeCastro & Donner					•	•	•	•	•	•	•	○	•	•	•	•	•	•	•	•
Dick & Meyer							•	•	•	•	•	•	•	•	•	•	•	•	•	•
Dowley, Corners & Co. (succ'd by	•	•	•	○	○	•	•	•												
Corner Bros. & Co.)									•	•	•	•								
Carsten Droge						•														
Chas. W. Durant			•	•	•	•	•	•	•	•	•	•	•	•	•	•	•			
Earle & Co.													•							
Electric S. R. Co.																	•	○	•	•
Empire S. Mfg. Co.															•	•				
J. M. & L. Escoriaza	•																			
Foote & Knevels																•				
Thos. Freeborn & Co.							•	•	•	•	•									
Greer, Turner & Co.	•	•	•	•	•	•	•	•	•											
Michael Hannon										•										
Harriman & Wallace (succ'd by	•	•																		
Wallace & Schomaker)			•	•	•															
John Harris	•																			
Sarah Harris	•																			
Havemeyer & Co. (succ'd by			•	•	•	•														
Havemeyers, Eastwick & Co., succ'd in turn							•	•	•	•	•	•	•							
by Havemeyer S. R. Co.														•	•	•	•	•	•	•
Havemeyer Bros. & Co. (succ'd by					•	•	•	•	•	•	•	•	•							
Havemeyer S. R. Co.)														•	•	•	•	•	•	•
Havemeyer & Elder	•	•	•	•	•	•	•	•	•	•	•	•	•	•	•	•	•	•	•	•
M. Hopke & Co.				•	•	•														
B. H. Howell, Sons & Co.															•	•	•	•	•	•
Hudson River Steam S. R.	•	•	•	•	•															
Johnson, Brodisk & Sons	•	•	•	•	•	•	•	•	○	•	•									
Johnson & Lazarus					•	•	•	•	•	•	•	•	•							
Katterhorn, Hopke, Offerman & Co.					•	•	•	•	•											
Frank Lazarus								•												
Long Island S. R. Co.	•	•	•	•	•	•														
F. O. Matthiessen & Wiechers	•	•	•	•	•	•	•	•	•	•	•	•	•	•	•	•	•	•	•	•
Wm. Moller & Sons (succ'd by	•	•	•	•	•	•	•	•	•											
Wm. Moller)										○	○	○	•							
Moller, Odell & Co.	•	•	•	•	•	•	•	•	○	○	○	•								
Moller, Sierck, Hencken & Co. (succ'd by																				
Moller, Sierck & Co.)	•	•	•	•	•	•														

APPENDIX A (continued)
SUGAR REFINERIES LOCATED IN NEW YORK CITY
1868-87*

REFINERY	68	69	70	71	72	73	74	75	76	77	78	79	80	81	82	83	84	85	86	87
Mollers & Martens (succ'd by	●	●	●	●	●	●														
Moller, Sierck & Co.)							●	●	●	●	●	●	●	●	●	●	●	●	●	●
New Jersey S. R. Co.		●																		
New Jersey Ref. Co.													●	●						
New York Steam S. R. Co.	●	●	●	●	●	●	●	●	●	●										
New York S. R. Co.													●							
W. H. Nichols & Co.														●	●	●				
North River S. R. Co.	●	●	●	●	●	●	●	●	●	●	●	●	●	●	●	●	●	●	●	●
Ockershausen Bros.	●	●	●	●	●	●	●	●	●	●	●									
Ockershausen																		●		
Peninsular S. Co.																	●	●		
Plume & Lamont	●	●																		
John F. Reinecke						●	●	●	●	○	○	●	○	○	○	●				
N. Ross & Co.		●	●																	
Wm. Schroeder								●	●	●	●	●								
Hector Sears				●	●	○	○	●	●											
Smith, Griggs & Co.												●								
R. L. & A. Stuart	●	●	●	●	●															
Taussig & Hammerschlag								●	●	●	●	●	●	●						
P. B. Veiller	●	○	●	●	●	○	●	●												
Weston & Co.																	●			
Wheatley, Williams & Co.	●	●	●	●	●	●	●	●												
Williamson, Griffith & Co.	●	●	●	●	●	●	●													
Wintjen, Dick & Co. (succ'd by	●	○	○	●	○															
Wintjen, Harms & Co., succ'd in turn by						●	●	●	●	●	●									
Henry Harms)												●								
James Wood																●				
Wylie, Knevels & Co.					●	●														
Number of Firms Newly Listed	–	3	4	2	6	5	2	3	0	2	0	2	3	1	2	2	3	1	2	0
Number of Firms Newly Omitted	–	3	5	1	1	5	8	1	4	3	2	3	5	4	2	0	5	3	2	1
Number of Firms Temporarily De-listed	–	2	0	1	1	2	0	0	2	1	0	1	1	0	0	0	0	2	1	1
Number of Firms Re-listed	–	–	1	1	0	2	1	1	0	0	0	1	2	0	0	1	0	0	0	0
Number of Mergers	–	0	0	0	0	0	1	0	0	0	0	0	0	1	0	0	0	0	0	0
Total Number of Firms Listed	30	28	28	29	33	33	27	30	24	22	20	19	18	14	14	17	15	11	12	12

*As compiled from the *New York City Directory*, 1868-87. The symbol ● indicates a year in which the refinery specified was listed in the city directory. The table, however, should be interpreted as only an approximation of the actual number of sugar refineries in operation, for not all the firms listed in the directory were, in fact, operating refineries. Some were merely commision merchants, having no refining capacity of their own, while others were merely firms *in embryo* which never succeeded in actually producing sugar. It is impossible to determine what percentage of the firms listed during the twenty-year period fall into either of these categories. But of the twelve firms listed in the 1887 directory, four–Joseph Bensel, Burden Control S. R. Co., Electric S. R. Co., and B. H. Howell, Sons & Co.–definitely were not operating refineries. This high percentage, however, probably was not typical for the twenty-year period. On the other hand, the directory did not always list every sugar refinery in New York City. For example, it consistently failed to include the Oxnard Sugar Refining Company. Moreover, in certain years, refineries that had been listed in prior or subsequent years were not included. This fact has been indicated in the table by the symbol ○ rather than the symbol ●. One possible interpretation is that the refineries not listed were temporarily closed down. But an equally possible interpretation is that they were not listed for the same unknown reason that the Oxnard refinery was not listed.

APPENDIX B

SUGAR REFINERIES LOCATED IN PHILADELPHIA

1869-87*

REFINERY	69	70	71	72	73	74	75		77	78	79		81	82	83	84		87
Armstrong & Winebrener					●	●												
J. Baker & Co.	●	●	●	●														
Henry W. Bartel (succ'd by	●	●	●	●	●	●	●		●	●	●		●	●	●	●		
George Bartel)																		●
Churchman & Mitchell							●											
Edward F. Cruse				●														
Dallett & Son				●	○	○	●											
Davis, McKean & Co. and	●	●	●															
Newhall, Borie & Co., succ'd by	●	●	●															
McKean, Newhall, Borie & Co., in turn succ'd by				●	●	●	●		●	●	●		●	●				
McKean, Borie & Co.															●	●		●
Delaware Sugar House			●	○	○	●	○		●	●	○		●	●	●	●		●
Chas. Donoghue	●																	
Easby & Mitchell (succ'd by						●	○											
Wm. Easby)									●	●	○		●	●	●			
J. H. Easby														●	●	●		
Enterprise S. R. Co.																		●
Feltus, Zimmerling & Co. (succ'd by	●																	
Feltus & Woodville)		●	●															
Ficher & Williams (succ'd by	●	●	●															
Williams, Fielding & Co.)				●	●													
Franklin Sugar Refinery		●	●	○	○	○	○		●	○	●		○	●	●	●		
Frazier & Rogers		●																
Girard S. R. Co.														●				
Harkness & Thompson (succ'd by	●	●	●	●	●	●	●		●	●	●		●	●	●	●		
Harkness & Co.)																		●
Harris, Heyl & Co. (succ'd by		●																
Heyl, Gibbons & Co., in turn succ'd by			●	○	●	●	●		●	●	●		●					
Heyl Bros.)														●	●	●		●
Harrison, Havemeyer & Co. (succ'd by	●	●	●	●	●	●	●		●	●	●		●	●	●	●		
Harrison, Frazier)																		●
George Harrison		●	●															
Herr & Wagner		●	●	●														
John Hilgert & Sons		●	●	●	●	●	●		●	●	●		●	●				
B. H. Howell, Sons & Co.					●	○	●		●	○	●							
Hutter, Frangkenhoff (succ'd by						●												
Robert Hutter)							●											
James B. Jewett						●												
Louis Kaston							●											
E. C. Knight & Co.	●	●	●	●	●	●	●		●	●	●		●	●	●	●		●
Alfred Kusenberg	●																	
Wm. Long		●	●															
Maderia & Cabada		●																
W. J. McCahan & Co.					●	●	●		●	●	●		●	●	●	●		●
George McGill						●												
George Mossop, Perkioman		●	●															
Pennsylvania S.R. Co.																●		●
George Potts																		●
Quaker City Ref.										●								
Rio Grande S. Co.																●		●
Rogers & Mitchell	●	●	●															
Gustave Schwoeri									●									
Wm. M. Sinclair				●														
Southwork S.R.				●	○	●												
Taylor, Gillespie & Co.	●	●	●	○	●													
Williams, Fielding & Co.				●	●													
Wiseman & McGill									●									
Chas. Zimmerling					●	●	●											
Number of Firms Newly Listed	–	9	1	5	4	4	2		2	1	0		0	2	0	2		2
Number of Firms Newly Omitted	–	2	2	5	4	3	4		5	2	1		1	0	2	1		2
Number of Firms Temporarily De-listed	–	0	0	4	2	1	2		0	2	2		1	0	0	0		0
Number of Firms Re-listed	–	–	0	0	2	2	2		3	0	2		2	1	0	0		0
Number of Mergers	–	0	0	1	0	0	0		0	0	0		0	0	0	0		0
Total Number of Firms Listed	13	20	19	14	14	16	14		14	11	10		10	13	11	12		12

*As compiled from the *Philadelphia City Directory*, 1869-87. The symbol ● indicates a year in which the refinery specified was listed in the directory; the symbol ○, a year in which the refinery specified was omitted though listed in both the preceding and following years. The table, however, as noted in the compilation for New York City (Appendix A), should be interpreted as only an approximation of the actual number of refineries in operation, for not all firms listed in the directory were, in fact, operating refineries. In the case of the 12 firms listed in the Philadelphia directory for 1887, all but two—Harrison, Frazier and E. C. Knight & Co.—definitely were not operating refineries. Again, although it is doubtful that such a high percentage of firms that were either commission merchants or firms *in embryo* was typical of the entire 19-year period, it does raise serious though unanswerable questions as to the accuracy of the over-all figures. For certain years no copy of the *Philadelphia City Directory* could be found. Those years were simply ignored, thus introducing a further source of error.

APPENDIX C

SUGAR REFINERIES LOCATED IN BOSTON
1868-87*

REFINERY	68	69	70	71	72	73	74	75	76	77	78	79	80	81	82	83	84	85	86	87
Adams S. R. Co.	•	•	•	•	•	•														
American S. R. Co.								•												
Bay State S. R. Co.	•	•	•	•	•	•	•	•	•	•	•	•	•	•	•	•	•	•	•	•
Boston S. R. Co.	•	•	•	•	•	•	•	•	•	•	•	•	•	•	•	•	•	•	•	•
Bristol S. R. Co.	•	•																		
Continental S. R. Co.	•	•	•	•	•	•	•	•	•	•	•	•	•	•	•	•	•	•	•	•
Eagle S. R. Co.	•	•																		
Jasper S. R. Co.									•	•	•	•	•							
Revere S. R. Co.						•	•	•	•	•	•	•	•	•	•	•	•	•	•	•
Standard S. R. Co.				•	•	•	•	•	•	•	•	•	•	•	•	•	•	•	•	•
Union S. R. Co.	•	•	•	•	•	•	•													
Number of Firms Newly Listed	–	0	0	1	0	1	0	1	1	0	0	0	0	0	0	0	0	0	0	0
Number of Firms Newly Omitted	–	0	2	0	0	0	1	1	1	0	0	0	0	1	0	0	0	0	0	0
Total Number of Firms Listed	7	7	5	6	6	7	6	6	6	6	6	6	6	5	5	5	5	5	5	5

*As compiled from the *Boston City Directory*, 1868–87. The symbol • indicates a year in which the refinery specified was listed in the directory. The problem of distinguishing between actual refineries, on the one hand, and commission merchants and firms *in embryo*, on the other, appears to be less serious than in the case of Appendixes A and B. All five of the firms listed in the *Boston City Directory* for 1887 were, in fact, operating refineries.

APPENDIX D

AVERAGE PRICES OF RAW AND REFINED SUGAR FOR SELECTED YEARS, AND THE MARGIN BETWEEN THEM

Year	*Raw (96° Test)*	*Refined (Granulated)*	*Margin*
1879	7.423¢	8.785¢	1.362¢
1880	8.206	9.602	1.396
1881	8.251	9.667	1.416
1882	7.797	9.234	1.437
1883	7.423	8.506	1.083
1884	5.857	6.780	0.923
1885	5.729	6.441	0.712
1886	5.336	6.117	0.781
1887	5.245	6.013	0.768
1888	5.749	7.007	1.258
1889	6.433	7.640	1.207
1890	5.451	6.171	0.720
1891	3.863	4.691	0.828
1892	3.311	4.346	1.035
1893	3.689	4.842	1.153
1894	3.240	4.120	0.880
1895	3.270	4.152	0.882
1896	3.624	4.532	0.908
1897	3.557	4.503	0.946
1898	4.235	4.965	0.730
1899	4.419	4.919	0.500
1900	4.566	5.320	0.754
1901	4.047	5.050	1.003
1902	3.542	4.455	0.913
1903	3.720	4.638	0.918
1904	3.974	4.772	0.798
1905	4.278	5.256	0.978
1906	3.686	4.515	0.829
1907	3.756	4.649	0.893
1908	4.073	4.957	0.884
1909	4.007	4.765	0.758
1910	4.188	4.972	0.784
1911	5.345	4.453	0.892
1912	5.041	4.162	0.879
1913	4.278	3.506	0.772
1914	4.683	3.814	0.869
1915	5.559	4.642	0.917
1916	6.862	5.786	1.076
1917	7.663	6.228	1.435

Source: Willett & Gray's *Weekly Statistical Sugar Trade Journal,* as reprinted in *United States* v. *American Sugar Refining Co. et al.: Testimony Before William B. Brice, Special Examiner,* pp. 4643–44.

DOMESTIC SUGAR-MARKET SHARES

Year	American S. R. Co.	National S. R. Co.	Other Cane Producers	Beet Sugar	Imports
1899	67.9	—	28.7	3.1	0.3
1900	67.3	—	28.7	3.1	0.9
1901	57.9	12.1	23.4	4.7	1.9
1902	57.0	13.8	22.8	5.4	1.0
1903	55.2	12.3	22.3	10.0	0.2
1904	58.1	11.8	23.4	6.5	0.2
1905	52.9	11.8	26.4	8.8	0.1
1906	51.0	11.8	26.2	10.9	0.1
1907	49.3	10.8	26.7	13.2	0.1
1908	45.1	10.4	27.6	16.3	0.6
1909	43.1	10.6	31.8	14.0	0.5
1910	42.1	11.1	32.4	13.9	0.5
1911	42.1	—*	41.9	15.5	0.5
1912	38.5	—*	46.1	15.0	0.4
1913	36.3	—*	46.3	17.0	0.4
1914	35.5	—*	47.1	17.0	0.4
1915	34.0	—*	44.4	21.1	0.5
1916	33.6	—*	46.0	20.0	0.5
1917	28.0	—*	49.3	22.6	0.1
1918	31.5	—*	52.3	16.2	—

* Share of market accounted for by National Sugar Refining Company included in share of market accounted for by other cane producers.

Source: Willett & Gray's *Weekly Statistical Sugar Trade Journal,* first issue of each succeeding year.

HAVEMEYER AND AMERICAN SUGAR REFINING COMPANY HOLDINGS IN SUGAR BEET COMPANIES, 1907

UTAH-IDAHO

Company[a]	Plant Locations[a]	Slicing Capacity (daily tons)[a]	Percentage of Interest in Company[b]
*Utah-Idaho Sugar Co.	Lehi, Utah	1,350	
	Garland, Utah	1,200	
	Idaho Falls, Idaho	600	
	Sugar City, Idaho	700	
	Blackfoot, Idaho	600	
	Nampa, Idaho	600	
	Total	5,050	51
*Amalgamated Sugar Co.	Ogden, Utah	600	
	Logan, Utah	500	
	Total	1,100	50
*Lewiston Sugar Co.	Lewiston, Utah	600	37
Total Slicing Capacity in Area		6,750	
Percentage under Havemeyer-American Control		100	

NORTHERN COLORADO

Company[a]	Plant Locations[a]	Slicing Capacity (daily tons)[a]	Percentage of Interest in Company[b]
*Great Western Sugar Co.	Loveland, Colo.	1,200	
	Greeley, Colo.	800	
	Eaton, Colo.	600	
	Fort Collins, Colo.	1,200	
	Windsor, Colo.	600	
	Sterling, Colo.	600	
	Brush, Colo.	600	
	Fort Morgan, Colo.	600	
	Total	6,200	68
Total Slicing Capacity in Area		6,200	
Percentage under Havemeyer-American Control		100	

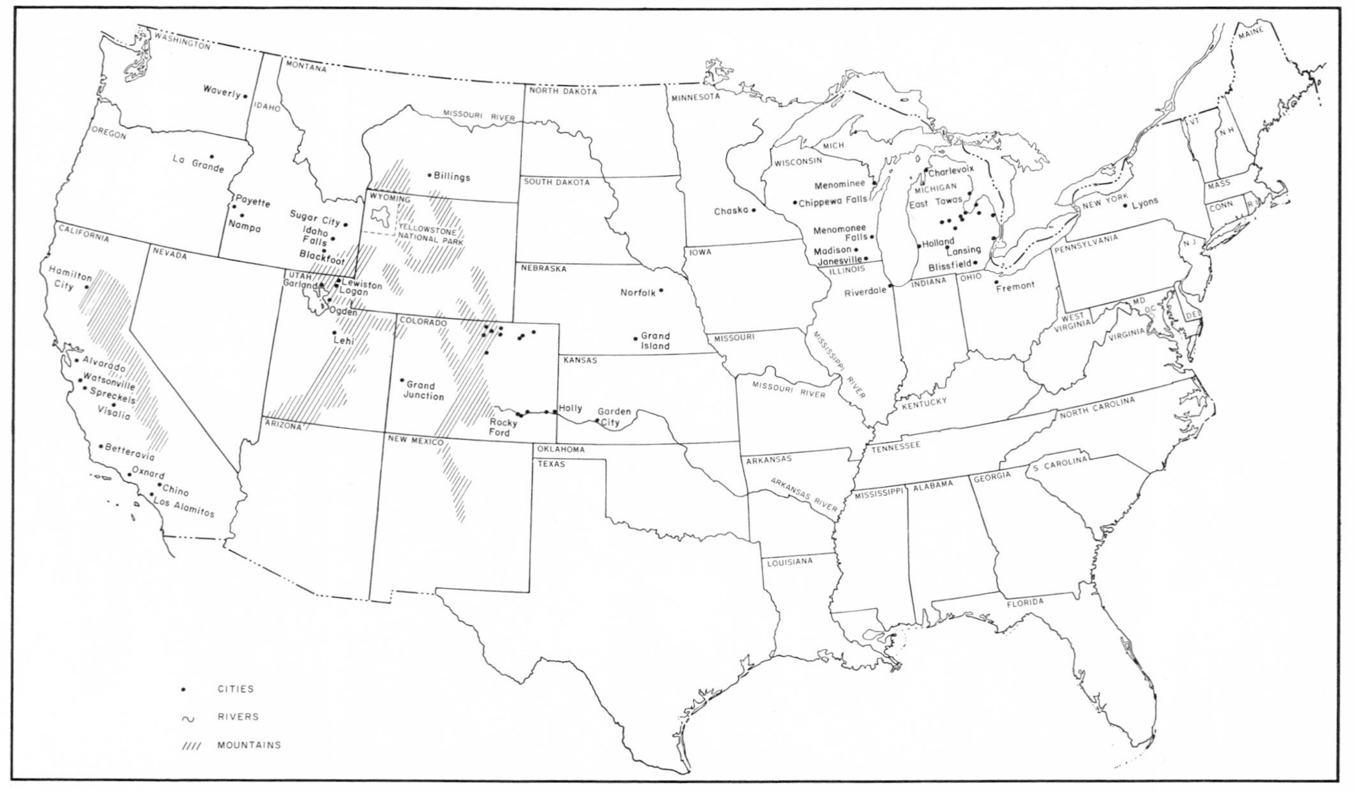

MAP 5. BEET FACTORY SITES IN THE UNITED STATES, 1907

MICHIGAN

Company[a]	Plant Locations[a]	Slicing Capacity (daily tons)[a]	Percentage of Interest in Company[b]
*Michigan Sugar Co.	Bay City, Mich.	600	55[c]
	Caro, Mich.	1,100	
	Alma, Mich.	750	
	Sebewaing, Mich.	600	
	Carrollton, Mich.	800	
	Crosswell, Mich.	600	
	Total	4,450	
*Continental Sugar Co.	Fremont, Ohio	400	51
	Blissfield, Mich.	600	
	Total	1,000	
Holland Sugar Co.	Holland, Mich.	350	—
Owosso Sugar Co.	Owosso, Mich.	1,100	
	Lansing, Mich.	600	
	Total	1,700	
West Bay City Sugar Co.	Bay City, Mich.	600	—
German-American Sugar Co.	Salzburg, Mich.	600	—
Mount Clemens Sugar Co.	Mount Clemens, Mich.	600	—
St. Louis Sugar Co.	St. Louis, Mich.	600	—
West Michigan Sugar Co.	Charlevoix, Mich.	600	—
Total Slicing Capacity in Area		10,500	
Percentage under Havemeyer-American Control		52	

CALIFORNIA

Company[a]	Plant Locations[a]	Slicing Capacity (daily tons)[a]	Percentage of Interest in Company[b]
*Spreckels Sugar Co.	Spreckels, Calif.	3,000	50
*American Beet Sugar Co.	Chino, Calif.	700	50[c]
	Oxnard, Calif.	2,000	
	Total	2,700	

CALIFORNIA—*Continued*

Company[a]	Plant Locations[a]	Slicing Capacity (daily tons)[a]	Percentage of Interest in Company[b]
*Alameda Sugar Co.	Alvarado, Calif.	800	49
*Union Sugar Co.	Betteravia, Calif.	600	—
Los Alamitos Sugar Co.	Los Alamitos, Calif.	700	—
Sacramento Valley Sugar Co.	Hamilton City, Calif.	600	—
Pacific Sugar Co.	Visalia, Calif.	350	—
Total Slicing Capacity in Area		8,750	
Percentage under Havemeyer-American Control		81	

SOUTHERN COLORADO

Company[a]	Plant Locations[a]	Slicing Capacity (daily tons)[a]	Percentage of Interest in Company[b]
*American Beet Sugar Co.	Rocky Ford, Colo.	1,000	50[c]
	Lamar, Colo.	400	
	Total	1,400	
*Las Animas Sugar Co.	Las Animas, Colo. (plant leased to American Beet Sugar Co.)	800	—
Holly Sugar Co.	Holly, Colo.	600	
	Swink, Colo.	1,200	
	Total	1,800	—
National Sugar Mfg. Co.	Sugar City, Colo.	500	—
United States Sugar and Land Co.	Garden City, Kan.	800	—
Total Slicing Capacity in Area		5,300	
Percentage under Havemeyer-American Control		42	

MISCELLANEOUS

Company[a]	Plant Locations[a]	Slicing Capacity (daily tons)[a]	Percentage of Interest in Company[b]
Washington State Sugar Co.	Waverly, Wash.	500	—
*Amalgamated Sugar Co.	La Grande, Ore.	350	50
*Billings Sugar Co.	Billings, Mont.	1,200	68
Western Sugar and Land Co.	Grand Junction, Colo.	700	—
*American Beet Sugar Co.	Grand Island, Neb.	350	50[c]
*Iowa Sugar Co.	Waverly, Iowa	400	75
*Carver County Sugar Co.	Chaska, Minn.	600	80
Wisconsin Sugar Co.	Menomonee Falls, Wis.	600	—
Chippewa Sugar Co.	Chippewa Falls, Wis.	500	—
Rock County Sugar Co.	Janesville, Wis.	600	—
United States Sugar Co.	Madison, Wis.	600	—
*Menominee River Sugar Co.	Menominee, Mich.	1,100	50
Charles Pope	Riverdale, Ill.	350	—
Lyons Beet Sugar Ref. Co.	Lyons, N.Y.	600	—
Total Slicing Capacity Indicated under Miscellaneous		8,450	
Percentage under Havemeyer-American Control		47	
Total Slicing Capacity in the United States		45,950	
Percentage Under Havemeyer-American Control		69	

* Denotes company under Havemeyer-American control.

[a] *United States* v. *American Sugar Refining Co. et al.*, pretrial testimony, 1912, p. 286.

[b] See pp. 240–42 and 247–48 above, as well as Hardwick committee investigation, 1911, p. 100.

[c] Preferred stock only. Holdings of common stock were, in the Michigan Sugar Company, only 35 per cent; in the American Beet Sugar Company, nil.

BIBLIOGRAPHY

The items below are listed in alphabetical order, with the exception of legal cases and statutes. The latter appear separately at the end. A numeral follows each entry, indicating the subject matter of the item. The code is as follows: **I**, Sugar Refining; **II**, Industries Other than Sugar Refining; **III**, General History; **IV**, Biography; **V**, Industrial Organization and Other Economic Subjects; **VI**, Miscellaneous.

Adler, Jacob. "Claus Spreckels, Sugar King of Hawaii," Ph.D. dissertation, Columbia University, 1959. This work was published under the title *Claus Spreckels: The Sugar King in Hawaii* in 1965 by the University of Hawaii Press. The pagination cited in the present text, however, is that of the dissertation. **IV**

Allen, Frederick Lewis. *The Great Pierpont Morgan.* New York: Harper & Bros., 1949. **IV**

American Sugar Family, 1917–22. This is the house organ of the American Sugar Company, successor to the American Sugar Refining Company. **I**

American Sugar Refining Company. *Annual Report*, 1891–1922. **I**

American Sugar Refining Company. *A Century of Sugar Refining in the United States, 1816–1916.* New York: n.p., 1916. **I**

Bain, Joe S. *Barriers to New Competition.* Cambridge: Harvard University Press, 1956. **V**

———. "Industrial Concentration and Government Anti-Trust Policy." In *The Growth of the American Economy*, ed. Harold F. Williamson. New York: Prentice-Hall, 1951. **V**

———. *Industrial Organization.* New York: John Wiley & Sons, 1959. **V**

Baker, Ray S. *Woodrow Wilson, Life and Letters*, vol. 4. 8 vols. Garden City, N.Y.: Doubleday, 1931. **IV**

Benson, G. Lee. *Merchants, Railroads & Farmers, Railroad Regulation and New York Politics, 1850–1877.* Cambridge: Harvard University Press, 1955. **III**

Bergh, Albert E., ed. *Addresses, State Papers and Letters of Grover Cleveland.* New York: Unity, 1908. **IV**

Berle, Adolph A., and Means, Gardiner C. *The Modern Corporation and Private Property.* New York: Commerce Clearing House, 1932. **V**

Bernhardt, Joshua. *Government Control of the Sugar Industry in the United States.* New York: Macmillan, 1920. **I**

Berry, Thomas S. "The Effect of Business Conditions on Early Judicial Decisions Concerning Restraint on Trade." *Journal of Economic History,* 30 (1950). **V**

Bezanson, Anne; Gray, Robert D.; and Hussey, Miriam. *Prices in Colonial Pennsylvania.* Philadelphia: University of Pennsylvania Press, 1935. **III**

Biographical Sketch of Robert L. and Alexander Stuart. Reprinted from the *Encyclopedia of Contemporary Biography of New York.* New York: Atlantic, 1882. The reprint can be found in the New York City Public Library. **IV**

Bishop, J. Leander. *A History of American Manufactures from 1608 to 1860.* 3 vols. Philadelphia: Edward Young & Co., 1868. **II**

Bishop, Joseph. *Theodore Roosevelt and His Times, Shown in His Own Letters.* New York: Scribner's, 1920. **IV**

Blakey, Roy G. *The United States Beet-Sugar Industry and the Tariff.* New York: Columbia University Press, 1912. **I**

Blum, John M. *The Republican Roosevelt.* Cambridge: Harvard University Press, 1954. **IV**

Bogen, Jules. *The Anthracite Railroads.* New York: Ronald Press, 1927. **II**

Boston City Directory, 1868–87. **II**

Bowker, R. R. "A Lump of Sugar." *Harper's Magazine,* 73 (June, 1886). **I**

Boynton, H. V. "Whiskey Ring." *North American Review,* 123 (October, 1876). **III**

Bradstreet's Journal, 1881–1900. **II**

Brandeis, Louis D. "Trusts and Efficiency." *Business—A Profession.* Boston: Hale, Cushman & Flint, 1927. **V**

Brown, Henry A. *Revised Analysis of the Sugar Question.* Somerville, Mass.: n.p., 1879. **I**

———. *Statement Made Before the Committee of Ways and Means on the Sugar Question.* Washington: Judd & Detweiler, 1880. **I**

———. *Sugar Frauds.* n.p., 1878. **I**

Burgess, George H., and Kennedy, Miles C. *Centennial History of the Pennsylvania Railroad Company.* Philadelphia: Pennsylvania Railroad Company, 1949. **II**

Burns, Arthur R. *The Decline of Competition.* New York: McGraw-Hill, 1936. **V**

Carlson, Oliver, and Bates, Ernest S. *Hearst, Lord of San Simeon.* New York: Viking, 1936. **IV**

Carmen, Harry J., and Syrett, Harold C. *A History of the American People.* 2 vols. New York: Alfred A. Knopf, 1955. **III**

Chicago Tribune, 1887–95. **III**

Champomier, P. A. *Statement of the Sugar Crop of Louisiana of 1860–61.* New York: Cook, Young, 1861. **I**

Chandler, Alfred D., Jr. *Strategy and Structure: Chapters in the History of the Industrial Enterprise.* Cambridge: M.I.T. Press, 1962. **V**

———. "The Large Industrial Corporation and the Making of the Modern American Economy." In *Institutions in Modern America,* ed. Stephen E. Ambrose. Baltimore: The Johns Hopkins Press, 1967. **V**

Clark, John D. *The Federal Anti-Trust Policy.* Baltimore: The Johns Hopkins Press, 1931. **V**

Cole, Arthur H., ed. *Industrial and Commercial Correspondence of Alexander Hamilton.* Chicago: A. W. Shaw, 1928. **III**

Commercial and Financial Chronicle, 1865–1922. **II**

Commons, John R. *The Legal Foundations of Capitalism.* Madison: University of Wisconsin Press, 1957. **V**

Cone, Andrew, and Johns, Walter R. *Petrolia: A Brief History of the Pennsylvania Petroleum Region.* New York: Appleton, 1870. **II**

Connecticut, Legislature, General Assembly. *Special Acts and Resolutions of the General Assembly,* 1889. **III**

Cordray, William W. "Claus Spreckels of California." Ph.D. dissertation, University of Southern California, 1955. **IV**

Cosmopolitan. **III**

Coxe, Trench. *Arts and Manufactures of the United States of America for the Year 1810.* Philadelphia: A. Gorman, 1814. **III**

David, Paul A. "The Growth of Real Product in the United States Before 1840: New Evidence, Controlled Conjectures," *Journal of Economic History,* 27 (June, 1967). **III**

DeBow, J. B. D. *The Industrial Resources, Etc. of the Southern and Western States,* vol. 2. New Orleans: DeBow's Review, 1852. **III**

DeBow's Review, 1846–60. **III**

Department of Justice (JD) File No. 59–8–13. *See* U.S., Department of Justice Official Papers.

Department of Justice (JD) File No. 60–104–0. *See* U.S., Department of Justice. Official Papers.

Department of Justice (JD) File No. 8247. *See* U.S., Department of Justice. Official Papers.

Department of Justice (JD) File No. 121616. *See* U.S., Department of Justice. Official Papers.

DeSantis, Vincent P. *Republicans Face the Southern Question: The New Departure Years, 1877–1897.* Baltimore: The Johns Hopkins Press, 1959. **III**

Destler, Chester M. *American Radicalism, 1865–1901.* New London: Connecticut College, 1946. **III**

Dewey, Donald. *Monopoly in Economics and Law.* Chicago: Rand McNally, 1959. **V**

Dewing, Arthur S. *A History of the National Cordage Company.* Cambridge: Harvard University Press, 1913. **II**

———. *Corporate Promotion and Reorganizations.* Cambridge: Harvard University Press, 1914. **II**

Dictionary of American Biography. **IV**

Digest of Accounts of Manufacturing Establishments. Washington: Gales & Seaton, 1823. **III**

Dill, James. *Statutory and Case Law Applicable to Private Companies Under the General Incorporation Act of New Jersey.* New York: Baker, Voorhis, 1901. **V**

Donner, J. O. Letter to the *New York Evening Post,* March 13, 1880. A reprint of the letter can be found at the New York Historical Society. **I**

Dos Passos, John R. *Commercial Trusts.* New York: Putnam's, 1901. **V**

Dudden, Arthur P. "Antimonopolism, 1865–1890: The Historical Background and Intellectual Origins of the Antitrust Movement in the United States." Ph.D. dissertation, University of Michigan, 1950. **V**

Eames, Francis A. *The New York Stock Exchange.* New York: Thomas Hall, 1894. **III**

Eichner, Alfred S. "Business Concentration and Its Significance." In *The Business of America,* ed. Ivar Berg. New York: Harcourt, Brace & World, 1968. **V**

———. *The Theory of Oligopoly.* In preparation. **V**

Encyclopedia Britannica. 11th ed. **I**

Evans, ——. "Sugar Refining." *DeBow's Review,* 6 (1849). **I**

Fels, Rendig. *American Business Cycles.* Chapel Hill: University of North Carolina Press, 1959. **III**

Fine, Sidney. *Laissez-Faire and the General-Welfare State.* Ann Arbor: University of Michigan Press, 1956. **III**

Fishlow, Albert. "Antebellum Interregional Trade Reconsidered." *American Economic Review,* 59 (May, 1964). Reprinted in *New Views on American Economic Development,* ed. Ralph Andreano. Cambridge: Schenkman, 1965. **III**

Flynn, John T. *God's Gold: The Story of Rockefeller and His Times.* New York: Harcourt, Brace, 1932. **IV**

Freedland, Fred. "History of Holding Company Legislation in New York State." *Fordham Law Review,* 24 (1955). **V**

Friedley, Edwin. *Philadelphia and Its Manufactures.* Philadelphia: Edwin Young, 1859. **II**

Garraty, John A. *Right-Hand Man: The Life of George W. Perkins.* New York: Harper & Bros., 1957. **IV**

Giddens, Paul H. *The Birth of the Oil Industry.* New York: Macmillan, 1938. **II**

Ginzberg, Eli, and Eichner, Alfred S. *The Troublesome Presence: American Democray and the Negro.* New York: Free Press, 1964. **III**

Gordon, Patricia J. "The Livingstons of New York." Master's thesis, Columbia University, 1959. **IV**

Goss, John D. *History of Tariff Administration in the United States.* New York: Columbia University Press, 1891. **III**

Gottesman, Rita S. *The Arts and Crafts in New York, 1726–1776.* New York: New York Historical Society, 1938. **III**

Gresham, Matilda. *Life of Walter Q. Gresham.* 2 vols. Chicago: Rand McNally, 1919. **IV**

Guese, Lucius E. "St. Louis and the Great Whiskey Ring." *Missouri Historical Review,* 36 (January, 1942). **III**

Gunton, George. "The Economic and Social Aspects of Trusts." *Political Science Quarterly,* 3 (September, 1888). **V**

Hardwick committee investigation, 1911. *See* U.S., Congress, House of Representatives, Special Committee on the Investigation of the American Sugar Refining Company and Others.

Havemeyer, Henry O., Jr. *Biographical Record of the Havemeyer Family, 1606–1943.* New York: privately printed, 1944. The work can be found at the New York Historical Society. **IV**

Havemeyer, Theodore A. *Letters to J. R. Tucker and Jas. G. Carlisle.* Washington: Globe, 1880. The pamphlet can be found at the New York City Public Library. **I**

———. *Papers Relative to Drawback Rates on Exported Sugar.* New York: *Evening Post* Press, 1887. **I**

Hawley, Ellis W. *The New Deal and the Problem of Monopoly.* Princeton: Princeton University Press, 1966. **III**

Hicks, John D. *The Populist Revolt.* Minneapolis: University of Minnesota Press, 1931. **III**

Hofstadter, Richard. *The Age of Reform.* New York: Alfred A. Knopf, 1955. **III**

Howe, George F. "The New York Custom-House Controversy, 1877–1879." *Mississippi Valley Historical Review,* XVIII (December, 1931). **III**

Howland, Harold J. "The Case of the Seventeen Holes." *Outlook,* XCII (May 1, 1909). **I**

Hunt's Merchant Magazine, 1839–60. **III**

James, Henry, *Richard Olney and His Public Service.* Boston: Houghton Mifflin, 1923. **IV**

JD File No. 59–8–13. *See* U.S., Department of Justice. Official Papers.

JD File No. 60–104–0. *See* U.S., Department of Justice. Official Papers.

JD File No. 8247. *See* U.S., Department of Justice. Official Papers.

JD File No 121616. *See* U.S., Department of Justice. Official Papers.

Jenks, Jeremiah W. "The Development of the Whiskey Trust." In *Trusts, Pools, and Corporations,* ed. William Z. Ripley. Boston: Ginn & Co., 1916. **II**

———. "The Michigan Salt Association." In *Trusts, Pools, and Corporations,* ed. William Z. Ripley. Boston: Ginn & Co., 1916. **II**

Johnston, J. *Statistical Cost Analysis.* New York: McGraw-Hill, 1960. **V**

Jones, Chester A. *The Economic History of the Anthracite-Tidewater Canals.* Philadelphia: n.p., 1908. **II**

Jones, Eliot. *The Anthracite Coal Combination in the United States.* Cambridge: Harvard University Press, 1914. **II**

———. *The Trust Problem in the United States.* New York: Macmillan, 1928. **V**

Josephson, Matthew. *The Politicos.* New York: Harcourt, Brace, 1938. **III**

Keasbey, Edward Q. "New Jersey and the Great Corporations." *Harvard Law Review,* 13 (November, 1899). **V**

Kirkland, Edward C. *A History of American Economic Life.* 3d ed. New York: Appleton-Century-Crofts, 1951. **III**

Knight, Frank H. *Risk, Uncertainty and Profit.* London: University of London Reprint, 1933. **V**

Kolko, Gabriel. *Railroads and Regulation, 1877–1916.* Princeton: Princeton University Press, 1965. **III**

Langtry, Albert P., ed. *Metropolitan Boston: A Modern History,* vol. 2. New York: Lewis Historical Publishing, 1929. **IV**

Larcom, Russell C. *The Delaware Corporation.* Baltimore: The Johns Hopkins Press, 1937. **V**

Leavitt, John B. *Memorial of S. C. T. Dodd.* n.p. n.d. A copy of the work can be found at the New York City Public Library. **IV**

Leftwich, Richard H. *The Price System and Resource Allocation.* New York: Holt, Rinehart & Winston, 1960. **V**

Letwin, William. *Law and Economic Policy in America: The Evolution of the Sherman Antitrust Act.* New York: Random House, 1965. **V**

Lexow committee investigation, 1897. *See* New York, Legislature, Joint Committee to Investigate Trusts.

Link, Arthur S. *Wilson: The New Freedom.* Princeton: Princeton University Press, 1956. **IV**

MacBean, William M. *Biographical Register of Saint Andrew's Society of New York,* vol. 2. New York: privately printed, 1925. The work can be found at the New York City Public Library. **IV**

McDonald, John. *Secrets of the Great Whiskey Ring.* Chicago: Belford, Clarke & Co., 1880. **III**

Machlup, Fritz. "Marginal Analysis and Empirical Research." *American Economic Review,* 36 (September, 1946). **V**

McLauren, John J. *Sketches in Crude Oil.* Harrisburg: n.p., 1890. **II**

Mark, Shelley M., and Adler, Jacob. "Claus Spreckels in Hawaii." *Explorations in Entrepreneurial History,* 10 (October, 1957). **IV**

Markham, Jesse. "Survey of the Evidence and Findings on Mergers." In *Business Concentration and Public Policy.* Princeton: National Bureau of Economic Research, 1955. **V**

Marshall, Alfred. *Industry and Trade.* London: Macmillan & Co., 1920. **V**

———. *Principles of Economics.* London: Macmillan & Co., 1920. **V**

Maybee, Rolland. *Railroad Competition and the Oil Trade, 1855–1873.* Mount Pleasant, Michigan: Extension Press, 1940. **II**

Means, Gardiner C. *The Corporate Revolution in America.* New York: Collier Books, 1964. **V**

———. "The Large Corporation." *American Economic Review,* 21 (March, 1931). **V**

Merton, Robert K. "Social Structure and Anomie," *American Sociological Review,* 3 (October, 1938). Reprinted in *Sociological Analysis,* ed. Logan Wilson and William L. Kolb. New York: Harcourt, Brace, 1949. **VI**

Moody, John. *The Truth About the Trusts.* New York: Moody Publishing, 1904. **V**

Moody's Manual, 1909. **II**

Moore, Austin L. *Life of John D. Archbold.* New York: Macmillan, 193?. **IV**

Morison, Elting E. *Turmoil and Tradition: A Study of the Life and Times of Henry L. Stimson.* Boston: Houghton Mifflin, 1960. **IV**

Mowry, George E. *The Era of Theodore Roosevelt.* New York: Harper & Row, 1958. **III**

———. "The First World War and American Democracy." In *War as a Social Institution,* ed. Jesse D. Clarkson and Thomas C. Cochran. New York: Columbia University Press, 1941. **III**

National Cyclopedia of American Biography. **IV**

Navin, T. R. and Sears, M. V. "The Rise of a Market for Industrial Securities, 1877–1902." *Business History Review,* 29 (June, 1955). **V**

Nelson, Ralph. *Merger Movements in American Industry, 1895–1956.* Princeton: Princeton University Press, 1959. **V**

Nevins, Allan. *Grover Cleveland: A Study in Courage.* New York: Dodd, Mead, 1932. **IV**

———. *John D. Rockefeller: The Heroic Age of American Enterprise.* 2 vols. New York: Scribner's, 1940. **IV**

———. *Study in Power: John D. Rockefeller, Industrialist and Philanthropist.* 2 vols. New York: Charles Scribner's Sons, 1953. This is a revision of Nevins' 1940 biography of Rockefeller. **IV**

New York American, 1907. **III**

New York City Business Directory, 1868–87. **II**

New York Evening Post, 1880. **III**

New York, Legislature, Assembly, Special Committee Appointed to Investigate Alleged Abuses in the Management of Railroads Chartered by the State of New York (Hepburn committee). *Report Together with Testimony.* Albany: n.p., 1880. **II**

New York, Legislature, *Legislative Journal.* 111th sess., 1888. **III**

New York, Legislature, Joint Committee to Investigate Trusts (Lexow committee). *Report and Proceedings.* Albany: Wynkorp, Hallenbreck, Crawford, 1897. **V**

New York, Legislature, Senate Committee on General Laws. *Report on Investigation Relative to Trusts.* 111th sess., 1888, S. Rept. 50. **V**

New York, New York, Chamber of Commerce. *Annual Report,* 1870–90. **III**

New York Penal Code, 1888. **III**

New York Times, 1865–1922. **III**

New York Tribune, 1878–90. **III**

New York World, 1907. **III**

Noble, Ransom E., Jr. *New Jersey Progressivism Before Wilson.* Princeton: Princeton University Press, 1946. **III**

Norman B. Tooker et al. v. *National Sugar Refining Co.: Answer and Crossbill of Louisine W. Havemeyer et al.* This and other documents in the case have been printed in one volume, which was generously made available by the American Sugar Company, successor to the American Sugar Refining Company. **I**

Norman B. Tooker et al. v. *National Sugar Refining Co.: Bill of Complaint. See* preceding item.

Norman B. Tooker et al. v. *National Sugar Refining Co.: Final Decree. See* preceding item.

North, Douglass C. *The Economic Growth of the United States, 1790–1860.* Englewood Cliffs, N.J.: Prentice-Hall, 1961. **III**

North, Douglass C.; Fogel, Robert; Supple, Barry E.; Easterlin, Richard A.; Gallman, Robert E.; and Cameron, Rondo E. "Economic History: Its Contribution to Economic Education, Research and Policy." *American Economic Review* 55 (May, 1965). **II**

Papers Relative to the Drawback Rates on Exported Sugar. New York: *Evening Post* Press, 1877. **I**

Pennsylvania, Legislature, Senate, Committee on the Judiciary, General. *Report in Relation to the Anthracite Coal Difficulties with the Accompanying Testimony.* Harrisburg: B. Singerly, 1871. **II**

———. *Report Relative to Extortionate Charges by the Railroad Companies of the State.* Harrisburg: Singerly & Myers, 1868. **II**

Pennsylvania Magazine of History and Biography. **III**

Penrose, Edith T. *The Theory of the Growth of the Firm.* London: Blackwell, 1959. **V**

People v. *North River Sugar Refining Co.: Appellants' and Respondents' Briefs.* On file at the New York Court of Appeals, First Division, vol. 31 (April 14–May 9, 1890). This document can be found at the Court of Appeals in Albany. **I**

People v. *North River Sugar Refining Co.: Record. See* preceding item.

Petroleum Producers Association. *A History of the Rise and Fall of the South Improvement Company.* Lancaster, Pennslyvania: n.p., 1875. **II**

Philadelphia City Directory, 1869–87. **II**

Pringle, Henry F. *The Life and Times of William Howard Taft.* 2 vols. New York: Farrar & Rinehart, 1939. **IV**

Pryor, Roger A. *Essays and Addresses.* New York: Neale, 1912. **IV**

Railway & Corporate Law Journal, 1887–92. **II**

Rightor, Henry, ed. *Standard History of New Orleans.* Chicago: Lewis Publishing, 1900. **III**

Ripley, William Z., ed. *Trusts, Pools and Corporations.* Boston: Ginn & Co., 1916. **V**

Roosevelt, Theodore. *An Autobiography.* New York: Macmillan, 1916. **IV**

———. *The Letters of Theodore Roosevelt*, ed. Elting E. Morison. 8 vols. Cambridge: Harvard University Press, 1951–54. **IV**

Sackett, William E. *Modern Battles of Trenton.* 2 vols. Trenton, N.J.: J. L. Murphy, 1914. **III**

Schlegel, Marvin B. *Ruler of the Reading: The Life of Franklin B. Gowan.* Harrisburg: Archives Publishing, 1947. **IV**

Schmidt, Louis B. "Internal Commerce and the Development of the National Economy Before 1860." *Journal of Political Economy,* 47 (1939). **III**

Schriftgiesser, Karl. *The Amazing Roosevelt Family, 1613–1942.* New York: W. Funk, 1942. **IV**

Schumpeter, Joseph. *Capitalism, Socialism and Democracy.* New York: Harper & Bros., 1942. **V**

———. *The Theory of Economic Development.* Cambridge: Harvard University Press, 1934. The work was originally published in German in 1911 as *Theorie der wirtschaftlichen Entwicklung.* Munich: Duncker. **V**

Seager, Henry R., and Gulick, Charles A., Jr. *Trust and Corporation Problems.* New York: Harper & Bros., 1929. **V**

Searles, John E., Jr. "American Sugar." In *One Hundred Years of American Commerce,* vol. 1, ed. Chauncey M. Depew. New York: D. O. Haynes & Co., 1895. **I**

Searles, John E., Jr., and Eastwick, Edward P. *Memorial Presented to the Committee on Ways and Means on the Sugar Tariff.* Washington: McGill, 1880. **I**

Sharfman, I. L. *The Interstate Commerce Commission.* 4 vols. New York: The Commonwealth Fund, 1931. **III**

Simons, Henry. *Economic Policy for a Free Society.* Chicago: University of Chicago Press, 1949. **V**

Sitterson, J. Carlyle. *Sugar County: The Cane Sugar Industry in the South, 1753–1950.* Frankfort: University of Kentucky Press, 1953. **I**

Smith, Adam. *Wealth of Nations.* New York: Modern Library, 1937. **V**

Stevens, William S. "A Classification of Pools and Associations Based on American Experience." *American Economic Review,* 3 (September, 1913). **V**

———. *Industrial Combinations and Trusts.* New York: Macmillan, 1913. **V**

Stigler, George J. "Monopoly and Oligopoly by Merger." *American Economic Review,* 40 (May, 1950). **V**

———. "Perfect Competition, Historically Contemplated." *Journal of Political Economy,* 65 (February, 1957). **V**

Stimson, Henry L., and Bundy, McGeorge. *On Active Service in Peace and War.* New York: Harper & Bros., 1948. **IV**

Stimson Papers. These are available at the Yale University Library, New Haven, Conn. **IV**

Stoke, H. W. "Economic Influences Upon the Corporation Laws of New Jersey." *Journal of Political Economy*, 38 (October, 1930). **V**

Stokes, I. N. Phelps. *The Iconography of Manhattan Island.* New York: R. H. Dodd, 1915–28. Vols. 4 and 5. **III**

Swanberg, W. A. *Citizen Hearst.* New York: Charles Scribner's Sons, 1961. **IV**

Taft, William H. *The Antitrust Law and the Supreme Court.* New York: Harper & Bros., 1914. **V**

———. *Presidential Addresses and State Papers.* New York: Doubleday, Page & Co., 1910. **IV**

Tarbell, Ida M. *The History of the Standard Oil Company.* 2 vols. New York: McClure, Phillips, 1904. **II**

———. *The Life of Elbert H. Gary: The Story of Steel.* New York: Appleton, 1925. **IV**

Taylor, F. H. *The Derrick's Handbook of Petroleum.* Oil City, Pa.: Derrick Publishing, 1884. **II**

Taylor, George R. "American Economic Growth Before 1840: An Exploratory Essay." *Journal of Economic History*, 24 (December, 1964). **III**

———. *The Transportation Revolution, 1815–1860.* New York: Rinehart, 1951. **III**

Taylor, George R., and Neu, Irene D. *The American Railroad Network, 1861–1890.* Cambridge: Harvard University Press, 1956. **III**

Tennant, Richard B. *The American Cigarette Industry.* New Haven, Conn.: Yale University Press, 1950. **II**

Thorelli, Hans B. *The Federal Anti-Trust Policy.* Baltimore: The Johns Hopkins Press, 1955. **V**

Thorp, Willard L. *Business Annals.* New York: National Bureau of Economic Research, 1926. **V**

U.S., Attorney General. *Annual Report*, 1888–1922. **III**

U.S., Attorney General. *Bills and Debates in Congress Relative to Trusts.* 57th Cong., 1st sess., 1903, S. Rept. 147. **V**

U.S., Congress. *Congressional Record*, 1888–90. **III**

U.S., Congress, House of Representatives, Committee on Expenditures in the Treasury Department. *Hearings of Sugar Frauds.* 62d Cong., 1st sess., 1911. **I**

U.S., Congress, House of Representatives, Committee on Manufactures. *Report on Trusts.* 50th Cong., 1st sess., 1888, H. Rept. 3112. **V**

U.S., Congress, House of Representatives, Select Committee Concerning the Whiskey Frauds. *Whiskey Frauds.* 44th Cong., 1st sess., 1876, H. Misc. Doc. 186. **III**

U.S., Congress, House of Representatives, Special Committee on the Investigation of the American Sugar Refining Company and Others. *Hearings.* 62d Cong., 2d sess., 1912. **I**

U.S., Congress, Senate, Committee on Finance. *Replies to Tariff Inquiries on Schedule E, Sugar.* 53d Cong., 2d sess., 1894, S. Rept. 452. **I**

U.S., Congress, Senate, Committee on Interstate Commerce. *Investigation of Meat Transportation.* 50th Cong., 2d sess., 1889. **II**

U.S., Congress, Senate, Special Committee to Investigate Attempts at Bribery. *Report.* 53d Cong., 2d sess., 1894, S. Rept. 606. **I**

U.S., Department of Commerce, Bureau of the Census. *Fourteenth Census: Population, 1920.* Washington, D.C.: Government Printing Office, 1921. **III**

U.S., Department of Commerce, Bureau of the Census. *Historical Statistics of the United States, 1789–1945.* Washington, D.C.: Government Printing Office, 1949. **III**

U.S., Department of Interior. *Abstract of Statistics of Manufacturing According to the Returns of the Seventh Census.* 35th Cong., 1st sess., 1858, S. Exec. Doc. 39. **III**

U.S., Department of Justice. Official Papers, File No. 59–8–13 (sugar rebates). National Archives, Washington, D.C. **I**

U.S., Department of Justice. Official Papers, File No. 60–104–0 *(United States* v. *American Sugar Refining Co. et al.,* antitrust prosecution). National Archives, Washington, D.C. **I**

U.S., Department of Justice. Official Papers, File No. 8247 *(United States* v. *E. C. Knight et al.).* National Archives, Washington, D.C. **I**

U.S., Department of Justice. Official Papers, File No. 121616 (sugar customs frauds). National Archives, Washington, D.C. **I**

U.S., Department of Labor, Bureau of Labor Statistics. *History of Wages in the United States from Colonial Times to 1928,* Bulletin No. 499. Washington, D.C.: Government Printing Office, 1929. **III**

U.S., District Court for the Southern District of New York. Official Records, File Equity 7–8 *(United States* v. *American Sugar Refining Company et al.,* antitrust prosecution). National Archives, Washington, D.C. **I**

U.S., Treasury Department. *Documents Relative to the Manufactures in the United States,* vol. 1. Washington: Duff Green, 1833. **III**

U.S., Treasury Department. *Report of the Secretary, 1863,* H. Exec. Doc. 3, 38th Cong., 1st sess., 1863. **III**

U.S. Industrial Commission. *Reports,* vols. 1, 13, and 14. Washington, D.C.: Government Printing Office, 1900. **V**

United States Railroad and Mining Registrar (Philadelphia), 1865–81. **II**

United States v. *American Sugar Refining Co. et al.: Exhibits.* 7 vols. New York: J. W. Pratt, 1913. These volumes were generously made available by the American Sugar Company, successor to the American Sugar Refining Company. **I**

United States v. *American Sugar Refining Co. et al: Final Decree.* A copy was generously made available by the American Sugar Company, successor to the American Sugar Refining Company. **I**

United States v. *American Sugar Refining Co. et al.: Plaintiff's Petition.* A copy can be found on file at the National Archives, under District Court for the Southern District of New York, File Equity 7–8. **I**

United States v. *American Sugar Refining Co. et al: Testimony Before William B. Brice, Special Examiner.* A typewritten copy of the testimony can be found on file at the National Archives, under District Court for the Southern District of New York, File Equity 7–8. A printed copy of the testimony was generously made available by the American Sugar Company, successor to the American Sugar Refining Company. The pagination cited in the present text, however, is that of the typewritten copy. **I**

United States v. *E. C. Knight et al.: Brief for the United States.* U.S. Circuit Court of Appeals for the Third Circuit, March term, 1894, no. 3. A copy of the document can be found in Department of Justice File No. 8247, National Archives, Washington, D.C. **I**

United States v. *E. C. Knight et al.: Transcript of Record. See* preceding item.

United States v. *Sugar Institute et al.: Transcript of Testimony.* This document was generously made available by the American Sugar Company, successor to the American Sugar Refining Company. **I**

Viener, John D. "A Sense of Obligation: Henry L. Stimson as United States Attorney, 1906–1909." Honors thesis, Yale University, 1961. The thesis can be found with the Stimson Papers at the Yale University Library, New Haven, Conn. **IV**

Vogt, Paul L. *The Sugar Refining Industry in the United States, Its Development and Present Position.* University of Pennsylvania Series in Political Economy and Public Law, no. 21. Philadelphia: University of Pennsylvania Press, 1908. **I**

Walker, Albert W. *History of the Sherman Act.* New York: Equity Press, 1910. **V**

Walker, Francis A. "Recent Progress in Political Economy in the United States." *American Economic Review*, 4 (1889). **III**

Warren, Charles. *The Supreme Court in United States History.* 2 vols. Boston: Little, Brown, 1926. **III**

Watkins, Myron. *Industrial Combination and Public Policy.* Boston: Houghton Mifflin, 1927. **V**

Watson, Donald. *Price Theory and Its Uses.* Boston: Houghton Mifflin, 1963. **V**

Weber, Thomas. *The Northern Railroads in the Civil War.* New York: Kings Crown Press, 1952. **III**

Weiss, Leonard W. *Case Studies in American Industry.* New York: John Wiley & Sons, 1967. **V**

Wells, David A. *The Sugar Industry and the Tariff.* New York: n.p., 1878. **I**

Who's Who, 1899–1920. **IV**

Willett and Gray's *Weekly Statistical Sugar Trade Journal*, 1883–1923. The issues for the years before 1890 can be found only at the New York offices of Willett & Gray, Inc. **I**

Williamson, Harold F., and Daum, Arnold. *The American Petroleum Industry,* vol. 1. Evanston: Northwestern University Press, 1959. **II**
Winsor, Justin, ed. *The Memorial History of Boston,* vol. 4. Boston: J. R. Osgood, 1881. **III**
Woodward, C. Van. *Reunion and Reaction, The Compromise of 1877 and the End of Reconstruction.* Boston: Little, Brown, 1951. **III**
Woolman, Henry. "John R. Dos Passos." *Cases and Comments,* 24 (July, 1917). **IV**
Wright, Carroll D. *History of Wages and Prices in Massachusetts, 1752–1860.* Prepared for the Massachusetts Bureau of Statistics of Labor, 16th Annual Report, 1885. **III**
Wright, William. *The Oil Regions of Pennsylvania.* New York: Harper & Bros., 1865. **II**

Legal Cases and Statutes

American Sugar Refining Co. v. *United States,* 223 U.S. 743 (1911).
Chappell v. *Brockway,* 21 Wend. 157 (1839).
Connecticut, *Statutes,* 1888–90.
Heike v. *United States,* 227 U.S. 131 (1913).
Hooker v. *Vandewater,* 4 Denio 349 (1847).
India Bagging Association v. *Kock,* 14 La. Ann. 168 (1859).
In re Greene, 52 Fed. 104.
In re Sugar Rebates, 14 I.C.C. Reports 622 (1908).
Merritt v. *Welsh,* 104 U.S. 694 (1881).
Mogul Steamship Co. v. *McGregor, Gow & Co.* (1892), A.C. 25 (H.L.).
New Jersey, *Statutes,* 1888–90.
Northern Securities Company v. *United States,* 193 U.S. 197 (1904).
Pennsylvania Sugar Refining Co. v. *American Sugar Refining Co.* Reprinted in S. Doc. 718, 60th Cong., 2d sess., 1909.
People v. *Chicago Gas Trust Co.,* 130 Ill. 268 (1889).
People v. *North River Sugar Refining Co.,* 3 N.Y. Sup. 401 (1889); 6 N.Y. Sup. 408 (1889); 24 N.E. 891 (1890).
Stanton v. *Allen,* 5 Denio 434 (1848).
State v. *Standard Oil Company,* 49 Ohio State 137 (1892).
United States, *Statutes at Large,* 1789–1920.
United States v. *Addyston Pipe & Steel Co.,* 1 F.A.D. 631 (1898); 175 U.S. 211 (1899).
United States v. *American Tobacco Co.,* 164 Fed. 700 (1908); 221 U.S. 106 (1911).
United States v. *E. C. Knight et al.,* 60 Fed. 306 (1894); 60 Fed. 934 (1894); 156 U.S. 1 (1895).
United States v. *E. I. Dupont de Nemours & Co.,* 188 Fed. 127 (1911).
United States v. *International Harvester Co.,* 214 Fed. 987 (1914); 274 U.S. 693 (1927).

United States v. *Jellico Mountain Coal Co.*, 43 Fed. 898 (1890); 46 Fed. 432 (1891).

United States v. *Kissel and Harned*, 218 U.S. 601 (1910).

United States v. *Nelson et al.*, 52 Fed. 646 (1892).

United States v. *New York Central Railroad.* Reprinted in Department of Justice File No. 59–8–13, sec. 1, National Archives, Washington, D.C.

United States v. *Standard Oil Co. of New Jersey*, 173 Fed. 177 (1909); 221 U.S. 1 (1911).

United States v. *Sugar Institute*, 15 Fed. Sup. 817 (1934); 297 U.S. 553 (1936).

United States v. *United States Steel Corp.*, 223 Fed. 55 (1915); 251 U.S. 417 (1920).

Wabash v. *Illinois*, 118 U.S. 557 (1886).

INDEX

Adams refinery: erected, 41; name changed and plant modernized, 73

Addyston Pipe & Steel case: role of in Corporate Revolution, 8–9, 17, 152; prohibits cartels, 187; Taft's role in, 299

Advertising: as barrier to entry of competitive firms, 19; pushed by American Sugar Refining Co., 327

American, the. *See* American Sugar Refining Company

American Beet Sugar Company: organized as merger of Oxnard enterprises, 244; conflict with American Sugar Refining Co., 244–46; saved by affluence of stockholders, 246; and working arrangement with the American, 246–47; ventures of in southern Colorado, 247–48; Havemeyer insists Robert Oxnard take over, 250; as price leader, 262; ends commission payments to the American, 272–73; the American sells interest in, 312

American Can case: and consent decree in sugar industry, 319; abandoned by Harding administration, 324

American Sugar Refinery (California): one of two West Coast firms, 89; and market-sharing arrangement with California Sugar Refining Co., 89–90; aided by Hawaiian growers, 90; joins trust, 92; charter annulled, 140–41, 153–54; and battle with Spreckels, 153–58; leased to Western Sugar Refining Co., 166

American Sugar Refining case: points up difficulty of applying Sherman Act, 291; criminal suit stymied, 302–3, 312; civil suit stymied, 303–4; bill of complaint prepared for, 304; delayed until other cases decided, 304–5, 316; pretrial testimony begun, 306–7; government's objectives in, 307–12; criminal prosecution of abandoned, 312; government testimony completed, 312–14; affects company behavior, 314–15; out-of-court settlement rejected, 316, 319; pretrial testimony ends, 316; and *International Harvester* precedent, 318; government resists consent decree in, 319; and *United States Steel* precedent, 324; ended, 324

American Sugar Refining Company: early profits of, 118; organized, 150; capital debt structure of, 151; as combination, unchanged from trust form, 151; purchases Philadelphia rivals, 152, 169–72; reaches understanding with Spreckels, 166; capital stock of, increased, 170; and advantages gained from Philadelphia acquisitions, 172; reaction to company's purchases, 174; and *E. C. Knight* case, 176–77, 179–80; accused of senatorial bribery, 180–84; faces problem of entry, 188–90; and working arrangement with wholesale grocers, 188, 191–95; obtains concessions from railroads, 196–206; agrees to act as "evener," 196–202; and railroad rebates 197–206; interest of in Mollenhauer refinery, 208–9; as price leader, 210–11, 329; extends special advantages to independents, 211; reasons for avoiding price wars, 211–12; seemingly solves problem of entry, 213; threatened by Arbuckle Brothers' packaging machine, 214–15; enters coffee business, 216; price war with Arbuckle Brothers begins, 216–22; aided by railroads, 220–21; begins selling sugar in cotton bags, 221; forced to tap reserves, 221; acquires major interest in National Sugar Refining Co. of N.J., 224–25; working arrangement with the National, 225; price war with Arbuckle Brothers ends, 226–27; retains dominant position in industry, 227–28; supplies capital funds to sugar beet firms, 229, 249; share of sugar market, 229, 259; acquires half-interest in Utah factories, 235–37; interest held in beet sugar enterprises, 240–43, 248; and American Beet Sugar Co., 245–47; marketing arrangement with Alameda Sugar Co., 247; fears overinvolvement in sugar beet industry, 248; stimulates efficiency in sugar beet industry, 250; and disposal of surplus raw sugar, 255–56; affiliates of agree to division-of-markets plan, 257–58; prosecuted for receiving illegal rebates, 264, 278–82; shows characteristics of megacorp, 265–66; as sixth-largest U.S. industrial corporation, 265–66; dividends after price war with Arbuckle Brothers, 268; and long-term contract with Hawaiian growers, 268–69; commission payments by American Beet Sugar Co. ended, 272–73; scraps factor plans, 276; experiments with other barriers to competition, 276; forces railroads to continue rebates, 277; settles rebate case, 281–82; purchases Camden refinery, 283; and Segel affair, 282–88; and difficulties with Baltimore refinery's minority stockholders, 286; seeks to prevent erection of refinery in New Orleans, 286; antitrust suits against, 291, 300–304, 307, 314–16, 324–25; co-operates in war effort, 291, 320–21; prosecuted for customs frauds, 291–94; refining costs of, 294–95n*10*; fined for customs frauds, 295; and settlement of private antitrust suit, 300–302; change in management of, 307–8; congressional investigation of, 308; effect of Havemeyer's death on, 307–10; builds new refinery at Chalmette, La., 310; threatened by Horace Havemeyer, 310–11; and control of the National of N.J., 311–12; Babst becomes president of, 320; accepts consent decree, 324–25; changes in organizational structure of, 325–28; finds it difficult to re-establish hegemony after war, 329–30; forced to surrender voice in other companies, 330

American Tobacco case: marks end of Corporate Revolution's first phase, 18; decision in, 20, 305–6; causes delay in *American Sugar Refining* case, 304–5; importance of, 305; Taft administration's handling of criticized, 313, 315

American Tobacco Company: one of six largest industrial corporations, 265–66; provides example for American Sugar Refining Co., 276; antitrust prosecution of, 20, 305–6

Anthracite coal industry: pioneers in consolidation techniques, 15

Antitrust laws: role of in Corporate Revolution, 8–9; difficulty of enforcing, 21, 176, 330, 334; introduced by New York legislature in 1888, 133–35; weighed by Congress, 142–44; effect of *E. C. Knight* case on, 186–87; effect of *Addyston Pipe & Steel* case on, 187; hamper Havemeyer's control, 264; *Northern Securities* case as precedent for, 298–305; first funds voted to enforce, 303; immunity granted under, 303; principle of compelling corporations to produce records established under, 304;

American Tobacco and *Standard Oil* cases set precedent for, 305–6; importance of *International Harvester* case to, 318; *United States Steel* case as precedent for, 324; fail to restore competitive conditions in sugar refining, 330. *See also* Sherman Act

Arbuckle, John: and conflict with American Sugar Refining Co., 214–17; agrees informally to end price war, 227

Arbuckle & Company, Pittsburgh wholesaler, 213. *See also* Arbuckle Brothers

Arbuckle Brothers: enters sugar refining, 188, 214–15; nation's largest coffee roaster, 213; and price war with American Sugar Refining Co., 216–22, 226–27; qualifies for railroad rebates, 277

Arnold Committee. *See* New York State legislature, investigation of trusts

Atkins, Edward F.: opposes sugar beet acquisitions, 268n22; second in command at American Sugar Refining Co., 307; points out change in the American's management, 308

B. H. Howell, Sons & Co., encourages building of new refineries, 209; ties of with American Sugar Refining Co., 209–10; adversely affected by price war, 222; joins Henry Havemeyer in Cuban ventures, 309–10; cancellation of its commission agreement threatened, 310–11

Babst, Earl D.: becomes president of American Sugar Refining Co., 320; represents U.S. on wartime International Sugar Committee, 320; pushes advertising strategy, 327; legal background of, 328

Bacon Committee. *See* U.S. Congress, investigation of trusts

Bain, Joe S.: on Corporate Revolution, 5–6

Baltimore Sugar Refining Company: taken over by American Sugar Refining Co., 172–73; minority stockholders give the American trouble, 286, 288

Barriers to entry: factor in evolution of market structure, 10; during Period of Imperfect Competition, 11; during Golden Age of Competition, 13, 44–45; during Corporate Revolution, 19; during colonial period, 29; created by Federal officials in whisky industry, 51; in sugar refining, 188–208; wholesale distribution outlets as, 193–95; railroad rebates as, 204, 206; economies of scale as, 207; absolute cost advantages as, 207–8; product differentiation as, 208; factor plans as, scrapped by American Sugar Refining Co., 276; experiments with retail outlets and advertising as, 276, 327; in agricultural implements, 317; in steel, 323

Bayard, Nicholas: erects first refinery in New York City, 26

Bay State Sugar Refining Company: joins trust, 74; shut down, 114

Belcher Sugar Refinery: purchased by trust, 82; high cost of operation of, 115; shut down, 115

Berle, Adolph A., 1

Big business: World War I leads to change in attitude toward, 320. *See also* Consolidation

Bliss, Colonel George: counsel to Arnold committee, 127

Bonaparte, Charles J.: rules out government prosecution of American Sugar Refining Co., 300–301

Booth, William T.: charges customs frauds, 52

Boston: first refineries in, 27; refineries in 1887, 73–74; refiners balk at trust agreement after Greenpoint refinery burns, 83; Knapp suggests that the American dispose of refinery in, 315

Boston Sugar Refining Company: joins trust, 74; turned into warehouse, 114

Brandeis, Louis D.: shapes Wilson antitrust policies, 313

Brooklyn Cooperage Company: subsidiary of American Sugar Refining Co., 206; obtains railroad rebates, 206–7

Brooklyn Eastern District Terminal: built, 197; source of conflict with Pennsylvania R. R., 201–2; receives "transfer" allowance from railroads, 277; important Havemeyer property, 309, 311

Brooklyn Sugar Refining Company, 65, 68, 71

Bunker, George: head of Delaware Sugar House, 170; sells out to American Sugar Refining Co., 170–71; organizes National Sugar Refining Co. in Yonkers, 190; on Doscher's effect on industry, 226

Burr, Edmund: urges working arrangement with American Sugar Refining Co., 247

California: sugar beet industry founded in, 230–32; largest beet factories in America located in, 243–44; sugar beet season in, 256; factories agree to division-of-markets plan, 257–58

California & Hawaiian Sugar Company: organized by Hawaiian growers, 270; has difficulty operating Crockett refinery, 270–71; agrees to market-sharing plan, 271–72

California Sugar Refining Company: owned by Claus Spreckels, 87; one of two surviving West Coast firms, 89; and price war with American Sugar Refinery, 90; leased to Western Sugar Refining Co., 166, 173

Capital: manufacturers' fear of expropriation of, 14, 101–2, 333; lack of mobility of in sugar refining in 1880's, 56–57, 67

Capital funds: supplied to sugar beet companies, 229, 249; Cutler search for, 234

Capital markets: role of in Corporate Revolution, 3, 97, 100; during Golden Age of Competition, 13; as affected by trust certificates, 16, 99–100; advantages of liquidity provided by, 91, 100; industrial-securities market created, 99. *See also* New York Stock Exchange

Capital requirements: as obstacle to consolidation, 3; during colonial period, 29. *See also* Barriers to entry

Carnegie, Andrew: refuses to join steel combination, 72; deprecates importance of trusts, 189

Centrifugal machine: invention of, 35; leads to charges of customs frauds, 53

Chandler, Alfred D., Jr.: on Corporate Revolution, 4–5; and concept of multi-departmental enterprise, 325

Civil War: effect of on sugar industry, 41–42

Cleveland, Grover: antitrust attitude of, 177–78; appoints Olney attorney general, 178

Coffee-roasting industry: Arbuckle Brothers pre-eminent in, 213; American Sugar Refining Co. enters in retaliation, 216; price war in, 216–17, 226

Colonial Sugars Company: Gramercy, La., refinery acquired by Cuban-American Sugar Co., 309–10

Colorado: beet sugar industry established in, 232; beet factories consolidated, 241; Havemeyer and American Sugar Refining Co. acquire interest in industry of, 241; factories agree to division-of-markets plan, 257–58

Community of interests: on West Coast in 1884, 89–90; in sugar in 1890's, 208–12; re-established, 226; threatened by Henry Havemeyer's death, 310

Competition, resurrection of: impossibility of, 16; considered in sugar refining, 147–48; Wilson administration seeks, 315; in sugar refining

falsely claimed by Justice Department, 329
–"ruinous": role of in Corporate Revolution, 6–7, 100–101; during Golden Age of Competition, 13–15; after 1873 in sugar refining, 56–57, 62–63, 69; cited in defense of sugar trust, 137; in coffee-roasting, 217; desire to avoid as motive in formation of International Harvester Co., 317; desire to avoid as cause of Corporate Revolution, 332. *See also* Market control, desire for; Excess supply relative to demand
–unfair: charges of in 1870's, 50, 59–60; English view on, 286; not evident in *International Harvester* case, 317; not evident in *United States Steel* case, 322–23
Competitive ethic: trust form strikes at, 125
Competitive model: approximated in immediate post–Civil War period, 43–46, 48; approaches perfection, 69; railroads help make possible, 93–94; leads to instability, 101, 333–34
Congress, U.S.: bribery of charged, 62, 180–84; and railroad legislation, 121; reaction of to trusts, 126, 130–31; investigates trusts, 126, 130; looks to states for solution to trust problem, 131; public pressure on, 142; considers Sherman Act, 142–44; reaction of to American Sugar Refining Co.'s Philadelphia acquisitions, 174; and antitrust funds, 176, 303; investigation of the American and U.S. Steel Corp., 303
Consolidation: initial plan for in sugar refining, 76; almost sabotaged, 83–84; arguments for, 90; due to desire for control over prices, 101–2, 332–33; economies from, 110–16; unchanged by trust's reorganization, 151; effect of independent refineries on, 159; of independent refineries, 223–24; of Utah beet factories, 239–41; changing court attitude toward, 291; power of courts to break up established, 306; in agricultural implements, 317; in steel, 322. *See also* Corporate Revolution; Price Control; Trust device
Continental Sugar Company: Havemeyer and American Sugar Refining Co. acquire interest in, 242, 309, 311; Havemeyer forces change in management of, 250
Continental Sugar Refining Company (Boston): joins trust, 74; connected to Standard Sugar Refining Co.'s plant, 114
Cordage trust: reportedly organized, 124; suffers financial ruin, 189
Corporate form: appearance of in sugar refining, 46
Corporate laws, changes in: role of in Corporate Revolution, 8; made by New Jersey, 16, 148–49; New York willing to make, 148
Corporate Revolution: suggested causes of, 1–10; third stage of industrial evolution, 17–23; causes of in sugar refining, 93; begins, 187; end of first phase of, 264; results of, 331; lessons of, 332–35. *See also* Consolidation
Costs. *See* Sugar beets, cost of processing; Sugar refining costs
Cottonseed oil trust: and industrial-securities market, 99; existence revealed, 123; linked to Standard Oil Co., 123–24; legal attack on, 141; reorganizes as holding company, 149–50
Court of Appeals, U. S., for the Second Circuit: overturns *E. C. Knight* precedent, 301–2
–for the Sixth Circuit: decision of in *Addyston Pipe & Steel* case, 299
–for the Third Circuit: decision of in *E. C. Knight* case, 180
Cuban-American Sugar Company: Havemeyer's ties to, 309, 311; acquires Colonial Sugars Co. refinery, 310

Cuban cane sugar: takes up Louisiana slack, 39; faces monopsony, 108; marketing season for, 255
Customs frauds: charges of in 1870's, 50, 54; investigation of, 52, 294nn9, *10*; difficulty of preventing, 61; evidence of discovered at Havemeyer & Elder, 290–93; extent of in sugar refining, 294; Earle reports suspicions of, 300
Cutler, Thomas R.: ties of to American Sugar Refining Co., 234–35; develops Utah beet industry, 234–39; organizes consolidation of Utah and Idaho beet factories, 239–40
Cutting family: joins Oxnard in sugar beet venture, 230; becomes stockholder in American Beet Sugar Co., 244; Bayard seeks accommodation with Havemeyer, 246

DeCastro & Donner: part of Havemeyer holdings, 71; placed in reserve, 114
Delaware Sugar House: sells out to American Sugar Refining Co., 170–71; combined with Spreckels refinery, 179
Department of Justice, U.S.: separate antitrust division established in, 303; officials await *Standard Oil* and *American Tobacco* decisions, 304–5; officials oppose out-of-court settlement, 314–15; claims competition restored, 329
Depression of 1893: onset marked by collapse of National Cordage Co., 16–17; demonstrates strength of consolidations, 17; economy's emergence from helps launch first phase of Corporate Revolution, 187
Dewey, Donald: on causes of Corporate Revolution, 8–9
Dick, William: role of in 1886 output-limitation scheme, 67; trustee of Sugar Refineries Co., 78; holds interest in Mollenhauer refinery, 208
Dick & Meyer Refinery: agrees to join trust, 75; burns down, 114
Dill, James: role of in revision of New Jersey corporate statutes, 148–49
Dissolution suits: against American Sugar Refining Co., 291; against American Tobacco and Standard Oil companies, 305–6; James Knapp's proposals with regard to, 315; against International Harvester Co., 317
Distribution network; role of in Corporate Revolution, 4–5; as barrier to entry, 18, 188, 195; American Sugar Refining Co. adopts rebate system initially to protect, 192; cost of maintaining in sugar industry, 193; poses problem for Arbuckle Brothers, 219–20. *See also* Wholesale grocers
Dividends: under sugar trust, 118; paid by American Sugar Refining Co., 118, 213, 221, 268n*21*; the American forced to pass, 329
Doscher, Claus: on reasons for joining trust, 71; re-enters sugar refining business, 218–19; influence of eliminated from industry, 226
Dos Passos, John R.: role of in devising trust agreement, 76–78; as outside promoter, 98; approaches Adolph Segel about selling out, 283
Drawback allowances: as competitive ameliorative, 57; bring British protest, 58; reduced, 66–67
Dutch Standard: for determining sugar purity, 52; demands for elimination of, 54, 62

E. C. Knight & Co.: initially agrees to join trust, 75; decides to stay out, 80; profits after trust formed, 161; hurt by competition with Spreckels, 163; sold to American Sugar Refining Co., 170–71; refinery combined with Franklin plant, 179
E. C. Knight case: gives legal sanction to holding company, 17, 152; government's complaint in, 176–77; Harrison administration's handling of, 176–77; temporarily suspended, 177; intervening developments,

179; revived under Cleveland, 179; decision in announced by lower courts, 179–80; appealed to U.S. Supreme Court, 180; Supreme Court decision in, 184–86; as part of larger judicial pattern, 185; forces American Sugar Refining Co. to tolerate rivals, 211; discourages subsequent prosecution of the American, 300–301, 315; precedent of overturned in Earle suit, 301–2

Earle, George H., Jr.: appointed receiver of Segel enterprises, 289; sues American Sugar Refining Co. under Sherman Act, 289; wins civil suit against the American, 298, 301–2; fails to persuade Roosevelt administration to prosecute the American, 300; asks government to end suit against the American, 321

East Boston refinery: adopts use of steam in sugar refining, 34

East Coast refineries: benefit from relative decline in Louisiana output, 39; Civil War's effect on, 41–42; number of in post–Civil War period, 43; enter into pooling arrangement, 63–64; and 1886 output-limitation agreement, 67; marketing area of delineated, 251; sources of raw sugar, 255

Eastwick, Edward P.: argues for uniform tariff, 61; spokesman for William Havemeyer's interests, 61

Economies of scale: role of in Corporate Revolution, 2–6, 102; analyzed, 102–3; role of in sugar consolidation, 103–4, 119; trust's nature precludes, 107; as barrier to entry into sugar refining industry, 207; resulting from consolidation of Utah beet factories, 239

Efficiency: stimulated in sugar beet industry, 249–50

Elkins Act: passage secured by Theodore Roosevelt, 274; forces railroads to cancel rebates, 277; prosecution of American Sugar Refining Co. under, 278–82; convictions under obtained, 279, 281–82; unsettled issues under cleared up, 279, 282

Entrepreneurship: in building first steam-powered refinery, 32–33; in erecting first waterfront plant, 40, 61; displayed by Havemeyer, 229; American Sugar Refining Co.'s contribution to diminished, 330

Entry into industry: ease of in immediate post–Civil War period, 44; as factor limiting monopoly, 97; argument that monopoly precludes, 137, 179–80; American Sugar Refining Co. grapples with problem of, 188–90; success of in sugar refining, 188, 208–9, 212, 214–19, 228, 253–54, 273, 310, 328; undermines cordage combination, 189; relation of to sugar margins, 212–13; discouraged by price war, 227; threatened, 273, 282–83, 288; Havemeyer's efforts to discourage, 285–86

Era of the Conglomerate: described, 23

Erie Railroad: grants secret rebates to American Sugar Refining Co., 197

Excess supply relative to demand: during Golden Age of Competition, 50; gives rise to whiskey ring, 51; in 1870's and 1880's, 62–63; as factor in sugar consolidation, 70–71, 117; and dumping in Missouri River area, 244–45, 253; seasonal nature of, 255. *See also* Competition, "ruinous"

Export of refined sugar: temporarily stimulated by drawbacks, 57–58; importance of to industry, 66–67; increases during World War I, 327–28

Firms, marginal: effect of on industry price, 63

Forest City Sugar Refining Company: purchased by trust, 82; shut down, 115

Franklin Sugar Refining Company: merged with American Sugar Refining Co., 161, 171; agrees to rebates for wholesale grocers, 192; and relationship with McCahan Sugar Refining Co., 210. *See also* Harrison, Frazier & Co.
Fuller, Melville W.: and decision in *E. C. Knight* case, 184

Gary, Elbert H.: sets policies with public opinion in mind, 323
Gilded Age of Politics: affected by competitive struggle of business, 15
Golden Age of Competition: described, 12–17; first phase of in sugar refining, 34–49; second phase of in sugar refining, 50–70; impossibility of re-creating, 334
Grant, Ulysses S.: administration tarnished by whiskey-ring scandal, 51
Great Merger movement. *See* Corporate Revolution
Great Western Sugar Refining Company (New Jersey): formed, 241; Havemeyer and American Sugar Refining Co. interest in, 241, 309, 311; as price leader, 262; the American sells interest in, 312
Gulick, Charles A., Jr. *See* Seager, Henry R.
Gunton, George: argues merits of consolidation, 145

Handicraft techniques: prevalence of during Period of Imperfect Competition, 11
Harding, Warren G.: antitrust policies of, 324; administration agrees to consent decree in *American Sugar Refining* case, 324
Hardwick committee: investigates American Sugar Refining Co., 308
Harlan, John M.: writes dissent in *E. C. Knight* case, 185–86
Harrison, Benjamin: signs Sherman Act, 144, 175; antitrust policies of administration criticized, 175–76; handling of *E. C. Knight* case, 176–77
Harrison, Charles: initially refuses to join trust, 73–75; sells out to American Sugar Refining Co., 169–71
Harrison, Frazier & Co.: largest refinery in Philadelphia, 73; refuses to join trust, 80; profits after trust formed, 161; hurt by competition with Spreckels, 163; name changed to Franklin Sugar Refining Co., 169; agrees to merge with American Sugar Refining Co., 169, 171; plant combined with E. C. Knight refinery, 179
Havemeyer, Hector: partner of brother William, 61; trustee of Sugar Refineries Co., 78; member of appraisal committee for Sugar Refineries Co., 79; forced to rebuild refinery, 83
Havemeyer, Henry O.: started in business, 40; role of in 1880 pooling arrangement, 63; on industry profits in 1880's, 66; on importance of exports, 67; attitude toward joining trust, 71–73, 75; hostility toward, 74; reports consolidation set, 75–76; trustee of Sugar Refineries Co., 78; and appraisal of properties, 79; first to sign trust agreement, 84; boasts of power over Cuban growers, 108; on tariffs and trusts, 95–96; on limitations to raising sugar prices, 97; on economies from consolidation, 104; on independence of trust members, 106; cites steadier work provided by trust, 109; on savings from stabilization, 117; relates profits to economies, 118; rejects competition as norm, 125; testimony of before Arnold committee, 126–28; points out advantages of New Jersey corporate laws, 150; president of American Sugar Refining Co., 151; sends Oxnard to West Coast, 153; thwarts Matthiessen take-over bid, 164; reaches accommodation with Spreckels, 166; involved in 1894 bribery charges, 182–84; on *E. C. Knight* case, 186;

promotes merger to form National Sugar Refining Co. of N.J., 188, 223–24, 228; uses wholesale grocers as entry barrier, 193–95; obtains concessions from railroads, 196–206; personal interest of in rebate arrangements, 201–2; extends special advantages to independent refineries, 211; reasons for avoiding price wars, 211–12; exercises price control, 212, 250–63; practices stay-out pricing, 212–13; and Arbuckle challenge, 214–17, 219–21; anger of over Doscher entry, 218–19; receives common stock of the National of N.J., 223–24; and control over the National, 225; eliminates Doscher influence, 226; reaches informal understanding with John Arbuckle, 227; fails in policy of stay-out pricing, 228; supplies funds to sugar beet companies, 229, 249; overcomes sugar beet challenge, 229–50; interest in sugar beet factories, 241–43, 248, 309; and American Beet Sugar Co., 245–47; supervises sales for beet companies, 246–47; forces change in beet factory management, 250; insensitivity of to change, 264; hampered by fear of antitrust laws, 264, 271; among the last of his generation active in the American, 264–65; interest in the National of N.J. criticized by Lowell Palmer, 265; holds few shares in the American, 266–67; personal methods of in directing the American, 267–68; negotiates settlement of conflict in West, 270–71; protests end of commission payments, 272; and loan to Adolph Segel, 284–88; efforts of to discourage new entry, 285–86; discounts significance of rebate and Earle suits, 289–90; dies, 290; held responsible for customs frauds, 293, 294n*10*; not succeeded by son, 307; death of diminishes the American's influence over industry, 308–10; ties of to Cuban-American company, 309–10

Havemeyer, Horace: slated to succeed father in business, 267; fails to take over after father's death, 307; seeks to establish rival interest to American Sugar Refining Co., 310–11; foiled in attempt to take over National Sugar Refining Co. of N.J., 311

Havemeyer, Theodore A.: started in business, 40; on investment needed to work lower-grade sugars, 56; on drawback allowances, 57; as leader of major refiners, 60–61; argues against uniform tariff, 62; attitude of toward joining trust, 71–73, 75; partner in Harrison, Frazier & Co., 73; trustee of Sugar Refineries Co., 78; dies, 264

Havemeyer, William: leads smaller refiners, 61; role of in 1880 pooling arrangement, 63; on reasons for winter losses, 66; role of in 1886 output-limitation scheme, 67–68; asks Searles to work for consolidation, 69; on Searles' efforts in organizing trust, 72; on reason for including all firms in trust, 72, 75; on how refining properties were valued, 80; on Revere Sugar Refining Co.'s decision to stay out of trust, 80; forced to rebuild refinery, 83

Havemeyer & Elder: origin of, 40; capacity of in immediate post–Civil War period, 44; joins 1881 price-fixing scheme, 64–65; destroyed by fire and rebuilt, 65; as low-cost producer, 65–66, 71; impact of on industry prices, 66; represented on board of trustees of Sugar Refineries Co., 78; expanded, 114–15; takes title to West Coast plant, 154–55; customs frauds discovered at, 290–93; becomes high-cost refinery, 294n*10*

Havemeyer family: arrives in United States, 28, 31; first generation of enters business for itself, 31; second generation of retires, 33; Frederick C. re-enters sugar refining, 39–40; builds first waterfront refinery, 40; provides leaders of opposing industry factions, 60–61; regrets sale of trust certificates, 266–67; influence in American Sugar Refining Co. dwindles, 307

Havemeyer Sugar Refining Company: Hector Havemeyer's properties consolidated into, 61; Greenpoint refinery of burns down, 83; rebuilt, 114; plants of connected with others, 114

Hawaiian sugar growers: Spreckels' dominance over, 88–89; join forces with Spreckels' rival, 90; crop of committed to Spreckels, 154; trust outbids Spreckels for crop of, 155; buy rival refinery, 253; marketing season of, 255; enter into long-term contract with American Sugar Refining Co., 268–69; begin producing "washed" sugars, 269; seek to put pressure on Spreckels, 269–70; organize Sugar Factors Association, 270; reopen Crockett refinery, 270

Hayes, Rutherford B.: attempts to refurbish party image, 51–52

Hearst, William Randolph: as political threat to Theodore Roosevelt, 275–76; his *New York American* obtains evidence of secret rebating, 276; trumpets role in rebate cases, 278; capitalizes on publicity of rebate convictions, 280

Heike, Charles R.: on Havemeyer's dominant role in American Sugar Refining Co., 265; convicted in customs fraud case, 296n*15*; called to testify in civil suit against the American, 303

Higginson, Henry Lee: intervenes with President Taft on behalf of American Sugar Refining Co., 307–8

Holding company: first developed, 15; solves problem of competition from within, 18; New Jersey sanction of, 16, 149; passes antitrust scrutiny, 17, 152, 187; cottonseed oil and lead trusts reorganize under, 149–50; advantages of, 150; susceptibility of to legal attack, 152; sugar trust reorganizes as, 158

Holt, George C.: castigates New York Central R. R., 279; refuses to sustain conspiracy indictment against American Sugar Refining Co. and railroads, 279, 303

Idaho. *See* Utah; Utah-Idaho Sugar Company

Ingham, Ellery P.: prosecutes *E. C. Knight* case, 176–77; reopens case, 179; handling of case assayed, 185

International Harvester case: delayed by World War I, 21; causes delay in *American Sugar Refining* case, 316; history of, 317–19; importance of, 318

International Harvester Company: one of six largest U.S. industrial corporations, 265–66; formation of, 317; antitrust suit against, 317–19

Interstate Commerce Act: strengthening of, 18; reasons for passage of, 122n*4*; violation of conceded, 202–3. *See also* Elkins Act

Inventories: regulation of and costs, 112–13

Jackson, Howell B.: jurist in whiskey-trust prosecutions, 179; cited in *E. C. Knight* decision, 180

Jarvie, James N.: on Arbuckle Brothers' frustration, 214; visited by Lowell Palmer, 215

Jay, John: heads customs-house investigation, 52

Justice Department. *See* Department of Justice, U.S.

Kidder, Peabody & Company: role of in sugar trust's reorganization, 151

Knapp, James: as Henry Wise's assistant, 303; gathers evidence against American Sugar Refining Co. in West, 303; outlines basis for out-of-court settlement, 314–15

Knickerbocker Sugar Refining Company: refinery built, 273; acquired by Adolph Segel, 288
Knight, E. C.: agrees to sell out to American Sugar Refining Co., 170–71

Labor relations: trust and, 108–9
Lead trust: and industrial-securities market, 99; reportedly organized, 124; reorganizes as holding company, 150
Legal environment: pools difficult to sustain in, 64; and trust device's legal status, 141; as affected by *E. C. Knight* and *Addyston Pipe* cases, 152, 186–87; change in brings end to Great Merger movement, 264; with regard to "unfair" competition, 286; reflects changing attitude toward consolidation, 291, 298; effect of *Northern Securities* case on, 298, 305; reflects changing presidential attitudes, 298–99; effect of *American Tobacco* and *Standard Oil* cases on, 305–6; effect of *United States Steel* case on, 324
Livingston family: early involvement of in sugar refining, 29; retirement of from sugar refining, 30–31
Lloyd, Henry D.: and *Atlantic Monthly* article on Standard Oil Co. monopoly, 122
Louisiana cane: loses markets to East Coast refineries, 37–38; reaches production limits, 38–39; effect of Civil War on, 41–42; impact of on prices of refined sugar, 47, 66; harvesting season of, 254–55
Louisiana Sugar Refining Company: history of, 81; forms pool, 81; joins trust, 82; connected with Planters refinery, 115, 254

Management: early separation of from ownership in American Sugar Refining Co., 266; change in the American's after Havemeyer's death, 307–8; structure of the American's in 1922, 325–28
Management techniques: as factor in Era of the Conglomerate, 24; of sugar trust, 105–6; introduced on West Coast, 153; in sugar beet industry, 249–50
Market, share of: independent refineries' in immediate post–Civil War period, 44; sugar trust's at its formation, 84; trust's during winter months, 160; trust's if Spreckels' competition not met, 161; American Sugar Refining Co.'s after Philadelphia acquisitions, 172–73; the American's reduced by entry of new firms, 190; beet sugar's, 232, 248–49; the American's if out-of-court settlement in trust suit agreed to, 314, 319; U.S. Steel's declines, 323; the American's after 1907, 328
—sugar: broadened during 1850's, 36–38; as factor limiting monopoly, 97; growth of in West, 328
Market areas, sugar: increased by railroads, 36–38; as affected by railroads, 93–94; for Utah beet factories, 237–38; Missouri River points as dumping ground for surplus sugar, 244–45; of refining centers delineated, 251; agreed to under division-of-markets plan, 257–58
Market control, desire for: role of in Corporate Revolution, 7, 101; as motive in sugar consolidation, 84, 90, 119. *See also* Competition, "ruinous"; Price control
Marketing arrangements: between American Beet Sugar Co. and American Sugar Refining Co., 246–47; division-of-markets plan, 257–58
Markham, Jesse: on Corporate Revolution, 5
Marshall, F. Snowden: replaces Henry Wise as U.S. attorney for Southern District of New York, 313
Matthiessen, F. O.: trustee of Sugar Refineries Co., 78; seeks to end

price war between trust and Spreckels, 163–64; thwarted in effort to gain control of American Sugar Refining Co., 164; approaches John Arbuckle about packaging-machine patent, 214–15; departure of from the American, 265; dies, 265
Matthiessen & Wiechers: second-largest sugar refinery in U.S., 73; agrees to join trust, 75; expanded, 114–15
McCahan, William J.: converts molasses house into sugar refinery, 189–90; on his relations with Franklin Sugar Refining Co., 210; at meetings to assure uniform sugar prices, 211
McCahan Sugar Refining Company: organized, 190; co-operation of with Franklin Sugar Refining Co., 210; role of high margins in firm's entry, 213; quarter-interest in purchased by National Sugar Refining Co. of N.J., 224
Means, Garginer C., 1
Megacorp: representative oligopolistic firm, 2; emerges from Corporate Revolution, 18, 22–24, 331; operational costs of, 116; American Sugar Refining Co. as in 1907, 265–66; reason for emergence of, 332
Mertonian innovation, 125n*15*
Metropolitan Sugar Refining Company, 288
Michigan: beet sugar industry established in, 232; consolidation of beet factories in, 241; Havemeyer and American Sugar Refining Co. become involved with beet factories of, 241
Michigan Sugar Company: formed as consolidation of Michigan beet factories, 241; as area price leader, 262; American Sugar Refining Co. sells interest in, 312
Miller, William H.: criticized for policy of "cautious" antitrust enforcement, 174–76; on difficulty of enforcing antitrust law, 176; forced to prosecute American Sugar Refining Co., 176; his handling of *E. C. Knight* case, 176–77
Missouri River markets: disposal of West Coast sugar in, 90–91; dumping of surplus sugar in, 244–45, 253; dumping of surplus sugar creates need for co-ordination among, 254; plan for selling in, 257–58; prices in co-ordinated through brokers, 272
Modern corporation: emerges from Corporate Revolution, 1, 3, 18. *See also* Megacorp
Mogul Steamship case, 286 and n97
Mollenhauer family: converts molasses house into refinery, 190; ties of to American Sugar Refining Co., 208–9; effect of Havemeyer-Arbuckle price war on refinery of, 222; replaces Doscher family in management of New York Sugar Refining Co., 226
Moller, George: on willingness to join trust, 70–71; on North River stockholders' unhappiness, 85; signs trust deed despite opposition, 86; testifies before Arnold committee, 128
Moller, Joe: on profits in sugar refining, 67
Moller, William: inventions of, 35; partner of Frederick C. Havemeyer, 40
Monopoly: result of Corporate Revolution, 18; and competitive tail, 19; transformed into oligopoly, 22, 188; goal of sugar trust, 91; economies of, 107–9, 116–17; role of assurances of in formation of trust, 117; benefits from, 118; public hostility toward, 120–22, 134; railroads viewed as, 120; Standard Oil Co. as new form of, 122; sugar trust described as, 137; trust's power of diminished by Spreckels, 162; of sugar refining industry achieved by American Sugar Refining Co., 173; *E. C. Knight* decision viewed as denying that exists in sugar in-

dustry, 186; transformed into oligopoly in sugar refining, 188; no longer insisted upon, 228; on West Coast enjoyed by Western Sugar Refining Co., 251, 253

Moody, William H.: explains to Henry Stimson importance of office of U.S. attorney for Southern District of New York, 275; cites usefulness of unfavorable publicity as weapon against corporate abuses, 278–79, 282; agrees to out-of-court settlement in rebate cases, 282; appointed to U.S. Supreme Court, 300

Morey, Chester A.: heads Havemeyer–American Sugar Refining Co. interests in Colorado, 241

Morgan, J. P.: role of in Corporate Revolution, 3, 17–18, 97, 266; selects Elbert Gary to head U.S. Steel Corp., 323

Mormon Church: involvement of in Utah beet industry, 234, 239; begins buying out American Sugar Refining Co.'s interest in Utah and Idaho companies, 316

National Cordage Company: financial collapse of, 16, 189; insolvancy of depresses industrial stocks, 187

National Sugar Refining Company (N.Y.): established, 190; ties of to American Sugar Refining Co., 209; role of high margins in firm's entry, 213; effect of Havemeyer-Arbuckle price war on, 222

National Sugar Refining Company of New Jersey: organized through consolidation of Mollenhauer, National (N.Y.), and New York refineries, 223–24; purchases quarter-interest in McCahan refinery, 224; working relationship of with American Sugar Refining Co., 224–26; Horace Havemeyer seeks to take over, 310; preferred shareholders in block take-over bid, 311; the American emerges as principal owner of, 311–12; attempts to buy the American's holdings of its stock, 316; becomes the American's chief rival, 330

Nelson, Ralph: on causes of Corporate Revolution, 4–9

New Orleans: refineries join trust, 81–82; refineries' marketing area, 251; refineries affected by dumping, 254; refinery outside of, at Gramercy, 310; new American Sugar Refining Co. plant near, at Chalmette, 310

New York Central Railroad: grants secret rebates to American Sugar Refining Co., 197, 220; defendant in rebate cases, 278–82; found guilty and fined, 279

New York City: first sugar refinery in, 26; sudden increase in number of refineries in, 34; pre-eminence of among East Coast refining centers, 42; advantages of as refining center, 43; refineries attempt to limit output, 64–65; refineries agree to join trust, 81; extent of customs frauds among refineries in, 294; newspapers fail to publicize sugar fraud convictions, 297; newspapers pick up *Outlook* article, 297

New York State legislature: investigation of trusts, 126–30; antitrust legislation of, 133–35

New York Stock Exchange: growth of in 1880's and 1890's, 3; as affected by trust certificates, 16, 99–100. *See also* Capital markets

New York Sugar Refining Company: enters industry, 219; effect of Havemeyer-Arbuckle price war on, 222; becomes part of National Sugar Refining Co. of N.J., 223–24

New York Times: reaction of to trusts, 123–24; criticizes sugar trust's secretiveness, 128–29; seeks state action against trusts, 132, 135; criticizes American Sugar Refining Co.'s Philadelphia acquisitions, 174; complains about handling of *E. C. Knight* case, 176

New York Tribune: reports customs frauds, 50, 52; reaction of to sugar trust's formation, 126

North, Douglass C.: on role of demand in early American economic growth, 11n*36*

Northern Securities case: effect of on antitrust law, 20, 298

North River Sugar Refining case: renders trust form illegal, 16, 120; argued before courts, 136–40; decisions in, 139–40, 145–46

North River Sugar Refining Company: agrees to join trust, 75; forced to suspend operations, 75; stockholders imperil consolidation scheme, 84–87; plant shut down, 114; as focal point of state action against trusts, 135–40; charter annulled, 139–40

Number of competing firms: as factor in evolution of industry structure, 10; during Period of Imperfect Competition, 11; in mid-nineteenth century, 34; in immediate post–Civil War period, 43; reduced by low margins after 1873, 56; in 1887, 83; increased by coming of railroad, 95; advantages of increasing, 334

Oligopoly: emerges from Corporate Revolution, 22; price competition under temporary, 162; emerges in sugar refining, 188, 228; gives way to classical duopoly behavior during Havemeyer-Arbuckle price war, 227; acceptance of, 291; given judicial approval in *United States Steel* case, 324; acquiesced to in sugar refining, 329–31

Olney, Richard: views of on antitrust law, 178; role of in whiskey-trust suit, 178; presses *E. C. Knight* case, 179; appeals lower court decision in *Knight* case, 180

Osborn, William F.: acts to enlist support of wholesale grocers, 194; works with Thomas Riley, 205; at meetings to assure uniform sugar prices, 211

Output limitations. *See* Price-fixing

Overhead costs: as factor leading to "excessive" competition, 13, 101; impact of on competition in sugar refining, 50; economies in, 102–4; responsible for railroad abuses, 121; as factor causing breakdown of competition, 333

Oxnard, Henry T.: successfully grows sugar beets, 230; builds new factory in California, 244; sugar beet enterprises merged to form American Beet Sugar Co., 244; on nature of working arrangement with American Sugar Refining Co., 246; contacts California beet companies concerning the American's offer to act as supervising selling agent, 247

Oxnard, Robert: trust representative on West Coast, 153; on working with Spreckels, 167; takes over American Beet Sugar Co.'s management, 250

Oxnard Brothers: agrees to join trust, 75; forced to suspend operations, 75; shut down, 114

Palmer, Lowell M.: role of in promoting trust, 74; and association with Havemeyers, 197; handles railroad affairs, 197–206; and cooperage business, 206–7; supplies American Sugar Refining Co. with other inputs, 207; as emissary to Arbuckle Brothers, 215; refers Wallace Willett to Henry Havemeyer, 233; forced out of the American, 265; member of committee to supervise sugar beet activities, 267

Palmer's Dock: source of conflict with Pennsylvania Railroad, 201–2. *See also* Brooklyn Eastern District Terminal

Panic of 1873: ends first phase of Golden Age of Competition, 13–14; depression leads to decline in sugar margins, 56

Parsons, John E.: role of in drawing up sugar trust deed, 77–78; on control over trust members, 106; refuses to hand over trust deed, 127–28; and arguments in *North River* case, 136–37, 145; approaches Charles Harrison of Franklin Sugar Refining Co. on subject of selling out, 169–71; and formation of National Sugar Refining Co. of N.J., 224; still associated with Henry Havemeyer in 1907, 265; cites *Mogul Steamship* case, 286; explains American Sugar Refining Co.'s refusal to let Pennsylvania refinery operate, 287; indicated under Sherman Act, 302; prosecution of dropped, 312–13

Pennsylvania Railroad: and conflict with American Sugar Refining Co., 201–2

Pennsylvania Sugar Refining Company: organized to build refinery in Philadelphia, 283; forced to close down refinery as condition of loan, 284

Period of Imperfect Competition: nature of, 11–12; in sugar refining, 26–34

Petroleum industry: pioneer in consolidation techniques, 70; contrasted with sugar refining, 77. *See also* Standard Oil Company

Philadelphia: first refineries in, 27; sugar prices in during colonial period, 28–29; increase in number of refineries in during 1850's, 34; largest refinery in, in 1887, 73; competition of refineries of against trust, 153, 159; Spreckels locates new refinery in, 156–57

Philadelphia Press: charges bribery by sugar officials, 180; reports on Treasury secretary's role in tariff controversy, 183

Planters Sugar Refining Company: forms pool, 81; history of, 81; joins trust, 82; connected with Louisiana refinery, 115, 254

Political influence: of American Sugar Refining Co., 182–84, 294n8; brought to bear on Henry Stimson, 281

Pooling arrangements: among East Coast refiners, 50; between New Orleans firms, 81; among sugar beet companies, 258. *See also* Price-fixing

Post, James: encourages formation of new firms, 209; partner in B. H. Howell, Sons & Co., 209; co-operates with American Sugar Refining Co., 209–10; on difficulty of eliminating independent refineries, 212; on losses as result of price war, 222; promotes merger of independent refineries, 222–23; brings McCahan refinery into consolidation, 224; co-ordinates pricing with Henry Havemeyer, 225; persuades Havemeyer to invest in Cuban properties, 309

Price control: how exercised by trust, 105; economies of, 110; with independent refineries, 159; exercised by Havemeyer and American Sugar Refining Co., 212, 225, 229, 250–63; re-established in sugar refining, 227; marketing arrangements as means of establishing, 246–47; threatened by Henry Havemeyer's death, 308–11; by government during World War I, 321, 328; by U.S. Steel, 323; American Sugar Refining Co.'s weakened but maintained, 328–30; desire for as fundamental cause of Corporate Revolution, 332–33; advantages of, 334. *See also* Market control, desire for; Price-fixing

Price-fixing: during Golden Age of Competition, 14; in sugar refining, 50, 59, 63–65, 67–68, 89–90; made difficult by common law, 64; by sugar trust, 105, 159; market-sharing plan agreed to in West, 271–72. *See also* Pooling arrangements

Price leadership: exercised by American Suger Refining Co., 210, 212,

227, 329; practiced by Henry Havemeyer, 261; by various beet sugar companies, 262; exercised by Elbert Gary in steel industry, 323; disadvantage of for the American, 328

Price maintenance: meetings to assure, 210–11; achieved in sugar refining, 262–63; weakened, 328–29

Prices, paid for refineries by sugar trust, 82, 85, 92

Prices, sugar: in colonial period, 28–29; in first decades of nineteenth century, 30; fall during 1840's, 36; importance of margins in, 47–48; in post–Civil War period, 48–49; after Panic of 1873, 56; in 1880, 63; as result of 1882 fire, 65; in 1886, 67–68; those in West geared to those in New York, 89; upper limit on set by tariff, 96; limits on, 97; after trust formed, 118–19, 159; with Spreckels competing in East, 161–63; in 1890's, 212–13; encourage new entry, 213; after entry of Arbuckle Brothers, 218, 221; after Havemeyer-Arbuckle price war ended, 227–28; after World War I, 329

Price war: on West Coast in 1886, 90; between Spreckels and trust, 152–55, 157, 162–65; avoided in East before 1890, 159–60; ended in East, 165; between Arbuckle and American Sugar Refining Co., 188, 218–22, 226–27; in coffee-roasting industry, 216–17; predicted but fails to occur in West, 270–71

Pricing policies: of trust, 159–60; Spreckels entry forces change in, 161; of independent refineries in 1890's, 210–11; stay-out pricing practiced by Henry Havemeyer, 212; by Arbuckle Brothers in coffee, 217; fail to deter entry, 228; American Sugar Refining Co.'s posting of prices, 261

Private warehouses, system of: Havemeyers take advantage of, 40; abolition of called for, 55, 61–62

Product differentiation: as factor in evolution of industry structure, 10; during Period of Imperfect Competition, 11; during Golden Age of Competition, 12, 46; in first decades of nineteenth century, 30; brand name sugars, 35–36; as barrier to entry in sugar refining, 208; pressed by American Sugar Refining Co., 327

Production regularity: desire for as cause of Corporate Revolution, 6; and employment, 109

Profits, excessive: difficulty of determining, 7, 118; in sugar refining, 119

—sugar refining: in colonial period, 29; Civil War's effect on, 41; squandered, 56; in 1880's, 65–68; after trust formed, 118; price war in 1890 puts end to, 162; of American Sugar Refining Co. in 1890's, 213; as result of Havemeyer-Arbuckle price war, 221–22

Progressive movement: as factor in Corporate Revolution, 19; effect of World War I on, 21; misguided emphasis of on antitrust approach, 330; fatal shortcomings of "trust-busting" program of, 334

Promoters: role of in Corporate Revolution, 3; role of in sugar consolidation, 97–99

Pryor, Roger: attacks sugar trust, 132–33, 135; seeks legal precedent against trusts, 136; arguments of in *North River* case, 136–39; on *North River* case's implications, 141, 146; seeks to re-create competition in sugar, 147; forced to accept reorganized trust, 151

Public opinion: and trusts, 120, 123–26; aroused by Arnold committee testimony, 128; forces Congress to act, 142; and Philadelphia acquisitions, 174; and bribery charges, 184; American Sugar Refining Co. avoids criticism in consolidation of independent refineries, 226; Henry Havemeyer ignores, 267; as factor in rebate prosecution strategy, 278–79; as weapon against the American, 293; Henry Stimson disappointed over failure to arouse in customs-fraud cases, 297; *Outlook* article stirs, 297; puts pressure on Taft administration to prosecute the American, 298; change in toward big business as result of war, 320; guides U.S. Steel policies, 323

Railroads: role of in Corporate Revolution, 5–6, 93; alter interregional commodity flows, 37–38; strengthen competitive nature of sugar refining, 93–94; target of antimonopolist attack, 121–22; and American Sugar Refining Co., 188; importance of sugar traffic to, 195; competition among, 195–96; the American acts as "evener" for, 196–202; and rebate arrangements with the American, 197–203; concerned over violation of law, 203; sugar marketing areas defined by freight rates of, 251; marketing plan influenced by freight rates of, 257; attempt to conceal rebates, 277; defendants in rebate cases, 278–82; taught a painful lesson, 282

Real Estate Trust Company: Adolph Segel brings ruin to, 288–89

Rebates, railroad: in petroleum industry, 15, 18; Theodore Roosevelt's attitude toward, 20; in sugar refining, 188, 195–206; received by Brooklyn Cooperage Company, 206–7; factor in Arbuckle–American Sugar Refining Co. conflict, 220–21; the American found guilty of receiving, 264; prohibition of helps end Great Merger movement, 264; outlawed by Elkins Act, 274; remain as most important barriers in sugar refining, 276; railroads attempt to conceal, 277; lead to prosecution, 278–82; end of seen as solution to trust problem, 280

Refineries, cost of: in 1850's, 34; in immediate post–Civil War period, 44; on West Coast in 1884, 89; Spreckels' Philadelphia plant, 157; by 1892, 207

–independent: and railroad rebates, 205–6; difficulty of eliminating, 211; accept American Sugar Refining Co.'s price leadership, 212, 262–63; merged, 222–26

–size of: in immediate post–Civil War period, 44; rebuilt Havemeyer & Elder plant, 65; Spreckels' Philadelphia plant, 157; independent refineries in 1888, 159; by 1892, 207; of American Sugar Refining Co.'s New Orleans plant, 254

Refining techniques: in colonial period, 27–28; in 1830's, 31–34; final-stage bottleneck in eliminated, 35; importance of waterfront site to, 40–41, 55; improved on West Coast, 153

Revere Sugar Refining Company: agrees to join trust, 74; reverses decision, 80; only independent refinery after 1891, 173

Rich Man's Panic of 1907: marks end of first phase of Corporate Revolution, 18, 187, 264

Riley, Thomas P.: handles railroad matters for American Sugar Refining Co., 197–206; on cooperage rebates, 207; arranges meeting to assure uniform sugar prices, 211; takes evidence of rebating to Hearst's *New York American*, 276–77; co-operates with Henry Stimson, 277

Rockefeller, John D.: as pioneer in consolidation techniques, 15, 70, 90; role of in Corporate Revolution, 17–18; portrayed as robber-baron, 122; rejects competition as norm, 125; appears before Arnold committee, 129.

Roosevelt, Theodore: attitude of toward "trusts," 18, 20, 274; administration's policies help bring end to Great Merger movement, 264; brings about change in role of government, 273–74; Hearst poses political threat to, 275–76; arranges to have *Outlook* publicize customs frauds, 297; succeeds in reviving Sherman Act, 298; reluctant to use antitrust approach, 298–99; administration brings suits under Sherman Act, 299, 305; administration refuses to prosecute American Sugar Refining Co., 300–301; antitrust policy of criticized by Wilson, 313–14; administration clears Tennessee Coal and Iron purchase, 323; wisdom of his approach to trust problem, 335

Roosevelt family: early involvement of in sugar refining, 29; retires from industry, 30

Root, Elihu: reaction of to rebate convictions, 280

St. Louis Globe-Democrat: reaction of to American Sugar Refining Co.'s Philadelphia acquisitions, 174

Schumpeter, Joseph: on dynamic competition, 229

Schumpeterian innovation, 125n*15*

Seager, Henry R., and Gulick, Charles A., Jr.: on causes of Corporate Revolution, 6; on economies of consolidation, 116

Searles, John E., Jr.: spokesman for William Havemeyer interests, 61; role of in 1886 output-limitation scheme, 67; asked to work for consolidation, 69; organizes trust, 70–76; trustee of Sugar Refineries Co., 78; approaches New Orleans refineries, 82; buys out North River stockholders, 86–87; asks Spreckels to sell out to trust, 90; his arguments for consolidation, 90–91; not an outside promoter, 97–98; on economies from consolidation, 102, 104, 110; boasts of power over Cuban growers, 108; on inventory management, 112–13; on shutting down inefficient plants, 113; avoids Arnold committee subpeona, 128; approaches Spreckels to end price war with trust, 165–66; criticizes younger Spreckels for cutting price, 168; negotiates sale of Philadelphia refineries, 171–72; secretly acquires control of Baltimore refinery, 173; refuses to testify in *E. C. Knight* case, 177; involved in 1894 bribery charges, 182–84; on American Sugar Refining Co.'s desire to protect distribution network, 192; organizes Brooklyn Cooperage Company, 206; forced out of the American, 265

Secrecy: of trust device, 77; need for in merger negotiations, 79–80; fans hostile reaction to trusts, 124, 128–29; surrounding Havemeyer-Spreckels understanding, 166–67; Havemeyer's penchant for, 267

Securities market. *See* Capital markets

Segel, Adolph: career of as promoter, 282; builds refinery in Camden, 282–83; builds second refinery, 283; sells out to American Sugar Refining Co., 283, 285; and financial involvement with the American, 283–89; loan to forms basis of government antitrust suit, 303

Senff, Charles H.: partner in Havemeyer & Elder, 40; attitude of toward joining trust, 71–73; trustee of Sugar Refineries Co., 78; acquires interest in Mollenhauer refinery, 208–9; still with American Sugar Refining Co. in 1907, 265; indicted under Sherman Act, 302

Shareholders: dispersed nature of American Sugar Refining Co.'s, 266; lack of opposition to Henry Havemeyer's leadership among the American's, 268; Havemeyer's troubles with minority, 216n*101*, 286, 288

Shares: of American Sugar Refining Co. widely dispersed by 1907, 266; Havemeyer family holds few in the American, 266–67

Sherman, John: antitrust bill considered by Congress, 141–44; responsibility of for antitrust law, 144; on revised measure, 144

Sherman Act: enacted, 16, 144; and holding-company device, 16, 152, 186–87; Theodore Roosevelt's attitude toward, 20, 298–99; Taft's attitude toward, 20, 299; Congress weighs, 142–44; immediate need for obviated, 144–45; purpose of defeated by *E. C. Knight* case, 186; discourages formal agreement ending Havemeyer-Arbuckle price war, 227; Roosevelt's willingness to enforce helps end Great Merger movement, 264; American Sugar Refining Co. accused of violating, 291. *See also* Antitrust laws

Simons, Henry C.: on cause of Corporate Revolution, 2

Social control: problem of re-establishing, 334–35

Speculation: engaged in by trust's organizers, 98; at time of American Sugar Refining Co.'s Philadelphia acquisitions, 173–74

Spreckels, Claus, Jr.: on Searles's arguments for consolidation, 90–91; on competition in 1890, 163; meets with F. O. Matthiessen to end price war, 163–64; approached by Searles to end struggle, 165–66; resists outside direction, 167–68; quit's father's enterprises, 168; organizes Federal Sugar Refining Co., 228

Spreckels, Claus, Sr.: his background in sugar refining, 87–88, 89–90; comes to dominate Hawaiian cane industry, 88–89; output-limiting policy of, 89, 251–52; interest of in rival American refinery, 89–90; refuses to sell out to trust, 90–91; influence of used to annul rival's charter, 140, 153–54; builds competing refinery in Philadelphia, 152, 155–57; and struggle with trust, 152–58, 161–65; viewed as defender against trust, 156, 161; denies plan to sell out, 157–58, 174; makes trip east to open new plant, 158; reaches accommodation with Henry Havemeyer, 166; proves difficult to work with, 167; forced to sell Philadelphia refinery, 168–69, 172; sale of refinery revealed, 174; successfully grows sugar beets, 230; beet sugar enterprises, 243–44; price leader in beets, 262. *See also* California Sugar Refining Company

Spreckels Sugar Refining Company: plant built in Philadelphia, 155–57; and competition with American Sugar Refining Co., 161–65; Havemeyers purchase minority interest in, 166; plant combined with Delaware Sugar House, 179; provokes increased railroad competition, 196

Standard Oil case: marks end of Corporate Revolution, 18; decision in handed down, 20, 305–6; causes delay in *American Sugar Refining* case, 304–5; importance of, 305; Taft administration's handling of criticized, 313

Standard Oil Company: pioneer in consolidation techniques, 15–16; model for sugar refining industry, 70, 195, 276; leads to acceptance of trust certificates, 99; seen as new form of monopoly, 122; example condemned, 123; linked to other consolidations, 123–24; and railroad rebates, 195; one of six largest industrial corporations, 265–66; fine for rebating found excessive, 282. *See also* Rockefeller, John D.

Standard Sugar Refining Company: largest refinery in Boston, 73–74; joins trust, 74; expanded, 114–15

Stanley committee: and investigation of U.S. Steel, 308

Stigler, George J.: on causes of Corporate Revolution, 3

Stimson, Henry L.: named U.S. attorney for Southern District of New York, 274–75; prepares rebate cases, 277–78; strategy followed in rebate cases, 278; obtains convictions, 279–81; sees end of rebates as solution to trust problem, 280; reacts to political intrusion, 281; arranges out-of-court settlement,

281–82; accomplishes goal in rebate cases, 282; prosecutes customs frauds, 293, 295–97; and results of prosecution, 297; succeeded by Henry Wise, 302; on Wise, 313
Stock. *See* Shares
Stock values: effect of dissolution on, 21; factor in handling of sugar trust, 147; of American Sugar Refining Co., 213; question of raised, 318n*86*
Structure of American industry, evolution of: as four-stage process, 9–24; lessons to be learned from, 332–35
Stuart, Robert L. and Alexander: adapt steam power to sugar refining, 32–33; firm of prospers, 33–34; effect of Civil War on business of, 41; withdraw from sugar refining industry, 56
Stursberg, Julius A.: on winter losses, 66; joins and offers to promote trust, 71; trustee of Sugar Refineries Co., 78; on independence of trust members, 106; on economies of consolidation, 117
Sugar: as a luxury item of consumption, 28–30; market for broadened, 36–38; shortage of during World War I, 320
—adulteration of: charges of in 1870's, 50, 58–59
Sugar beet companies: Havemeyer and American Sugar Refining Co. interest in, 229, 240–42, 247–48; agree to division-of-markets plan, 257–58; seek out-of-court settlement in antitrust suit, 314; the American eschews voting its stock in, 314–15; agree to maximum price during World War I, 321
Sugar beet factories: in Utah, 234–41; in Colorado, 241; in Michigan, 241–42; in California, 243–44; elsewhere, 242
Sugar beets: as threat to cane refiners, 228; early efforts to grow in U.S., 230; and tariff protection, 232; share of domestic sugar market of, 248–49; harvesting seasons of, 256–57; prices of geared to those of refined sugar, 261–62
—cost of processing: in 1901, 233; Havemeyer complains of execessive, 250
Sugar cane: early processing techniques for, 27–28; production limits of in Louisiana reached, 38–39; growing seasons of, 254–55. *See also* Sugar refining industry; Tariff, on raw sugar
Sugar Factors Association: organized by independent Hawaiian cane growers, 270; Western Sugar Refining Co. fails to reach agreement with, 271
Sugar importers: join forces with smaller refiners, 54, 60; bypassed by larger refiners, 60; eliminated by trust, 107–8
Sugar Refineries Company, The. *See* Sugar trust
Sugar refining, costs of: at new Havemeyer & Elder plant, 65, 71; as result of consolidation, 110–12; at American Sugar Refining Co. in 1890's, 213; at the American's plants in early 1900's, 294–95n*10*
Sugar refining industry: role of in evolution of industrial organization, 24; during colonial period, 26–30; in Period of Imperfect Competition, 26–34; early production methods of, 27–28; early fortunes in, 29–30; in first decades of nineteenth century, 30; technological change in during 1830's, 31–33; during first phase of Golden Age of Competition, 34–49; technological change in during 1850's, 35–36; rapid expansion of in 1850's, 39; Civil War's effect on, 41–42; preeminance of New York firms in, 42–43; competitive character of, 43–49; during second phase of Golden Age of Competition, 50–69; racked by charges of customs frauds, 52–54; conflict between small and large refiners in, 54–56, 60–62; competition in after

1873, 56–69; attempts to gain export assistance, 57–58; complaints of product adulteration arise in, 58–59; first price-fixing scheme proposed in, 59; attempts at credit destruction in, 59–60; bypassing of importing merchants in, 60; and pooling arrangement of 1880, 63–64; and output-limiting scheme of 1881, 64–65; temporary relief from competitive pressures in brought by Havemeyer & Elder fire and New York strike, 65–69; other output-limitation agreements in, 67–68, 271–72; Golden Age of Competition in ends, 70; trust organized in, 70–92; price wars in, 90, 152–55, 157, 162–65, 188, 218–22; how affected by railroads, 93–94; necessarily confined to major seaports, 94; limitations on monopoly in, 97; role of promoters in consolidation of, 97–99; raw-sugar brokers eliminated from, 107–8; trust in declared illegal, 139–40, 145–46; trust in reorganized as holding company, 150; and *E. C. Knight* case, 176–77, 179–80; faces problem of entry, 188–90; and railroads, 195–96; community of interests in during 1890's, 208–12; entry of new firms into, 214–19, 270–71, 273; merger of independent refineries in, 222–26; challenged by sugar beet industry, 229–350; Henry Havemeyer's control over, 250–63; co-ordination of marketing in, 254–56; effect of Theodore Roosevelt's policies on, 264; factor plans abandoned by, 276; rebates prosecution in, 278–82; Adolph Segel's effect on, 282–89; discovery of customs frauds in, 290–98; antitrust suits in, 300–304, 306–7, 312–16, 319–20; effect of Havemeyer's death on, 307–9; initial involvement of in Cuban land holdings, 309; co-operates with government during World War I, 320–21; consent decree in, 324–25; change in structure of, 328

Sugar trust: created, 78; formation of revealed, 84; threatened by North River Sugar Refining Co. stockholders' withdrawal, 84; Spreckels refuses to join, 91; purchases American Sugar Refinery, 92; certificates of help create industrial-securities market, 99; organization of described, 104–5; and fixing of prices, 105; independence of members of, 106; its adjustment to long-run demand, 113; reorganized as New Jersey corporation, 120, 150; public reaction to formation of, 126; New York State investigation of, 126–30; U.S. House investigation of, 130–31; agrees to "deal" in *North River* suit, 135–36; social desirability of argued and answered, 137–39; Barrett and Finch decisions in New York State's suit against, 139–40, 145–46; obtains Connecticut charter, 146; reorganization of thwarted by New York injunction, 147; ponders reorganization alternatives, 150; reorganizes as New Jersey corporation, 150; and struggle with Spreckels, 152–58, 161–65

Supreme Court, U.S.: and *E. C. Knight* case, 17, 184–86; and *United States Steel* case, 21–22, 324; mood of in 1890's, 185; and *Addyston Pipe & Steel* case, 187; decision in *American Tobacco* and *Standard Oil* cases, 306

Tabor, Charles F.: pressed to act against sugar trust, 132; agrees to bring suit, 135; willing to change New York corporate law, 148; forced to accept reorganized trust, 151

Taft, William H.: attitude of toward industrial consolidation, 20–21, 299; pressure on administration to prosecute American Sugar Refining Co., 298; administration decides to bring suit against the American, 302; antitrust record of criticized,

313; orders prosecution of International Harvester Co., 317
Take-over efforts: by F. O. Matthiessen, 164–65; by Nash, Spalding & Co., 165; by Horace Havemeyer, 310–11
Tammany Hall: attacks sugar trust, 132
Tariff, on raw sugar: Civil War brings increase in, 41; controversy over uniform *v.* ad valorem duties, in 1870's, 50, 55–60; changes in demanded to end customs frauds, 53–55, 60; legislation of stymied, 62; involved in bribery allegations, 181–82; encourages sugar beet production, 232
Tariff protection: role of in Corporate Revolution, 8, 95; as ameliorative for competition, 15; stimulates ante bellum Louisiana production, 38; extent of in sugar refining, 95–96; as factor in sugar consolidation, 95–97; sets upper limit on sugar prices, 96
Technological progress: exogenous force affecting evolution of industry structure, 10–11; effect of during Golden Age of Competition, 12–13, 26; during Era of the Conglomerate, 23–24; transforms sugar refining in 1830's, 31–33; resistance to, 33; behind rapid expansion of sugar refining industry in 1850's, 35–36; drives outmoded refineries from industry, 48–49; effect of telegraph and cable on refining industry, 69
Technology: of colonial sugar-making, 27–28; application of steam to sugar refining, 31–33; centrifugal machine developed, 35; causes breakdown of competition, 333
Thomas, Joseph B.: head of Standard Sugar Refining Co., 73; agrees to join trust, 74–75; trustee of Sugar Refineries Co., 78
Thomas, Washington B.: succeeds father as official of American Sugar Refining Co., 265; on reasons for deferring to Henry Havemeyer, 268; indicted under Sherman Act, 302; succeeds Havemeyer as head of the American, 307; inaugurates less-personal administration, 307; points out changes in management, 308
Transportation costs: role of in Corporate Revolution, 5–6; lowering of stimulates competition, 93
Transportation revolution: as cause of Corporate Revolution, 11; affects market for sugar, 36–38
Trust device: pioneered by Standard Oil Co., 15, 70; mechanics of, 15–16, 76–77; declared illegal, 16, 141, 145–56; organized in sugar refining industry, 70–92; public reaction to, 123–26; legality of argued, 136–40, 145; states take action against, 140–41, 153
Trust problem: end of rebates seen as solution to, 280; difficulty of dealing with, 291. *See also* Consolidation

United States Steel case: decision in, 21–22, 322–24; leads to acceptance of oligopoly, 291, 324; effect of consent decree in sugar case on feared, 319; ruling on issue of unfair competition in, 322–23; rule of reason upheld in, 324
United States Steel Corporation: as consolidation, 17, 322; one of six largest U.S. industrial corporations, 265–66; congressional investigation of, 308; antitrust suit against, 322–24
Untermyer, Samuel: retained by Adolph Segel, 287
Utah: beet sugar industry established in, 232, 234; beet factories consolidated, 239–41; beet factories agree to division-of-markets plan, 257–58
Utah-Idaho Sugar Company: antecedent history of constituent mem-

bers of, 235–39; reasons for consolidation of, 239; organized, 239–41; Havemeyer and American Sugar Refining Co. interest in, 240, 309, 311; as price leader, 262; Mormon Church begins buying out the American's interest in, 316

Valuation of property: creates problem at trust's formation, 79

Wages: trust's effect on, 108–9
Warner Sugar Refining Company: acquires Knickerbocker Sugar Refining Co. plant, 273n*46*; only New York refinery not involved in customs frauds, 294
Warren, Charles B.: heads Havemeyer–American Sugar Refining Co. interests in Michigan, 241
Watkins, Myron: on cause of Corporate Revolution, 7
Wells, David A.: on need for ad valorem duties, 55
West Coast refineries: only two left in 1887, 89; rivalry between increased by trust's actions, 92; and Spreckels-trust conflict, 152, 166; marketing area of described, 251; agree to market-sharing plan, 271–72
Western Sugar Refining Company: organization of ends price war in West, 166; involves American Sugar Refining Co. in beets, 243; output-limiting policy of, 251–52; maintains West Coast monopoly, 253; and disposal of surplus sugar, 255; pressure from Hawaiian growers abated by, 268–69; cuts prices to meet competition of "washed" sugars, 269; unable to reach agreement with Hawaiian growers, 270–71; agrees to market-sharing plan, 271–72; the American sells interest in, 312
Whiskey industry: political scandal involving, 51
Whiskey trust: and industrial-securities market, 99; its formation revealed, 123; linked to Standard Oil Co., 124; antitrust suit against, 175
Wholesale grocers: on West Coast warned not to buy trust sugar, 153; and working arrangement with American Sugar Refining Co., 188, 191–95; competition among, 191; the American realizes it cannot eliminate, 192–93, 327; used as barrier to entry, 193–95; undermine the American's rebate agreements with railroads, 200; become embroiled in Havemeyer-Arbuckle conflict, 219–21; as defendants in rebate cases, 278–82; profits in sugar voluntarily limited during World War I, 321; breach-of-contract suits against, 329
Wickersham, George: seeks to convict individuals responsible for customs frauds, 296; expresses regret over prominent men indicted, 302; instructs Henry Wise to prosecute American Sugar Refining Co., 302; agrees to end criminal suit against the American, 312–13
Willet, Wallace: promotes sugar beets, 232; approaches Thomas Cutler as Havemeyer emissary, 233
Wilson, Woodrow: antitrust policy of, 3, 20–21, 313–14; administration's handling of *American Sugar Refining* case, 314–16; administration backs down from goals in *International Harvester* case, 319; administration still refuses consent decree in *American Sugar Refining* case, 319; supporters' hopes for antitrust approach frustrated, 330
Wise, Henry A.: assists Henry Stimson in rebate cases, 277; succeeds Stimson, 302; and antitrust prosecution of American Sugar Refining Co., 302–4, 306, 308, 311–13
Wood, Fernando: heads customs-house investigation, 52
Woolson Spice Company: Henry Havemeyer purchases controlling

interest in, 216–17; receives rebates, 220; replaced by American Coffee Co., 221
World War I: affects attitudes toward big business, 21, 291, 320–21; forces government to accept consent decree in *International Harvester* case, 318; American Sugar Refining Co.'s assistance to government during, 320; food controls during, 320; leads to postponement of *American Sugar Refining* case, 320; obscures decline in the American's influence, 328–29

Designer: James Wageman
Typesetter: Monotype Composition Company
Typefaces: Linotype Caledonia and Melior
Printer: Universal Lithographers, Inc.
Paper: P&S R 55 lb. offset
Binder: Moore and Company
Cover Material: Interlaken Arco Linen AL3 945
Manuscript Editor: Penny James